T0301547

Chinese Money in Global Context

Chinese Money in Global Context

Historic Junctures Between 600 BCE and 2012

Niv Horesh

Stanford Economics and Finance

AN IMPRINT OF STANFORD UNIVERSITY PRESS

STANFORD, CALIFORNIA

Stanford University Press
Stanford, California

Printed and bound by CPI Group (UK) Ltd,
Croydon, CR0 4YY

Library of Congress Cataloging-in-Publication Data
Horesh, Niv, author.
Chinese money in global context : historic junctures between 600 BCE
and 2012 / Niv Horesh.
    pages cm
Includes bibliographical references and index.
ISBN 978-0-8047-8719-2 (cloth : alk. paper)
    1. Money—China—History. I. Title.
HG1282.H76 2014
332.4'951—dc23
2013017257
ISBN 978-0-8047-8854-0 (electronic)

Typeset by Thompson Type in 10/12 Sabon

For Sivaan, Dekel, and Heli with Love

Contents

Tables and Figures, ix

Acknowledgments, xi

Introduction, 1

PART I

1. A Common Origin for Coinage?, 19

2. From Coinage to Paper Money: The Origins and Evolution of
Chinese and Western Banknotes in Comparison, 41

3. The Great Money Divergence: European and Chinese
Coinage before the Age of Steam, 83

PART II

4. Paper Money in Qing China: Exactly How Common and
Reliable Was It by the Early Twentieth Century?, 121

5. British Banknote Issuance in China:
Cross-Imperial Connections, 148

6. Japanese Colonial Banking and Monetary Reform:
China, Korea, and Taiwan, 1879–1937, 183

7. Will the Renminbi Go Global?, 210

Conclusions, 239

Notes, 251

Bibliography, 293

Glossary, 339

Index, 343

List of Tables and Figures

Tables

4.1 The Stock of Currency in the Late Qing (c. 1900s), 138

6.1 YSB Note Circulation in China Proper (Excluding Manchuria) versus YSB Total Note Circulation, 1906–1912 Year End, 187

6.2 YSB Deposits and Loans versus Other Banks, 189

6.3 Yokohama Specie Bank Select Midyear Balance-Sheet Entries, 1915–1923, 192

6.4 BoTW Paid-Up Capital, Year-End Balance Sheet Totals, Note Circulation (End-of-Month Average), and Note Reserves, 205

6.5 Bank of Taiwan Deposits, Regional Breakdown, 206

Figures

5.1 A Shanghai Activists' Bill Explaining the Aims of the May 30th Movement, 174

5.2 A Caricature Capturing the Prevailing Mood among British Residents of Shanghai Soon after the Mid-1925 Disturbances, 175

5.3 An Advertisement by the Chinese Patriotic Tobacco Co. Promoting the *Wusa* ("May 30th") Cigarette Brand on the Heels of Antiforeign Sentiments, 176

6.1 YSB Total Note Circulation, 1906–1944 Year-End, 195

6.2 Estimated Distribution of the Stock of Currency in the Environs of Jilin City, 199

7.1   U.S. Dollar to RMB Official Exchange Rate, 1949–2010, 222

7.2   Hong Kong Dollar to RMB Official Exchange Rate,
        1949–2010, 228

7.3   Yen to RMB Official Exchange Rate, 1949–2010, 229

Acknowledgments

Had it not been for the support of colleagues and friends, I would not have been able to beat a path back into the doors of Australian academia. Once there, three individuals went well beyond the call of duty to ensure in various ways that I would eventually be able to winkle out some teaching relief, as well as the minimal headspace and institutional recognition without which a project such as this cannot be sustained over a long period of time: Emeritus Professor Mark Elvin (Oxfordshire), Professor Hans Hendrischke (University of Sydney), and Professor Louise Edwards (HKU). I am deeply grateful to Mark, Hans, and Louise for their confidence in my research potential, their professional integrity, and the intellectual guidance they have provided me with over the years.

The following passages in comparative monetary history also owe much to the intellectual generosity of scholars with whom I have been fortunate enough to work, brainstorm, and share office gossip on occasion. As a lecturer at UNSW, I could always bank on help from Bufang (Betty) Zhang, Greg Evon, Jean Gelman Taylor, Jon von Kowallis, Wang Ping, Haiqing Yu, Jim Levy, Peter Collins, Mengistu Amberber, Julien Cayla, and Peter Sheldon. Later on, at UWS, I have been privileged to collaborate with another very talented, hard-working, and erudite group of individuals: Emilian Kavalski, Peter Mauch, Edmund Fung, David Walton, Sarah Graham, George Karliychuk, Brett Bennett, and Brett Bowden.

Wan Wong, Di Ouyang, and Mayumi Shinozaki at the National Library of Australia; Darrell Dorrington at ANU; and Bick-har Yeung and Michelle Hall at the University of Melbourne spared no effort in acceding to my many pesky book orders and niggly database inquiries. Yingjie Guo (UTS), Hyun Jin Kim, Graeme Smith, and Alison Betts (University of Sydney); Chi-kong Lai (UQ), Samuel Lieu, and David Christian (Macquarie University); and Robert Cribb, Pierre van der Eng,

and Luigi Tomba (ANU) were always generous with their knowledge of
the "trade."

My notion of world history has, in turn, been greatly enriched over
the years through discussions or correspondence with—among others—
Zhou Weirong, Yuri Pines, Yishai Yaffe, Walter Scheidel, Victor Mair,
Jerry Bentley, Wayne Farris, Roger Ames, Nick Hudson, Khaled Fahmy,
Ethan Segal, Leith Morton, Jabin Jacob, Ute Wartenberg Kagan, Helen
Wang, John Samuel, Joe Cribb, Robert Bracey, Kevin Butcher, Constan-
tina Katsari, Guicai (Gavin) He, Long Denggao, Chang Jianhua, Chen
Zhiwu, Debin Ma, Kent Deng, Barbara Krug, Yitzhak Shichor, Jon Sul-
livan, Shuyu (Susie) Wu, Liu Yanhong, Wang Zhengxu, Andreas Fulda,
Chun-Yi Lee, and Steve Tsang. The Taiwan Studies Programme at the
University of Nottingham's China Policy Institute generously provided
me with a subvention that helped cover part of this book's production
costs.

Though the corny logic of travel and research funding in academe has
meant we could not necessarily meet face to face, a number of colleagues
overseas have nonetheless taken the time out of their busy schedule to
either directly or indirectly offer invaluable extensive feedback on parts
of this book project. I am particularly grateful to Mark Elvin, Richard
Burdekin, Hans Ulrich Vogel, Michael Schiltz, and Akinobu Kuroda for
teaching me so much more about money, its "whys" and "whereofs."
At Stanford University Press, I am indebted to Margo Fleming and her
editorial team—and to two anonymous referees—for leaving no stone
unturned in a bid to help make this book project more robust and accessible to wider audiences. Any remaining errata are, of course, exclusively
my own.

Finally, all members of the Horesh-Khoursheedi *'hamula* did their
best to ensure I wise up to the "real world" from time to time, as did my
Ravid, Avdar, and Grady relatives. But my children, Sivaan (nine) and
Dekel (six) could always be trusted to do so particularly amiably. I dedi-
cate this book to Sivaan, Dekel, and their mother, Heli, who over the
past decade all shared with me the highs and lows of life Down Under.

Chinese Money in Global Context

Introduction

The state can ordinarily expect one-third in profit as some of the
paper money it issues is bound to be burnt, drenched or stolen; and
as some other paper money is deposited along the way, the state
can arrogate one-third of coin proceeds to itself. Only two-thirds
need to be kept in coin as reserve against the amount issued in
notes each year.   —Zhou Xingji (b. 1067; *Fuzhi ji* chapter 1, p. 32)

I do not know which makes a man more conservative—to know
nothing but the present, or nothing but the past.
                    —John Maynard Keynes (1926, p. 21)

The Chinese economy has always operated by its own monetary
rules, which were usually created and enforced by a powerful state
with a large bureaucracy and a strong army.
                    —Jack Weatherford (1997, p. 125)

THEMES

This book seeks to offer a fresh reinterpretation of important junctures
in Chinese monetary history by placing them in a broader global context and by pointing to critical linkages between the past and the present. Partly inspired by Keynes's famous insight of 1926, it posits that to
adequately appreciate the current transformation of the renminbi possibly into one of the next global reserve currencies one would *first* need
to consider the broader sweep of Chinese monetary history hitherto,
with particular emphasis on the late imperial (1368–1911), Republican
(1912–1949), and Mao eras (1949–1976).

Equally important, one would need to go beyond the many miscon-
ceptions and clichés about the inscrutability and exceptionalism of China's ancient "monetary rules," or about the supposedly all-powerful and

omnipresent nature of its emperors, that still riddle popular literature; as will be later argued, in relative terms, the reach of the Chinese late imperial polity was not nearly as extensive as Weatherford might have us believe, and nowhere was this more evident than in the monetary realm. By the same token, the following chapters are directed against the tendency to treat Chinese monetary history as sui generis by some numismatists and area specialists. Often considered "separate," Chinese monetary history might offer in fact many instructive parallels, as well as on occasion some revealing counterpoints to conventional wisdom.[1]

What is proposed here instead is a framework for understanding those Chinese "monetary rules" as part of a much wider global progression through which the notion of money had initially been all but synonymous with coined metal, then supplemented with paper bills, and how this notion of money has more recently become associated with much more abstract constructs such as public debt, the nation-state, or transnational monetary unions. It may therefore be justified to start this Introduction *not* with an episode in Chinese monetary history, strictly speaking, but with a brief reminder from elsewhere of when that millennial linkage between metal and money was formally severed. This severance will be briefly revisited in the Conclusions from a Chinese perspective; what will be discussed there is whether the renminbi's rise to global prominence betokens an entrenchment of the nation-state as the ultimate arbiter of money. Or is it the case that concerns about the Chinese economy might lead, in fact, to the reestablishment of metal as the ultimate arbiter of money? After all, both the "national" (U.S. dollar) and "transnational" (euro) incumbents of the global monetary system are not formally backed by metal but have weakened considerably following the global financial crisis.

When President Richard M. Nixon announced in August 1971 that the United States was no longer committed to the convertibility of the dollar to gold, the sky did not quite fall down from above, for although gold convertibility had been underwritten, or implicitly assumed to be, for much of the preceding century, America's move off gold was in gestation for several months prior, as the greenback was being dumped by speculators. Incensed by French attempts to erode the credibility of the greenback by persistently exchanging it for gold and weakened by the large military outlay in Vietnam and a severe balance of payment deficit, the Nixon administration responded to this financial instability by trumping the Bretton Woods monetary system almost overnight, with relatively little by way of subsequent disruption.[2] Ever since the so-called Nixon Shock, which not only brought an end to the Bretton Woods system but also put paid to all variants of the historic gold standard, economic agents have by and large acquiesced in the morphing of money into one of the abstractions of the nation-state itself.[3] China's modern currency is certainly no exception in that regard even if the delinking of renminbi from metal has more to do with the fact that the country was part of the newly formed Communist bloc on its establishment in 1949 than with the Nixon Shock per se.

Yet, as "technocratic" or "ephemeral" as the Nixon Shock might appear forty years on, and however respectably "conservative" fiat currency may be deemed from a twenty-first-century perspective, it is worth tracing back what is—for all intents and purposes—a rather novel state of affairs in recorded human history. Although previous phases in which currency inconvertible to metal had been recorded in different parts of the world—Marco Polo's or Ibn Battuta's impressions of China under Mongol rule might perhaps spring to mind right away—never before had full-blown fiat money been so universally and sustainably accepted, and never before had the inconvertibility of currency into specie seemed so unquestionable as in our age. In the face of Irving Fisher's dire predictions in the late 1910s, even celebrated free-marketeers such as Milton Friedman and Anna Schwartz would come to conclude by 1986 that government monopolies over currency in the developed world was to remain in effect and that modern fiat money would be free of inflation for a long time to come.[4]

That geopolitics played a critical role in international monetary affairs leading up to the Nixon Shock is of itself not so surprising: After all, "money" (read: coinage) has been from almost its very inception in Lydia around 600 BCE associated, at least in the West, with *regnum* and the finance of war through debasement.[5]

What was to be enduringly unique after the collapse of the Bretton Woods accords is, however, of great magnitude: For the last four decades we have grown accustomed to think of and value money virtually inextricably from the nation-state as its ultimate arbiter, whereas through much of the previous 2,600-odd-year period, money ultimately implied base or precious metal mostly in the form of round metal coinage or in the form of metallic reserves backing notes. The premodern insignia of rulership on coinage had represented, in that context, a guarantee of *metallic* quality much more than of value par excellence.[6]

Yet the fact that a watershed event such as the Nixon Shock did not prove all that earth shattering might suggest that the "metahistoric" knots binding metal to money might have been fraying, at least in the

West, during the early modern period. It is this conjecture that provided the preliminary impetus for the writing of this book. China then firmly reassumes the front stage across which much of the rest of the storyline unfolds. For where this book might contribute a little to the already sizeable body of literature on world monetary history is in venturing a comparative analysis of the ways and means by which the conceptualization, creation, and regulation of currency in premodern China followed, or departed from, the more widely studied Western monetary evolution, beginning with strictly metallic standards through to the Nixon Shock and its aftermath.[7]

Indeed, in recent years, several important works have helped us piece together more effectively the dialectics whereby—well before the breakdown of Bretton Woods—early modern Western currencies had started to gradually shed their conceptual metallic anchorage. Suffice it to crudely flag at this point what were arguably few of the critical junctures in that regard: Nicholas Oresme's (1320–1382) exhortations against the scourge of medieval debasements, and his calls for an unadulterated currency belonging with the public; Jean Bodin's (1530–1596) envisioning of money creation as the prerogative of the sovereign irrespective of coin fineness;[8] Thomas Mun's (1571–1641) advocacy of the East India Company's specie trade;[9] the lengthy debates between John Locke (1632–1704) and William Lowndes (1652–1724) on whether newly minted British coinage might have denominative potential beyond its metallic content;[10] the first short-lived European experience with paper money (*kreditivsedlar*), issued by Johan Palmstruch's (1611–1671) royally chartered bank (Stockholms Banco);[11] David Hume's (1711–1776) and Adam Smith's (1723–1790) criticisms of bullion hoarding as a measure of enhancing state wealth;[12] the notorious overissue of *assignats* during the French Revolution;[13] the establishment of the Bank of England (1694) as principal bank of issue, creditor to the throne, and lender of last resort, as well as the suspension of its banknotes' convertibility into gold during the Napoleonic Wars; the great debates between British "currency-school" bullionists and their "banking-school" opponents throughout the nineteenth century over the desirability of restoring Bank of England note convertibility and maintaining 100 percent gold reserve against the note issues;[14] the resuspension of the sterling and greenback's gold convertibility and the establishment of colonial currency boards during the interwar period, and—last but not least—the growing popularity of "heterodox" Keynesian principles in the 1930s.[15]

Resonant across much of Oresme's and Bodin's seminal work were questions about money's geographical mandate: whether overseas bullion supply drove the secular deterioration in its value, or what one might nowadays call "inflation."

Crown Agent Thomas Gresham (1519–1579), to whom the famous "Gresham's Law" is somewhat erroneously attributed ("bad money will drive out good"), was similarly concerned about the pound's deteriorating intrinsic value as compared with continental currencies and the effect of this deterioration on England's foreign debts.[16] In that sense, it is worth recalling—following Eric Helleiner's recent groundbreaking study—that before the twentieth century foreign currencies had always made up a relatively large share of the money stock across different Western polities, partly as safeguard against domestic coinage debasement.[17]

That being the case, it would seem logical to examine—as this book does, particularly in Part I—whether the premodern Chinese monetary experience might reveal an equal degree of anxiety concerning debasement or concerning foreign currency substitution. Might any differences or commonalities concerning debasement or the flow of foreign coinage across Eurasian polities tell us about the political economy of either region in premodern times? Quite naturally, such exploration must also entail by definition a cursory look at how the political economy of money was couched within the "real"—largely agrarian—economies of premodern Eurasia and whether the nature of these premodern economies can be borne out by, for example, prosaic indices such as historic interest rates.

When delving into the minutiae of money regulation in times past, this research project aimed to eschew grand narratives of materialistic determinism inasmuch as possible. The reason is that much of the recent authoritative work in the field, particularly that which encompasses the 1930s, might lead one to accept that the crux of transnational finance has been at once highly political and very unpredictable to its protagonists.[18]

At least since the voyages leading to the discovery of the New World, empire building has been intimately associated with, if not driven by, the pursuit of precious metals. Empires would certainly try to control specie, but because its supply and demand never proved fully tractable, empire builders were rarely in agreement on what precise monetary arrangements would ensure the metropole's enduring hegemony. Indeed, it was "largely by accident"—to borrow Barry Eichengreen's words—that the London-centric international gold standard, which ended up entrenching British hegemony in the prewar era, had come about domestically.[19]

Similarly, it was only when Germany and the United States decided in the 1870s that they, too, would leave silver for gold that a truly international gold standard started taking shape. China was the last major country in the world to go off silver, but it never quite joined the prewar international gold standard and thus did *not* embrace fiduciary silver coinage as Germany and the United States had in the 1870s. And once it became Communist, China could not be party to the Bretton Woods arrangements, either.[20]

Yet polemics between gold monometallists and silver-gold bimetallists were one of the salient characteristics of British economic debates even after the move off silver. It was only after British India's currency switched from the precolonial time-honored silver base to a gold one in 1898 that the bimetallist cause at home weakened considerably. British bimetallists had been convinced that an overvalued gold sterling would disrupt British exports to India, but their views did not sway the Treasury, which held that recourse to silver would blemish the stability of British currency and London's position as the hub of international finance.[21]

At the root of the global move off silver before World War I were severe fluctuations in metal prices. Silver and gold discoveries in Nevada, California, and West Africa during the mid-nineteenth century altered bullion stock ratios, triggering a chain reaction that saw Germany, Scandinavia, the Netherlands, and the Latin Union going off silver as a monetary base one after the other. Attendant monetary tremors were equally felt in East Asia, prodding Japan to rebase the yen on gold at the turn of the twentieth century, partly to position itself on an equal footing vis-à-vis its Western trading partners.[22]

ARGUMENTS

Although much has been written (and disputed) concerning the factors behind Japan's adoption of the gold standard, Part II of this book aims to reapproach this important episode from a "peripheral" perspective: It will explain what Japan's move on gold meant for China in monetary terms by highlighting the more limited degree to which the yen was convertible to gold in Japan's contiguous colonial possessions and how Japanese colonial monetary policy hastened—for better and worse—the delinking of paper money from metal while marginalizing traditional metallic coinage across the region.

More generally, the thrust of this book implies that this prewar episode in East Asian monetary history is critical to our understanding of the universalization of fiat currencies in the postwar era. At heart is not merely the diffusion of the gold standard per se but the means whereby paper money was diffused across the region, paving the way in no small measure for the acceptance of today's fiat currencies and modern "national debt" instruments. Thus, Chapter Five builds on my earlier work to recapitulate the immense qualitative contribution that private British bank fiduciary note issuance had made to the popularization of paper money in both Japan and China as of the mid-nineteenth century and the ways in which modern Japanese banks built on that experience as they ventured into China's and Korea's monetary realms in the early twentieth century. Other Western financial institutions either entered East Asian markets much later or were of much smaller size locally than their British or Japanese competitors; they therefore left a much smaller "footprint" on the Chinese prewar economy and will be mentioned only briefly in the following pages.

In evolutionary terms, it is argued that any robust examination of the impact Japanese colonial monetary reform had on prewar China—as is attempted in Chapter Six—must be prefaced by a discussion of British bank operations in East Asia. Only then should attention be paid, more generally, to the triumph of Chartalist views over Hayekian ones in early twentieth-century Western economic thought by way of explaining bank note popularization across East Asia and the spread of central banks.[23] After all, the two main contenders slated to replace or complement the U.S. dollar as global reserve currency in the future—the renminbi and (by-now much tarnished) euro—can perhaps both be seen as more quintessentially "Chartalist" than the U.S. dollar in that, unlike the U.S. dollar, neither of them had been historically issued by private financial institutions or convertible into metal.

In the interest of brevity and focus, this study is little concerned with the philosophical question of what money is. Instead, it asks readers to assume—in the Aristotelian tradition— that money simply came about to facilitate trade and that it does not always embody wealth in and of itself; indeed, Aristotle, suggested that money could become "worthless" when replaced by another type of money—a proverbial insight that might conceptually offer a befitting backdrop for our exploration of currency substitution in prewar China later on.[24]

As already mentioned, this research project emerged quite naturally from my first book, *Shanghai's Bund and Beyond*, where I explored how and why British overseas banks like HSBC were able to disburse fiduciary banknotes in China's treaty ports as of the latter part of the nineteenth century.[25] What intrigued me then was that foreign banks could issue currency at will in a relatively sophisticated, large, and sovereign economy such as China's, where paper money had been in use long before Europe. Technologically speaking, there seemed little to recommend HSBC notes over Chinese bank notes at the time, and so a foray into the divergent institutional setting that had historically conditioned both fiduciary and fiat banknote issuance on either extreme of the Eurasian land mass was called for. Peter Bernholz's seminal 1997 study seemed like an appropriate point of departure as it is one of very few that would discuss in the same breath individuals like John Law (1671–1729)—the Scottish speculator who famously introduced the concepts of banknotes and join-stock enterprise to Louis XV of France—and the Chinese premodern experience with paper money, albeit in brief.[26]

This book, in turn, enlarges the comparative scope of that foray both temporally and thematically. In the process of writing it, it became clear to me that the millennium-long Chinese experience with banknote issuance might perhaps confirm at least one of John K. Galbraith's many proverbial insights, even though Galbraith himself did not discuss China much in his work: "The fear of inflation which inflation leaves in its wake can be as damaging as the inflation itself."[27]

THEORY

When pressed on why his influential books appear to avoid any semblance of grand theory, prominent China historian Jonathan Spence replied:[28]

My personal opinion is that [any] kind of overstatement of a theoretical approach is somehow limiting. We know from experience, or just from history, that most social science theories are quite fleeting. They were quite transitory. They were taken immensely seriously by scholars of the time. But very occasionally you have someone like Marx or Weber. Most of the others might have a strong impact more recently, but usually did not last for very long. And to simply impose a social science analysis would not be appropriate, whatever it might be—whether it is deconstructional, or post-colonialism, or postmodernism, or subaltern studies, or the "public sphere." Most of these are already passing us by.

Arguably, the historian's scepticism as expressed by Spence, among others, could and should have loomed larger in academia once the magnitude of the global financial crisis has sunk in, eclipsing along the way many of our economist colleagues' neoclassical dicta as well as much of their enthusiasm for deregulation and "small government." Still, in sketching out a suitable theoretical framework for this work, Galbraith's insight seemed like the basis on which New Institutional Economics (NIE) could perhaps shed more light, even though NIE has been fairly rarely applied outside the Western monetary setting so far. Ordinarily, NIE places great emphasis on the evolution of property rights as determinant of early modern economic growth. Herein, the challenge was to bring the explanatory powers of property rights to bear on the emergence of the modern national-debt economy, entailing the transition from purely metallic money to its later abstractions.

Insofar as the production, dissemination, and *regulation* of money were concerned, it was often the case that institutions proved not merely "the rules of the game," as Douglass C. North might cast them but were—to paraphrase Avner Greif—the very "engine of history."[29] Of course, this is not to discount demographic and other factors that may have also been at play but about which less conclusive data exits: It is reasonable to assume, for example, that the fourteenth-century Black Death turned labor in Europe exceedingly dear and interest rates lower, thus perhaps spurring the mechanization of mining. On the other hand, relative to other parts of the world, the plague might have meant that the existing European stock of metallic money rose on a per capita basis, arguably offsetting any incentives for bullion prospecting.[30]

Because the skein of causation may not always untangle in readers' eyes straight away, it is important to clearly put forward the simple premises of this book right at the beginning. As is discussed particularly explicitly throughout Chapters Two and Three, the quantity of money in the premodern world was intimately tied up with the structure, strictures, and evolution of mining and metallurgy. Mining entrepreneurs were by and large able to secure their possession of mineral wealth in premodern China to a *lesser* degree than in Europe. This, in turn, might at the very least help explain why early modern European pits clearly were more extensive and mechanized, while Chinese mining ventures were rather diffuse and labor-intensive.

Technological advancement aside, the reach of the state—both ideologically and practically—was more circumscribed in late imperial China (1368–1911 CE) as compared with the early (221 BCE–588 CE) and mid-imperial (589–1367 CE) eras. Yet it would be difficult to find instances across these three eras that might echo Dennis Kehoe's recent description of the Roman mining industry as "significant . . . but not only in state hands, private operated ventures were particularly important in the Republican era." Even when imperial Rome moved to take over the most important mines within its reach, it did so in partnership with private enterprise. Kehoe also emphasizes in this context the extensive use of water removal devices like Archimedes screws and water wheels, which allowed miners in Rome to reach depths of up to 200 meters below the ground.[31]

To be sure, under Tiberius's reign (14–37 CE), the early Roman Empire attempted for a time to seize not just more important mines but also foundries. In contrast to early imperial China, however, the Roman state did not aim to monopolize metal production; there was always a large free market for all kinds of metals within its midst, even if it was slave labor that was widely used to extract ore there, as in Han China.[32]

Comparative advantages in mining, then, should *not* be exclusively seen as the corollary of divergent natural endowment. Indeed, as Chapters Two and Three would indicate, European mining may have been more capital intensive as far back as Greco-Roman times because of relatively looser state intervention, even if the transition from republic to empire ushered in greater penetration of the mining sector by the central Roman government. In that sense, the outflow of precious metal from the Greco-Roman world eastward, famously lamented by Pliny the Elder some two millennia ago, is of great significance, as it presaged more numerous European observations to that effect as of the late medieval era.

In any event, it could have scarcely been accidental that the apex of coin output in premodern China occurred during the Northern Song (960–1127) dynasty, at a rather aberrant moment when the state greatly relaxed its control and taxation of the mining sector, while at the same time vigorously promoting the monetization and commercialization of society. Strikingly, some of the applications in mining technology that had been developed as part of the "Song Industrial Revolution" were still used in China as late as the nineteenth century. And even more strikingly, Northern Song per capita coin output levels were not to be matched any time before the introduction of steam-powered mints into China at the turn of the twentieth century. That this was the case is explained for the most part in terms of the post-Song tightening up of central government control over mining and in terms of the restrictions on the free flow of metal (copper of which bronze coinage was made, in particular) and on commoners' possession thereof.

Paper money was also popularized across China during the Northern Song dynasty, some six centuries before Europe. However, despite its great comparative value, the monetary thought that informed the emergence of paper money in China remains relatively little studied in English. Neither is Zhou Xingji—already quoted—a household name among Western historians of political economy, I suspect. Zhou conceived of a metallic reserve ratio (2:3) to support note circulation that would turn out very close by chance to the ratio many European banks of issue adhered to in the latter part of the nineteenth century.[33] By implication, the first British banks to issue notes on Chinese soil in the latter part of the nineteenth century eventually embraced similar reserve principles, as explained in Chapter Five.

Chapter Two will therefore aim at elucidating the institutions—both bureaucratic and those intangible—that propped up Chinese paper money fairly successfully, not only during the Northern Song era but also during the Southern Song era (1127–1279) and under the reign of the Mongol Yuan dynasty (1271–1368). They will explain why those institutions came unstuck during the early Ming dynasty (1368–1644) and how modern bank note issuance came about in China in the face of historic sediments associating fiduciary currency with inflation in the popular as well as intellectual mind-set.

That six centuries divided the onset of Chinese and European paper money can perhaps be simply understood in terms of "path dependency," among other conceptual frameworks. Unlike neoclassical theory, NIE posits that the range of effective policy responses to any given problematic is limited by past policy decisions, even though past circumstances may no longer obtain. Put baldly, "path dependency" suggests that history and habits matter a great deal more than allowed for in neoclassical theory; they can often invalidate what is otherwise the optimal policy response.

Notably, although much silver was injected into the Northern Song economy, it remained largely uncoined, as had been the convention hitherto. Instead, as explained in more detail in Chapter Two, the Northern Song economy primarily relied on low-value bronze coinage to the benefit of the impecunious; notes, too, were denominated at the time in multiples of bronze (or iron) coins. Over time, that convention became progressively entrenched, so that silver was not coined in China's economic heartland even when it denominated Yuan note values or when it became more abundant and cheaper relative to other metals in the late imperial era.

We know that silver and gold were coined in Xinjiang and Tibet by the Qing dynasty (1644–1911); we also know from official records that suggestions for the coining of silver proper did emerge at times, but they were always rebuffed. The lack of coined precious metal may have therefore precipitated China's perspicacious recourse to a new form of higher-value currency in the image of paper money. By the same token, the deficit in standard high-value coinage likely translated into higher capital and transaction costs.

To be sure, there was probably no a priori reason why early Chinese paper money could not have eventually shed off its conceptual metallic anchorage and gradually have been transformed into a form of public debt, as was the case in early modern Europe. The breakdown of popular trust in late Yuan and early Ming paper money has, in that sense, to do with technological factors only inasmuch as paper could be printed off all too easily, whereas mining copper and casting it into coins was much more onerous. Of more significance here, it seems, was the lack of institutional levers that might have effectively constrained the imperial treasury from abusing the prerogative to print money over and above its revenue stream.

Neither can the causality proposed in subsequent chapters boil down to a simplistic, linear technological decline in post-Song mining as opposed to a linear ascent in early modern Europe. For, as Joseph Needham famously argued, it was not only the case that the know-how for producing cupro-nickel (*baitong*) may have reached Bactria from early imperial China, but it may also have been the case that zinc was first imported into early modern Europe from China.[34]

The flip side, of course, was that as of the fourteenth century European coinage consisted of different precious metals and alloys at once. Precious metal coinage presents, in turn, more opportunities to rulers for remunerative debasement. Thus, state-minted base metal coinage was always in short supply in Europe to the detriment of the impecunious, and banknotes spread relatively late, somewhat contrary to the Chinese experience. But, either way, European debasement and Chinese overprinting were similarly driven by premodern rulers' hunger for additional revenue, as the following pages make clear.

Fortunately, as this book project was venturing out from nineteenth century banknote issuance into the wider pastures of world monetary history, it became possible to tap into many insights of senior colleagues, who had been working—largely outside NIE circles—on other aspects of the topic. If at first it seemed as though infinitely more popular titles had been written about "how to make money" than scholarly titles on "how money came about," it gradually became apparent to me that world monetary history, as a subfield of world history, was in fact beginning to thrive in no small measure thanks to the decompartmentalization of area studies and the globalization of academe more generally.

Needless to say, questions such as "what is money?"; "who should create money, and for whom?" and "can money creation beget prosperity?" were in one way or another uppermost on the minds of previous generations of economic historians. After all, it is no coincidence that three identically titled studies pursuing precisely this theme were published between 1980 and 1997, namely, "The Power of Money."[35]

Still, if we were to consider "The Power of Money" eponymous triplet as a kind of cross-section of the English-language body of work on monetary history two decades ago, we might easily conclude that it was fairly Eurocentric and geared toward either antiquity or twentieth-century Western "money doctoring" in the developing world with little by way of global or temporal comparative overview. Granted, early twentieth-century Western "money doctors" left behind valuable commentaries on China's traditional monetary system, but ones that are inevitably colored by the gold-standard orthodoxy of the times and are otherwise devoid of reference to original Chinese sources.[36]

Important studies have since been published, on which the following chapters draw at length, in addition to the familiar classics in Chinese and Japanese by Xiao Qing, Ye Shichang, Kato Shigeru, and—above all—Peng Xinwei. For an understanding of the late imperial Chinese monetary system in its global context, I have relied on more recent work by Professor Kuroda Akinobu and his collaborators at Tokyo University; by Dennis Flynn, Arturo Giráldez, and other prominent scholars more loosely affiliated with the "California School," such as Richard Von Glahn; by Hans-Ulrich Vogel and his collaborators at Tübingen University; by Zhou Weirong and his fellow researchers at the Chinese Museum of Numismatics; and by Joe Cribb and his fellow curators at the British Museum, to name but few. My understanding of modern Chinese banking and of world finance owes, in turn, a good deal to recent pathbreaking work by Cheng Linsun, Brett Sheehan, Richard C. Burdekin, Chen Zhiwu, Marc Flandreau, and Niall Ferguson.

At the same time, I have tried to complement this body of work in at least three meaningful ways:

1. This book attempts to highlight surprising commonalities across Chinese and European monetary history no less than it searches for the "Great Divergence" therein.
2. Although it is informed by the invaluable contributions of "California School" historians to our understanding of the role bullion

flows played in the making of the early modern world, this book's interpretation of China's position therein remains fairly diametrically opposed to theirs. Namely, I see the European exchange of Latin American silver for Chinese commodities like silk and tea as essentially a marker of Chinese comparative weakness in the late imperial era rather than a marker of strength. Europe's comparative advantage is cast here as largely emanating from the possession of superior information on global bullion flows. Jesuit observations aside, I cannot find much clear-cut evidence indicating that the Yangzi Delta and English economies were on par on the eve of the Industrial Revolution or that per capita money supply—as a very rough proxy for respective income levels—was similar around 1750. Conversely, I do see some evidence to suggest that the Northern Song economy had been in fact more technologically advanced and considerably more monetized than the medieval European economy and that, absent a military threat from the steppe, it might well have charted an alternative (read: non-Western) path to economic modernity.

3. This is to my knowledge the first book in the English language that considers the very topical internationalization of the renminbi as *not* just one link in China's postwar resurgence on the world stage but *also* as part of a long-term global monetary evolution, which saw money shedding off its age-old metallic anchorage to assume the mantle of the modern nation-state. And because the rise of modern nationalism is inextricably tied to the creation of nation-states, it is vital to show how modern Chinese monetary history has fed into modern Chinese nationalism, not least by way of highlighting the popular resistance with which British and Japanese bank note issuance in prewar China was met.

SCOPE, ORGANISATION, AND STRUCTURE

The relevance of historic narratives to Chinese perceptions of the role the country naturally ought to play on the world stage in the future can perhaps be borne out here by the fact that ancient Chinese spade-shaped coinage embellishes the logos of both the People's Bank of China (headquartered in Beijing) and the Central Bank of the Republic of China (headquartered in Taipei). At the same time, many in China would view spade coinage not merely as "ancient" but also as the *oldest* form of currency *anywhere* in the world. Chapter One will take issue with such

exceptionalist views, based on a critical analysis of the latest archaeological evidence. Surprisingly, such comparative considerations of the
origins of metallic money are quite hard to come by in the pertinent
literature.

Culturally, too, premodern Chinese currencies are still resonant with
many: Imitations of late imperial *sycee* (hoof-shaped silver ingots) can
often be seen in public venues and households as amulets and mascots
propitiating good fortune. And premodern round bronze coins, typically with square holes—popularized in China as far back as the third
century BCE—can be witnessed not just as household amulets and in
many souvenir shops; the shape of these coins informs in fact the logos
of three of China's largest state-run commercial banks. The round rims
of such coins are *traditionally* thought to represent "heaven," and the
square holes, "earth." The combination of "heaven" and "earth" po-
tently suggests, in turn, a "mandate from heaven" to imperial rule and,
by implication, the right to exclusively issue coinage.[37]

As previously indicated, *Chinese Money in Global Context* is divided
into two parts with different thematic emphases. Part I (Chapters One
through Three) is aimed at critically integrating the specialized scholarship on money in antiquity with new insights from the field of world
history and with arguably better-known studies of early modern developments in a bid to overcome what Jerry Bentley aptly described as
"modernocentrism" in some of the scholarly literature on the origins
of globalization.[38] Here, ardent students of Chinese monetary history
might well note a fundamental commonality, that over two and a half
millennia round metal slabs with diameter of roughly 1 to 6 cm and
weighing around 1 to 6 grams prevailed as currency not just in China
but across a large swath of Eurasia.

Chapters One through Three therefore cast a sidelight on this millennial commonality, as they trace back its origins and geographical variants in terms of coin production technology; the metal or alloy used;
the designs embedded; the identity of issuer and counterfeiters; and the
overall level of monetization in society. Part II (Chapters Four through
Seven) is on the whole more focused on the recent past, as it examines
for the most part specific historic junctures in the evolution of money in
China since the mid-nineteenth century.

By no means exhaustive, this conjunctural narrative has nonetheless
been selected because it might more readily afford the lessons of the
past when broaching questions in large global perspective: For example,
how could private-order paper money (re)emerge in China as of the late
eighteenth century, and how reliable and widespread was it (discussed
in Chapter Four)? Why and how was imperial Japan attempting to

establish a greater East Asian (inconvertible) yen bloc, and what popular reaction did it elicit in the region (discussed in Chapter Six)? And is history anything to go by when assessing the RMB's chances of becoming the next global reserve currency or indeed when pondering the future of the nation-state construct (discussed in Chapter Seven)?

The Conclusions will aim to thread all of these questions together in as unadorned a manner as possible. Here, not only will the RMB's internationalization process be placed against the backdrop of the U.S. dollar's postwar trajectory, but an answer to the question of "what's in it?" for China will also be sought. In pursuing the ramifications and problematics of modern monetary hegemony, I will indirectly draw on insights by Jonathan Kirshner. Notably, Kirshner has explained that the creation of a "sterling area" in the late 1930s eventually allowed Britain to mobilize crucial resources to fight World War II and that the existence of a "sterling block" in the early postwar era helped sustain London's vital financial industry alive in the face of competition from New York.[39] But is this historic exposition relevant at all to the future of the U.S. dollar, the RMB, or both?

Ultimately, therefore, this book cannot purport to offer a "new" comprehensive world history of money or make for a chronologically informed undergraduate primer. Neither does it claim to revolutionize monetary theory. Rather, this book aims to underscore important episodes in the evolution of money in China that are worth revisiting from a fresh (often diachronic) global perspective. Accordingly, each of the following seven chapters features an introduction and provisional conclusions, so that it can be read and assessed on its own merits as an originally framed, self-contained study. That said, it is hoped that the book as a whole will present as larger than the sum of its parts insofar as construing the significance of the earlier junctures in Chinese monetary history within the broader sweep of global convergence on fiat currency and in view of China's resurgence in the twenty-first century.

PART I

CHAPTER ONE

A Common Origin for Coinage?

Popular literature often depicts a vigorous thrust of globalization that has "flattened" the world economy ever since the fall of the Berlin Wall in 1989. In the realm of scholarship, the present thrust of globalization is compared on occasions with the previous and much longer thrust of globalization, which had arguably started with the discovery of the New World and ended with the parceling up of the global economy into three separate economic blocs following World War II.[1] Studies of the current and previous thrusts of globalization mostly discuss changing trade volumes and standards of living, yet some attention to the changing media of currency in antiquity is also at issue. Although ground-breaking studies have recently discussed how the Mongol use of paper money and, later, the discovery of rich silver deposits in Mexico and Peru brought about a sweeping overhaul of the monetary order across Eurasia from the thirteenth century onward and how this helped shape Eurasian trade in the era of High Imperialism and the edifice of modern nation-statehood, much less interdisciplinary attention has been paid to the transmission of currency across Eurasia *before* the Common Era.[2]

The purpose of this chapter is, therefore, to examine the precursors of monetary globalization as far as the conceptualization and standardization of currency are concerned. The following passages survey the transmission of currency design and production technology across Eurasia in antiquity. In addition, they cast a sidelight on the present ("postmodern") and previous ("early modern") thrusts of globalization through a discussion of the premodern universalization of round coinage.

Postmodern interpretations of globalization often ascribe a minor role to the mastery of mineral wealth or the production of means of payment. In their influential books Hobson and Frank suggested, for example, that the mass flow of silver from Latin America to China in the early modern era was not a marker of Chinese economic passivity but rather a testament to the "magnetic" qualities and the inherently more advanced nature of the Chinese economy.[3] A hundred years ago, European views of the Chinese early modern economy were of course much dimmer if not bluntly "Orientalist." Thus, if Hobson's aforementioned book is titled *The Eastern Origins of Western Civilization* (2004), Terrien Lacouperie's is provocatively titled *Western Origin of the Early Chinese Civilization* (1894).[4]

Lacouperie's typical nineteenth-century bias should not detain us here. Of more relevance was his suggestion, based on apocryphal sources, that the premodern Chinese currency system had in fact been directly modeled on earlier Hellenistic coinage. Furthermore, he claimed that the Western Han (206 BCE–6 CE) monopoly of coinage production had in fact derived from Greco-Roman governance patterns, even though later on the production of coinage ended up much less centralized in medieval Europe than in, for example, Tang China (618–907 CE).[5]

This chapter will therefore aim at taking a fresh integrative look at the origins and standardization of Chinese round coinage from a global perspective. It will show in passing that the various theories arguing for an exclusively endogenous impetus behind the spread and development of Chinese round coinage vouched for by many scholars in either East Asia or the West all carry inherent contradictions. In contrast, circumstantial and archaeological evidence in support of partly exogenous origins seem to be mounting. Evidence from the Middle East points to the early invention and wide circulation of round coinage in Lydia, Greece, and the Achaemenid Empire. The expansion of the Persians into India in the sixth century BCE and the later incursions by Alexander and the Greco-Bactrians in the fourth and third centuries BCE may have all facilitated or, indeed, decisively contributed to India's adoption of round coinage. Similarly, the flow of ideas, artistic motifs, and metallurgic know-how from West Asia to China via Central Asia had occurred much earlier than the third century BCE. Active adoption of foreign (Central Eurasian steppe) customs in the fourth century BCE is recorded in Chinese preimperial records and confirmed by recent archaeological findings across Eurasia.

In essence, therefore, this chapter questions the endogeneity of Chinese premodern round coinage with Lacouperie's improbable claim serving as a point of entry. The remaining sections are framed with a view toward testing argument and counterarguments to that effect. The second section will briefly chart the key characteristics of China's Bronze Age and the transition to iron casting there; the third section critiques prevailing views of the origins of Chinese round coinage among leading scholars in the People's Republic of China (PRC); short of providing an exhaustive numismatic survey, the fourth section aims to place the Chinese monetary experience in antiquity in broader Eurasian perspective; the fifth section presents later but equally pertinent numismatic evidence from the Silk Road. Finally, the Conclusions section will reassess the spread of round coinage across Eurasia in antiquity in light of the evidence presented here.

CHINA'S BRONZE AGE

Archaeological evidence suggests that the Bronze Age began in China's north and northwest regions no later than 2500 BCE, even though the south generally had more abundant copper deposits. It is generally acknowledged that Mesopotamia and Anatolia had developed a distinct bronze material culture at least five centuries earlier, yet most archaeologists would also agree that the level of sophistication in bronze vessel production reached during China's Shang dynasty (1600–1046 BCE) was unparalleled in the ancient world.[6]

Bronze coin casting began in China in earnest during the late Spring and Autumn period (722–481 BCE). Copper had previously been alloyed to produce bronze weaponry and sacrificial vessels, which proved far superior to their stone equivalents in sharpness, durability, and gleam.[7]

Much of the preimperial paraphernalia of Chinese currency retained the idiosyncrasies of that era. The famous spadelike (*bubi*) or knifelike (*daobi*) bronze coin designs were, for example, a Spring and Autumn refinement of the stone axes that had served as a medium of exchange in Neolithic times. In turn, the complex version of the ideograph denoting "quality" or "value" (*zhi*) in modern Chinese still conveys the exchange of two stone axes for one piece of cowrie, a much rarer item that was first introduced into the Yellow River basin as an exotic decoration from the tropical south. Arguably, cowrie morphed into a sumptuary medium of exchange in its own right sometime between the late Shang and early Zhou Dynasties (1100–256 BCE).[8] Gold had been recognized as a precious metal back in the Shang era and could have hypothetically contributed to the gradual diminution in coin size. Yet it was too scarce in North China to become an inherent component of China's imperial monetary system.

The introduction of cast-iron weaponry, as from the mid-Spring and Autumn periods on, meant that sufficient amounts of copper could be freed up to serve as medium of exchange, thereby relegating most of China's nonmetallic protocurrencies—cowrie, silk, and animal hide—to the sidelines of mercantile activity. At the same time, most early designs of bronze money in north China continued to simulate tools that had initially been made of bronze (like spades or knives), possibly because these could be recast into useful articles and draw value from that utility.⁹ In parts of south China like the kingdom of Chu, however, currency in the form of flat golden plates (*yingyuan*), miniatures of cowrie (known as "ant-nose money" or *yibi qian*) made mostly of bronze, and spade-shaped currency made of silver had been concurrent until the Qin unification.¹⁰

During the Warring States era (403–221 BCE), practical considerations led to the gradual attenuation of tool-shaped designs—generally designated by numismatists as "shovel-like" (*chanxing*) coins—into easier-to-carry, hollow designs such as that of the "level-head" (*pingshoubu*) currency or the flatter "pointed-feet" (*jianzubu*) currency. In the early imperial Qin (221–206 BCE) and subsequent Western Han dynastic reigns (206–8 BCE), this type of currency had gradually made way for the introduction of the flat, round alloy coins (*yuanqian*), which were appreciably lighter than most Warring State copper currencies and ultimately became the hallmark of Chinese coinage for almost two millennia thereafter.¹¹

The convergence on round coinage across Eurasia roughly at that point in time suggests a degree of influence by Greco-Bactrian designs over Indian ones. It might also suggest that earlier contact with Greek coinage may have had something to do with the emergence of *yuanqian*, although this is much harder to prove. China's imperial age is conventionally thought to have begun with the unification of the "Middle Kingdom" by the notoriously ruthless First Emperor of Qin in 221 BCE. Traditionally, China's history is perceived from then on as a long sequence of dynastic reigns punctuated by bouts of chaotic disunion. Dynastic patriarchs are often framed in popular literature as ushering order into a disorderly world, while the last rulers in each dynasty are presented as degenerates who plunged all under heaven into chaos.

Within this narrative, political union and disunion have each assumed an auxiliary swag of similes. The dissemination of round *banliang* coins with square holes by the First Emperor of Qin, as part of an all-embracing standardization campaign, came to serve as one of the most evocative symbols of a strong unified China and as a benchmark for much of the Confucian discourse on monetary policy in subsequent dynasties. In reality, of course, the standardization of round coinage took much longer: Following the sudden collapse of the Qin, during the early Western-Han reign, "private coinage" was permitted; gold and silver ingots were readily exchanged, and the weight of the *banliang* was drastically reduced. Even Emperor Wudi (r. 141–87 BCE), who restored the state monopoly on coinage, tried at first to introduce "new" types of money—including ones made of silver alloy and the notoriously inflationary deer-hide currency (*lupibi*)—before embracing in 118 BCE a round variant of the *banliang*.[12] Then, during usurper Wang Mang's brief reign (9–23 CE), there had also been famous attempts to reinstitute noncircular and nonmetallic currency alongside *yuanqian*; the hoarding of cowrie in elaborate bronze vessels as a symbol of wealth and status otherwise even survived a few decades thereafter.[13]

But the early *banliang* design is nevertheless traditionally deemed to have entrenched the design of Chinese imperial coinage for almost two millennia afterward, perhaps because nonround forms of base-metal money seemed to have disappeared by the end of the first century CE, and the monetary use of silver and gold greatly diminished for several centuries thereafter. Concomitantly, the imperial regulation of copper mines and a monopoly of hearths had, from then on, become the most salient feature of China's monetary system in the premodern era.[14]

HOW DISTINCT WAS CHINESE PREMODERN METALLIC CURRENCY?

However implausible the notion of a single West Asian origin of round metallic currency in the world must seem at first glance, it must *not* be rejected straightaway. This is not least because today's scholars need to know more about earlier thrusts of "globalization" to contextualize the present one. In Chinese academia, at any rate, the discourse on the precursors of globalization is still in its infancy, and the premise that China's ancient metallic currency is distinct goes almost without saying. That preimperial coinage is perceived as distinctly "Chinese" in design is perhaps best attested to by the fact Spring- and Autumn-era (722–479 BCE) spade-shaped coins, which had preceded round bronze coinage, were chosen to make up the People's Bank logo.

To be sure, knife- or axe-shaped currencies were recorded at different periods elsewhere. In some parts of Africa, sickle axes, axes, and knives were used as currency even after the onset of the continent's first indigenous round coinage, the Ethiopian gold *aksum* coin (200 CE). Earlier on, in Pharaonic Egypt bronze-ring armlets strung on metal loops had served as protocurrency long before China adopted the stringing of round bronze coinage. Even in the early modern era, when round coinage had already become universally entrenched, other designs could resurface in certain currency circuits: One is reminded for example of the extensive circulation of Southeast Asian cowrie in Yunnan in the early Ming era. Another example might be the appearance of the "fish-hook" gold *larin* coins of the Persian Gulf in the seventeenth century, whereas most other Islamic coins were round.[15]

Short of piecing together an exhaustive survey of global countercurrents in numismatics, what should perhaps concern us at this stage is why and how the shape of Chinese currency became round at much the same time as other parts of Eurasia were adopting round coinage, that is, the third century BCE. Is this *design* convergence across Eurasia simply a coincidence? Design convergence might conceivably reflect, in the first instance, a technological convergence emanating from the advantages of casting round coinage over more complex shapes of metallic money in terms of molding or wear and tear. Other explanations for the extensive spread of round design across Eurasia within a relatively short space of time might bring to mind metahistoric, cultural, or ecological factors. But the present chapter does not concern the complex economies of technology or transmission of production know-how as much as it is an attempt to underscore the plausibility of *design* diffusion and similarities in the conceptualization of currency. In that sense, it goes against much of the conventional wisdom both in the West and in East Asia postulating that two inexorably separate monetary traditions had existed across Eurasia before the universalization of steam-powered mints in the mid-nineteenth century.[16]

Granted, minting technology never quite carried over from West Asia to East Asia prior to the nineteenth century, and in that sense a modicum of separateness can be argued for; Chinese round coins traditionally were cast from molten bronze while western Eurasian round coin production involved, in the main, striking a die on a solid metal flan.[17] Neither could extant Chinese sources, archaeological findings, or our present knowledge of the scope of intercivilizational contact before the common era allow for an exhaustive delineation of the conditions in which Chinese craftspeople might have attempted to (re)produce round coinage.[18] Yet the archaeological, epigraphic, and circumstantial evidence presented in the following discussion would clearly suggest that a form of "stimulus diffusion" of round-coinage design could have transpired across Eurasia. In other words, there seems to be a strong case that during the mid-fourth century Chinese craftspeople—having encountered foreign precious-metal round coinage or having heard about it from their superiors—attempted to produce round coinage for the first time, while relying on preexisting metallurgical know-how and while maintaining a preference for bronze.[19]

It is otherwise often alleged that the "separateness" of premodern Chinese coinage derived from its being made out of copper or bronze, while European coinage was usually made of silver or gold. This seems, however, an overstatement from today's vantage point: To begin with, large quantities of imperial Chinese round coinage were at times made of iron, although bronze always remained the mainstay; there have even been found rare specimens of ancient spade-shaped coinage made out of silver, quite apart from the aforementioned gold-plate coinage that was current in the southern state of Chu during the preimperial era.[20] But, perhaps more important, recent studies have shown that cast bronze coinage was at times *also* an important part of the European premodern money system alongside silver and gold: Such for example was the famous Roman *aes* coinage.[21] And after about 1300 CE, copper again played an important role both as means of adulterating (read: debasing) European precious metal coinage or as token money in its own right, as will be explained in Chapter Three.

Similarly, if Aristophanes' (427–386 BCE) *The Frogs* contains the most ancient of recorded Western diatribes against the scourges of debasement, then nobleman Shan Qi's exhortations in China—although different in approach and tenor perhaps—are equally revealing. Aristophanes famously decried the replacing of full-bodied Athenian gold coins with poor-quality copper alloys of the same nominal value, probably in the context of fiscal exigencies arising from the Peloponnesian Wars (431–404 BCE).[22] Contained as a passage in the ancient classic *Discourse of the States* (*Guoyu*), Shan Qi warned King Jing of the Zhou Dynasty (r. 544–520 BCE) not to abolish all existing variants of knife-shaped bronze coinage in favor of new bigger and heavier bronze coinage that was probably intended to pass at a much higher nominal value than its weight would warrant. Instead, Shan Qi suggested that a duality of both light and heavy coinage should obtain in the marketplace; he further recommended that the supply of either type of coinage should be adjusted by the king from time to time, so as to shore up prices and facilitate market transactions.[23]

Aristophanes may have ably presaged Gresham's more explicit early modern "law," postulating that a bad currency would always drive out good ones in the marketplace. Yet here, too, one can arguably find proximate Chinese premodern articulations. Deemed a Confucianist, Han-era statesman Jia Yi (201–169 BCE) was, for example, concerned that state inertia might lead to peasants abandoning their fields and engaging in lucrative, illicit coin casting. In this context, he admonished: "As de-based bronze coins proliferate, they will full-bodied coins obliterate" (*Jianqian rifan zhengqian riwang*). On the other hand, if the state it-self attempted to issue excessively "heavy" (read: fiduciary) coinage and thrust it on commoners, it would lead to a proliferation of forgeries of that very same coinage, Jia warned.[24]

Guoyu and the *Frogs* can be seen, in a sense, to be formatively mark-ing both monetary differences and commonalities that would remain in force across Eurasia. In the West, debasement was to entail not just an attenuation of round and struck coinage but quite often *also* a manipu-lation of the exchange rate between different metals so as to defray the cost of warfare. In China, cast base-metal coinage remained the main-stay, at least conceptually, both in peace and at times of war; it concep-tually remained so even when raw precious metal started flowing in en masse during the late imperial era.

In practice, however, a multiplicity of weights and inscriptions was tolerated even after coinage turned decidedly round in China; pre-cious metal was otherwise never to be widely coined there before the late nineteenth century. Thus, subsequent Chinese sources continue to bespeak arguably greater preoccupation than in the West with issuing "light" and "heavy" forms of the same coinage as principally a means of stabilizing the prices of everyday necessities, keeping commoners well fed, and averting popular rebellions. References in Chinese preimperial sources to issuing heavier fiduciary coinage as a means of supporting in-creased military outlay are rare, by comparison, even if debasement can be read through these sources on occasion. Rather, the principle of coin-weight variation as price and tax-levy stabilizer and as a social leveller of sorts was often rearticulated in statecraft classics in terms of "child and mother [coins] complementing each other" (*zimu xiangquan*).[25]

In fact, "child and mother" tropes would remain frequently cited in Chinese monetary policy debates right until the twentieth century. As explained in the next chapter, they would also be invoked in later de-bates about the merits of issuing high-denomination paper money along-side standard bronze or peripheral iron coinage, wherein coinage was more often than not cast as "mother" due to its vitality to the rural economy.[26] Yet, for all its distinctiveness, this premodern child–mother discourse on coin *multiplicity* cannot overshadow another deep vein in ancient Chinese statecraft, which affirms the *singularity* of the state as the provenance of money. To be sure, this vein is much more em-phatically reflected in the first-century BCE classic, the *Yantielun* ("Dis-courses on the Salt and Iron Monopolies") than in the *Guanzi* ("The Book of Master Guan"), compiled around the same time. Nevertheless, it was only rarely questioned at times of political and territorial unity later in the imperial era. Indeed, this important vein is not only Chinese in nature; it runs parallel to sentiments found in many Greco-Roman sources as well as in ancient Indian political thought, namely, that coinage and mining are the most fundamental of state prerogatives.[27]

That the notion of two inexorably "separate" coin traditions is nevertheless so entrenched among numismatists is otherwise quite surprising, given the broad agreement among Western and Chinese archaeologists that premodern metallurgy—that is, bronze casting in its earliest forms—had spread beforehand from ancient Mesopotamia both to the east and to the west. In his seminal study, Shaughnessy, for example, has argued that Shang chariots (1200–1046 BCE)—"the most sophisticated of all Chinese bronze age artefacts"—were in all likelihood an adaptation of Central Asian design and know-how well before the appearance of metallic coinage, and Kuz'mina's more recent work broadly supports this view. That basic Hittite chariot design also spread westward to the Levant.[28]

Other instances of metallurgic know-how, art motifs, ideas, and crops being transmitted from western Asia via Siberia to eastern Asia (and vice versa) before the fourth century BCE can arguably be found. Maspéro, for example, famously believed there had been strong Achaemenid influence on Chinese astronomy, geography, myth, and folklore in pre-Han times. More recently, Jessica Rawson alluded to the possible influence of steppe cultures on the style of early Zhou bronze sacrificial vessels.[29]

Exceptionalist arguments, particularly in PRC scholarship, are perhaps best summed up by Xiao Qing's important 1984 work: Xiao alleged that even if scholars commonly accepted the seventh century BCE as the dating for the appearance of the world's first (round) metallic currency in Lydia, China's currency system was in fact older than the Hellenistic one because knife-shaped and spade-shaped metallic miniatures had already circulated by then.[30] The fact that most Western experts and some Chinese ones date the *daobi* and *bubi* no earlier than the sixth century BCE might still not completely undermine Xiao's argument because no comparative radiocarbon analysis of Lydian and early Chinese coinage seems to have been carried out yet. Notably, prominent Chinese archaeologist Hua Jueming, although implicitly accepting the precedence of Lydian coinage, has nevertheless insisted bronze casting developed completely autochthonously in China.[31] It would appear, at any rate, that greater scholarly attention to this dating issue might be called for, if only to put Lacouperie's assertions in perspective.

Renowned Chinese numismatist Wang Yuquan believed that early Chinese cast-bronze coinage, which typically had a round and later a square hole for stringing (*yuanqian*), endogenously evolved during the late Warring States era (475–221 BCE) from the spade-miniature design without any foreign influence. For Wang, the proof for such endogenous evolution was the fact that many of the early Chinese round coins excavated in areas once pertaining to the preimperial Qin State had been cast with the character *liang* to denote weight—the same character that many older *bubi* coins of the same area carried. In areas pertaining to the Wei Warring State, however, round coins often carried place names, leading Wang to speculate that the transition to round coinage, which swept China from the Qin southward during the third century BCE, also had to do with assertion of regional loyalties.[32]

The doyen of Chinese numismatics, Peng Xinwei, was somewhat less confident about the distinct origin and evolution of preimperial Chinese currency. Peng implicitly rejected the notion that cowrie or *bubi* could serve as proof for the earlier formation of currency in China compared with the West. Yet he stopped short of explicitly conceding a possible West Asian influence on the Chinese transition to round coinage. The first variants of *yuanqian* conveyed, in his view, *not* regional loyalties or affinity with the *bubi* but rather a stark conceptual departure from the emulation of metallic tools like spades and knives to signifying the value implicit in the utility of a spinning whorl. By suggesting that the stone spinning whorl was the mainspring of *yuanqian*, Peng also gave short shrift to another once-dominant school of thought in Japan, which posited sacrificial jade discs as the subject of *yuanqian* emulation.[33]

More recently, Dai Zhiqiang and Zhou Weirong have noted in their important brief survey that the emergence of spade currency in China closely matched the onset of Lydian coinage. They attributed this cotemporality to similarities in the formation of polities vying for commercial supremacy in either Asia Minor or the Yellow River basin. Yet Dai and Zhou believe, too, that the subsequent monetary trajectory on either extreme of the Eurasian landmass was "separate"; hence they do not discuss the universalization of round currency in its own right. In other words, they see the invention of coinage in either case as purely endogenous, as was, in their view, the evolution of Chinese and Greco-Roman metallurgy.[34]

To my mind, however, all of the main theories that suggest a purely endogenous transition to round coinage in China carry weak links. By contrast, I argue that a closer examination of archaeological, demographic, and circumstantial evidence found in more recent studies might occasion a reassessment of the plausibility of exogenous factors in triggering the transition to round coinage in China.

The evidence will be presented in the following two sections in more detail. Suffice it to say here that the proverbial linkage of *yuanqian* round currency to jade discs is commonly supported by a reference to the *Erya*, a Chinese lexical compilation of no earlier than the third century BCE. The *Erya* famously contains a taxonomy of three jade discs, based on the proportion of the hole to the rim.[35] But, strangely enough, this commonly cited entry does not feature any reference to metal. In fact the whole *Erya* segment in which this entry appears, along with subsequent premodern exegeses, scarcely carries any characters formed of the radical for metal or anything that might allude to copper casting.

Indeed, citing the *Erya* to support an essentially numismatic argument brings to mind another questionable convention: The first *yuanqian* specimens feature in fact a round hole rather than a square one. Traditionally, the First Emperor's reversion to a square hole is explained in terms of enforcing his "mandate from heaven" to exclusively issue currency. That notion is supported, in turn, by a famous segment of the *Lüshi chunqiu* ("Master Lü's Spring and Autumn Annals," ca. 239 BCE), which is similarly devoid of any specific reference to currency or metallurgy. Rather, the segment generally establishes roundness as a symbol of "heaven" and squareness as a symbol of the "earth." Yet, Hua Jueming has more recently argued the transition from round *yuanqian* holes to square ones had little to do with symbolism but ensued in the main from technological considerations. Namely, coinage with square-hole inner rims was easier to polish with a file.[36]

One might find fault with Peng's rationale precisely on the same grounds: Why would *yuanqian* emulate a spinning whorl typically made of stone at that era, when the earlier *bubi* and *daobi* were miniatures of cast-bronze tools, presumably deriving their value from the fact that they could be recast into real knives and spades? Finally, it is odd that none of the leading Chinese numismatists entertained the possibility of an exogenous impact, when all knew full well that one of the main *older* bronze currencies of the Warring State of Chu was in fact modeled on cowrie, commonly believed to have been imported from Southeast Asia.[37]

That *yuanqian* has remained associated with a "separate" monetary tradition may implicitly be predicated, at least in part, on the common assumption that this type of coinage had first emerged in the state of Wei around the mid-fourth century BCE, Qin's immediate neighbor to the east, rather than on Qin's western frontier. However, even proponents of the "separate" school concede that round coinage spread to the far west (and east) of Wei within a decade or so. To my knowledge, no extensive radiocarbon dating or extensive archaeological surveys have been carried out to substantiate the case for clear Wei precedence. Neither would Wei precedence, if proven beyond doubt, completely rule out the possibility of foreign impact from the north.[38]

The Eurasia-wide transition to round coinage at roughly that point in time, not just in China but, as we shall show in the following pages, also in India, is quite striking and may possibly be indicative of the impact of Western or West Asian (Lydian, Ionian-Greek, and Achaemenid) monetary traditions on East and South Asian currency systems. It might perhaps suggest that earlier contacts with West Asian coinage (most likely the Greco-Bactrian variety) may have had something to do with the emergence of *yuanqian* in China. Indeed several ancient observers— Pliny the Elder (ca. 43–79 CE) is perhaps the best-known one—seem to suggest that Greco-Roman coinage had habitually flowed eastward in return for Chinese and Indian luxury commodities.[39]

Scheidel's pioneering study of the level of monetization in Rome calls for a more detailed account of the technological as well as organizational development of mining in either region, not least because the European economy relied on metal coinage right up to the appearance of paper money there in the mid-seventeenth century. A cursory comparison would suggest that, despite broadly similar excavation tools, Roman mining ventures were far more extensive and went vertically deeper into the ground than those in early imperial China. Many mines gradually became the property of the Roman state but—somewhat contrary to the overall Chinese pattern—cities and private individuals continued to own and operate large-scale mines. Even in its state-owned mines, Rome sometimes leased out operating contracts to individuals, small associations, or the larger *societates publicanorum* (or *publicani*), with slaves and wage laborers making up the actual workforce.[40]

Publicani consisted of *socii* (partners), who put up the capital and were governed by one or more *magistri*, who bought the contract. By the late republic, they acted as bankers to the state, and their messengers would transport mail for officials and important private individuals. In the late republican era, there was even a market for unregistered shares (*partes*) in Roman *publicani*, which by now operated much like a cartel.[41] It would be difficult to find in imperial Chinese history a parallel to the role played by *publicani* in the Roman polity either in the mining sector or as tax collectors for the state.

In comparative terms, it is worth remembering that bronze casting had been practiced in Lydia at least 1,500 years before coinage emerged, and iron had been smelted at least 500 years beforehand. Right from its inception, the production of Lydian coinage was different from the techniques traditionally used in China: Lydian and later most Western blanks were individually cast and then struck with images using metal pellets and engraved hammering, whereas most Chinese round coinage was mass-cast with minimalist inscription as part of the mold itself. Around the second century BCE there is evidence for the spread of chaplet casting in coin production in some parts of Europe, a technique not unlike the ancient Chinese coin production mode, but the practice definitively disappeared in the Middle Ages. In thirteenth-century England, there was a further technological departure, as "moneyers" began to use precision shears to cut identical square coin blanks off long iron or gold-cast bars and then rework them into sturdy round coins through hammering and blanching. The last important technological departure in Europe before steam-powered mints was the transition in the sixteenth century to mechanized coin production using rolling-mills and the screw presses, which allowed for higher-quality rimming to combat clipping, chipping, and other forms of debasement.[42]

METALLURGIC EVIDENCE FROM ASIA MINOR, IRAN, AND INDIA

New archaeological evidence from Nush-i-Jan in Western Iran suggests that Babylonian-inspired "ring money" had already been in use in the Median Empire (728–549 BCE). Some of these rings seem to be of standardized design, and it is likely that their weights were also standard across the region.[43] It is evident that the lands constituting the subsequent Achaemenid Empire (550–330 BCE) had inherited from earlier centuries two entirely separate currency systems, which coexisted side by side until the last decades of the empire. On the one hand, the territories south and east of the Taurus based their currency on a Sumer-Babylonian–derived silver standard. That standard then expanded under the Assyrians, and later under the Achaemenids, to embrace Egypt, Syria, Eastern Anatolia, the Iranian Plateau, and the Indo-Iranian borderlands. Though commodities such as gold, lead, corn, meat, or wine served from time to time as media of payment in the eastern reaches of the Achaemenid Empire, the standard of worth there was mostly provided by fine silver. The same standard could have influenced India's ancient punch-marked silver coinage.[44]

By way of contrast, the satrapy of Lydia embodied the electrum/gold-coin standard that was to define the northwestern reaches of the Achaemenid Empire. Though interchangeable by a fixed exchange rate

(1:20), the lower-denomination silver sigloi (derived from *shekel*) seems to have been the imperial coinage of the East, whereas the gold daric was more commonly the coinage of the western parts of the Iranian Empire and beyond. Daric coins have been excavated mostly in Asia Minor, Greece, Macedonia, and Italy. The sigloi denomination has been found mostly further eastward in hoards in Asia Minor to Pakistan, making it an important issue for the region.[45]

Moreover, the Greek Attic tetradrachm was likely designed for conversion into the units of the silver-standard Achaemenid East. In Achaemenid Egypt, the circulation of Greek-Athenian coinage attained an enormous volume. In contrast to the East, which had an Assyrian heritage, the Achaemenid satrapies of Western Anatolia evolved a currency of gold, either mixed or pure. In that region the earliest true coins had been struck in electrum, the natural alloy of silver and gold.[46]

The new evidence from Nush-i-Jan suggests quite persuasively that the monetary use of silver ingots arose well before the emergence of round Lydian electrum coinage and persisted in the face of increasing competition from the innovation of coined silver. However, the ultimate adaptation of the round golden daric across the Achaemenid Empire is a testament to the powerful influence of the Anatolian innovation of round currency.[47]

To complete this complex picture, one must consider the extent to which this seventh-century Lydian innovation had an impact on the early forms of Indian currency within the next two centuries, that is, decidedly prior to the emergence of Chinese round coinage (*yuanqian*). The archaeological evidence seems to suggest that the use of silver as money was introduced into India, as in Greece, through the medium of Mesopotamian material culture, even if the motifs on Indian "bent-bar" or later "punch-marked" silver coinage are considered unquestionably indigenous. To be sure, the ingots found at Nush-i-Jan bear resemblance to Indian silver "bent bars" excavated in Afghanistan. Notably, even Professor Schaps—whose important recent study rejected the notion of possible Western impact on the Chinese transition to round currency—conceded that the putatively indigenous ancient coinage of India could have in fact been engendered by Mesopotamian–Acahaemenid contact because monetary silver itself was hardly mentioned in the Vedic literature and must have been introduced from an alien civilization.[48]

Several numismatists pointed to Babylonian influence on early Indian coinage. There is noticeable resemblance between Babylonian shekels and the punch-marked coins; both are irregular in shape but conform to a certain weight standard; neither bears inscription. As such, Babylonian silver bars have not been excavated in India proper; neither are there explicit records of trade contacts between India and Mesopotamia in Buddhist literature. There are many more records, however, attesting to the Achaemenid invasion of India and to the introduction of many elements of Persian culture, of which the Indian mints may have drawn more direct inspiration.[49]

Although round coinage of the Hellenistic type is conventionally thought to have been introduced on the Iranian Plateau no earlier than the reign of Seleucus I (r. 305–281 BCE), it is important to note that round daric and sigloi coins had circulated in Asia Minor well before Alexander's defeat of the Achaemenid Empire and its invasion of India. The daric was likely struck only in Western satrapies, but it was a recognized imperial unit of account across the Iranian-Afghan satrapies, too, and even "far beyond" the Persian empire, so much so that it later served as a model for the currency standard Alexander established in that region. By contrast, fifth-century BCE sigloi were more of a local currency grounded in Asia Minor and only seldom found their way to Egypt or Syria. Therefore, the fact that Achaemenid coins have not yet been excavated on China's western frontier or in India proper cannot resolutely nullify the hypothesis of vicarious Lydian-Achaemenid impact on China's transition to round coinage in the third century BCE, even before the spread of Greco-Bactrian round coinage across Central Asia. This hypothesis, in turn, gains credence when examining the Indian transition to round coinage, which occurred about the same time as China's and in similar circumstances.[50]

Echoing Lacouperie, a few nineteenth-century European scholars mistakenly attributed the emergence of Indian coinage to Alexander's invasion of India, thus dating it around the fourth century BCE. However, more recent radiocarbon examinations suggest the first bent bars and punch-marked coins of India date as far back as the sixth century BCE. The largest Indian polity issuing these coins was Magadha, whose ancient capital of Pataliputra was situated not very far from the modern city of Patna. Yet such coins have been excavated right throughout the Indo-Gangetic plane and as far west as Afghanistan. Most of these coins are irregular (or rectangular) in shape, but oval (or circular specimens) also exist. Indian coinage remained rectangular and *silver*-cast for the most part even after Alexander's invasion, for example the Karshapana variant of the Mauryan era (321–185 BCE), but rectangular *copper* coins with similar motifs were also cast during that era.[51]

Indian-Iranian cultural and economic contacts long predate the eastern conquests of Cyrus (558–530 BCE), who annexed to his empire the Indian region of Gandhara (in contemporary Punjab). During Darius's reign (552–486 BCE), another military foray into northwestern India was launched. There are recorded contacts with India in Achaemenid inscriptions at Persepolis and at Naksh-i-Rustam. The Iranian occupation of that region continued well into the early fifth century BCE, thus predating the onset of Hellenic hegemony (Achaemenid rule over India, however, had all but vanished by the time Alexander reached the Punjab, and there is no clear evidence of Iranian impact in the region into the fourth century). Though daric coins have not been excavated in India proper, it is likely that Achaemenid currency was well known in India during the fifth century BCE, and silver may have flowed into the country in exchange for gold dust.

Irrespective of whether the early coinage of Maghada had been vicariously inspired by Babylonian or Achaemenid unstruck silver bars, the fact is that the Mauryan (321–185 BCE) bent-bar and punch-marked coinage of India seems to have slowly but consistently transmuted into more circular shapes during Ashoka's reign (304–232 BCE), and this was likely through expanding trade contacts with Western coinage as well as Buddhist missionary traffic around entrepôts such as Taxila.[52] Notably, by the first century CE bent-bar and punch-marked coinage had been completely supplanted by round coinage of the Greco-Bactrian streak. Though Buddhist missionaries had not yet reached China at that stage, putative early Qin contact with round coinage in Central Asia may also explain why knife and spade coinage was giving way to *yuanqian* at roughly the same time.

On Alexander's conquest of Bactria, Indian coinage also started shedding semiabstract endogenous motifs for anthropogenic Greek ones. The Hellenization of Indian coinage culminated during the reign of Kanishka (r. second century CE), of the Kushan empire.[53] Surprisingly enough, this cross-Eurasian temporal and archaeological set of circumstances has not been widely discussed in the numismatic literature, which on the whole still seems regionally compartmentalized, if not somewhat resistant to the new discourses of world history. Yet, recent archaeological evidence supports the enlargement of the scope within which early Hellenistic coinage (and possibly Achaemenid coinage) is known to have circulated—well into South India.[54] Archaeological evidence confirming the flow of Hellenistic coinage into China's west before the Common Era has, on the other hand, not yet emerged.

LATER EVIDENCE FROM THE SILK ROAD

The Kushans who brought about this final transformation in Indian coinage would rule an empire that covered most of what is now Central Asia, Xinjiang, and northern India during the reign of the famous Kanishka previously mentioned. Their territory would during this period border the western extremity of Chinese Han Empire. In 161 CE a Kushan subking named Xie in Chinese was sent out by the Kushan king to attack the Han Chinese military commander in the Tarim basin, Ban Chao.[55] What is very relevant for our purposes is the fact that these Kushans were one of the five Da Yuezhi tribes who had conquered the Greco-Bactrian kingdom centuries earlier.[56] The Da Yuezhi were steppe nomads of Scythian-Tocharian extraction,[57] driven out of what is now Gansu and Xinjiang provinces of China by the Xiongnu in about 162 BCE.[58] Prior to that they had been the immediate western neighbors of the Xiongnu and the Warring States kingdom of Qin. Their migration west caused a chain reaction that drove the Sai (Saka) into Parthia and the conquest of Bactria by the Yuezhi themselves.[59] The Parthian kings Phraates II (Justin XLII 1.5) and Artabanus II (Justin XLII 2.2, combating the Tochari) were killed by the invading "Scythians,"[60] and only in the reign of Mithradates II (beginning ca. 124 BCE) could the Parthians contain them in Sistan.[61]

Rebuffed in Iran, the Yuezhi would later in the first and second centuries CE clash with the Han Empire and the Xiongnu in Western Turkestan and the Tarim basin. Chinese sources refer to the five lords of the Yuezhi who ruled the five tribes of their imperial confederation.[62] Of these five, the lord of the Guishuang/Kushan tribe would gradually emerge as the ruling power under King Kujula Kadphises.[63] The Kushans, who on their coins proudly depicted themselves wearing the typical Central Asian/Scythian peaked headdress and long boots, thereby highlighting their origins,[64] are perhaps best known for having been primarily responsible in transmitting Buddhism to China. Having situated themselves at the very center of the vast trade networks between the Mediterranean world and East Asia, the Kushans would use the Greek alphabet as part of their writing system and trade actively with both the Greco-Roman world and the Chinese.[65] Greco-Roman artistic traditions would have a significant impact on the art and architecture of the Kushans, especially in the realms of sculpture and ornamentation,[66] and via them between the second century BCE and the third century CE on the Buddhist artistic tradition of East Asia.[67]

Given this later evidence of the dramatic impact of Kushan-sponsored Buddhist Gandhara art on Chinese culture and art, there is no reason to deny the possibility that before the second century BCE these same Yuezhi-Kushans, when situated right next to Qin, could have potentially fulfilled a similar role in the transmission of ideas and material culture between China and West Asia. Between the death of Alexander and the imposition of the round coinage across China by the First Emperor of Qin, the areas immediately adjacent to both the Greco-Bactrian kingdom and Qin (Gansu and Xinjiang) had been inhabited by the Yuezhi and related Scythian-Tocharian peoples such as the Saka and Wusun.[68] They would no doubt have traded with the peoples of Sogdia and Bactria, who during this period used the round coins of the Greco-Bactrian kings. It would be almost inconceivable that none of this trade traffic involving goods and coins found its way east to Qin.

Even more important perhaps is the fact that it is during this very period (late fourth to mid-third centuries BCE) that the Chinese Warring States, especially Qin and Zhao, were most open and receptive to influences from the steppe. King Wuling of Zhao (325–299 BCE), right after the death of Alexander in the West, would scandalize more conservative states to the east by adopting so-called Hu (that is, nomadic Inner Asian steppe) customs and even clothing in an effort to update his military along the lines of steppe cavalry.[69] Such was the prevailing mood in these western and northern Warring States, and it is entirely probable that currency reforms in imitation of practices found in Bactria (that is, round coinage) and possibly also among the Yuezhi may have taken place in Qin, which was the closest of the Warring States to the Yuezhi.

The earliest historic record attesting to minute Chinese knowledge of the trappings of Hellenistic coinage is quite revealing. Ban Gu's (32?–92 CE) famous *Hanshu* ("History of the Former Han Dynasty") was sealed around 111 CE but relates in the main events that had occurred between 206 BCE and 6 CE. In his portrayal of central Asia, Ban refers to the kingdom of Jibin that was probably situated in modern eastern Afghanistan as a place where coinage was typically made of gold and silver and inscribed with a mounted warrior on one side and a human face on the other.[70]

In sum, strong circumstantial evidence speaks to the plausibility of the transmission of round coinage from Bactria to China. Yet the earliest archaeological evidence from the silk road that might suggest West Asian impact on the transition to round coinage in China, or at the very least mutual awareness of the distinct currency systems across Eurasia, does not go much further back than the beginning of the common era. Nicola Di Cosmo, in turn, has persuasively shown that the nomadic peoples living in present-day Mongolia around the fourth century BCE traded extensively with China and greatly valued knife coins, as evidenced in burial hoards. These peoples could also cast copper and iron, although metallurgic know-how itself reached them not from China but probably from the Pamirs.[71]

In eastern Scythian tombs from the fourth century BCE, electrum jugs bearing Bactrian patterns were found but not Bactrian coins. In excavations of Xiongnu tombs in present-day Mongolia, golden jewelry from the West was found alongside Chinese silk, but, again, Hellenistic coinage was nowhere to be seen. In sites as faraway east as the Feng Sufu tombs (Beipiao, Liaoning) glassware of Roman origin was found dating back to fifth century CE, yet even in a site of that later era no Roman coinage has been found to date.[72] Sassanid and Roman gold coins were found, by contrast, near Huhehot in Inner Mongolia.[73] Therefore, in the absence of clear-cut archaeological findings that might better define the perimeters of world trade around the third century BCE, the most compelling numismatic finding pertinent to this study is that which emerged in the beginning of the last century in Shaanxi province and in the Xinjiang oasis of Khotan (Hetian).

Between CE 30 and CE 150 the Buddhist kings of Khotan issued their own hybrid coinage, which clearly attests to the knowledge and fusion of Greek and Chinese motifs and, to a lesser extent, of production techniques. These copper coins were struck rather than mass cast for the most part, with Chinese characters on one side conveying standard weight and Sino-Kharosthi script on the other side denoting the king's name. The coins appear to have been designed in a way that could make them convertible to both Bactrian *tetradrachm* and Chinese *liang* standard—notably, Kushan and Chinese coins of the same era were also found alongside the Khotan hybrid. Similar hybrid coinage was also found in the oasis of Kucha, but the latter carried more inscriptions. Elsewhere in the region, Sassanid coinage was used quite extensively from the fourth century CE until the spread of the popular Chinese *kaiyuan tongbao* coin during the early Tang era (seventh century CE).[74]

The coins found in Shaanxi in the early twentieth century do not carry Chinese characters at all but a script thought until recently to have been a variant of classical Greek. The dating of these coins is not in dispute as much as their origin. In a recent article, Mark Whaley suggested, for example, that the inscriptions the coins carry are in fact a variant of Sino-Kharosthi. The Kharoshthi script was a derivative of the Kushan lingua franca (Prakrit) popularized in Central Asia as a medium for government, trade, and the transmission of Buddhism. It was used in Ashokan inscriptions in northwest India and may have been initially modelled on Aramaic. For Whaley, this was evidence that the Wei River Valley in Shaanxi, where the coins were found, had strong trade contact with northwest India mediated by the Tocharian minority that resided in present-day Gansu around 120 BCE.[75] The existence of these Sino-Kharosthi coins may be a testament to early extensive trade between India and Bactria in the west and China in the east. Whether such contacts existed as early as the fourth and third centuries BCE is a moot point. Yet even if trade and the transmission of Buddhism into Central Asia had nothing to do with China's transition to round coinage, one can by no means rule out earlier Chinese contact with Achaemenid currency.

CONCLUSIONS

The origin of the inspiration behind the *yuanqian* round coinage standardized across China by the First Emperor of Qin in the third century BCE has remained obscure and is still a contentious issue. Yet this chapter has demonstrated that the various theories for endogenous inspiration vouched for by many scholars in either East Asia or the West all carry inherent contradictions. In contrast, circumstantial and archaeological evidence in support of exogenous origin is quite compelling.

We have observed how evidence from the Middle East points to the early invention and wide circulation of round coinage in Lydia, Greece, and the Achaemenid Empire. The expansion of the Persians into India in the sixth century BCE and the later incursions by Alexander and the Greco-Bactrians in the fourth and third centuries BCE all facilitated and may have decisively contributed to India's adoption of round coinage, which was completed under the aegis of the Kushan kings in the second century CE. Given the strong likelihood, if not certainty, of West Asian inspiration for India's monetary transformation, it would be unwarranted to completely rule out a similar scenario for China, which during the same period (third century BCE) also experienced the transition to round currency.

The flow of ideas, artistic motifs, and metallurgic know-how from West Asia to China via Central Asia had occurred much earlier than the third century BCE. Active adoption of foreign (Central Eurasian steppe) customs in the fourth century BCE is recorded in Chinese preimperial records and evidenced in recent archaeological findings across Eurasia.

Unlike Europe, Chinese coin production remained until the nineteenth century CE grounded in base metal use and (perhaps consequently) was based on casting rather than minting techniques. Yet it is fairly widely accepted that the transmission of rudimentary metallurgical know-how from west Asia to China had occurred long before the adoption of round coinage by Qin. That being the case, acknowledging the probable external origin of Chinese round coinage becomes less problematic.

The case for exogenous impact gains further credence when we consider the fact that the very people who helped seal India's adoption of round coinage, the Kushans and their Scythian-Tocharian vassals, had been earlier in the third century BCE the immediate western neighbors of the nascent Qin Empire and other states where round coinage first emerged. Thus, much of the circumstantial and historical evidence seems to support the hypothesis that the introduction of round coinage to China was part of the monetary revolution that swept across the whole of Eurasia. Ongoing archaeological work in China's western provinces could further highlight this ancient phase of globalization that, quite literally, still shapes our most fundamental grasp of money.

But what have the origins of round coinage got to do with subsequent chapters' emphasis on the pursuit of revenue through debasement by medieval and early modern rulers across Eurasia? I would argue that an examination of the political economy of today's fiat currencies cannot be separated from the vitality of monetary standardization to the extraction of coin seigniorage within the premodern polity. If monetary distinctiveness was the corollary of territorial sovereignty in the twentieth century, then we would need to better demarcate the ways in which the former departed from much earlier phases of monetary standardization within and across different polities. In this context, important studies such as that of Angela Redish have greatly advanced our understanding of the diffusion of mechanized minting across early modern Europe in terms of the need to produce a more uniformly round coinage, one that would be more resistant to wear and tear and pervasive clipping.[76]

Implicitly, it is otherwise assumed that all around the world "roundness" had been found to be practically superior to other forms of coinage in antiquity, long before Leonardo da Vinci explicitly stated so; the Renaissance, after all, was at a time when the mechanization of European round coin production was just beginning.[77] Whether the recognition of the superior quality of round coinage had been reached through trial and error or cross-fertilization beforehand is rarely discussed. It might then follow that premodern rulers resorted to "roundness" as one of the key means of combating forgeries and enhancing durability and reputation. Yet, in the European context, monetary sovereignty also implied the need to keep coinage distinct from that of other polities through elaborate insignia. As will be shown in the following pages, the ways and means by which these competing thrusts of convergence and divergence were historically negotiated in China reveal not just the compelling allure of material or technological benefit but also the significance of historic precedent (read: "path dependency") in determining the acceptable perimeters of what money should be like. In that sense, the contribution of this chapter to the literature is not so much in providing a definitive answer to the question of precisely where and when money first originated or why its shape converged. Rather, the contribution may lie in explicitly and loudly articulating these very same questions and perusing the pertinent literature in their light.

CHAPTER TWO

From Coinage to Paper Money

The Origins and Evolution of Chinese and Western Banknotes in Comparison

ORIGINS

To better explain the different numismatic traditions across Eurasia leading up to the emergence of paper money in the early modern era, and to account for their permutations afterward, one must view early imperial China and the Greco-Roman world in a broader perspective. Rome developed without the use of coinage right until the late fourth century BCE, trailing behind much of the Hellenic world. Before it cast its first bronze coins, Rome had embraced the coinage of Magna Graecia. It was only after the first Pyrrhic War (280–275 BCE) that the Roman silver didrachm appeared alongside bronze coins, sustained by a conversion ratio (1:120) that was more than eightfold lower than the one normally prevalent between the standard silver weight unit and bronze coinage in imperial China (1:1,000).[1]

By the early second century CE, the vast majority of coins cast in Rome were made of bronze; cast bronze coinage saw continued use as a form of token currency used to pay soldiers or divide war booty, whereas struck bronze became a subsidiary of silver coinage.[2] The Mediterranean is replete with place names that are associated with metal production. The Romans, who decisively supplanted Macedonian hegemony in 197 BCE, first mined copper—the main component of bronze—in Cyprus (Kypris), whence the Latin name for this metal derives. Likewise, the provenance of Roman bronze was the homophonous city of Brundisium (today, Brindisi), where the Romans processed Cypriot copper. Silver and gold were largely mined further to the west in Gaul and Rio Tinto in the Iberian Peninsula.

As more silver mines were brought back to life in Macedonia by the Roman Republic, the silver denarii were set to become the monetary pillar of the nascent Augustine Empire. It is estimated that, between 85 to 50 BCE, over 400 million of these silver coins had been in circulation.[3] Crude ingots and cast bronze coins had become all but defunct by then across the Western flank of the Roman empire, but the variety of coinage was otherwise kaleidoscopic—it was augmented by hundreds of types of strictly city-minted and locality-bound coins in the Eastern reaches of the empire up until the third century CE. It would therefore be plausible to assume that the later Roman Empire (284–602 CE) did *not* form a single circulation area.

The political vacuum that befell Europe after the disintegration of Rome in the fifth century left large areas of the western empire, including the British Isles, without coinage for almost 200 years. Roman gold coinage all but disappeared from sight, the first English silver penny having been struck only in 765. Thereafter, English silver coinage served as a model for the first indigenous coinages of Poland and much of Scandinavia.[4] However, it was only in the tenth century that England's new "sterling" (that is, superior) silver coinage emerged. The units of account that medieval English silver pennies were ultimately measured against, "shillings," were in fact derived from a much older Roman gold coin, the solidus; shillings did not become tangible coins themselves until the Tudor era. In fact, the first English gold coin to circulate widely, the noble, would appear only as late as 1351.[5]

The breakup of the Eastern Han Empire and the ensuing political disunion in China did not result in a comparable monetary upheaval. Rather, a long continuum of monetary advances had arguably put China ahead of both Europe and the Middle East within five centuries, so that by the time banknotes began appearing in Europe in the seventeenth century they had already been widely experimented with in East Asia. In the greater scheme of things, what set China's early monetary evolution most notably apart from the rest of the civilized world was its reliance on cast-bronze coinage and the rare occurrence of gold as a standard means of payment in the Common Era.[6]

To be sure, Dong Zhuo (?–192 CE) the notorious warlord who had brought the Eastern Han empire to its end, greatly debased its standard *wuzhu* coinage in favor of smaller, clipped coinage of the same nominal value. The Eastern Han monetary system had been fairly stable up to this point, with relatively rare incidence of illicit "private coinage." On the other end of the debasement spectrum, Sun Quan, who established himself as the breakaway king of Wu, issued between 238 and 246 CE slightly bigger (about 7 gram) coinage than the *wuzhu* but declared it to be worth no less than a thousand older coins each (*daquan dangqian*).[7]

Lower levels of monetization occurred for the most part during the Six Dynasties era of political disintegration (222–589 CE), particularly north of the Yellow River. Weaker central authority than the one prevalent during the Eastern Han led to the spread of "private coinage," along with a greater tolerance of it by the authorities. Once effectively in private hands, coin-mold casting technology improved considerably even as overall coin output diminished.[8]

In response to the diminishing output of standard coinage, rife debasement and concomitant forgeries a few eminent contemporaries like warlord Huan Xuan (369–404 CE) or scholar and statesman Shen Yue (441–513 CE) proposed that coinage be replaced entirely by commodity moneys like grain or silk. Others, like General Shen Qingzhi (386–465 CE), recommended the legitimization of private coinage at the expense of the state's prerogative to issue money. Yet, despite political disunion and such dissenting standpoints, the convention of Chinese statecraft that placed bronze coinage as a mainstay of the economy remained largely in force. It was reflected in for example Lu Bao's (c. 300 CE) famous *Qianshenlun*, a satire of the tendency of the time to fetishize bronze coinage, or in the influential polemics against commodity money by scholar Kong Linzhi (369–422 CE).[9]

Professor Mark E. Lewis has noted, more broadly, that arable land was comparatively scarcer in early imperial China and natural deepwater ports few and far between, resulting in fairly insular population concentrations. In the Roman Empire it was cheaper to ship grain than it was in China because grain-basket regions in the Mediterranean region were strung together in close proximity to one another.[10] But perhaps a more important difference from a numismatic perspective was the fact that the city-state modality and coinage issued by city-states was paramount in the Greco-Roman world, whereas in China cities were—to use Lewis's description—physically and ideologically "evanescent." Unlike in ancient Rome, medieval Europe, or India, Chinese emperors avoided revealing themselves to the inhabitants of their capital cities; hence the absence of anthropomorphic images on East Asian coinage.[11]

Walter Scheidel weighed into the equation with factors such as the comparatively loose connection between ideology and political power in Rome as opposed to the pervasive Confucian-legalist narrative underlying state authority in Qin-Han China. Perhaps for that reason, the power of the warrior class in China "was mostly contained"; a relatively large civilian bureaucracy emerged in China, and there was less reliance on slave labor. Scheidel then marshals disparate secondary sources to suggest that, by 400 CE, the Roman empire employed 30,000 civilian officials as compared to around four times that many in Western Han China (206 BCE–9 CE).[12]

But, from a numismatic perspective, another of Scheidel's observations is more compelling: Based on various sources he reached the tentative conclusion that Rome, with the vast mineral riches it possessed in tandem with the preponderance of precious metals in postrepublican coinage, was a far more monetized polity than China.[13]

Nevertheless, monetary paper instruments appeared in China earlier; indeed, paper itself had been invented there (in the Han period).[14] Some of the earliest precursors of banking and fiduciary currency in China date back to the commercial heyday of the Tang dynasty (617–907 CE). A case in point is the appearance of *guifang* or "counting houses" where, for a small service charge, merchants could deposit liquid funds to protect them from fire or theft and draft checks to a third party against the deposits whenever necessary. The proprietors of these early financial institutions are believed to have devised call loan schemes resourced on their clients' deposits to increase house turnover. By the early tenth century, however, the *guifang* allegedly had become associated with dubious speculators who habitually debased coin deposits for quick gains or turned the counting houses they owned into gambling dens.[15]

The *guifang* was concurrent with another notable Tang monetary innovation: "flying cash" (*feiqian*), introduced during the emperor Xianzong's (r. 806–820 CE) reign. Flying cash comprised a public-order mechanism whereby merchants received from the imperial treasury against liquid deposits a paper scrip that could be carried into other provinces easily and cashed in local flying cash depots as the need arose. *Guifang* and flying cash depots dotted the Tang capital of Chang'an and other urban centers. They became the most visible sign of an increasingly sophisticated credit economy. But while private-order counting houses were gradually falling from grace, variants of flying cash continued to be used throughout the subsequent Five Dynasties era (907–960 CE), laying the groundwork for the dissemination of the world's first full-fledged fiduciary paper money during the Northern Song era (960–1127 CE).[16]

THE "SONG INDUSTRIAL REVOLUTION"

The concept of fiduciary money in China drew on the first monetary uses of paper scrip during the latter part of the Tang era, as well as from the variegated occurrence of base metals in interregional trade after the collapse of the Tang and the ensuing political disunion of the Five Dynasties. That period saw extensive internecine warfare that brought copper mining to a near standstill in the north. Because copper was becoming more and more scarce, almost all the contending warlords of the time attempted to prevent bronze coinage from flowing into their rivals' hands as a result of cross-border trade. Their respective kingdoms—Southern Han, Min, Wu Yue, Southern Tang, Chu, Later Tang, and Later Shu—cast heavily debased or token coinage from lead, iron, or even clay so that it could be used domestically, for example, to pay soldiers' salaries. These coins were, of course, of very little intrinsic value, and ipso facto constitute the first step toward ridding Chinese currency of its metallic anchorage.

With the reestablishment of political unity in China by the Northern Song era in the tenth and eleventh centuries, a whole new range of credit instruments surfaced; there was, for example, a private-order arrangement dubbed *she* whereby buyers would issue wholesale vendors a one-month promissory note (*qiyue*) made payable after the resale of goods. The circulation of these promissory notes lent the backdrop against which use of the Sichuan iron-denominated notes could become widespread.[17]

As the Northern Song armies were consolidating their power in Sichuan at the end of the tenth century, the cumbersome form of iron currency prevalent in the Later Shu could not be adequately replaced with the new dynastic bronze standard mainly due to an unrealistic official exchange rate proclaimed by the authorities. Consequently, the heavy Sichuan iron coins were deposited in bulk in return for promissory notes that had since been issued and regulated by sixteen of the wealthiest families in the region.[18] Critically, note regulation was taken over by officialdom once the Song dynasty had firmly asserted its authority in the Southwest. This unceremonious turnaround provided the setting in which the world's first fiduciary paper money tender surfaced.[19]

That sequence of events that led to the Song takeover of the private-order notes circulating in the Sichuan region (then called Yizhou) is meandering and therefore hard to follow, but it is critical to our understanding of monetary history in comparative terms. When Song administrators took over the Later Shu in 965, they discovered that the kingdom's domestic iron coinage had by then driven out better-quality bronze coinage from circulation as Gresham's Law might have predicted. Nevertheless, by 979, they indicated that they would introduce a *gradual* commutation of tax liabilities from iron coinage to standard bronze coinage. Yet these intentions immediately sparked a free fall in the relative price of iron coinage as the local population scrambled to source bronze coinage wherever possible. In 982, Song administrators therefore decided to avert the unrest in the marketplace and to allow for a separate currency zone in Sichuan where Later Shu iron coinage would continue to be admissible for tax purposes and where provincial mints would continue to cast new Northern Song coinage made of iron. Sichuan merchants in need of bronze coinage to purchase goods in bulk from other provinces were accordingly forced to exchange iron coinage at government-approved depots.[20]

In 993, despite the Song's willingness to accommodate heavier iron coinage, its plummeting exchange rate against bronze coinage, as well as excessive central-government fiscal extraction in the province, provoked a peasant rebellion around the provincial capital of Chengdu, resulting in the closure of local imperial mint for a year. These circumstances further disrupted the mobility of bulky iron coinage and its supply so that some merchants started disbursing iron-coinage denominated bills instead.[21]

Contrary to expectation perhaps, these bills (*jiaozi*)took hold over the next ten years despite frequent forgery. In 1005, the new Song prefect at Chengdu, Zhang Yong (946–1015), aimed to shore up the value of private-order *jiaozi* by limiting their issue to sixteen of the leading local merchant houses. Limiting issue licences was meant to help the bills gain more traction despite frequent supervisory problems: Tighter local-government oversight did appear to have extended the use of notes.[22]

By 1020, however, private-order *jiaozi* had been rapidly depreciating again and thus were not always honored by the issuing houses; as a result those houses were shut down by Zhang's successor Kou Jian despite much popular protest against their closure. Indeed, China's experience with paper money could have been a very short one if the newly appointed Chengdu prefect, Xue Tian, had not decided to reinstate *jiaozi* as a public-order currency in 1023 and to set up provincial exchange bureaus to administer the conversion between *jiaozi* and metallic currencies for a modest commission of 3 percent. Furthermore, Xue aimed to limit each issue of notes to a three-year period and to a maximum value of 1.25 million strings (*guan*) while requiring that the bureaus hold 360,000 *guan* in metallic reserves at all times.[23]

Before long Song administrators realized that this local Sichuan experiment in official paper money issuance could be expanded to the benefit of the imperial treasury. Merchants who were willing to carry provisions to the northern frontier, where the Song was pitted against Khitans and Tanguts, were often paid with various bills that were convertible to iron coinage or *jiaozi* in Sichuan and backed against state

revenue from its monopoly of the local tea and salt trade. However, by
1105, *jiaozi* notes in Sichuan were depreciating again to the extent they
were declared void unless exchanged for government bronze-coin denominated notes (*qianyin*) at a whopping discount of four to one. Soon
afterward, the costly exigencies of war against the invading Jurchens,
who founded the Jin dynasty, led the Song to overprint *qianyin* until
these notes became next to worthless as well.[24]

An expansion of the credit economy had been part and parcel of what
Mark Elvin and others termed "China's medieval economic revolution"
during the Northern and Southern Song dynasties (960–1127, 1127–
1279).[25] Based in Kaifeng before the Jin onslaught of 1126, the Song
government demonstrated an unparalleled interest in economic reform.
Momentous advancements in metallurgy, weaponry, print, and maritime
navigation defined much of this era. The types and quantity of both fiduciary and metallic money proliferated to the extent that silver bullion
was occasionally required as a high-denomination means of payment.[26]
    Perhaps the most remarkable indicator for the globally unprecedented
level of monetization that the Northern Song economic order ushered
into China is the fact that, overall, up to 70 percent of imperial revenue at the time was levied in the form of metal or paper instruments,
whereas in the preimperial era corvée labor and commodities such as
grain arguably made up the bulk of these revenues. It might be argued
that such a monetized economy could not have emerged by tax conversion alone—it went hand in hand with greater coin output, with innovations such as public-order paper money, and most importantly, with
new marketplace dynamics. Around 1077, for example, annual imperial
revenue was conservatively estimated at 64.5 million strings of cash, of
which only 36.2 percent was levied in the form of traditional land taxes;
this is an impressive total compared with the makeup of Ming and Qing
imperial revenue, considering that China was much more populous in
the later imperial era.[27]
    Notably, other sources of imperial tax revenue in 1077 came from
the salt, wine and tea monopolies (34 percent), from mining activity (6.2
percent), and from commercial imposts (13.5 percent). In other words,
commercial sources of tax adding up to such more traditional sources as
land taxes were becoming very important at the time, even if their overall share was arguably smaller than in early-modern English fiscals. In
any event, during the Southern Song era the ratio of grain to monetary

receipts within imperial revenue was smaller still because the Southern Song lost much taxable arable land to the Jurchen and later to Mongol invaders.[28]

By way of comparison, on the Norman occupation of England in the eleventh century, royal revenue is believed to have relied on land taxes; overall revenue totalled only around 1.7 million pounds annually, of which as much as 64 percent were directed toward military outlay. The Normans therefore introduced a poll tax and a swag of customs and excises that heralded a secular diminution in the share of land taxes of overall royal revenue. While Chinese imperial revenue does not seem to have grown much at all after its Northern Song peak, English royal revenue reached £5 million annually by the early seventeenth century. Equally important, commercial taxes in England had by then made up around 70 percent of revenue; by the early eighteenth century, interest rates in England had been considerably lower than in the eleventh century, and the Crown had begun to accumulate a "national debt" both to foreign lenders and its own subjects through the Bank of England.[29]

Elsewhere in Europe during the late medieval era it could be argued that a ruler's reliance on land taxes was more pronounced than in Northern Song China. Frequent warfare and a bigger military outlay, however, meant that European rulers scrambled to find new sources of revenue by the advent of the early modern era—these ranged from debasement through the sale of aristocratic degrees and charters to commercial exactions such as those imposed at turnpikes.[30]

To sustain the unprecedented pace of monetization of production relations, the Northern Song authorities first aimed at enhancing the output of coinage. The famous reformer Wang Anshi (1021–1086), whom later generations of neo-Confucians would castigate as overly "statist," in fact aimed at enlisting the private sector to ensure that increased output of coinage would be met with sufficient amounts of raw material. To that end, he considerably relaxed the state's monopoly on copper mining (tongjin); he replaced forced labor with recruited miners, gave more autonomy to local pit managers, lifted metal price and transport controls, and reduced taxes on mineral-wealth possession from around 30 percent to only 20 percent, thus enticing more prospectors into the industry.[31]

Once he had acceded to a position of power next to the Emperor Shenzong, Wang Anshi turned the supply of standard coin into one of his key policy planks. Wang vigorously pooled metallurgic know-how and, as previously indicated, provided market incentives to the extent that imperial mines and foundries eventually managed to double their output, extracting 9,000 tons of copper and churning out as many as 5 million bronze coin strings annually, that is, 5 billion individual coins. To understand the sheer scale of Northern Song output, it might be useful to recall that, in the late thirteenth century, the central London Mint is thought to have annually produced only around 50 million silver pennies, England's main currency at the time.[32]

Even output such as Wang Anshi called for did not prove adequate in meeting the demand for bronze coinage because many of the newly produced coins found their way to Korea, Japan, and Southeast Asia, where they were prized as superior media of exchange. Demand for bronze coinage in the vast agricultural sector also put severe pressures on the state-controlled mining industry. Compounding the difficulty in meeting the demand for cash were the relatively high costs of maintaining mint hearths, as opposed to the low seigniorage revenue that the provincial authorities could extract from low-denomination coinage. This set of circumstances resulted in prolonged periods of "coin famine" (*qianhuang*). It was by no means confined to Wang's era: In fact, "coin famines" partly explain the resurgence of iron coinage earlier in the Tang era, as well as later in the Song era.[33]

The difficulty of obtaining cash militated scholars like Zhou Xingji (1067–1125), who supported supplementary paper money issues, to deride the significance people attach to cash, as opposed to "grain." Cash, he averred in terms that would have been familiar to his readers, "cannot be fed on when starving" (*ji bu ke shi*).[34] As mentioned in the Introduction, Zhou concluded (well ahead of his time) that paper money could be stably and profitably maintained as long as the government kept two-thirds of its overall value in coin reserve so that notes would be redeemed on demand. He was correspondingly leery of allowing too much "tenfold-bigger" fiduciary coinage (*dangshiqian*) to circulate in the marketplace lest it unleash inflation. Short of completely ruling out "bigger cash" that was much higher in value than its increased metallic content (*daqian*), or of negating the state's need to raise revenue through seigniorage, Zhou thought that its issue embodied a drastic form of debasement. When taken to its extreme, such bigger coinage could destabilize the entire monetary system. In that sense, he presaged much of the discourse on ideal specie and bullion reserves to support paper money that was to emerge six centuries later in Europe.[35]

As will be discussed in Chapter Five, as late as the nineteenth century the European notion of the right reserve ratio for private-order notes *also* hovered between one- to two-thirds. Yet, what seems largely missing from the premodern European setting is the concept and practise of *daqian*: Rarely was coinage debased there in a way that would reduce its metallic content to just one-third of its nominal value overnight. In terms of size and content, perhaps the closest equivalent to *daqian* were the large bronze coins issued in multiple nummi units under Byzantine emperor Anastasius I (r. 491–518 CE). Yet, a forty-nummi coin (known as follis) could, for example, weigh 9.34 grams, whereas a 10-nummi piece could weigh 2.05 grams. In other words, the metal content of the follis could be higher than what its nominal value might have indicated, the exact opposite of the rational underlying the issue of *daqian*.[36]

Precisely why "coin famines" had come about and how to tackle them were questions right at the fulcrum of statecraft debates in the eleventh century; these intense debates galvanized much of the seminal neo-Confucian backlash against Wang Anshi and account in no small measure for the fact that coinage output was ultimately much smaller in per capita terms during the late imperial era. Polymath Shen Kuo (1033–1097), a Wang Anshi supporter, perceptively recognized that the dearth of coins was engendered partly by overseas demand and partly by population growth; he suggested that the best way to satiate the growing demand for money without further investment in mining and mints was to issue new higher-value coins from gold and silver that would not carry a premium overseas and to issue more notes to be backed by imperial revenue from the salt trade (*yanchao*).[37]

A few opponents of Wang Anshi at the court also recognized overseas demand as an important contributor to the "famine" but nevertheless blamed Wang's relaxation of the state's copper monopoly for making the hemorrhage of coins possible. For Sima Guang, Wang's neo-Confucian archrival, there was nonetheless only one folly at the heart of the matter, namely, the thrust toward greater monetization of the rural economy that disrupted in his view time-honored production relations and made commodities dearer. Moreover, Sima rejected the notion that economic growth can occur as a result of extraneous stimulants; he believed that only population growth could enlarge the output "pie" and that any attempt at reallocation of existing resources seemingly in the interest of productivity was a zero-sum game where wealth would be unproductively redistributed in favor of the government and vested interests.[38]

Coin famines remained a pernicious problem right until the fourteenth century, and so Wang's supply-side solutions lost favor. In the subsequent Southern Song era, there was greater reliance on large fiduciary coinage (*daqian*), on paper instruments, and on iron coinage (well beyond Sichuan), to a large extent as a result of the Northern Song government's failure to ensure that enough full-bodied bronze coinage would remain in circulation locally so that the monetization of the tax base could be balanced off. Yet, the proliferation of paper instruments was not limited to state-backed scrip: Private-order scrip and commodity bills of exchange continued to be widespread too. Later, the dearth of "cash" led both the Southern Song officialdom and some merchants to try disbursing shorter strings of cash (*duanmo*), containing around eighty coins, at the same nominal value of a *guan* substring (*mo*)ordinarily comprising one hundred coins.[39]

Historically, the Song formalization of "short" strings is an important juncture because the conceptualization of 1,000 full-bodied bronze coins on par with a "string" was not only an ideal that later dynasties pursued; this parity may have evolved from the ancient custom of stringing cowrie in early-imperial times. That 1:1,000 parity was mentioned as early as the Western Han era in Sima Qian's famous *Records of the Grand Historian*. Smaller strings could be found in the marketplace during the Tang era, perhaps as a consequence of similar shortage of cash, although they were not openly formalized by the state in the same way.[40]

More to the point, the definitive defeat of Wang Anshi's reform faction on the dethronement of Emperor Huizong (r. 1100–1126) by Jin invaders set in train a secular decline in coin output; it also engendered an enduring statecraft legacy in that the economic latitude of the state, for example, its ability to partake of gentry enterprise, was thenceforth constrained, even if the semblance of all-powerful emperors was carefully preserved. But it was not just economic policy that turned around: Despite his statism and promotion of peasant militias, Wang Anshi was a strategic realist who was also open to Buddhist and Daoist ideas of statecraft. His bureaucratic vision implicitly prized technocratic skills over Confucian moral hermeneutics, and he sought changes in China's famous imperial examination system in that spirit. That his fairly short-lived procommerce measures and irredentist rhetoric had not of themselves translated into a stronger imperial army that might have conceivably fended off the later invasions of steppe peoples from the north tended to unfairly cloud his followers' reform-faction legacy in the eyes of both contemporary and future generations of imperial policy makers.[41]

Tellingly, Wang Anshi's detractors accused him of embracing the rapacity of the notorious Qin official Shang Yang (390–338 BCE), in that Wang, too, was allegedly aiming to "enrich the state and strengthen its army" (*fuguo qiangbing*) at the expense of the people (read: gentry) and in violation of humane Confucian injunctions.[42] As it turned out, precisely the same slogan in its Japanese rendition (*fukoku kyōhei*) would become the rallying cry of the sweeping Meiji reforms in Japan eight centuries later. It epitomized the Meiji oligarchs turning away from Confucian learning. As heavily as it drew on Anglo-American and Prussian precepts of modernity at the time, it is instructive to note that Meiji Japan was aiming to become the first non-Western society to industrialize with an ideal actually borrowed from premodern Chinese statecraft—an ideal that in China had by then become fraught with negative connotations. Otherwise put, Meiji Japan articulated modernity unto itself not merely by transposing Western liberal thought but also by construing the very essence of Western primacy at the time in terms of concrete policy measures that had been put in place at certain moments in Chinese premodern history. For the Meiji oligarchs, modernity was not primarily about withdrawing monarchical prerogatives, or entrenching popular participation in government, as the English model might have potentially been interpreted; on the contrary, modernity was to be found in allowing the state to penetrate much deeper into society than was the case during the preceding Tokugawa era. American ideals celebrating "small government" were, at any rate, not much entertained.[43]

Throughout the Northern Song era, bronze coinage was the standard except for Sichuan, where it was initially the mainstay of the money stock, whereby ten iron coins were nominally made convertible to one standard bronze coin. In other parts of China, Song iron coinage—to the extent it was current there—served merely as "token" or subsidiary money. However, the value of iron coinage depreciated precipitously, so that much of it flowed back to Sichuan, where the authorities effectively discouraged the use of bronze coinage alongside.[44]

Sichuan iron coinage predated the establishment of the Song, but it was the Song dynasty's attempt to regulate the private issue of iron coin–denominated bills in Sichuan that heralded the evolution of paper money into an acceptable, large–scale, and state-backed medium of payment. Before 1073, the perception of full convertibility of state-backed notes to coin was quite sound, but over time the Song geared its bureaucracy toward issuing notes against tax payment in coin rather than handing over coins to individuals in return for its own notes (*naqian qingjiao*). Because premodern paper as a raw material eroded quickly, the Northern Song could also find a pretext to limit the validity of each of its issues to only a few years (*jie*), quite apart from the geographical constraints it imposed on where some of the issue could circulate. On expiry, the notes then had to be exchanged at a considerable discount for a new issue, a stratagem later used by the Yuan and Ming treasuries too. Notably, as of 1073, because of the mounting fiscal pressures of maintaining peace with the steppe peoples to its north, the Song government started issuing unbacked *jiaozi*, that is, notes that were disbursed without any commensurate amount of coinage received by the treasury. However, even prior to 1073, the use of paper instruments was not always tied to coinage receipts: Because the Song government constantly needed merchants to convey supplies to garrisons in the northwest, that region ran a trade deficit with the rest of China. Hence, in return for their services, merchants who made the journey west from the economic heartland of China in the east were often paid not in coin but in exemption bills that could reduce their tax liability in their home province or in certificates that allowed them to join in the heavily government-regulated salt trade.[45]

Shen Kuo's suggestion that bills denominated in silver or gold coinage be issued as a means of meeting the demands of monetization across the Northern Song society and of defraying the costs of a growing state apparatus is critical precisely because it was not acted on; instead, where medieval rulers might have resorted to silver or gold coin debasement elsewhere in Eurasia, Song governments in the main resorted to paper money.

What was then the position of silver in the Song economy? Was the notion of silver as a potentially sound means of payment fraught in any way? Or was it peripheral simply because this was the case in the early imperial era? The answers to these questions are all fairly straightforward: In contrast to the Five Dynasties era, for example, silver was in fact becoming monetized by the Song era in the form of flat bars (*ting*). Such bars were also made admissible by weight rather than by unit in tax payments. Yet, because the use of silver was largely confined to merchants and moneylenders, it circulated in urban centers where the inflow of bullion from overseas was significant. Paper money, on the other hand, was a more common medium of payment even though its value was mostly denominated in hundreds or even thousands of bronze coins. Peasants, who advanced much of the tax revenue, were largely outside the realms of this credit economy. Critically, whereas the Song intake of bullion via overland and maritime trade increased, the output of its domestic silver mines was in proportional decline after the defeat of Wang Anshi's reforms.[46]

And what of the economic theory that might have accompanied the spread of an innovation such as paper money? The later European

historic experience with paper money, briefly touched on in the Introduction, would suggest that popular receptivity to government-issued
notes was first predicated on the fleshing out of sound metallic-reserve
principles. On examination, and as ahead of the times as Xue Tian and
Zhou Xingji's were, the earlier Chinese experience seems on the whole
somewhat less pronounced in terms of setting out the minutiae of ample
reserve.[47]

The imperative of holding sufficient reserves to ensure the convertibility and popular receptivity of paper money was discussed in general terms under the somewhat obscure label of *chengti*, which might
roughly translate as "revaluation." During the Southern Song era, as the
empire shrank in size and paper money depreciated, *chengti* discussions
usually connoted the need to produce more bronze coins with which to
shore up the relative value of paper money. There was otherwise less
willingness on the part of bureaucrats to overtly criticize the throne
for the overproduction of notes or to articulate specific reserve ratios
of bullion and specie to the issue of notes. Either way, the rationale for
increased coin output was often discussed in terms of the early-imperial
"Child and Mother" (*zimu xiangquan*) trope, an expression that had
originally been applied to different coin weights in a purely metallic setting. Contrary to intuition perhaps, the "mother" in Song monetary discourse was in fact petty bronze cash, while high-denomination paper
money was cast as the "son": In this distinction one may also observe
the enduring vitality of low-denomination bronze coinage. By the same
token, paper money was often cast as "empty" (*xu*), while bronze coinage was "real" (*shi*) money. And in an adaptation of Shan Qi's preimperial duality, which originally concerned coinage alone, when Song paper
money was overissued it was either deemed "light" (*qing*) or "heavy"
(*zhong*) when well regulated.[48]

Clearly, then, one of the most intriguing facets of Song paper money
is its regional private-order provenance, as was the case in Europe too.
Private-order paper instruments would generally indicate the growth of
a credit economy quite apart from the monetization of tax base. Yet it
was only with state takeover that the same paper money could become
current beyond the locality where it had been issued. Progressively, state-
issued notes had been losing their metallic anchorage: The main form
of paper money in the Southern Song, for example, (*huizi*) was more
fiduciary in nature than *jiaozi* or *qianyin* if only due to the fact that the
coinage with which it was denominated had been produced much less
than in the Northern Song era. Bronze coin-denominated *qianyin* had
been circulating at a discount during the Northern Song era, yet they
were still fairly sought after by merchants—perhaps it was this experi-

ence that led Southern Song officialdom to conclude that *huizi* would not need to be fully convertible on demand. In that sense, the transition from the Northern to Southern Song might betoken the first few steps toward annunciating fiat currency in practice, although at the conceptual level the link between paper money and metal was never fully severed in premodern China.[49]

By the same token, that the Song increasingly resorted to unbacked notes, and to iron coinage—not just in Sichuan but throughout the Huainan region as well—as its armies retreated south might have cemented a trope that subtly linked, in later Chinese statecraft, fiat-money tendencies with dynastic decline (*shuaishu*).[50] Following Zhou Xingji, however, references to specific reserve requirements became rare in statecraft discourse, even though reserve principles remained well understood. Yuan Xie (1144–1224) of the Southern Song era was perhaps one of the most representative in this discursive vein as he postulated:

Paper money will be of lowly esteem when aplenty, and become prized when scarce; thus redeeming some of it out of circulation, will make it appreciate in value; for when it is lowly its circulation languishes; when it is prized, it will be widely used; thus redeeming some of it will boost its circulation.[51]

The Northern Song move away from solid reserve holdings seems to have come around 1127 as the Song armies retreated south in the face of Tangut (Xixia) and later Jurchen (Jin) invasions. Now based in Hangzhou, the Southern Song bureaucracy was split by spiraling military expenditure. Hawkish officials were calling to recover China's territorial integrity, while doves sought to maintain the status quo with the nomadic peoples of the northern steppe lands and avoid a fiscal nemesis. In 1135, the court had tried to introduce inconvertible notes only in frontier areas as a way of striking a balance between the two camps. However, the rejection of the new notes by merchants and provincial administrators alike resulted in, by 1160, the restoration of convertibility to specie.[52]

Steppe peoples who posed constant threat to the Song were, at the same time, imitating Song institutions and material culture and incorporating more and more ethnic Han sedentary communities within their midst. But the pattern of imitation was not identical at least insofar as coinage design was concerned. For example, the Mongols, who eventually annihilated the Song, had occasionally inscribed their bronze coins with 'Phags-pa script. By comparison, the Jurchen Jin Dynasty exclusively used Chinese script on its coinage. In 1157, the Jin also printed Song-style paper money denominated in bronze coinage units for the first time. This was followed in 1197 with silver-denominated Jin notes. But little is known about the degree to which the Jin applied metallic reserve principles to their notes.[53]

What *is* known about the Jin-Southern Song fray in monetary terms is that it resembled in no small measure the protomercantilist setting of the Five Dynasties era: Each side tried to use fiduciary notes as a way of preventing copper and silver from flowing in the other direction, but the dearth of bronze coinage made both Jin and Southern Song paper money lose value rapidly. In response, the Jin introduced baser iron coinage and tried to revitalize mining by relaxing its government monopoly on mining and foundries, much as the Northern Song had attempted earlier. Jin paper money finally came undone in 1206, as the Mongols were consolidating their power in the north and pushing into Jurchen occupied territory. The Jin financed the cost of defence against the Mongols by printing more paper money, while at the same time forcing commoners to render their tax liability in hard currency. Soon afterward, Jin paper money effectively became worthless. Yet in some ways it informed the Mongol monetary experience: Both Jin and Yuan paper money, for example, bore greater relation to silver than had Song paper money, which had been denominated in bronze and iron units.[54]

THE MONGOL LEGACY

That paper money had been invented in China was a fact known in early modern Europe thanks to Marco Polo's influential travelogue. Until recently, therefore, much of the classic monetary literature touching on China focused on the Mongol Yuan dynasty (1271–1368) and its founder, the Khublai Khan (r. 1260–1294), at whose behest Polo seems to have worked.[55] There is therefore no pressing need to belabor the observations of previous studies. Instead, this section will try to contribute to the existing literature by underscoring the ways in which Yuan monetary policy differed from that of the Song and why it was undermined shortly after Marco Polo's tour of duty ended.

On Genghis Khan's death (1227), his vast Eurasian empire fragmented into four domains or khanates that were effectively independently governed by his descendants. In modern territorial terms, these domains would roughly correspond with Central Asia (Chagatai), Russia (Golden Horde), China (Yuan), and Iran (Ilkhanate). Each of these domains similarly maintained a separate silver-based currency and a separate silver- and gold-based tax system, yet cross-linkages existed, and the pan-Mongol preference for silver generally meant that the aggregate demand for, and the relative price of, silver rose globally.[56]

Where Song monetary experience counts, in this context, is the fact that while the Mongols tried to issue paper money in China and later in Iran, it was only in China that their paper money issue prevailed and remained fairly stable right until the latter part of the thirteenth century. Ultimately, it was this relative stability, the vast scale of circulation, and popular trust in paper money that Marco Polo was so impressed with and that set China's monetary experience apart from the rest of Eurasia at that time.

What might account for popular receptivity to Yuan notes in the face of previous Song and Jin paper money overissues? At heart, it would seem, the success of Yuan paper money derived from political stability and expanding Eurasian trade just as much as from sound metallic reserves. In 1276, Khubali Khan was able to resolutely defeat remnants of the Southern Song imperial army in the south and thus turn the Yuan into the first non-Chinese imperial line to rule all of China. From then on, as Morris Rossabi has observed, the Khublai Khan maintained stability across his empire and fostered linkages with the other khanates by extending protection to long-distance merchant convoys to a much greater degree than Chinese emperors, under the influence of Confucianism or Legalism, might have. Merchants, in turn, paid homage to Mongol military prowess by accepting Yuan government notes across the empire, so that in the Khublai's reign the use of paper money reached a scale much greater than in the Song. Yet, so as not to undermine the very concept of fiduciary currency, Khublai did not simply declare Southern Song notes (*huizi*) invalid but judiciously allowed for their gradual commutation into Yuan paper money at a discount for a period of several years after the Southern Song downfall.[57]

To further understand Yuan monetary policy, one would also have to take account of the fact that intermittent coin famines continued in China during the thirteenth and fourteenth centuries as a consequence of monetization in other parts of East Asia and Southeast Asia where Chinese bronze coins became popular. Silver, on the other hand, was trickling into China in ever-growing quantities along both the eastern and western principal trade routes as a result of China's trade surplus. Faced with a narrowing of its base-metal money base, the Yuan dynasty eventually decided to all but abandon bronze coin mints. And although they continued to issue silver coins elsewhere, the Mongols did not mint any silver coins in China proper after 1259. Instead, from as early as 1260, the nascent Yuan dynasty was able to increasingly rely on the issue of nominally convertible paper notes, while in actual fact discouraging the free circulation of coinage and bullion and constricting their use in mercantile activity except when handed over to the treasury in return for notes.[58]

Yet the main departure from Song practice was the fact that Yuan paper money followed the Jin precedent: It was partly denominated by and mostly backed against silver reserves. In addition, at least conceptually, early Yuan issues were also denominated and backed by silk yarn. The corollary was that the Yuan cast many fewer bronze coins even as compared with the diminished Southern Song output. On the other hand, the Yuan demanded that tax be paid not just in its own notes but also partly in silver bullion.[59]

Conceptually, the most important Yuan unit of account was *yuanbao*, often rendered as one *yinding* silver bar, and ordinarily commensurate with 50 taels (Tls.) or around two kilograms of silver by weight. Thus, while most Yuan notes were formally denominated by *guan* units, that is, strings of 1,000 bronze coins, they would more often than not be valued in the marketplace based on the decreed exchange rate between *guan* and silver, whereby one tael was officially worth two guan.[60]

There were other departures from Southern Song policy too. The latter was, for example, characterized by hiving off different currency zones—a measure largely designed to stem the outflow of bronze coinage to the frontier. As previously indicated, during the Northern Song era, iron coins were mostly confined to Sichuan and the northwest, but after 1189 the Southern Song issued iron coinage for use in some parts of the Lower Yangzi basin too. Often, Song notes would be redeemable in cash only in one zone but not in another. By contrast, Yuan notes were usually legal tender wherever they ended up circulating across the empire.[61]

As for coinage, much less of it was cast during the Yuan so as to entrench notes as the main circulating medium of payment. Similarly, the use of bullion in everyday transactions was discouraged. This meant that the Yuan had to somehow satisfy the demand for petty cash in the agrarian sector with notes. Thus, whereas most Song notes were usually denominated in thousands of coins—200 bronze coins was probably the minimal note denomination—Yuan note values varied from several *guan*, or "strings" of a thousand coins, right down to the equivalent of just two individual bronze coins (*wen*).[62]

By far the most important Yuan issue was that of silver-backed notes (*zhongtong yuanbao chao*). The Khublai Khan is thought to have chosen the title *zhongtong* (moderate rule) to allay the concerns of his many Han-Chinese subjects about the ruthlessness of the Mongol conquerors and about the rapaciousness of his first treasurer, Ahmad Fanakati. Yet from 1277 onward, immediately after the completion of China's occupation, Yuan measures to sustain the circulation of the notes were quite unprecedented: The free flow of tangible bullion and specie was greatly restricted. Moreover, in 1287 Khublai's new Tibetan treasurer, Sangha, declared *zhongtong* notes would no longer be redeemable unless exchanged for newly issued *zhiyuan* notes at a disadvantageous rate of one to five.[63]

The year 1287, then, as famously underscored by Marco Polo, signifies the end of the golden age of Yuan paper money. Unlike the thrust toward inconvertibility during the mid-Song transition, however, this Yuan milestone does not seem to have been driven by *defense*-outlay pressures. Rather, the initial thrust toward inconvertibility may have been catalyzed by dwindling specie in state coffers as a result of *offensive* outlay, namely, the expensive and unsuccessful Mongol attempts to conquer Japan (in 1274 and 1281).

Subsequently, the thrust toward inconvertibility was much catalyzed by the Mongol custom of constantly granting tribute to relatives of the imperial clan. Such bestowals became more frequent after Khublai Khan's death in 1294. On the other hand, his successor, Temür (r. 1294–1307) was generally reluctant to raise taxes so that the bestowals had to be funded by clawing back regional bullion reserves otherwise kept against the note issue. Reserves were thus transferred to the central imperial treasury in the Yuan capital near modern Beijing. Consequently, the total amount of the reserve held at various regional depots (*pingzhunku*) to redeem notes and shore up their value dropped from Tls. 936,950 to only Tls. 192,450 by the early fourteenth century. Needless to say, the transfer of reserves unleashed breakaway inflation that the Yuan would not be able to contain.[64]

On the eve of Mongol defeat at the hands of Ming Dynasty founder, Zhu Yuanzhang, the fiscal situation had become so catastrophic that the Yuan decided to further reduce the few vestigial links between its paper money and metallic reserves. When the *zhongtong* notes had first been issued in 1260, well before the completion of China's occupation by the Mongols, the total volume of issue that year was valued at Tls. 3.6 million; by 1287, annual issue values had hovered around Tls. 250 million. While *zhongtong* notes were phased out then, *zhiyuan* and other notes' annual issues remained at much the same level right until 1341. Critically, in 1351, Toghto, the Grand Counsellor to Toghun Temür, the last Yuan emperor, decided to defray urgent flood repair work in the Yellow River with retired *zhongtong* notes reprinted with a new caption (*zhizheng jiaochao*). Toghun Temür further decreed that the reprinted *zhizheng jiaochao* notes would be worth twice as much as older *zhiyuan* notes without assigning any new reserves against them, thus turning already inflationary conditions into hyperinflation.[65]

What is interesting in the Yuan transition to a silver-reserve based currency is, then, the fact that bronze coinage *conceptually* remained so central to monetary policy. This is reflected not just in the fact that most notes carried *guan* values; there was also frequent depiction of actual "strings" of bronze coinage on the notes whereas the latter contained hardly any depiction of silver bars. Also, it was reflected in the contemporary discourse on the adequate metallic reserve needed to prop up the greater volume of Yuan paper money in everyday commerce and in imperial emoluments. For example, when criticizing the overprinting of notes, the official Hu Zhiyu (1227–1295) would invoke Song conceptual conventions in casting inconvertible Yuan notes as "children" without a mother currency (that is, bronze coinage) to back them up. In fact, Hu's position was rather prudent because, unlike other critics at the time, he did not negate the functionality of paper money altogether. Zheng Jiefu, his contemporary, was arguably even more lenient in calling for the restoration of cast coinage production, for Zheng turned convention on its head by explaining that bronze coinage was merely a "child" designed to assist (*yi*), the main currency of the day, namely, "mother" notes.[66]

Ye Li (1242–1292), who served as official both in the Southern Song and Yuan courts, arguably came closest to envisioning premodern paper money as fiat currency, for, short of shedding off the metallic anchorage of money, Ye suggested that the metallic reserves held against the Yuan note issue must be immobilized in state coffers and that commoners should not have the option of readily converting notes into bullion. Thus, one cannot quite speak of a concrete fiat standard either having emerged or having been conceived in premodern China centuries before such a turnaround coalesced in the post–Bretton Woods world. Rather than an epistemological breakthrough in the understanding of money, the transition from fiduciary notes to effectively inconvertible notes embodied either monetary practicality or fiscal urgency.[67]

On the other end of the spectrum, there were more strident criticisms of paper-money issuance. Early on, scholar Xu Heng (1209–1281), for example, called for the abolition of "empty notes" (*xuquan*). Drawing on the previous dynasty's experience, Xu declared that the lack of metallic reserves was a scourge and that popular trust in paper money was quickly eroding, although he stopped short of discussing the ideal reserve ratio or other monetary measures.[68] Later, playwright Gao Ze-cheng (1310–1380) would lampoon the proliferation of notes and people's trust in such "flimsy" (*bao*) currency in his satire, *Wubaozhuan*.[69]

These works reflected the Yuan's departure from the Northern Song intellectual setting, where the notion of *chengti* had implied the need to keep anywhere between 66.6 percent and 100 percent in metallic reserves against note issues. Later in the Southern Song, the notion of *chengti* became more abstract still.[70] By the Yuan era, silk, silver, or gold conceptually replaced bronze coinage as the reserve mainstay, and the notion of having to keep a reserve was also differently termed with the expression *chaoben* (literally, "note substance").[71]

Late Yuan officials could not resist the temptation of excessive note issues, thereby unleashing repeated waves of inflation and consistently undermining popular trust in paper currency. Court proclivity toward the use of note issuance as a cheap means of generating fiscal revenue became a feature of imperial policy that would surface time and again. Inevitably, commoners had to resort to imported silver bullion as the sole reliable store of value, ultimately forcing the imperial bureaucracy to adapt its finances along the same lines.[72]

From the fifteenth century on, government note issuance—as a moot policy measure—was therefore subject to deep-seated suspicion both within the imperial bureaucracy and in popular discourse. Full resumption of bronze coin casting by the Ming dynasty (1368–1644) occurred only in 1522. By then, the Chinese economy had been drawing in an immense overflow of Japanese silver. But unlike Tokugawa Japan, Chinese late imperial governments did not attempt to mine and to coin silver before the late nineteenth century.

Yuan monetary policy is fairly well studied, but its ramifications in Central Asia are much less so. For example, Gaykhatu (?–1295), the profligate fifth Mongol ruler of Iran, introduced paper notes in Tabriz in 1294 to replenish his notoriously depleted treasury. These notes featured the Chinese character *chao* (meaning bill) alongside Arabic script in allusion to the relative stability of Yuan currency. *Chao* was conveniently transcribed into *čāw* in Farsi, and so the first word used to describe paper money in the Islamic world was of Chinese origin (notwithstanding its arcane status in modern Farsi). Chinese script also featured on the coinage that the Mongols introduced into Central Asia. The introduction of notes was made possible by importing Chinese block-printing technology. Block printing eventually spread westward, but paper money was overwhelmingly rejected by Persians and was taken out of circulation within a few months.[73]

The *čāw* was made of the bark of the mulberry tree. It was oblong in shape and, in addition, bore the *shahāda*. Underneath this was the name "Īrīndjīn tūrčī" (meaning "very costly pearl") and, inside a circle, the designation of the value ranging from one to ten dinars. *Čāw* bills also bore the red impression of the state seal in jade (the Altamġa), granted by the Genghis Khan to the Ilkhan.[74]

Chinese numismatic studies quite often point to the Delhi sultanate as another part of the world that was directly impacted by the "Chinese" (that is, Mongol) experience with the issuance of paper money. Some sources assert in this context that Yuan notes were imitated by Sultan Muhammad ibn Tughlaq (r. 1324–1351).[75] However, Sultan Tughlaq's pattern of issuing fiduciary currency had little to do with paper money as such. Rather, he famously introduced token copper coinage, which was meant to circulate on a par with older silver and gold coins and committed to accepting in return this copper coinage at face value in tax payments. Yet soon after it was issued, Tughlaq's copper coinage was forged on a vast scale. The sultanate's landed aristocracy who possessed of the coin first could benefit immensely by deploying the new currency immediately and purchasing "horses, arms and luxuries." In a short time, however, token coin value plummeted in the marketplace. Inflation ensued, and government revenue was hit hard because most of the coins were later used in tax payments at face value. These losses eventually led to the abolition of copper-token coinage in the sultanate.[76]

THE MING LEGACY (1368–1644)

The Yuan was the shortest dynasty to have ruled China; the reasons for its downfall were complex, and monetary excesses should be seen as just one of many catalysts. The dynasty's senior bureaucracy comprised, for example, more foreigners than ever before, a factor that invariably alienated Han subjects. Yet, interestingly enough, after the Ming dynasty founder, Zhu Yuanzhang, had overthrown the Mongols and restored ethnic Han suzerainty, he chose nevertheless to cling to the Yuan practice of paper note issuance (now called *baochao*), as well as to limit the circulation of specie and bullion. Furthermore, Ming notes were from the beginning effectively inconvertible, that is, they were only notionally backed against silver reserves. Generally, throughout Ming reign, fewer coins were cast in both absolute and per capita terms compared with the Song era, so that mint operational know-how continued to decline.

As might be expected, in the absence of sound reserve principles, *bao-chao* issues became inflationary almost from inception, so much so that the Ming was forced to abandon the issuance of paper money altogether in 1430.[77] From then on, China's late imperial economy became progressively reliant on silver mined overseas to oil the wheels of commerce and facilitate government tax revenue. White metal came to eclipse both paper money and bronze coinage in the late Ming to the extent that *it* was now often deemed the "mother" currency.[78]

The *lijia* reform launched by Zhu Yuanzhang (r. 1368–1398) and Emperor Jiajing's (r. 1521–1566) "Single Whip" reform (*yi tiao bianfa*) formalized over the course of Ming rule a gradual commutation of tax-in-kind and corvée labor into silver-denominated land tax, levied by an increasingly decentralized provincial apparatus. Foreign silver became the preferred monetary standard in urban areas and was acquiesced to by an imperial court that nominally espoused locally cast bronze coinage as legal tender.[79]

That said, the Ming court had little grasp of the global trade dynamic that caused so great an inflow of silver into China. It accepted the availability of silver rather passively: Some Ming officials even toyed with the idea of disbursing state-held silver to peasants as a fast-and-ready form of famine relief. Silver was collected and disbursed by the state, but there was no overarching imperial scheme regulating the sourcing, casting, or distribution of the precious metal.[80]

Much of the silver monetized in China during the first half of the sixteenth century was, in fact, mined in Japan and traded for raw Chinese silk. Thereafter, in the seventeenth century, as the Tokugawa shogunate restricted Japan's overseas trade and bolstered its indigenous coinage system, the Spanish galleon traffic nourished China with silver mined in Latin America. Silver produced in Latin America was often carried on board galleons sailing from Acapulco to Manila, then transshipped to Southeast China by local seafarers. It is roughly estimated that around 5 million pieces-of-eight (later known as Carolus dollars)—commensurate with 120 tons of silver—found their way to Asia during the early seventeenth century.[81]

Notably, until about 1500, Japan under the Muromachi shogunate (1137–1573) had been a net importer of silver, and its monetary system relied in no small measure on Song-style bronze coinage that had been imported from China. Song coinage could fetch a higher exchange value in Japan than in China once the Yuan discouraged bronze coin circulation. Nevertheless, Japan eventually moved to indigenize its coinage system and switched to a trimetallic standard, as the supply of Chinese bronze coinage dried up during the Ming and early Qing eras. Indeed, after 1500 Japanese silver mines saw vigorous expansion on the back of the arrival of ash-blowing technology from Korea, silver output having peaked as a result between 1575–1625. Unlike Japan under the early Tokugawa shoguns, however, the late Ming bureaucracy did not attempt to expand silver mining. In other words, the surge in Japanese silver output that facilitated the mid-Ming transition to a silver economy had occurred only a decade before the explosion in Spanish-American silver production—the latter having been achieved on the back of new mercurial amalgam techniques. Although such knowledge may have also been available in Japan, mercury was in short supply there so that less efficient extraction techniques prevailed instead.[82]

The Ming abandonment of *baochao* in favor of imported silver in 1430 effectively brought to a close China's premodern experiment with paper money. Calls for the restoration of paper money were made but were invariably dismissed by late Ming emperors, even when the imperial treasury found itself depleting as a result of the Manchu invasion. As will be examined in Chapter Four, the Manchu Qing dynasty (1644–1911) did issue notes, although only briefly, during the Shunzhi reign (1643–1661), preferring to resume bronze coin production instead. A return to state-backed notes as a desperate means of enhancing imperial revenue would occur again only in the mid-nineteenth century under the Xianfeng reign and against the backdrop of the Taiping rebellion and deeper European monetary inroads. China's monetary system thus became bimetallic in the Qing era—a system in which bronze coins and silver bullion maintained a parity whereby they were mutually convertible and universally accepted. The Qing monetary system was, in that sense, different from that prevalent in early-modern Europe where gold, paper instruments, and government regulation had by then begun to play a more significant monetary role.[83]

Though first issued in China as far back as the tenth century, paper money was not trusted there because successive dynasties had tampered with its convertibility into hard currency. In monetary policy debates at the court, the evocation of silver as an important pillar of the monetary system certainly overshadowed that of paper currency during the early and middle Qing.[84] Silver bullion was used as the most common medium of large transactions, foreign trade, and tax collection while round bronze coins continued to serve as a daily medium of exchange in retail.

Moreover, because the Qing imperial government preferred bullion to its own often-debased bronze coins, silver weights evolved into the most important units of account in China.[85] That much being said, it is important to recall that nonmonetary popular uses of paper money did not completely disappear after 1430. Indeed, the tradition of burning mock coins and notes made of paper (*mingzhi*) in Buddhist and Daoist burial rites to help propitiate the deceased's soul continued to be widespread from the fifteenth through the nineteenth centuries.[86]

To better understand how early Ming emperors could enforce paper money in the popular mind-set, it might be useful to recall the Yuan track record. In that context, it is often assumed that the inconvertibility of late Yuan issues simply doomed the fate of paper money. Yet Toghto's unbacked *zhizheng* notes were still accepted, in the payment of their wages, by laborers recruited to bolster dams along the Yellow River. Quite apart from insufficient reserves per se, what ultimately tarnished the Ming experiment with paper money was Emperor Yongle's (r. 1402–1424) lavish expenditure in relocating his capital to Beijing, in embarking on several military campaigns against Annam and the Mongolians, and in dispatching Zheng He's famous expeditions across the seas. Much like Temür's bestowal of additional tribute on imperial clan relatives, Yongle undermined popular trust in notes because of the consequent imbalance between imperial revenue and expenditure. A comparison between the Yuan and Ming paper money issuance might therefore suggest that note inconvertibility to specie or bullion was not as pernicious in itself as the popular perception of metallic-reserve violability. Inflation soon ensued from ever more new issues and from a precarious fiscal predicament.[87]

Yongle passed away in 1424, and his successor Xuande (r. 1425–1435) gradually wound down the expansionist policies, abandoning paper note issuance six years later. However, with the exception of a late rebound beginning in the waning days of Emperor Wanli (r. 1572–1620), the Ming did not move to drastically increase bronze-coin output to replace paper money. Rather, in the main, the dynasty allowed imported silver bullion to become the mainstay of the monetary system.[88]

Why did Emperor Xuande and his successors not opt to revive coin output on a larger scale? The costs associated with sourcing copper and rehabilitating imperial mints, now long in decline, immediately spring to mind as one reason. In addition, forged coinage had by then spread far and wide, driven in no small measure by the lack of reliable currency. At the same time, strong preference for bronze coinage in rural areas meant that Ming emperors had to tolerate the use of Song-era coinage (*guqian*), both genuine and forged. To be sure, Emperor Hongzhi (r. 1487–1505) attempted to ban forged coins and to set his new Ming coinage at twice the value of Song-era coinage, but these measures did not substantively detract from the centrality of silver bullion to the Ming economy.[89]

A formative plank in Ming statecraft that not even Yongle's expansionism could overturn was the aversion to large-scale mining as an activity that induces sedition and disrupts farming. There had of course been physiocratic or geomantic opposition to mining in previous eras, yet Ming founder Zhu Yuanzhang's origins as a commoner seem to have instilled in him a deep-seated suspicion of miners as would-be bandits, and of local mine administrators as fomenting popular resentment to their brutality and corruption. That this aversion had a lasting effect is manifest in the facts that not even Yongle's attempts to redevelop Yunnan's silver mines could offset the Ming's reliance on imported silver and that large-scale bronze coin casting resumed only under the Qing Emperor Qianlong.[90]

The atmospherics surrounding Zhu Yuanzhang's decision to cling to paper money issuance are, in turn, manifest in many extant statecraft compilations. Notably, the official Fan Ji, who had also served in the Yuan court, suggested that the Ming should carry on with paper note issuance and that these notes would be accepted by commoners despite Yuan excesses. To dissociate note issuance from Yuan particularities, Fan historically traced the rationale behind note issuance right back to Han Wudi's deer-hide currency and exaggerated the appeal of early-Ming issues as being "honoured by Chinese and foreigners alike across many kingdoms."[91]

Ye Ziqi (1327–1390) justified the early-Ming note issue in much the same vein. He invoked what he thought were previous uses of paper scrip in times past. These ranged from private-order exchange bills of the Han era (*zhiji*) and putative bronze-coin denominated notes (*qianyin*) in the Tang era through to the more historically verifiable occurrence of *jiaozi* and *huizi* during the Song era. At the same time, Ye stressed that Ming notes must be backed up by full-bodied bronze coinage and that heavier fiduciary coinage (*daqian*) should be avoided.[92]

Ye's insistence on bronze coinage as the ultimate pillar of money is important in view of the fact that the Ming had not restored bronze coinage on a large scale yet. Like Yuan notes, however, Ming *baochao* retained for the most part the conceptual link between bronze coinage and money in the nominal unit of account and in the inscriptions and iconography appearing on the notes.

That the Ming tax base became progressively silver denominated without silver coinage being minted was more a matter of practicality and acquiescence to the inflow of silver from overseas than a marker of a shift in statecraft. In fact, *baochao* notes were often denominated in *wen* or individual bronze "cash" coins; they carried at the same time a caption promising a reward of 250 silver taels (*liang*) to anyone who would turn in counterfeiters. The latter were threatened with beheading (*zhan*) much like the caption on Song and Yuan notes. Yuan notes, however, usually set out a reward for information on counterfeiters in silver bars (*yinding*) rather than in weight, although previously under the Southern Song reign ubiquitous *huizi* notes set out the same rewards in strings of "cash."[93]

Views like Fan Ji's and Ye Ziqi's continued to occupy the mainstream at the early Ming court even after *baochao* had begun to depreciate precipitously. The official Liu Dingzhi (1409–1469), for example, could not dismiss the functionality of paper money when current alongside bronze coinage. Quite apart from their significance to merchants, Liu averred that *baochao* benefited farmers too in being easier than heavy cash to carry. The trouble, Liu thought, was with their overissue, which unleashed inflation and precipitated the loss of popular faith in their use. In other words, he concluded, "When much printed, notes will lose value; when printed too much, notes will necessarily stop circulating."[94]

In 1436, the imperial ban on the use of silver in everyday commerce— originally designed to prop up *baochao* circulation—was lifted. This turnaround also signified the strengthening of bullionist tendencies in Chinese statecraft, although silver remained in practice beyond the pale of coining. Neo-Confucian scholar and statesman Qiu Jun (1421–1495) thought, for example, that it would be best not only to acquiesce in the spread of silver as media of payment in the marketplace but also to formally coin it into China's *main* currency alongside with a restoration of *baochao* and bronze "cash" in auxiliary roles. Yet, in a tone somewhat reminiscent of William Cobbett's (1763–1835) later invectives against English banknotes, Qiu adamantly argued that—when circulating on its own as main currency—paper money was similar to "heavy" fiduciary cash (*daqian*) in that both lacked real value, and both incentivized forgery. Moreover, he described them both as a form of state engrossment at the expense of undiscerning merchants and landlords. For these reasons, Qiu was also opposed to the desirability of state monopolies over mining, foundries, and salt.[95]

Nevertheless, once the late Ming polity came under sustained pressure by the steppe Manchu, who had set up a competing polity to the north and eventually conquered all of China, the fiscal situation at the imperial treasury was deteriorating quickly. Consequently, the prospect of casting *daqian* or a restoration of *baochao* issuance became more

compelling. The former monetary solution was eventually acted on, particularly in the waning years of Emperor Tianqi (r. 1621–1627), but the
latter proposition concerning paper money never did materialize during
the late Ming.[96]

The temporary spike in coin output during Tianqi's reign had been
preceded by intense debate as to whether *daqian* could raise seigniorage
revenue, given that it had historically given rise to forgeries, and whether
the toleration of old coinage (*guqian*) did not detract from potential seigniorage revenue. Scholar Hao Jing (1558–1629) suggested, for example,
that issuing *daqian* nominally worth hundreds of coins each was an effective way of averting higher mint costs. Yet, until the Tianqi reign,
Ming policy leaned toward low bronze coin output; it remained leery of
daqian issues and by and large lenient toward the spread of silver, as reflected in influential writings by scholars Li Zhizao (1565–1630) or Song
Yingxing (1587–1666). At the same time, late Ming proposals to reintroduce notes, either as replacement for bronze coinage or as fiduciary
currency alongside silver by officials such as Chen Zilong (1608–1647),
Jiang Chen (c. 1630), or Qian Bingdeng (1612–1694), were all rebuffed.[97]

Scholars such as Yang Cheng (1521–1600), although opposed to the
relinquishment of bronze coin production on account of mint costs, suggested that coining silver alongside bronze coinage would be a way of
better recovering production costs.[98] However, philosopher Wang Fuzhi
(1619–1692) arguably expressed a view closer to the prevailing Ming
norm. Wang begrudgingly accepted the popularization of silver across
society by suggesting that this precious metal was less scarce than gold
and at the same time more durable and easier to store and transport than
bronze. Neither was it sought after for utensil casting like bronze or iron.
Yet Wang Fuzhi vehemently opposed private silver mining or the formal
state coining of that metal as a form of engrossing peasants' livelihood.[99]

On the other end of the spectrum, toward the end of Ming reign,
there was on occasion more strident opposition to the inroads silver bullion had made into society. Notably, Huang Zongxi (1610–1695), who
was otherwise relatively supportive of private commerce, called in vain
for the resumption of *baochao* issues. Huang suggested the notes should
this time be backed by ample bronze coinage rather than by silver. Yet,
in order to repopularize bronze coinage, Huang suggested it would be
vital to lift the standard of workmanship in imperial mints and to improve coin quality. Though costly in the short run, for Huang, these
were essential measures designed to ensure imperial coins would not be
conflated with forged ones in the marketplace.[100]

Gu Yanwu (1613–1682) believed, by contrast, that although there was
nothing wrong with the inroads made into society by the use of silver

coinage, the market price of silver should be better regulated by government through routine permutations in the amount of bronze coinage cast. Gu thereby perceptively implied that once bronze coinage was officially promoted, its price would *perforce* rise, thus leveling off any undesirable spike in the price of silver due to external factors. Unlike Huang Zongxi, Gu was strongly opposed to the restoration of *baochao* or to the notion that paper money could serve as a "child" (read: auxiliary) currency alongside bronze coinage.[101] He argued that previous dynasties had resorted to note issuance as a kind of high-value money because—unlike the circumstances prevalent under the Ming—precious metal was too scarce then to fill that role. In that context, and arguably betraying a neo-Confucian bias, Gu invoked the spread of Buddhism and its penchant for erecting gilded shrines as the reason why gold for example had become rare in China by the Tang era, even though the metal had been used monetarily in previous epochs.[102]

THE EARLY EUROPEAN EXPERIENCE WITH

PAPER MONEY IN COMPARISON

Perhaps the most compelling difference between the Chinese premodern experience with paper money issuance and the experience that typified early modern Europe was the fact that the latter served as a gateway to the modern "national debt" economy. Chinese emperors, by comparison, issued banknotes but did not quite borrow from either the public or from foreign merchants before the nineteenth century. To be sure, positions in the bureaucracy, honorific titles, or certificates allowing private individuals to partake of the state's monopolized industries like salt, liquor, and mining were occasionally sold off so as to supplement imperial revenue. For example, Song-era merchants who were willing to carry provisions to the northern frontier were quite often paid with salt certificates called *yanyin*. These certificates allowed the merchants, in turn, to purchase salt in government-run mines and to on-sell it elsewhere.

Proceeds from the sale of such certificates became increasingly important once the mid-Ming polity was forced to abandon banknote issuance. During the early sixteenth century, a large secondary market for *yanyin* rights (*kaizhong*) emerged around Huizhou: At that time these certificates were characterized by a fairly high degree of fungibility. However, by 1617 the *kaizhong* market was undermined by a Ming bureaucracy that fairly arbitrarily decided to concentrate salt trade right in the hands of a coterie of favored merchants. As a result, *yanyin* circulation volumes shrank and the revenue therefrom never quite supplanted the bulk of Ming imperial receipts, which remained grounded in land tax.[103]

Patterns associated with the rise of England's "perpetual" national-debt economy after the Glorious Revolution (1688) are quite telling in this context. Much of that debt could be initially raised from the well-heeled against future tax receipts because increased parliamentary over-sight was perceived as a guarantee that interest payments would not be disrupted and that default would be unlikely. Notably, while late medi-eval English monarchs had frequently borrowed from foreign merchant families behind closed doors, by the early nineteenth century the En-glish national debt was in the main owed *diffusely* and on a *long-term* basis to *voluntary* bondholders in a clear departure from the patterns of medieval Italian city-states, where the concept of government bonds (*rivarolo*) had arguably first appeared in 1152.[104]

Between the late seventeenth century and the mid-eighteenth century, English national debt grew from a meagre £2 million to a whopping £834 million but was still seen as a much safer investment than other European government loans. Indeed, the English Crown's ability to bor-row funds more readily was to a large extent a determinant of English triumph in the Seven Years' War (1756–1763), which cemented in turn English domination of global trade and secured more future commercial tax therefrom.[105]

Indirect commercial tax revenue—such as farmed-out custom re-ceipts—contributed around 70 percent of all English tax revenue in the late eighteenth century, with individual income tax becoming important only in the twentieth century.[106] Indeed, this might help explain why, far from showing much interest in Chinese land-tax revenue, one of the first things British empire builders sought to foist on the defeated Qing following the Opium Wars was a mechanism for the extraction of com-mercial taxes, namely, the "Chinese" (effectively British-run) Imperial Maritime Customs (est. 1854).

If the eighteenth century was for China one of reliance on imported silver, it presaged in Britain both materially and culturally a transition into modern statehood, of which extensive paper-money use was one of several key characteristics. Cassis, for example, points to the fact that over the course of the eighteenth century British overseas trade more than doubled, spectacularly boosting demand for American and Asian consumer goods like sugar, tobacco, tea, and coffee. Concomitantly, the markets for British goods in American and African colonies greatly ex-panded well before the Industrial Revolution.[107]

In fact, by the late eighteenth century the non-European world as a whole was increasingly relying on Spanish-American silver and European coinage. At the same time, Europe's own economy was being unrecognizably and exceptionally transformed by paper money and exchange bills with the northwest clearly in the lead. Implicitly interest-bearing paper-made bills of exchange had been widely used between the Italian city states and the Low Countries, probably as early as the fifteenth century, and might account for both the relaxation in European invectives against "usury," as well as a secular downturn in European interest rates starting around that time.[108]

Those stark differences between the Chinese and early-modern European economies were vividly portrayed by Adam Smith, among others. Although acknowledging the great size and sophistication of China's domestic market, Smith deemed its economy "has been long stationary." Marco Polo's account of the country's fabled riches sounded in his ears very similar to more recent travelogues by "stupid and lying missionaries." In what might have been hyperbole, Smith further asserted that Chinese menial laborers lived in poverty much more abject than laborers in "the most beggarly nations in Europe."[109]

More importantly, Smith put what he saw as China's slow falling behind down to a premodern-like ("ancient") despising of foreign commerce and a repression of capital markets, which resulted in comparatively high interest rates.[110] Smith then contrasted the rise of European urban craft and far-flung trade missions with China's (and India's) agrarian societies, noting that European polities were ultimately driven by "corporation laws and the corporation spirit," which then augmented fiscal revenue.[111] By contrast, the Chinese polity relied on comparatively low land taxes for its revenue—between a tenth and a thirtieth of all produce, if we were to believe Adam Smith's estimate.[112]

What about other parts of the world? That financial paper instruments were known in China since at least the Tang era (618–907) has already been mentioned. Throughout the Islamic world, too, similar paper instruments (for examples, *'hawaala*, *suftajah*, and *sakk*) were used quite extensively, mostly as private-order payment methods, by the tenth century at the latest. It is quite possible that these played a role in the emergence of medieval European bills.[113] In India, these paper instruments were commonly known as *hundi*, which the British called "bazaar bills" when they first traded in the region.[114]

European exceptionalism, to the extent it can be plausibly argued, has therefore nothing to do with the use of financial paper instruments per se. Neither can it be associated with state-backed notes being the principal form of currency, considering the earlier Yuan experience. Rather, where early-modern northwestern Europe appears exceptional lies perhaps in the ways and means by which European paper instruments ushered in an explosive growth in sovereign debt and commercial tax revenue. That, in turn, placed immense resources at the disposal of central authorities, thereby underlying the emergence of much more fiscally powerful, mutually competitive polities ("fiscal-military states" to borrow John Brewer's term) that were often at war with one another. Somewhat paradoxically, Britain was the first of these fiscally empowered, rapidly centralizing polities even as its own self-perception remained hued with liberalism and aversion to absolute monarchy. Otherwise put, through its parliamentary constraints on the encroachment of the state on the individual, Britain was able to lure more individual resources in the service of its expanding state bureaucracy.[115]

Yet the buildup of "national debt" was contingent on persuasive demonstration of the state's ability to keep fiduciary money stable. After all, debasement and overprinting were the most pernicious means whereby the state encroached on individual wealth. Many European polities failed at that in the eighteenth century, but the continent as a whole saw the diffusion of reserve principles and managerial acumen from west to south, a factor that ultimately entrenched the use of paper money and popular trust in the state's credit-worthiness.

In England and Wales, financial paper instruments (including notes and drafts) totalled approximately £15 million—arguably a whopping 56 percent of the money stock—as early as 1698, while in France banknotes made up only 5 percent of the money stock at the turn of the nineteenth century.[116] If rather slow and uneven, the radiation of paper instruments from Britain to continental Europe in the eighteenth century was one expression of an emergent and sweeping credit economy comprising joint-stock corporate ownership and historically low interest rates; an economy that was later extended by the government issue of "perpetual" annuities. Sandra Sherman, for example, has contended that "long-term credit implicated [British] culture in a new kind of narrativity, since promises in stock annuities, and negotiable [paper] instruments were verifiable only with time."[117]

How stable state-backed fiduciary currency had conditioned the buildup of "national debt" and the emergence of modern Britain is perhaps best attested to in discussions surrounding the establishment of the Bank of England. It is instructive to recall, in that context, that the Bank's note issue prerogatives were not much discussed in its first Act. Rather, the Bank had been primarily envisioned as a channel of raising funds from the public so as to support the Crown's naval expansion and expansionist wars. Proceeds from the initial sale of Bank stock loomed large in the eyes of the Crown. To that end, the Crown was prepared to grant buyers a "sweetener" in the form of note issuance and a stake in future dividends; note issuance was therefore not much conceived as revenue generating in its own right but as a commercial privilege enticing lenders to the Crown. On the other hand, from the public's point of view, note issuance loomed much larger as it was a matter of everyday utility. Nonetheless, banknote issuance had until then been very desultory. Put otherwise, that the Bank of England would eventually become Britain's central bank was not preordained but more of a response to the demand of a nascent credit economy. In fact, much of the Bank's business in the early eighteenth century had to do with the issuance of high-denomination, personalized, and interest-bearing notes ("sealed bills") made against bullion deposits. These deposits, which before long would surpass in value the Bank's paid-up capital, were then on-lent to the Crown.

It was only in 1797 that £1 notes were being disbursed by the Bank of England for the first time in lieu of gold coinage. Yet this, too, was not preordained but a corollary of the temporary suspension of pound note convertibility by the Bank. The latter resulted in turn *not* from a breakdown in popular trust but from elite concerns about possibly massive withdrawals of gold from England after revolutionary France had reverted from a failed, de facto fiat standard (*assignats*) to a system based on gold coinage.[118]

In May 1821, on Napoleon's demise, the convertibility of the pound to gold was restored at the prewar parity, and it thus greatly strengthened its global status and reputation for stability. The pound would from then on be increasingly defined in terms of gold rather than silver and would remain convertible right until the outbreak World War I.[119] The 1821 resumption of convertibility is a milestone in monetary history that contrasts with the premodern Chinese experience, in which the dawning of inconvertibility would signal an irreversible downturn in imperial fortunes and the dwindling of bullion holdings.

For the sake of the argument, one might also wish to compare the evolution of metallic-reserve thought across both settings. While the Bank of England's note issue expanded exponentially in the eighteenth century, one might expect its formal reserve requirements to have hardened too. However, early eighteenth-century ledger data on *actual* bullion and specie holding is incomplete. Clapham suggested the volumes of Bank of England notes in circulation circa 1720 was £2.4 million against just £1 million in bullion, or around 40 percent cover, assuming no additional specie was kept in store. This is a ratio quite close to the lenient one-third cover that British colonial banks would be asked to abide by much later in the mid-nineteenth century. But it is a much lower ratio than the one idealistically envisioned by Zhou Xingji in the eleventh century, namely, two-thirds cover. By 1797, the note circulation volume of the Bank of England had reached £11 million against £4 million in bullion holding—still around 40 percent metallic cover in real terms. Note issuance was at that time the largest entry in the Bank's ledger, thereby confirming its evolution from a government creditor to a specialized bank of issue. Yet, the total value of the notes dwarfed in comparison to the size the national debt as a whole had reached.[120]

The uncovered portion of the issue represented, in one way or another, metallic proceeds lent to the Crown. But that portion, too, was swept up by the "national- debt" economy in that it became increasingly securitized. In 1832, Horsley Palmer, a Bank director, formally proposed that the Bank's issue should comprise one-third metallic cover and two-thirds cover in the form of interest-bearing government bonds instead of direct government debt.[121] It is extremely difficult to plot regulatory fluctuations thereafter, yet data presented by Tennant for 1852 do show that the Bank's maximum note issue was now capped at £34.7 million pounds, against as much as two-thirds metallic cover and one-third government securities. Furthermore, in practice, it was the case that excess bullion holdings could not be lent fast enough to match slumping demand for notes. Therefore, the circulating volume (£20 million) in 1852 actually turned out to be *lower* than the reserve (£23.1 million), in a clear sign that the statutory two-thirds metallic reserve requirement was honored to the letter.[122]

Notably, as England itself was switching to paper money use domestically, it relied on Spanish-American dollars in farther-flung parts of its trading empire. As already indicated, from 1497 the Spanish colonial government minted a large silver coin that through wide circulation not just in Asia became known as the Spanish silver dollar. Around the end of the eighteenth century, this coin was in wide circulation in the West Indies, eastern Canada, and the United States. The value of the coin varied in different locales but was highest in Halifax, capital of the Canadian province of Nova Scotia. Consequently, whenever merchants from the adjacent province of Prince Edward Island secured Spanish dollars, they sent them to Halifax to take advantage of the higher exchange rate there. The resulting shortage of money in on the island itself prompted the governor to gather in all the Spanish dollars he could and have their centers punched out and counterstamped with a sunburst. The punched centers passed as shillings and the outer rims as five-shilling pieces. The mutilated coins were thereafter no longer acceptable outside Prince Edward Island; so, as a consequence, they turned into a discrete provincial currency.[123]

The U.S. Congress established an exchange rate between the U.S. dollar and other foreign coins that circulated widely in the country in 1793; only the Spanish silver dollar, however, was considered legal tender and equated to the U.S. dollar, although its silver content differed slightly. This special status for the Spanish silver dollar in the United States was due to its ubiquity. After the decolonization of Latin America, the Mexican silver dollar appears to have become the chief metallic money used in the southern American states, and its use topped the U.S. dollar itself in popularity; Mexican dollars were also the most popular money in the American West as late as 1849.[124]

Similarly, when the colony of New South Wales was founded in Australia in 1788, it ran into the problem of a lack of coinage. In view of this, Governor Lachlan Macquarie (1761–1824) sought to emulate the Canadian experience and ordered some 40,000 Spanish silver dollar coins (worth £10,000 then). These were sent to Sydney by the British government with a view to launching a stable currency there. The dollar shipment arrived by sea via Madras on November 26, 1812. To stop dollar coins from leaving the colony, they were immediately holed out into subsidiary "dumps," which were valued at fifteen pence and restruck with a new design, while the dollar rims received an overstamp around the hole and were valued at five shillings. The "holey dollar" became the first official currency produced specifically for circulation in Australia. Yet as from 1822 these coins were recalled, melted down for sale in London as bullion, and replaced by proper sterling coinage in return.[125] During the same period, clipping of Spanish silver dollars was also common in China, but this was carried out there by individuals, pawnshops, and even foreign banks for assaying and validation purposes; it was *not* a stratagem used by the central authorities to increase money supply or propagate silver coinage.

Could these monetary developments have better disposed Western Europe for transition from a typically rural premodern society to an industrialized one, all other factors being roughly equal? The cost of capital seems to have been the key determinant here, as Clark and Allen have respectively argued.[126] Though wide gaps in income could be observed between the north and south of Europe around the middle of the seventeenth century, we have sufficient evidence from which to infer that, at least in the north, interest rates were by then considerably lower than the ones prevalent in China. Recent seminal work by Chinese economic historians points to upwards of 20 percent, as the common annualized interest rate for mercantile short-term loans in urban seventeenth-century China, while the same rate was lower than 8 percent for the Netherlands at that time.[127]

We can, in addition, turn to somewhat later Jesuit observations. Because their mission to China was controversial at the Vatican, the Jesuits were quite often at pains to heighten the significance of their work and, by implication, the relative magnitude and prosperity of the Chinese late imperial economy. It is thus instructive that Father Pierre-Martial Cibot, who had lived in Beijing in the 1760s, and who favorably compared the average Chinese standard of living with that of France ("if one does not let the social extremes skew the tally"), devoted much of his economic writing to apologetically explain to his ecclesiastical readership why higher interest rates were tolerated in China.[128]

Yet the historic transition from metal to paper money in Europe, which further decreased the cost of capital, was relatively slow. The recovery of mints during the Carolingian era after a protracted post-Roman hiatus paved the way for a significant increase in continental trade. Concomitantly, the emergence of Florentine banking in the twelfth century dispelled many of the papal interdictions on interest and capital accumulation. Widening trade links then provided the impetus for a distinctly European phenomenon: the rise of joint-stock enterprise.[129]

Joint-stock companies were emerging alongside guilds in Europe from the sixteenth century onward. Many had received a royal charter that helped them monopolize the most lucrative commodities in foreign trade. At the same time, the transferability and scope of share ownership consolidated the companies' purchasing power and institutionalized their independence from the sovereign. Politically, this new balance of power was reflected, for example, in the way the British Parliament displaced the Crown as the key agent of fiscal policy and in the legal articulation of private property rights.

Although commonalities between the mid-Ming and Tudor economies across both extremes of Eurasia may be hard to pin down, there is some similarity between the Sichuan setting in which the world's first paper money had emerged and that of Sweden, a peripheral European economy where banknotes were first used in the West. Much like iron-abundant late-tenth-century Sichuan, Sweden was a net exporter of raw metal (copper) in the mid-seventeenth century. Notably, in both instances paper money first emerged as a private-order mechanism designed to facilitate the settling of accounts within monetary systems grounded in heavier and lower-value coinage than the one used in surrounding regions: iron coinage in Sichuan, copper coinage in Sweden. Notable too is the fact that Sweden was a latecomer into the nascent Western European "national debt" economic mold; though it furnished much of the iron and copper that sustained Portuguese, Dutch, and English trade with Africa at the time, it was not the driving force behind that intercontinental trade. In fact, the Swedish National Debt Office was set up only in 1789 to help fund warfare with Russia.[130]

Furthermore, in both instances, private-order note value started depreciating dramatically a few years after they were issued and were only stabilized once the state took over their issuance. In 1656 a Dutch merchant by the name of Johan Palmstruch, who became chair of the fledgling Swedish Board of Trade, may have realized the potential profits he could make by helping Swedish merchants avoid the necessity of carrying cumbersome copper coinage; he repeatedly petitioned the Swedish throne to advance the establishment of banks in the kingdom and eventually received a royal charter that year to set up a private bank (Stockholms Banco) in return for committing half the profits to the Crown. However, the first type of interest-yielding notes the Bank issued against deposits did not prove popular because the balance of interest had to be settled before they could change hands.[131]

In 1661, this bank started granting loans against property collateral and against commensurate nonyielding deposits of copper coinage as well as disbursing notes (*kreditivsedlar*) to clients for a commission. This second type of nonyielding, impersonal, and more readily fungible private-order notes proved immensely popular to the extent that they circulated at a premium over metallic money. Palmstruch, however, could not resist the temptation of issues over and above the bank's receipts in metal. When Palmstruch's stratagem became known to the public, a serious run on Stockholms Banco ensued, leading to the latter's collapse in 1668 and to Palmstruch's imprisonment on embezzlement charges. The Swedish government was subsequently forced to intervene in order to assuage the anger of Palmstruch's depositors and note bearers; from then on, the Swedish government took over banknote issuance, initially as a public good and only much later as a form of national debt.[132]

A Swedish parliamentary central bank (Riksbank) was set up to replace Stockholms Banco and to deal with the trail of disgruntled debtors it left behind. By 1701 the Riksbank started to issue certified checks of its own, which circulated as paper money side-by-side with specie, so much so that much copper coinage was drawn out of circulation, and

Sweden went on an effectively inconvertible paper money standard in 1745. That year the Riksbank's metallic reserve against note issuance stood at 14 percent. After Sweden's entry into the Seven-Years' War in 1756, it experienced severe budget deficits and inflation to the extent that bulky copper coinage could circulate at a great premium above Riksbank notes. Much of the government's deficit was funded by the Riksbank through note issuance to the extent that the latter's metallic reserve sank from 24 percent in 1754 to just 4 percent in 1762.[133] Yet even the 1754 reserve peak seems very low compared with Bank of England reserve ratios around the same time.

The separation between banknote issuance and public debt occurred much later in Sweden than in England, where the state issued annuities as early as 1693.[134] In fact, banknote issuance and government debt were synonymous in Sweden through much of the eighteenth century. In 1789, the National Debt Office (Riksgäldskontoret) issued for the first time large quantities of small-denomination interest-bearing promissory notes, which circulated at the same time as the Riksbank notes for a period of forty years. Then, in 1831, a year after Sweden formally switched back to silver standard, *Enskilda* (private) banks began to issue notes which circulated side by side with the Riksbank notes for another seventy years. Besides these more officially sanctioned notes, the early-modern Swedish money supply also consisted of a mixture of notes issued by a variety of organizations and individuals; only a fraction of these notes were redeemable in silver, however. Swedish monetary "exceptionalism" formally ended in 1873, as it joined the British-led gold standard.[135] The country further converged with the rest of Western Europe in 1897, as private bank note issuance rights were abolished. This was a significant milestone not least because, unlike in England, private banking in Sweden had revolved up until the 1860s around currency exchange and note issuance rather than the provision of industrial or mercantile credit.[136]

As already indicated, the great bulk of coinage in seventeenth-century Sweden was made of copper, while Tudor coinage had been based on silver and gold. To raise the global price of copper, one of Sweden's main exports at the time, King Gustavus Adolphus (r. 1611–1632) decided to place the Swedish monetary system on a copper standard, a move that lasted until 1776. The increase in Swedish copper exports dovetailed with a growing demand for copper in Hapsburg Spain; the Spanish also aimed to debase their own domestic coinage while diverting silver and gold from their colonies in Latin America to be sold as raw material for currency in other parts of the world. On that score, at least, Sichuan in the Five Dynasties era appears somewhat removed from the European setting in question as iron coinage was used there as a mercantilist strat-agem initially by the Later Shu. This ploy, initiated against the back-drop of coin famine (*qianhuang*), prevented the more precious copper from crossing the border into competing kingdoms, while Spain adopted baser-metal coinage to actually facilitate the outflow of the more pre-cious metal overseas during an era that saw an upsurge in the output of precious metal.

Yet when seventeenth-century Sweden is compared directly with seventeenth-century East Asia rather than with the Later Shu, other re-vealing points of convergence emerge: It is interesting, for example, that in Sweden, too, copper mines were mostly state run (however, more pri-vate enterprise was allowed in the Swedish iron industry). Also of note is that although Swedish copper underpinned Spain's new domestic cur-rency, seventeenth-century Japanese copper furnished Chinese and In-dian imperial mints. That Japanese copper could not, on the other hand, substantively compete with Swedish copper in European markets attests to the limited scope of globalization before the age of steam, as will be discussed in the following chapter.[137]

Largely driven in the eighteenth century by the Bank of England (est. 1694), the spread of banknotes in Britain followed a rather different dynamic than in Sweden. Simply put, Swedish paper note issuance seems to be more inchoately associated with the rise of a modern credit econ-omy when comparison is drawn to England. To begin with, one has to recall that the Bank of England had first been set up with the brief of managing Crown debt, evolving into a singular bank of issue only much later. It aimed at expanding its own note issue at the expense of a mul-titude of other private-bank–issued notes in the eighteenth century, but its monopoly of paper money in England was formalized only in 1844. Elsewhere in continental Europe and Scotland, private banknotes prolif-erated well into the late nineteenth century. In Scotland and Hong Kong private banknote issuance has survived to this day.[138]

How did private bank notes emerge in England in the latter part of the seventeenth century, not long after Palmstruch introduced this in-novation in Sweden? The advanced Dutch credit economy may have fa-cilitated the introduction of the idea on the British Isles: It was perhaps no accident that Palmstruch himself had grown up in the Netherlands, where mercantile bills of exchange had long been in use and where the Bank of Amsterdam (established in 1609) was renowned for its intricate conversion system between silver and gold, as well as for its prowess in invoicing customer deposits in a multitude of foreign coins of varying quality. Those invoices could eventually be bought and sold in the marketplace for hard currency by those preferring the safety of the Bank's assay system. A few decades later, the Bank of Amsterdam also became an important creditor to the Dutch East India Company (VOC) and the municipality of Amsterdam.[139]

In the early seventeenth century, English long-distance merchants did not yet have a comparable exchange bank to turn to; deposit banking developed later in England than on the Continent where Venetian-style *giro* banks and Rialto specie exchanges had been in existence since the late medieval period. Rather, wealthy merchants often deposited their excess gold or silver at the London Tower Mint for safekeeping. This habit came to an abrupt end in 1640, when Charles I expropriated the Tower Mint private deposits to defray the cost of his campaigns against the English and Scottish parliamentary armies. Disillusioned, more and more of the city's merchants began to deposit their excess specie from then on with London's goldsmiths on Lombard Street. The latter would pay 5 percent interest on such fixed-term deposits and would issue written receipts as semiliquid proof of the amount brought in. Receipts immediately convertible into cash on demand appeared a few decades later and were known as "promissory notes." Some of the specie deposited would be lent out in turn by the goldsmiths at a higher interest rate while the receipts themselves started to pass from hand to hand until they evolved into a form of scrip. Small regional banks outside London began to emulate this arrangement in the latter part of the seventeenth century; it was also these country banks that pioneered the circulation of *modern* (read: impersonal and non-interest–yielding) paper money on the British Isles on the eve of the establishment of the Bank of England.[140]

Then, the popularization of notes in the West gathered much more momentum when improved printing technology had finally managed to keep forgeries at bay. During the early 1800s, Philadelphia inventor Jacob Perkins's steel plates and siderography began to change the world of note printing. By the 1860s, note printing in Britain and the United States had been mechanized, all but eliminating the need to manually date notes. Printers such as the London-based Bradbury, Wilkinson & Co., the American Banknote Company, and the Continental Bank Note Company of New York made use of these new applications to become the premium suppliers of notes to the rest of the world—China and Japan included.[141]

More generally, the nascent modern credit economy was advanced in no small measure thanks to an invigorated concept of corporate ownership. The latter evolved following the Renaissance as a means of affirming the concession of property rights by the monarch, the Bank of England included. The monarch tolerated the concept of corporate ownerships because the first joint-stock trading companies paid for their charters, thereby helping to raise tax revenue. Through the share capital they raised the founders of joint-stock companies achieved a degree of investment security and economies of scale that were quite unparalleled elsewhere in the early modern world. By the early nineteenth century, the British Parliament was *not* only tolerating joint-stock enterprise but also actively engaged in regulating it and laying down the legal foundations for its exponential growth in the twentieth century.[142]

CONCLUSIONS

The last millennium saw triumphal bouts and the decline and resurgence of paper money in China and the West. The world's first paper money owes its rise to monetary innovation as early as the Tang dynasty. These innovations came of age during the Northern Song era and culminated in the Yuan dynasty's de facto renunciation of coinage. However, the Chinese premodern experiment with paper money was not an enduring one. In 1430, the Ming polity was forced to relinquish paper money, and the Chinese economy became wholly dependent therefrom on imported silver as the main medium of exchange. Although bronze coinage conceptually remained the anchor of the late-imperial monetary system because of its importance to the peasantry, standardized silver bullion, largely measured by weight and quality rather than by tale, was in practice the currency used in higher-denomination transactions. Ironically, as Chapter Four will explain, it was not until the establishment of British banks in Shanghai in the latter half of the nineteenth century that paper money would reemerge in China on a large scale.

What hypotheses could this overview support? First it would suggest that extensive monetary use of silver or gold was not a prerequisite for paper money proliferation. On the contrary, in both the Sichuan and Swedish experience, the appearance of paper money was strongly associated with the use of base metals and private-order mercantile initiative. At the same time, when viewed comparatively, the European and Chinese experiences suggest that sustaining paper money involved sooner or later prompt central-authority intervention. Far from enshrining note convertibility in its own right, whether the premodern state would be able to entrench fiduciary or token currency seems to have been determined by its ability to project metallic-reserve inviolability and *moderate* debasement in the first instance.

Though crucial at first, private bank note issuance would become peripheral across premodern Eurasia. Once the state had taken over bank note issuance and was able to prop up circulation for some time, it would ultimately seek to borrow funds or issue more paper money against future tax earnings rather than against its present bullion holdings. In that sense, the reliability of state-backed notes ineffably underlay the state's ability to later disseminate other paper-based debt instruments like salt certificates and, in early modern England, corporate charters and bonds. The latter, in fact, still underwrite much of our twenty-first-century national-debt-driven monetary system.

CHAPTER THREE

The Great Money Divergence

European and Chinese Coinage before the Age of Steam

Economic historians have of late been preoccupied with mapping out and dating the "Great Divergence" between northwestern Europe and China. However, relatively few studies have examined the path dependencies of either region; the dynamics of monetization, the spread of fiduciary currency, or their implications for financial factor prices and domestic-market integration *before* the discovery of the New World. This chapter is designed to highlight the need for such a comprehensive scholarly undertaking by tracing out the varying modes of coin production and circulation across Eurasia before steam engines came on stream and by examining what the implications of this currency divergence might be for our understanding of the early modern English and Chinese economies.

California School historians often challenge the entrenched notion that European technological or economic superiority over China had become evident long before the Industrial Revolution. In their view, no clear-cut European departure from the premodern economic mold elsewhere in the world can be identified any time before 1800. Although a few tentative studies of monetary systems across Eurasia in antiquity have been attempted,[1] it is worth noting here that, to date, the Great Divergence debate has largely revolved around comparative wage and consumption data, maritime trade volumes, life-span estimates, land ownership inequalities, and agricultural productivity on the eve of Britain's Industrial Revolution. The debate has scarcely touched on monetary aggregates or financial indices in the intervening period, namely, the late Middle Ages.[2]

Here, I shall draw on the many stimulating insights and rich data that scholars associated to one degree or other with California School thought have contributed to our understanding of world monetary history, while insisting that the contours of that very history—when comparatively studied—do support in fact the notion that northwestern Europe's departure from the premodern mold had long predated 1800. Though our focus will be on global bullion flows, I will point to early-modern advancements in coin production and metallurgic technology by way of demonstrating how Europeans were able to sustain and further benefit from the flow of specie into Asia. Eric Helleiner has persuasively shown in this context that "territorial currency," namely the notion that foreign coinage cannot be used at will within another sovereign polity, normalized across Western Europe long after the concept of national sovereignty had first been envisioned in the Treaty of Westphalia (1648).[3]

By addressing endogenous mining output and divergent production modes of coinage, this chapter is intended to underscore Professor Helleiner's important insights from an East Asian perspective. It is also intended to complement Professor Akinobu Kuroda's important work. For, despite his resolute rejection of conventional Eurocentric monetary wisdom, Kuroda does otherwise seem to suggest that the unseemly roots of Europe's eventual sweeping uptake of "debt-based *single* [read: national] unit of account" in the early twentieth century can in fact be partly traced as far back as the mercantile restructuring of late medieval England.[4]

This chapter will survey in broad strokes the evolution of currency across Eurasia roughly from the Tang (in China) and Carolingian (in Western Europe) eras up to the age in which the aforementioned Terrien Lacouperie lived, namely, the age in which steam technology had revolutionized everything from the notion of distance to the notion of labor. Steam, of course, also changed our notion of money because it ushered in the standardization of coin production around the world. Between 1787 and 1797, Birmingham innovator Matthew Boulton introduced steam-powered steel collars to mints—a technology that greatly improved the quality, durability, roundness, and uniformity of British coinage. Boulton's new steam-powered minting machines were sold all over Britain and then purchased by Russian, French, American, Siamese, and Japanese mints. Across Europe and North America, steam thus quickly replaced less advanced minting technologies in the early nineteenth century, ranging from basic coin hammering practiced from the very inception to manual screw presses. Boulton's invention rapidly decreased minting costs, reduced forgeries, and made it easier and more attractive for the central-state apparatus to take over the private issuance of local base metal token currencies. Based on observation of mints in Europe, American technicians in Philadelphia had been able in 1836 to develop a steam-powered mint of their own; they later exported it to Latin America.[5]

Steam-powered minting had transformed China's monetary system by the early twentieth century. For over two millennia before that, imperially cast bronze coinage had remained the mainstay of Chinese currency. Distinctly known to Europeans as "copper cash" (*qian*) but often made of brass, these low-denomination coins typically had fairly simple raised rims to discourage clipping, with minimalistic inscription; they featured a square hole in the middle so that they could be stringed in big clusters of 1,000 pieces (mostly known as *diao* or *guan*) often subdivided into smaller cluster of 100 (*zumo qian*).[6] Since the sixteenth century, heavy silver ingots (sycee) and imported silver dollars had become indispensable in higher-denomination transactions. Yet in 1887 inveterate Chinese general and statesman Zhang Zhidong had ordered minting machinery from Birmingham, which within a decade would have an impact on both low- and high-tier currencies. By the early twentieth century, provincial mints had employed steam-powered machinery to not only issue limited amounts of imperial silver dollars but also flood the marketplace with better-quality bronze coins (*tongyuan*) that were not square-holed like traditional "cash." These looked very much like European currency at the time; namely, they were no longer holed and carried elaborate designs.[7]

The remaining sections of this chapter are framed with a view toward understanding the wider ramifications of coin production in Chinese and European early-modern societies. The following section analyses the evolution of currency across Eurasia following Rome's disintegration and the breakup of China's formative Han Empire. The next section after that explores why Western Europe had reverted to gold coinage in the late-medieval era, just at a time when late imperial China abandoned paper money. The section following that one then questions the notion that China's monetary role in the early-modern era was "magnetic" as California School studies might suggest; the next section will point to technological breakthroughs, which account for the quality of Western coinage well before the age of steam. Finally, I shall integrate the whole gamut of historic evidence in a bid to sketch in broad stokes the Great Monetary Divergence between East and West, dating back to the early Middle Ages; I will identify the ways in which European coin production departed from the rest of the world, beginning as early as the thirteenth century, and the implication of that departure on European statecraft. Whereas other studies have traced out the Great Divergence in terms of the European economies' overcoming of common Malthusian brakes, here I shall emphasize the global pursuit of trade, mineral resources, and the supply of metallic money as critical determinants of European prosperity.

THE GREAT MONETARY DIVERGENCE IN THE EARLY MIDDLE AGES: THE SILVER PENNY ERA

The three centuries of political disunion following the breakup of China's Han Empire saw, particularly in the northwest, diminishing levels of copper output, the spread of "free coinage," and rampant debasement by competing polities. Certainly, land taxes were still levied at that time in grain or cloth in the north, yet, contrary to previous Han practices, ordinary officials were rarely remunerated in copper "cash" even in the south. Nonetheless, on balance, the degree of demonetization and discursive discontinuity in south and northeast China during those three centuries may well have been less extensive than what ensued from the collapse of the Roman Empire in Western Europe.[8]

On the British Isles, for example, coinage fell into complete disuse as a medium of exchange by 450 CE, only to reemerge in the latter part of the seventh century. However, on the European continent no such clearcut break occurred: The Germanic tribes that overran Rome continued to operate its old mints, churning out the mainstay of gold tremisses and solidi coinage in the fifth century CE and retaining much of the original Roman imagery intact. Their rulers' own portraiture gradually surfaced on coinage only as of the mid-sixth century, so that early medieval coinage design came of age only at the onset of Carolingian power. The critical difference between the continental and English monetary trajectories became even more pronounced when minting resumed on the British Isles. Ironically, the management and production of currency became much more centrally controlled in England than across the Channel by the eighth century.[9]

Although the currencies of the Franks, Visigoths, and Lombards were based on golden tremisses and solidi, Italian principalities resorted to a range of autochthonous silver and bronze coins under Ostrogothic and Byzantine rule. Beginning in the late sixth century, Western European gold currency became increasingly debased as a whole, possibly as a result of the decline of mining in Eastern Europe or fewer trade links across the Continent. Much of the Frankish coinage in the late seventh century was made of 25 to 75 percent alloys of gold and silver. Byzantine mints in Italy produced debased gold coins between the seventh and eighth centuries, but by the end of the eighth century the coinage they produced was composed of copper alloy that had often been gilded perfunctorily. Strictly speaking, gold coinage survived the downfall of Rome only in Asia Minor and in North Africa, where gold could still be readily sourced from the long-standing mines of Nubia and brought to mints on trans-Saharan camel convoys.[10]

Both pseudo-Roman and self-identifying medieval rulers' gold tremisses gave way in the eighth century to new coinage of pure silver in Western Europe, which was less precious per unit. That new silver coinage had become known as *pennies* on the British Isles and *deniers* on the Continent in the ninth century. During the period between the eighth and thirteenth centuries, gold coinage further receded from circulation in much of the western reaches of the Continent, while the new silver coinage took root; this was Europe's first silver-coinage epoch.[11]

Why did Western Europe abandon gold coinage in the eighth century? It is plausible that the breakdown of central authority and feudalization weakened the ability to embark on large-scale mining operations to replenish the stock of currency. It may also be that this was exacerbated by shrinking trade volumes across the Mediterranean due to Arab conquest and monetary reform.[12]

Umayyad khalif 'Abd al-Malik ibn Marwan initiated a reform of Islamic currency in the late seventh century. Hitherto the Islamic world had relied on the Sassanid silver drachma and Byzantine solidi gold coinage, but from then on aniconic gold coinage predominated. Nevertheless, the Ummayads did strike silver after they reformed gold currency. At the same time, one would do well to remember silver had not yet been fully monetized in China; hence its relative price vis-à-vis copper and gold was low there. In turn, greater demand for gold in the Arab world might have led to an outflow of gold from Europe in return for silver from China via Asia Minor—but global metal-price arbitrage alone surely cannot sum up all the factors at play considering the relatively low volume of intercontinental trade at the time.[13]

Like early medieval European currency, which was pseudo-Roman in essence, the early Arab currency emulated almost precisely Sassanid silver coinage in territories occupied to the east, including central Asia, while in territories occupied to the west, including Egypt, Byzantine coinage—made up as it was of mostly gold and subsidiary copper—served as a model. Following 'Abd Al-Malik's monetary reforms, however, the design of Arab coinage of all metals was deanthropomorphized, featuring Kufic script exclusively. Notably, the transition from Sassanid-Byzantine coin design to purely Kufic verses due to Islamic prohibitions of imagery was faster than the transition from pseudo-Roman to avowedly medieval coinage in Europe.[14]

The Arab silver coinage of Central Asia carried over later into the medieval period by the Ilkhanid and Golden Horde authorities alongside copper subsidiary coinage. The original coinage of the Ottomans also consisted of silver coins (akçe, or asper as it was known to Europeans). It was not until the late fifteenth century that Ottoman gold coins were finally struck; in the interim, foreign gold coins—mainly the Venetian ducat—facilitated trade between Europe and the Mediterranean basin, circulating uninterruptedly in Muslim Asia Minor.[15]

Of equal importance, 'Abd Al-Malik prioritized, in areas adjacent to Europe, gold coinage over silver coinage so that, due to the Byzantine employment of the gold nomisma (a variant of the Roman solidus also known as bezant), the exchange rate in the Levant was between fourteen and eighteen silver units for one gold unit of equal weight, whereas in Europe the same rate was close to 12:1 in the early medieval period. In other words, gold was not just more widely monetized but also dearer in the East, even though Arabs and later the Ottomans could more readily tap into Nubian gold deposits. Indeed, the gold dinar served as staple currency in the East, while the silver dirham and copper coinage were subsidiary.[16]

Demand for gold in the Muslim Mediterranean coincides almost seamlessly with the European abandonment of gold coinage, which followed decades of debasement. As previously indicated, the gold tremisses standard employed by Anglo-Saxons and Franks had been wholly supplanted by pennies and deniers by the eighth century. Following 'Abd al-Malik's reforms, Byzantium, in turn, abandoned its minor silver-coin mintage for a purely gold standard with subsidiary copper coinage.[17] Byzantine gold coinage remained fairly stable thereafter until Constantine IX Monomachus (1042–1055) sharply reduced its gold content. That debasement was a desperate attempt to boost state revenue in the face of destructive Pecheneg invasions.

By the end of the eleventh century, the nomisma's gold content had fallen to just 10 percent, and it was replaced two centuries later by the florin as the trade currency of the Mediterranean basin. Notably, in Byzantium, coinage and bullion mining were monopolized by the central authorities, as was the case in China at the time, whereas in much of early medieval Europe localized mining and minting was commonplace.[18]

The decline in nomisma metallic content and the abandonment of gold coinage elsewhere in Europe occurred when, at the western extreme of the continent, English silver currency was quickly acquiring a reputation for quality and reliability; it was sought after in Scandinavia and the Baltic regions, which did not have their own currencies at the time. This was a remarkable turnaround in monetary history, given that the use of coinage had receded in England for nearly 200 years following the retreat of Roman governors. By the seventh century, coin production resumed with vigor on the British Isles: Mints were established by the Anglo-Saxons in London, Canterbury, and Winchester after two centuries of discontinued local production, as post-Roman gold coins gave way to local designs. In 928, a single consistent coinage system was proclaimed across England. Furthermore, in 973 King Alfred additionally reinforced the standardization and replenishment of circulating coinage by instating a system of reminting worn-out and clipped coins with official insignia every six years; these were brought to mints by private individuals and smelted. Those individuals would receive in return the equivalent amount in new coinage, an amount that was invariably smaller in intrinsic metallic content as a result of brassage and seigniorage extraction. Under the reign of Edward the Confessor (r. 1042–1066), the last Anglo-Saxon to rule England, the reminting of older coinage was carried out every three years.[19]

Crucially, rather than reverting to the continental mode of feudal free minting they had been more accustomed to, the Norman conquerors of England accepted in effect the Anglo-Saxon system and reinforced its centralizing tendency. The Tower of London Mint was established in 1299, firmly reinforcing the reputation of English currency for size consistency and metallic purity across the continent. That reputation was thrown into high relief because neighboring France experienced successive waves of debasement between 1290 and 1450, which accelerated a schism there between intrinsic and imperially decreed coin values. But it was not until the fifteenth century that English coinage was firmly rebased on gold again, and the use of foreign gold coins there started rapidly declining.[20]

The metallic content of English silver pennies remained stable right until the mid-fourteenth century when the first of major debasement of silver coinage occurred there too. It was under Henry VIII (r. 1509–1547) and Edward VI (r. 1547–1553) that the silver content of the English pound (as a unit of account rather than a tangible coin) was reduced more than ever before in pursuit of windfall of seigniorage revenue. The era between 1542 and 1551 saw the pound losing more than five-sixths of its silver content; it therefore became known to posterity as the era of "Great Debasement."[21]

Yet, unlike France, England had by the late seventeenth century also attempted to rebase and replenish its stock of silver coinage in part so as to maintain its relatively high reputation and in part to better reflect metal price movements. The latter aim proved harder to calibrate, and England did lose much of its silver coinage stock in those years because the metal price of English coins was often higher overseas than their imperially decreed value domestically.[22]

In our view, England and France's disparate experiences with debasement over those 250 years—though scarcely considered in comparative Eurasian terms hitherto—denote a veritable reconceptualization of money that laid the groundwork for the eventual emergence of "national debt" and modern nation-statehood. Destabilizing and only marginally remunerative in the long run, these debasements did nevertheless help monarchs amass resources with which to further entrench central authority at the expense of feudal lords. In France, the latter could up to that time issue coinage of their own, while foreign coins could similarly be used fairly uninterruptedly. Yet, in England, these debasement and (less frequent) reminting campaigns had already been accompanied by incipient central authority efforts to wipe out the use of all coinage except that which was approved by the monarchy.

If early modern England and France diverged in the *degree* to which their rulers pursued debasement as a source of short-term profit, China's earlier adoption of paper money as well as its path-dependent formulations of Confucian statecraft meant that coinage debasement was practiced by central governments there arguably less regularly. As already indicated, one way European rulers could aim to gain more seigniorage revenue was by delinking imperially decreed coin values from their metallic values. To a large extent, this could be achieved more easily than in China because both gold and silver coinage circulated in early-modern Europe, whereas successive late-imperial Chinese dynasties were for the most part reluctant to coin anything but traditional copper cash. In other words, seigniorage could be raised in the European setting by manipulating the imperially decreed exchange rate between silver and gold coins serving different functions in the economy. Yet, at the same time, early modern European rulers needed to find ways of offsetting the consequent outflow of coins of either metal to other polities where the decreed exchange rate was more favorable to that particular metal. Two corollary stratagems eventually emerged in response to this problem: limiting "free coinage" and private-order assaying and the espousal of greater monetary integrity that was manifest partly through the rise of mercantilism. At the turn of the seventeenth century, legal-tender coinage had not yet crystallized across Western Europe, of course. But the first attempts by central government at replacing intangible units ("ghost moneys") with tangible-currency units in national accounts were tentatively underway.[23]

In China, as both Kuroda and Dunstan have shown, copper "cash" was conceived of in imperial nomenclature as a "public good" of sorts; one that the central government must provide largely at its own expense and even at a net loss in order to facilitate commoners' livelihood (*bianmin*). More vigorous production of "cash" was envisioned, in turn, as the ideal stratagem for bringing down the price of grain, especially over the annual *soudure* period or at times of severe famine. In China therefore, somewhat contrary to conventional wisdom, the price of "cash" relative to silver ingots could at times rise even when more of it was produced because silver coinage was not minted, and silver ingots were too dear to be customarily used in rural areas to buy grain. Consequently, the silver-ingot weight and fineness preferred by the imperial bureaucracy increasingly came to be used as an intangible "money of account" against which tangible bronze coins (that is, copper "cash") of uneven size and provenance were tallied. To keep the price of "cash" at bay, the Chinese government did not just produce more of it but aimed to release more grain for sale from its many granaries at the same time, particularly in restive famine-stricken localities.[24]

Thus, perhaps because of the imperative to finance more frequent warfare, metallic debasement was probably much more pervasive in early modern European polities than in China as means of raising revenue. At any rate, English theorists and policy makers seem to have internalized first—well before the Industrial Revolution—the fiscal and monetary limits of debasement in a bimetallic setting. They knew that manipulation of the decreed exchange rate between coins made of gold and those made of silver—namely, "crying up" or "crying down" certain coins in a way that could cause a dramatic departure from their intrinsic metallic worth—could lead to the outflow of either overseas. For these reasons, they ensured that monarchs debased coinage relatively infrequently in the early modern era; debasements that proved too drastic were tempered with "rebasements"; at the same time, they enhanced the efficacy of debasement and shored up trust in domestic coinage by minimizing the availability of competing precious metal foreign coinage and curbing bullion exports.

The issue of subsidiary base metal coinage was, in turn, largely left to local nonstate actors. Although, strictly speaking, some precious metal foreign coinage was used in England, just as English domestic coinage could sometimes be reluctantly permitted in English colonies, this kind of currency substitution had been distinctly frowned on. More to the point, and in contrast to much of the rest of Europe, foreign currency substitution had been intermittently counteracted in England since the

Middle Ages and with particular vigor over the course of the eighteenth century.[25]

Eventually, England was first to unilaterally decree a monometallic gold standard, whereby its dwindling silver coinage was made "token" rather than full-bodied subsidiary of gold. Little studied in this context, the history of European taxation is nevertheless important because it broadly shows that early-modern England was—well before the Industrial Revolution—*also* the first large polity where urban mercantile taxes supplanted rural land taxes as fiscal mainstay, whereas (relatively low) land taxes remained the mainstay of the Chinese polity until the twentieth century. Indeed, one might well hypothesize that, by transitioning to a gold standard grounded in reality on fiduciary coinage and later on banknotes, eighteenth-century English political economists intuited from historic experience—and against the backdrop of intense continental rivalries—a more stable means of bolstering state coffers than debasement; one that preconditioned the popular uptake of "national debt."[26]

In China, by way of contrast, the path-dependent prescription of low-value bronze coinage narrowed down the seigniorage potential deriving from the purposeful delinking of intrinsic values from imperially decreed ones, so that high-denomination units of account, or their conversion rates, were not effectively determined by the Chinese emperor as in England. In fact, increasing the supply of coinage could be a liability to Chinese emperors because of higher relative production costs per unit. Though the state monopoly over coinage eventually became more enshrined in Chinese statecraft than was the case in medieval European praxis, calls for "free mining" and "free casting" as a means of supplementing state coinage with better-quality coinage were made by, for example, Premier Zhang Jiuling as late as in the Tang era. However, his views were ultimately rejected in favor of those who argued for banning the nonmonetary use of copper, so as to bring down the price of the raw material from which coinage was made. By implication, the latter argued that "free casting" would only make copper dearer.[27]

Neither did Chinese coinage face equally intense competition in the marketplace from foreign coins as it did elsewhere in Western Europe; on the contrary, it was usually drained by demand for coinage in the less monetized polities of Japan, Korea, and Southeast Asia at the time. Although China is famous to have been the birthplace of paper currency in the eleventh through the fifteenth centuries, the notes centrally issued by Chinese emperors had to be anchored in conversion to bronze coinage or silver ingots for the most part. On the other hand, Chinese imperial taxes were raised in kind and corvée labor to a greater extent than in France or England up until that time.[28]

When coinage debasement did occur in China it was usually in the form of issuing more "big cash" (*daqian*), namely bronze coins about four times as *heavy* as the standard coins but with a nominal (read: imperially decreed) value usually tenfold larger. The only exception to this pattern was perhaps partial recourse to cheaper iron-made coinage during the Han and Northern Song eras. However, careful reading of Song Yingxing's treatise *Tiangong kaiwu*, an influential late Ming-era economic compendium, would seem to suggest that *daqian* coinage had by then been rarely centrally issued because it was seen as disadvantaging commoners and because it aggravated forgery.[29]

Unlike China, late medieval and early modern continental European debasement usually consisted of issuing *lighter*, *smaller*, and more alloyed coins with the same nominal value as standard units rather than larger token coinage in the manner of *daqian*. In fact, the emergence of bigger silver coinage in late medieval Europe such as the famous central European groschen (also known as groats or grossi) was initially associated with a desire to offset the impact of long-term debasement with more unadulterated "white silver" in the monetary system.[30]

On the other hand, arguably because post-Song coin output levels were lower in China, Chinese emperors tolerated commoner use of standard-size coins genuinely or supposedly issued by previous dynasties. Except for Emperor Qianlong's vigorous efforts to recast deficient or forged "cash" and increase coin output, Chinese late-imperial large-scale recasting efforts were relatively rare. By contrast, late-medieval European debasements were often facilitated by the recall and remintage of older coinage, and thus coins from previous centuries were much harder to come by there even if coeval foreign coinage was rife.[31]

To be sure, bronze coin prices did rise relative to silver during Qianlong's reign, whereas the overall late-imperial trend was one of appreciating silver. However, Qianlong's efforts also resulted in higher raw copper prices, and probably for that reason higher coin output was not sustained thereafter.[32]

The dynamics in the Chinese late-imperial monetary system were such that lower coin output and lack of adequate investment in improving production technology or in counterforgery measures were of themselves dampening the price of imperial coinage relative to raw copper and silver, thereby further entrenching the spread of nominally illicit private imitations (*siqian*). Thus, seigniorage incentives for higher production were all but neutered a priori. In 1567, high-ranking Ming official Ge Shouli memorialized, for example, that lower coin output even spurred rumors in the marketplace that imperial bronze coinage was about to be abolished altogether, resulting in downright rejection of newly cast coinage in some localities.[33]

To be sure, desultory attempts at popularizing newly cast late-Ming coinage through *rebasement* were made at certain moments during the Hongzhi, Wanli, and Jiajing reigns. But they were all discontinued prematurely because the imperial bureaucracy could not muster the stamina to see through the displacement of *siqian* and to wait out the initial period of low returns. At first, rebased Ming coinage was all too often taken out of circulation and smelted into *siqian* coins and could therefore not gain the anticipated *agio* in the marketplace straight away. To gain a foothold in the marketplace, rebased coinage would have had to be made more distinguishable from *siqian* through better casting technology, not just higher copper content. Equally important, it would have required more proactive state backing in the form of making it admissible in tax payments. In the event, neither requirement was met. As fiscal pressures and external threats to the survival of the dynasty mounted during the Tianqi and Chongzhen reigns, Ming coinage was produced on a larger scale, but it was then characterized by desperate *debasement* measures rather than rebasement.[34]

That despite Qianlong's efforts "older" coinage genuinely or purportedly produced by previous dynasties (*guqian*) remained an important pillar of the Chinese late-imperial monetary system well into the Qing era is evident in arguably the most pertinent of Jesuit treatises on that theme: Du Halde's (1674–1743) chapter on money in his famous *Description of the Empire of China*, translated into English from the French in 1736. Notably, Du Halde himself had not been to China, so he relied on a great number of older sources brought over to Europe by fellow Jesuits over the years. Unlike other Jesuits, however, Du Halde was not only physiocratic in his approach but also stressed the importance of trade, possibly due to the influence of new European mercantilist theories. Thus, his praise for rustic China is somewhat more ambivalent. He referred to the "genius" of the Chinese monetary system, for example, and at the same time could describe in a separate segment the reign names (*nianhao*) minimalistically inscribed onto Chinese coins as "pompous":[35]

But what mark of inscription is on that money? That of Europe is stamp'd with the Head of the Prince; but in China it is otherwise. According to the genius of the [that] Nation, it would be deem'd indecent and disrespectful to the Majesty of the Prince, for his image to be perpetually passing thro' the hands of dealers, and the dregs of the people.

Du Halde goes on to suggest that forgery of bronze coinage was all too common in China despite the imposition of capital punishment in such cases. He did not see that necessarily as a drawback because he thought that if Chinese coinage had been made from precious metal as in Europe, it would invite still more forgery. More importantly, the subtext of Du Halde's implicit endorsement of late imperial emperors' tendency to condone counterfeit coins might underscore the fact that, by the early eighteenth century, Western European polities had started discouraging the use of "older" or "foreign" coinage so as to enhance seigniorage revenue and prop up their nascent public debt.[36]

These differences were of course thrown into relief by a Chinese political economy that was ordinarily more suspicious—particularly in its late-imperial, neo-Confucian iteration—of coin debasement and seigniorage as schemes designed to profit the state at the expense of commoners. In a practical sense, the Ming polity's ability to debase coinage was also constrained by its reluctance to coin silver and, more implicitly, by the dynasty's unsuccessful attempts at sustaining fiduciary paper money, as well as by the collective memory of the earlier Song and Yuan failures at preventing paper money from depreciating against copper "cash"; silver was thus strictly valued for tax purposes in the form of bullion, that is, according to its weight and purity, whereas the value of early modern European silver was often manipulated relative to the value of gold specie.[37]

Consequently, even as more Spanish American silver flowed into China in the late-Ming era, and despite the fact that this dynasty issued comparatively low quantities of bronze coinage, base copper "cash" remained exceedingly important in the popular mind-set. Liang Fang-zhong noted, for example, that Ming fiscals were from very early on geared toward maximizing silver receipts and that copper cash was less admissible for tax purposes, but commensurate imperial outlays were often paid out in much lower-quality silver ingots (*yinding*) or even in copper cash, so that high officialdom could possess of the margin in good-quality monetary silver (*yinzi*). As a result, the circulation of good-quality silver ingots remained the preserve of circles close to the imperial court, high officialdom, and wealthy merchants, whereas commoners overwhelmingly relied on copper cash. Moreover, silver had not yet conjured up any special mystique in the Ming popular mind-set, being the "distant" metal that it was.[38]

Perhaps contrary to what one might expect in this context, the late imperial Chinese monetary trajectory also departed in meaningful ways from that of coeval Korea and Japan, not just from that of northwest Europe. To be sure, before 1600, Korea and Japan drew heavily on

Chinese coinage to sustain their own monetary systems. However, as Lin Man-houng has indicated, by the eighteenth century about half of all Japanese coinage in circulation had been domestically produced from gold or silver—metals that remained uncoined in China proper, where coin output diminished and coin quality deteriorated fairly consistently between the fifteenth and the seventeenth centuries. Moreover, much of the new Japanese coinage issued by the *bakufu* government in the seventeenth century carried a higher decreed value than its metallic content, and many local *daimyō* were allowed to issue inconvertible paper money (*hansatsu*) in a bid to overcome metal supply shortfalls. Korea had, in turn, altogether *banned* the monetary use of silver (and banknotes) right until 1876, whereas China became after 1600 increasingly *reliant* on imported silver.[39]

Across East Asia one could detect difficulties in sourcing sufficient metal to meet the popular demand for coinage during the early eighteenth century. Yet banknotes had fallen out of grace by then as a credible means of payment in both Korea and China. As discussed in great detail by Professor Hans Ulrich Vogel, much of the copper needed to produce Chinese "cash" was imported from Japan between 1685 and 1715. But in 1726 the *bakufu* authorities prohibited further exports to China, in part so as to increase domestic coin output. Faced with its main source of copper supply drying up, the Chinese Qing dynasty was forced to develop alternative copper sources in remote Yunnan; hence the cost of copper transport and coin production increased even further.[40]

Indeed, a subsequent spike in the relative price of "cash" persisted fairly consistently until the late eighteenth century. Under young Emperor Qianlong (r. 1735–1796), the post-Song secular decline in Chinese per capita coin output levels was temporarily held back by virtue of newly sourced Yunnan copper and a vigorous expansionist policy. Yet Qianlong was otherwise wary of emulating his predecessor's fiscal expansion, which was carried out through greater tolerance of provincial surcharges on private ventures. At any rate, Chinese coin output level started dropping again after 1770s, and throughout the late imperial era coins genuinely or falsely pertaining to previous dynasties widely circulated in the Chinese marketplace.[41]

The post-Song decline can in turn be plausibly traced back to shifts in China's early modern mining industry, which was rigidly state controlled in comparative terms. Record Song copper output was achieved, for example, by the replacement of slave and corvée miners with paid ones and by allowing more private iron-ore mining ventures. As indicated in the previous chapter, the flat tax rate on private metal output was lowered by Song reformer Wang Anshi (1021–1086) to 20 percent, whereas it stood at around 30 percent later, quite apart from the fact that later dynasties turned in effect into a monopsony of all the metal produced, so that the government-decreed price of metal was invariably weighted down. In addition, later dynasties were also conditioned by a long-established physiocratic discourse and by suspicious founding emperors, who tended to associate "excessive" mining with lawlessness in the hinterland and local bailiff peculation.[42]

These vastly divergent political economies of mining and coinage across Eurasia begot by the early modern era a clear technological divide. They may have also had an impact on the means by which forgers operated and how counterforgery techniques evolved: For example, we have generally *fewer* references to clipping (*jianbian qian*) in late imperial Chinese sources than in early modern European sources, although records for the smelting of coinage (*xiaoqian*), or its illicit recasting into copper utensils, in late imperial China seem to be comparatively numerous, possibly due to a wide gap between the ("black") market price of copper and the state-decreed price. Similarly, the interdiction of private copper smelting of either utensils or articles of faith—in conjunction with the interdiction of private mining—were distinctly cited in China as means of reducing forgery, even though such measures could bring about the opposite outcome. This was because such measures put an upward pressure on the price of raw copper, which in turn could lift the intrinsic value of bronze coinage above its nominal value, thereby making underground debasement and forgery more lucrative still. In this context, Professor Vogel's recent insights further construe the distinct political economies emerging across either end of the continent:[43]

While many similarities in the [early-modern] mining techniques existed in Europe and China, one conspicuous difference can be observed in their varying degrees of mechanization, particularly in drainage, ore hauling and ore crushing. Although in China suitable basic technical devices were available, it seems that they were not systematically used and further developed for mining and smelting purposes. For instance, although waterpower was already being used to drive the bellows of Chinese blast furnaces in the first century CE, and although use of water-power for such purpose is also mentioned for the fourteenth century, the piston bellows at the eighteenth and early nineteenth-century Yunnan copper mines, then the leading mining region in China, appear to have been mainly man-powered.

Indeed, that before the tapping into Yunnan deposits China could become so dependent on imported Japanese silver and copper—even as its absolute coin output levels fell far below the North-Song peak—contrasts sharply with the effervescence in mining around the same time in central Europe, namely even *before* the discovery of New World deposits. This central European effervescence was likely driven by stronger property rights, as compared with the Chinese setting, where more often than not metal prices were set by a government monopsony and much mine output was otherwise repossessed. And by the early sixteenth century, a typical mine owner in central Europe, who had regularly paid contributions to the *Bergmeister,* was the sole claimant to whatever metal the mine yielded so long as he conformed "to the decrees of the laws relating to the metals, and to the orders of the *Bergmeister.*" Notably, the latter would not only register his title as legally binding but would also keep record of multiple shareholders in larger mines and when necessary adjudicated disputes commercial between them.[44]

That Japan could supply so much metal to China at a time it had not yet had strong central government is another testament to how competition between smaller polities—or in this case *daimyo*-led feudatories—as well as greater allowance for private mineral prospecting under the late Muromachi shoguns could lead to a more productive mining industry. Certainly, it would be hard to find any late imperial Chinese setting where nonroyals could *formally* wield so much power as the Medicis and Fuggars did in the late medieval European prospecting and mining.[45]

Also of note is the fact that Chinese emperors relied on state mining output to produce new bronze coins, while the "Great Debasement" in England was mostly underpinned by attracting individuals to voluntarily hand over their foreign and older coinage to government mints for *reminting* through legal and economic incentives. After reminting, these individuals received less in the way of pure silver, of course, but this was offset by the fact that newly minted coins carried a higher "legal tender" value when paying tax. Remarkably, commodity prices only partly caught up with the ratio of the debasement. Such debasements ceased by the early eighteenth century, as English monarchs found better means of raising revenue in the form of floating national debt—first through Bank of England (est. 1694) banknotes, then through bonds. In retrospect, therefore, the "Great Debasement" can be viewed as a one-off transformative event that set in train far-reaching monetary and socioeconomic developments in England, but it was nonetheless *not* sufficiently disruptive to have shaken popular trust in sovereign-backed media of payment. It may well explain the Bank of England's ability to successfully "market" the concept of national debt through banknote issuance in the early eighteenth century and the evolution of these banknotes into "legal tender" in the following century.[46]

As already indicated, English silver pennies were frequently recalled by kings and reminted. Yet despite varying metallic weight standards, they mostly preserved their market value because of the consistency of reminting. Elsewhere in Western Europe—and in China too—the value of the denier, copper "cash," and all other low-denomination currency depended more on their metallic content.

Although there were more mints in continental Europe than in England (reminting was common in fourteenth-century France), coinage became a visible feature of everyday commoner life to a greater degree in England than, for example, in the Iberian peninsula or areas under Frankish rule. In central Europe, coins were used intensively in the Rhineland and Bavaria but hardly seen elsewhere. In Scandinavia and Russia, silver dirhams from the Arab world were commonly used, but autochthonous coinage appeared much later. In sum, I suggest that the key to understanding the monetary divergence across Eurasia in the early middle ages is the concurrent multiplicity of silver coinage of varying quality and intrinsic values, as well as repeated debasements by dissimilar polities, which spawned what Luigi Einaudi famously called "imaginary money" or notional unit-of-account systems. This very divergence is what afforded late medieval French and English monarchs the latitude for remintage within their respective territories at higher seigniorage rates and for the gradual exclusion of competing overseas currencies as of the early modern era.[47]

That *after* the Song downfall there were no contending polities issuing moneys around China, coupled with the pervasiveness of low-value bronze coinage and in-kind taxation, meant that Chinese emperors' ability to extract seigniorage in the form of "legal tender" blandishments was limited.

THE WESTERN EUROPEAN RETURN TO GOLD

Probably the most important yet relatively little-studied upturn in premodern global monetary history is northwestern Europe's reversion to gold-based currency after about four centuries of silver penny domination. Granted, this upturn might have been of less consequence in

Southern Europe, and Spain in particular, where the minting of gold coins and the usage of Islamic dinars continued alongside silver pennies after the eighth century. In Andalucía, the Umayyad governors replaced the Visigothic system of coinage in Spain with an Arabic one, consisting initially of gold dinars and their fractions similar to those of North Africa but of inferior and very variable fineness. Thus, Spain and Byzantium-affiliated Italy were the only regions of Europe where a gold standard remained intact around the twelfth century.[48]

The Italian emporia of Genoa and Florence, which handled much of Europe's trade with West Asia and North Africa, also used Islamic gold dinars. But the dinar became heavily debased as of the twelfth century and was thus falling from grace as the preferred currency of international trade. In 1252, Genoa had begun minting its own gold coinage (genovino), to be immediately followed by the famous florins of Florence and the ducats of Venice, with all containing more gold than the contemporaneous Almoahed dinar. What afforded Genoa, Florence, and Venice the gold with which to trade on an even keel with the Islamic world, while the dinar was losing ground as a reliable currency? Booty brought back by the Crusaders might immediately spring to mind, yet surprisingly the economic effects of the Crusades on the balance of trade between Europe and the Levant have remained far from clear-cut. In turn, what much more clearly emerges from pertinent studies is that the Italians' ability to tap into the gold deposits of North Africa in return for European copper was an important factor in Europe's monetary transition.[49]

In the first instance, it was the Italians' ability to tap into the gold deposits of North Africa in return for European copper that might explain changes in the Italian city-states' monetary systems. Gold reached Italy via Hafsid Tunisia on trade routes pioneered by the Fatimids. In West Africa gold was considered a luxury royal item—it was rarely monetized or commoditized. As a mark of its success in replacing the Byzantine gold nomisma, the Venetian gold ducat had begun, by the fourteenth century, to circulate widely in Egypt and later reached other parts of the Muslim world. Later, the florin also began to be used more widely around the Mediterranean. In 1472, the Venetians too moved from a bimetallic standard to a gold standard domestically.[50]

Here, perhaps for the first time in the history, we have an example of trading (read: mercantilist) polities that strategically leveraged their advanced understanding of the *global* marketplace and of bullion flows to acquire economic superiority even when there was little bullion that they could mine domestically. Indeed, that information-based superiority presaged the way in which the Italian city-states, and later the Portuguese, Spanish, Dutch, and English, would manipulate global bullion stocks to gradually gain the upper hand over the economically preponderant East. Key to sustaining early asymmetric-knowledge advantages was the moderate rate of debasement of, for example fourteenth-century Venetian republican coinage, which partly resulted from local merchants' councilor powers but ultimately enhanced its popularity over other continental coinage. By contrast, Venetian colonial currency disbursed in Greece was comparatively much more debased than republican coinage, but it was regionally circumscribed, that is, it could not be converted into other coinage outside Greece. Either way, both metropolitan and colonial Venetian coins were minted from bullion mostly mined elsewhere; coeval Hungarian and Serbian coins were minted from domestically mined silver and yet did not prove as popular. More generally, foreign full-bodied coins as well as worn and clipped coins from all over Europe were brought to Venice for remintage precisely because of the premium that Venetian coinage carried over metal.[51]

There has traditionally been emphasis in the pertinent literature on how dreams of El Dorado propelled the exploration of the New World. But, following Vilar, it is important to recall that the thirst for African gold had in fact much earlier fueled competition between Genoese and Portuguese navigators, indirectly leading to the European rediscovery of the Canary Islands in the thirteenth century. In fact, the sourcing of West African gold would eventually be reflected in the naming of England's famous coins, the guineas, first struck in 1662. Although the literature emphasizes the effects of Latin American silver on the rest of the world, one would equally do well to recall that Columbus's diary is replete with allusions to gold, thus reflecting the impact of earlier expeditions across the Mediterranean and West Africa. Indeed, the latter was the *first* precious metal to be brought back from Latin America, mainly through looting and indigenous Caribbean forced labor in alluvial deposits, but it depleted by 1525.[52]

Portuguese precious metal transport qualitatively augmented the scale of Italian city-state trade in one very important sense: It directly reached out to India and East Asia by sea. Here, it is worth recalling Om Prakash's important observation that the mainstay of Portuguese maritime business in the sixteenth century—well ahead of the importation of indigo or silk—was the procurement of pepper from India initially in return for West African–sourced gold and later with Latin American gold and silver. In terms of cargo values, and excluding pepper and precious metals, base metals like copper were preponderant on Portuguese ships: Often that copper would be of Japanese rather than European provenance and would be offloaded by the Portuguese in China where it was used to produce "cash."[53]

For these reasons, it would be a mistake to overstate the significance of silver. Rather, at play in early modern Eurasian and Euro-African trade was a reallocation of metal from places where it had no monetary value to places where it had and thus was more precious. This transformation was evident in the European metropole as it gradually went on gold while buying off pepper, textiles, and tea with silver and copper. Yet within Europe one could also observe a secondary divergence between England, where debasement and base-metal petty cash were rare, to countries like France and Spain, which, as of the seventeenth century, introduced ever smaller coinage alloyed from silver and copper ("black money," "billon," or "vellon" variants) in an attempt to reserve silver coinage for trade overseas.[54]

Gold currencies were important to the Italians because most of the Muslim world with which it principally traded was on a gold standard. As a result, gold could be converted in the Muslim world to more silver, whereas in Europe silver was the standard and in high demand, and so it was worth a little less in terms of gold around the eleventh century. It is thus reasonable to assume that the Italians, who were acutely aware of exchange rate differentials, tapped whatever gold could still be found in Europe more cheaply, thus acquiring greater purchasing power in the East.[55]

In addition to debasements and the availability of African gold to the Italian city-states, the *third* factor at play in explaining Europe's monetary departure from the rest of Eurasia during the late Middle Ages concerns mining output. As famously argued by Peter Spufford, throughout the eleventh through the fourteenth centuries—or well before the discovery of silver and gold in the New World—Europe had experienced sustained mining output spurts, which added to the continent's mineral riches relative to other parts of the world; these booms arguably transformed Western Europe into a more monetized area than either India or China in per capita terms; they quenched the local demand for silver quite apart from the excess silver probably flowing westward into Europe as a result of Song and Yuan recourse to paper money at the same time. Output spiked up with the significant discovery of silver deposits in Goslar, followed by the discovery of the famous silver mines of Melle, Sardinia, and Kutna Hura.[56]

As a consequence of increased mining activity, by the mid-fifteenth century German mining engineers achieved two technological breakthroughs that spread crucially to the rest of the continent. These were mechanical drainage pumps to eliminate flooding and a lead-chemical process to separate the copper and silver commonly found intertwined in European ore. These developments long predate steam-powered pumps and furnaces but are seldom considered in accounts of the Great Divergence.[57]

Similarly, revolutionary improvements in mechanized minting techniques occurred in early modern Europe long before steam technology. The most notable progress was embodied in the screw press invented not long after Gutenberg's printing press toward the end of the fifteenth century. At first it made little inroads into traditional ways of hammering flans, as little had changed in method from Greek times to the medieval era. Later in the sixteenth century, however, the screw press spread from Italy to England, thus greatly improving European coin consistency and arguably placing the quality of European coinage ahead of Chinese coinage. The invention of the screw press is accredited to Italian architect Bramante, with the technique further systemized in Britain and France. In Spanish-ruled territories, however, the roller press was the more common technology until the early eighteenth century.[58]

As from the eleventh century, sub-Saharan trade routes afforded Europe increasing quantities of gold also from Nubia, Mali, Ethiopia, and later the Sofala (Mozambique). Equally noteworthy, however, are the commodities that those sub-Saharan convoys brought back from Europe to Africans, not least of which were copper alloys and copperware. These were often more prized than gold by Africans, not just as money but also as decoration. The fourteenth-century traveller Ibn Battuta noted this trade and commented on Malian prosperity as a result of gold exports.[59]

Although Mali flourished as a result of exporting gold, its own gold bar currency was devoid of the extensive international function that Spanish-American silver dollars would later play, for example, in the global economy beyond their mere intrinsic value. In fact, Ethiopia was the only major area of precolonial sub-Saharan Africa to have minted its own coinage (as opposed to bar currency), but this was before Ibn Battuta's time.[60] From the second to the ninth centuries, the Aksumite kings minted gold coinage, as well as smaller quantities of bronze and silver coinage; initially these coins carried Greek inscriptions to be replaced later by Amharic. However, indigenous Ethiopian coinage lapsed in the tenth century, so that by the eighteenth century the kingdom became dependent on imported currencies, principally the silver Maria Theresa

thalers (MTT) of Austria. Ethiopian indigenous coinage was only resumed by Emperor Menilek II (r. 1889–1913), with silver coins called
talaris (modeled on the MMT) and copper fractions, showing the Lion
of Judah—an allusion to the traditional belief that Menilek I had been
the son of King Solomon and the Queen of Sheba.[61]

Europe's ability to tap into African gold was compounded by an increase in its silver output. The Venetians had had their own mines at
home and in their colonies to begin with. Thus, by 1400 Venice had
become a major supplier of coins to the Levant. The generally accepted
gold to silver ratio for Italy in 1284 was 1:11. Then, an abundance of
silver from Bohemian mines began to cheapen silver so that the gold to
silver ratio in Venice between 1305 and 1310 reached 1:14. Later, between 1326 and 1328, silver became less plentiful—by 1326 the ratio of
gold to silver in Venice had rebounded to 1:10.[62]

Following Venice, in the fourteenth to sixteenth centuries other regions in Europe moved to minting gold coinage. As early as 1290, Philip
IV of France established new national gold coinage to circulate alongside
silver currencies (the chaise and agnel). In England, in the hundred years
following 1344—when domestic gold coinage was proclaimed after centuries of exclusively silver penny circulation—the value and even weight
of gold coinage produced exceeded that of silver coinage. By the end of
the fourteenth century, gold may have been used to supplement the silver
that was being remitted eastward to fund commodity purchases.[63]

It is important to note that although the Italians city-states appear
to have catalyzed Europe's reversion to gold coinage through their control of minting and mining interests across the continent, the leading
Mediterranean currency in the thirteenth century—the gold florin—was
actually modeled on English coinage; it featured corrugated rims to
combat sweating and clipping. Furthermore, medieval English coinage
maintained a high standard because the authorities there were known
to intermittently confiscate foreign bullion in ports and restrike it into
more uniform English coinage; in fourteenth-century England there
were strict regulations against debasement by private-order "moneyers"
(as opposed to monarchs) even if in Europe, more generally, "moneyer"
guilds had until the early-modern era much more power and independence from the state than their counterparts in China.[64]

In the 1360s, all English mints produced gold coins weighing a total
of about two tonnes of gold. This output can be nominally compared
with the peak of coin production in premodern China, particularly the
"Song Industrial Revolution" of the tenth through the twelfth centuries.
Based on a standard factoring of 1:10 European gold:silver ratio preva-

lent at the time, English gold coin output in the 1360s would have been roughly commensurate with 540 million Chinese bronze coins (silver had not yet been fully monetized in China in Song times). During the Wang Anshi era (in office 1070–1086), at the height of Chinese coin production, 5 million "cash" strings were produced annually, or an impressive 50 billion bronze coins for the entire decade. From these data, one can vaguely fathom perhaps the sheer extent of Song effervescence in comparative terms, notwithstanding that China was much more populous than England and that Chinese coin production fell precipitously thereafter never to attain the same level in per capita terms again before the import of steam technology. As Professor Vogel has shown, the only significant post-Song rebound resulted in its 1750s–1760s peak in an annual absolute output of 4 million strings, yet at that point China's population had been at least threefold bigger that during the Northern Song era.[65]

As late as the fourteenth century, Chinese steelmaking processes had been more advanced than in Europe. Air was blown from piston-blowing machines into furnaces. These fans were often water-driven; they were more efficient than the concertina bellows used in metallurgy in Europe at the time. The sixteenth-century European adoption of blast furnaces may have been influenced by knowledge of Chinese designs of bellow-powered blast furnaces originating in the thirteenth century. In the eleventh century, at the Song peak, as much as 125 tonnes of iron were produced in China annually, whereas in Europe as late as the eighteenth century about 150 tonnes were produced annually.[66]

So how did European mining and metallurgic technology eventually overtake China's? Modern European metallurgy is associated with the publication of theses first by Vannoccio Biringuccio (1480–1537) and then Georgius Agricola (1494–1555). The latter, of greater importance, recounted in Latin the advancement made by German metallurgy at the time insofar as furnaces were concerned. After Agricola's work was published in England, Elizabeth I invited German mining experts to help develop mining on the British Isles. In the early sixteenth century, concomitantly, blast furnaces were set up in the Sussex Weald and New-bridge alongside older Roman-style bloomery furnaces, with Sir Isaac Newton serving at one time as master of the Royal Mint. Thus, although the Chinese pioneered the use of cast iron and had more advanced furnaces in the early Ming era, the Ming *haijin* isolationist policy seems to have ultimately translated into technological stagnation and European advantage in metallurgic technology by the early Qing period.[67]

If limited to one single event, then the turnaround by which Europe overtook Chinese metallurgy was probably embodied in the transition to the use of coke and coal in European iron making in the early seventeenth century. These crucial technological breakthroughs in the production of iron by means of coal had been patented in England by Sturtevant (1611), Rovenson (1613), and Dudley (1665).[68] Later, in the eighteenth century, European water-driven cylinder blower furnaces operated on a large scale—predating steam technology per se by a century. These applications were far ahead of Chinese metallurgic practices at the time.

European flans were typically cast in individual pellets or roundels worked out from clay or sand molds, or shear-cut off bars in medieval times when coins became thinner. The Romans pioneered the serrated-edge indentation, which evolved into an incuse or beaded rim in the medieval era to combat clipping, whereas Chinese coinage resorted to raised rims for the same purpose. As of the mid-seventeenth century English and French coins featured a more elaborate "milled edge" effected with a file before striking, a technique little used in China except for a moderately incuse rim. Overstriking coins twice or even thrice was common in Europe but never experimented with in China as a means of reasserting imperial authority. Chinese round coinage remained remarkably similar to its antecedents in the early imperial era even through the early medieval era: It was made in the self-contained multiple chapalet known as "coin tree" molds (*qianshu*).[69]

The growing divergence in how coins were manufactured across Eurasia foregrounds a topic that is relatively little discussed in the pertinent literature: From the middle of the eighteenth century better-quality European coinage could enhance trade benefits already accruing to Europe as a result of the relocation of metal to places where it had monetary utility. Perhaps the clearest evidence for that was the first global coin, the Carolus silver dollar, which was made of Latin American silver and exported by Spain to the rest of the world, while Spain's own monetary system increasingly resorted to lower-value "vellon" coinage. In China, for example, after an introductory phase, Carolus dollars were valued "on their own reputation for consistency" well above their silver content even after their production was halted as a result of Latin American emancipation.[70] To be sure, by the 1860s, older Carolus dollar coins had started giving way in China to Mexican republican dollar coins, which were first minted in 1823 and therefore of better production quality. Yet because many new Latin American republican dollars were inconsistent in weight and size for some two decades after independence, and because it was harder to forge the more widely recognized Carolus dollars, the latter remained reputable in East Asia for its reliability right until the twentieth century.[71]

A similar premium (read: *agio*) of European coinage over its metallic content when traded overseas is observed by Şevket Pamuk's (1997) study of the seventeenth-century monetary system in the Ottoman Empire. Unlike China, the Ottomans at the time did coin silver, yet Pamuk shows that their long-standing, manually produced akçe had lost much of its esteem in the 1580s as a result of debasement. Similarly, Ottoman mining output declined sharply after 1600. Contrary to the European pattern at the time, Ottoman debasement was, however, not a long-term strategy of raising revenue but more of an emergency measure designed to meet unexpected military outlay as a result of rebellion. Neither did the Ottomans resort in the seventeenth century to imperially decreed near-token copper currency on the same scale as France or Spain. Against this backdrop, Carolus dollars—among many other European (but *not* English) gold and silver currencies—circulated widely and were highly prized in the Levant, too, in the seventeenth century.[72]

In sum, northwestern Europe, the Muslim world, and China followed diverging monetary trajectories in the Middle Ages. Europe came off a post-Roman gold standard to rely on silver pennies between the eighth and fourteenth centuries after two centuries of waning monetization, probably because of a decline in mining operations and shrinking trade volumes. European gold coinage remnants may have been smelted, in turn, and flowed to the Muslim world where gold was the mainstay along the southern Mediterranean. Initially bimetallic, the Islamic currency system was effectively rebased on gold by the tenth century, perhaps in part because silver had been continually drained: first by India and, and as of the fourteenth century, China's newfound voracious appetite for silver.[73] That being the case, there may have been another possibly important factor behind Europe's reversion to gold, quite apart from the mining booms in Goslar, Sardinia, and Kutna Hura and apart from the inflow of African gold deposits.

Following earlier studies, Professor Akinobu Kuroda has recently hypothesized that China's perspicacious adoption of paper money during the Southern Song and Yuan eras may have freed up immense silver assets in East Asia for movement westward. It could well be that the immense inflow of silver along open roads of the vast Mongol Empire— long before the European acquisition of Latin American silver—cata- lyzed the transition to a higher-value gold standard in late medieval Eu- rope; for silver abundance was widely recorded in the late thirteenth century not just in Europe but *across* the length and breadth of Eurasia, only to become scarce again in the 1360s. By and large, globally cheaper silver may have meant greater ability to rebase European currencies on imported gold.[74]

Yet, on the flip side, one must not forget that silver and gold ingots remained very important monetary components within China, too, af- ter the establishment of the Mongol Yuan dynasty. In fact, Yuan paper money—which Marco Polo was so impressed with—had been practi- cally based on silver reserves, although notionally denominated at times in "cash," or silk units. Mongol coinage was largely struck from sil- ver elsewhere in Eurasia. In that sense, the scale of silver outflow from China to the West under Mongol auspices should perhaps be qualified.[75] Epistemologically, Koruda's approach and important insight departs from other studies, which tend to foreground improvements in Euro- pean mining technology in the thirteenth through the fifteenth centuries as underpinning that continent's greater supply of silver over and above any putative exogenous shock.[76]

EARLY MODERN PATTERNS OF MONETARY HEGEMONY

As already indicated, when the Ming abandoned paper note issuance in China, silver may have become scarcer again in the rest of Eurasia. However, by then Western Europe had already been firmly anchored on a gold standard with access to African gold supplies and nascent control of global bullion and currency flows through early modern maritime traffic of, for example, cowrie shells. Cowries were widely used in Yun- nan, even as late as the early Ming period, as evidenced in contracts and stone tablets from the era. It was still in limited use toward the end of the dynasty. At the same time, Yunnan itself was actually sup- plying up to three-quarters of China's silver output. Yet, as Professor Hans-Ulrich Vogel has shown in his pathbreaking study, the price of cowries in Yunnan was in secular decline after the thirteenth century (when it was accepted as tax payments by local authorities) and suffered a more pronounced decline in the seventeenth century, when authorities decided—after several previous failed attempts—to introduce Chinese bronze coinage into the province more forcefully despite the exorbitant outlay of such measures. The introduction of "copper cash" into Yunnan at a high cost to the Ming imperial treasury is another reminder of the differences between Chinese late imperial statecraft and coeval European political thought, for in the Chinese case the spread of coinage served primarily a political purpose and was a net drain on central government resources. And once "cash" replaced cowrie as Yunnan's principal media of exchange, it may well be that some surplus cowries found their way from Yunnan to Africa, where cowries served as currency in some parts of the continent right until the early twentieth century.[77]

The Ming abandonment of nominally silver-backed paper notes—which is magisterially portrayed in Richard Von Glahn's study—paralleled the famous "single whip" tax reform. After initial discouragement of silver transaction in the early Ming dynasty, the reform entrenched the demand for silver by the populace because silver ingots were now needed to pay land tax. Short of actually coining silver, the Ming did nonetheless see a spike in silver mining in the periphery during the early fifteenth century under the Yongle Emperor.[78]

Ironically enough, from then on, as silver became more common in both tax payment and commercial transaction, and as China's population and commercial activity grew apace, less silver was mined domestically relative to imperial expenditure. Consequently less and less *domestic* silver reached Ming coffers. As noted in Flynn and Giráldez's influential work, that deficit was more than made up by a vast inflow of silver from Japan and later from Latin America. As a result of the commencement of the galleon trade between Acapulco, Manila, and China—and in the face of a domestic mining decline—the *total* amount of silver entering Ming coffers had in fact doubled by 1570s compared with previous decades. Receipts of overseas silver numbered around 100 tons per year toward the end of the Ming dynasty.[79]

The longer so-called second silver century, namely that which signifies the flow of Latin-American silver *into* China—postdating the putative flow of silver *from* China westward under Mongol auspices—coincided as of about 1738 with shifts in the procurement of copper as raw material for traditional coinage. That year, the Qing authorities reduced the amount of copper purchased from Japan for casting coinage in the imperial capital and allowed a greater degree of freedom for private copper mining in Yunnan.[80] However, some Japanese copper continued to be coined in provincial mints even after 1738; Yunnan copper veins had, at any rate, already depleted by the beginning of the nineteenth century.[81]

Until then, there were reports of a dearth of coins but no acute shortage of copper as raw material can be detected. On the other hand, there is little evidence of progress in the technology for copper mining during that era; Yunnan copper mining does not seem to have incorporated water-power devices, horsepower, or mechanized intervention. In fact, it was only in 1867 that officials started memorializing the throne about the need to employ modern mints like the one then operating in British-ruled Hong Kong so as to economize on raw material, improve coin consistency, and discourage forgeries.

As indicated at the outset of this chapter, modern minting machinery was purchased from Birmingham only in 1887 and was first used only in Guangdong. Yet by the 1900s modern copper coin minting under imperial and provincial auspices was so extensive and debased that the value of *tongyuan* dropped precipitously, heightening uncertainty and inflation in the marketplace. Although notional bimetallism survived in the Chinese hinterland in part as a safeguard against debasement until about 1935, the customary stringing of "cash" had in practice died out in the early twentieth century. This was because *tongyuan* coins were unholed and often denominated in multiple units well above their actual metallic value. Being full-bodied, traditional holed "cash" was thus gradually driven out from circulation in the early twentieth century in favor of ever-lighter types of modern-minted fractional coinage. Traditional "cash" was then often smelted or exported to Japan, where the demand for raw copper in the ammunition industry was on the increase.[82]

The long-term implications of the galleon trade that underpinned the "second silver century" and, to a lesser extent perhaps, Europe's earlier reversion to gold coinage, were such that the exchange rate between copper and silver in China declined from 320:1 in 1368 to the late imperial notional standard of 100:1 by 1621.[83] These 1621 figures are very instructive data that can be loosely compared with the other end of the continent around the same time. For example, by 1640 there similarly were many fewer mints and mines operating within the Ottoman Empire compared with previous centuries as a result of the flow of bullion from the New World. In the early seventeenth century, records show Ottoman copper coinage weighing 8 dirhams (3.072 grams × 8 = 24.576 grams of alloyed copper) was valued on par with one silver akçe (1 aksum, nominally 0.7 grams of alloyed silver). This in turn suggests a rough Ottoman silver to copper exchange ratio of 1:35. Saddled with a trimetallic standard at the time, the Ottoman Empire's gold to silver exchange rate was similar to Europe at the time at 1:10; however, this rate has less comparative value concerning China because in the latter gold was not monetized. In fact, the lack of demand for monetary gold as a moderating factor might have heightened the demand for silver in China. At any rate, the data suggest silver might have been up to three times dearer in relation to copper coinage in Beijing than it was in Constantinople around the seventeenth century—even though copper-made "cash" was the only coined currency of China and the one still widely preferred in China's vast rural hinterland.[84]

A century later, European confidence over the mastery of global bullion flows can be detected in, for example, Daniel Defoe's writings. Whilst Defoe's literary characters express on occasion anxiety about Europe's seeming marginality in the face of Chinese trade surplus, Defoe himself did not mince words in his more worldly work. For example, in the novel *New Voyage Round the World* (published in 1724), one of the British protagonists describes the Chinese as "despising our manufactures and filling us with their own."[85] But in the *Complete English Tradesman* (published 1738), Defoe clearly evinced acute awareness of the dynamics of global trade that is so conspicuously absent from contemporaneous Chinese writings. At the heart of his observation clearly lay confidence in Britain's dominion of the world economy:

This trade to our West Indies and American colonies, is very considerable, as it employs so many ships and sailors, and so much of the growth of those colonies is again exported by us to other parts of the world, over and above what is consumed among us at home; and, also, as all those goods, and a great deal of money in specie, is returned hither for and in balance of our own manufactures and merchandises exported thither—on these accounts some have insisted that more real wealth is brought into Great Britain every year from those colonies, than is brought from the Spanish West Indies to old Spain, notwithstanding the extent of their dominion is above twenty times as much, and notwithstanding the vast quantity of gold and silver which they bring from the mines of Mexico, and the mountains of Potosi . . . As the manufactures of England, particularly those of wool (cotton wool included), and of silk, are the greatest, and amount to the greatest value of any single manufacture in Europe, so they not only employ more people, but those people gain the most money, that is to say, have the best wages for their work of any people in the world; and yet, which is peculiar to England, the English manufactures are, allowing for their goodness, the cheapest at market of any in the world.[86]

In retrospect, Defoe pokes a hole in the attractive notion that trade with "the East" was paramount in the early modern European popular mind-set. In the monetary realm, too, more mundane observations can be found that might undermine, for example, the attractive notion that the trimetallic currency system of early Mughal India (est. 1526) was as advanced as northwestern Europe's before the introduction of steam technology. To be sure, the Mughals did *not* allow foreign coinage to circulate domestically, as French adventurer Jean-Baptiste Tavernier (1605–1689) famously observed;[87] in that sense, perhaps, the Mughal monetary system was ahead of the nascent English "territorial" currency. Rather like the late medieval European pattern of "free coinage," the Mughals were able to draw commoners with raw silver to their mints voluntarily and maintained consistently low debasement rates. For these reason, Richards for example framed their monetary system as "powerful, flexible, pervasive, and long-lived."[88]

Eventually, however, much of the silver brought to Mughal mints would be of Latin American provenance, almost to the same degree as in late Ming China. On the other hand, Mughal coinage—notwithstanding its putatively high quality—never played a significant role outside of India.[89] Dutch East India Company (VOC) factors who had come into close contact with Mughal minting techniques described them as early as the 1720s as being exceedingly labor intesive, "comparatively poor and wasteful," even though Mughal coinage, unlike Chinese coinage, was grounded in precious metal.[90] In Ceylon much of the circulating copper coinage in the latter half of the seventeenth century was Dutch minted. Similarly, in Goa, Portuguese-minted coinage was rife, as was other European coinage in coastal trading enclaves along the South Indian coastline.[91]

Following Headrick, one should recall that European colonial penetration into tropical terrain was an exceedingly difficult and slow process before steamboats (and railroads) allowed for upstream navigation in the nineteenth century.[92] Mughal prohibitions aside, this is one more reason why European coinage was rare in inland India (and Africa) before the nineteenth century. Because they were unfamiliar, British-minted coins in Surat, for example, proved unpopular in the mid-seventeenth century. Yet, as early as 1717, the British obtained permission to mint Mughal-style coins, and these in fact gradually seeped far and wide into the Indian monetary system. Though unrecognizably so, "British" (read: Mughal-style) coinage had in fact played an important role in the stability of the Mughal monetary system well before formal British dominion over India began; and by the time the Raj was proclaimed in 1858, some of the coinage circulating across British-ruled parts of India possessed increasingly "British" features, including royal portraiture and English-language inscriptions.[93]

By the early seventeenth century, European financial innovation had shifted from the Italian city-states to the Low Countries, though it was still driven by the exigencies of costly and recurrent warfare between equal-size polities and ambitions of monopolizing trade with the East. This spurt of European financial innovation had actually long preceded the English "Industrial Revolution," a complex but much better-studied spate of events. The financial and industrial revolutions then converged on the spread of joint-stock companies and prototypes of central banks in the latter half of the nineteenth century.[94]

Whether the premium that silver fetched in China over other metals, or for that matter China's trade surplus with Europe before the 1830s, can be viewed as evidence for the "magnetic" qualities of the Chinese economy should be examined in view of European monetary penetration patterns elsewhere. To understand China's monetary function in the early modern world, we must look beyond silver to the dynamics of monetization following contact with Europe. On this count, the flow of silver from Latin America as of the sixteenth and seventeenth centuries should be considered in tandem with Europe's takeover of the global cowrie trade, for the cowrie trade can help us gain an important insight on how the premeditated relocation of one form of money (not even a precious metal in this case) from one part of the world to another, where it was more coveted, could help Europeans plug trade deficits, as well as "subsidize" slave labor.[95]

What "subsidy" could the cowrie trade provide after the discovery of profuse New World gold and silver deposits? To be sure, gold exports from Africa to Europe did drop by the eighteenth century as a result of the ready availability of Latin American bullion. Cowrie exports, therefore, came to bankroll the purchase of slaves and African commodities like coffee. It was the one factor equalizing European trade deficits with Africa, in the same way perhaps that opium helped equalise European trade deficit with China in the early nineteenth century, a time when Western silver output temporarily declined due to the Napoleonic Wars and Latin American emancipation.[96]

However, that cowrie shells were drawn to Africa in such large quantities should not obfuscate the causality at play: Although cowrie shells from the Maldives had been used in the gold-rich Sudan as early as the fourteenth century, it was Europeans who after 1500 enlarged this trade much beyond Arab reaches to West Africa; the Portuguese are thought to have shipped up to 150 tonnes of cowrie out of Bengal annually as a rough indicator for the amount of shells reaching Africa. Even as late as the eighteenth century, cowrie was four times dearer in Africa relative to silver as compared with India. Europeans thus sourced cowrie from outside *both* Europe *and* Africa precisely because they identified it as a potentially trade "equalizer" with the African region and *not* because the African economy evinced any particular "magnetic" qualities at the time.[97]

Of course, in terms of early modern patterns of European hegemony, Maldives cowrie should be mentioned alongside the story of wampum so familiar to students of American history but more rarely woven into comparative studies in monetary history. Although these are different species of seashells, the monetization of wampum in the early stage of European settlement in North America bears much resemblance to the Portuguese monetization of cowrie in Africa. Both cowrie and wampum were first used by the indigenous population as decorative status symbols and commonly strung together. Both were at times mechanically forged with varying degree of success, and both were then mass-sourced by Europeans so as to purchase ever more key "commodities"—for example, fur from Native Americans or African slaves and gold.[98]

In most cases, Europeans did not establish these trade patterns but joined them alongside other local merchants or foreign hegemons, thereby enhancing their order of magnitude manyfold. For example, it was the Dutch East India Company that eventually positioned itself as an important supplier of Japanese silver and copper to Ming China, alongside Chinese seafarers. Similarly, it was Arab traders who first brought cowrie to Africa with which to buy slaves. However, only when the Portuguese gained maritime supremacy in the Indian Ocean did the importation of Southeast Asian cowrie into Africa as means of funding the purchase of slaves, who were subsequently sent to till Brazilian plantations, truly reach global dimensions.[99]

Arguably less known is the fact that Yunnan, the very same source of Ming-Qing copper, had in fact relied on cowrie as one of its own principal currencies until the mid-Ming. Cowrie and metallic cowrie-shaped casts were, of course, one of the principal currencies of the Chu kingdom as far back as the Spring and Autumn era, but Yunnan was the only part of China where cowrie emerged as an important medium of payment *after* the seventh century CE. In India, too, cowrie shells had served as common subsidiary money at least since the Mauryan dynasty: They were imported from the Maldives into Bengal and circulated in the Indus Valley as early as 1400 BCE. By the Middle Ages, eighty cowries were worth in Bengal 144 grams of copper, which was in turn tantamount to 14 grams of silver. In other words, the late medieval putative Bengali shell-copper-silver exchange rate of roughly 60:10:1 suggests that silver was considerably more abundant there at that time than in China. Either way, as coined copper became the norm in sixteenth-century Bengal, cowrie shells had lost much of their value there and were subsequently exported to Africa, where they could fetch a higher return in the slave trade. In that sense, contact with Europe expedited the monetization of both Bengal (coined copper) and sub-Saharan Africa (cowrie). Notably, in the Maldives, where cowrie was sourced to begin with, one gold dinar could fetch 10,000 shells in the sixteenth century, whereas in West Africa the same amount of gold could initially be bought off in return for just a few shells. [100]

Cowrie aside, what else could the Portuguese trade in Africa in return for gold (and slaves)? In return for gold, the most precious store of value in Europe and the Levant at the time, Africans contented with base-metal objects. The famous *Manilha* brassware ornaments were produced by the Portuguese—sometimes even from African-sourced brass—precisely to serve as a media of exchange with which to buy gold and slaves. However, imported copper rather than that locally mined was the mainstay: Copper was the most important monetary metal imported into sub-Saharan Africa between the sixteenth and seventeenth centuries, as gold itself was of little monetary use there and because hardly any silver was mined locally. In fact, silver was relatively dearer in Africa than in Europe: Around the sixteenth century, the African silver:gold ratio was in the vicinity of 8:1.[101]

It would be implausible to suggest that African economies possessed exceptionally "magnetic" qualities only because a mineral resource was the principal item Europeans could trade off there when purchasing local produce or "manpower." Although late medieval China's case is vastly different, the analogy drawn here would caution against depicting China's economy as possessing "magnetic" qualities or as being more advanced than Europe's on the eve of the Industrial Revolution because Europeans could equalize trade there only by using silver bullion.

On the contrary, the acquisition of asymmetric information on global bullion flows and dissimilar currency zones allowed Europeans to co-opt Africa and China into a wider trading system on preferential terms. In that sense, the mastery of global bullion and specie flows could perhaps be cast as an enduring early modern stratagem that allowed Europeans to buy in far-flung corners of the world those commodities they could not grow or produce themselves. Much was for European consumption, but a good deal was traded elsewhere. In due course, the wealth generated as a result of that trade could bankroll direct European colonization of parts of the world where coveted commodities like pepper, sugar, coffee, and even tea could be grown; what could not be directly colonized was over time substituted in part with nascent European industry—even Chinese porcelain or Indian cotton textiles.

CONCLUSIONS

Relatively little studied in that context hitherto, the mastery of late medieval bullion flows through extensive mining and the possession of asymmetric information on global supply and demand for precious metal seems, nevertheless, indispensable to our understanding of the "Great Divergence." When analyzed in conjunction, pertinent studies of the last three decades might suggest that the scramble for New World gold and silver had been long preceded by an outflow of silver from China in the thirteenth century, as well as an upturn in European domestic silver deposit yields. Only when silver from the East dried up, and once European domestic sources had been exhausted in the face of constant technological improvement, were more readily available sources sought externally. Thus, it would be a mistake to focus exclusively on the massive haulage of New World silver to China (or India) later in the seventeenth century as a marker of European dependence. On the contrary, the Portuguese, Dutch, and British—having based their domestic currencies on gold—all excelled in systematically marrying up lower-value "money" supplies outside Europe with particular demand for that "money"—which was not necessarily metallic, for example cowrie—in other locales outside Europe.

Yet the picture will still not be complete without a recognition of the significance of coin output and quality (read: minting consistency) as underpinning the Divergence in the early modern era, that is, long before the universalization of steam-powered minting, for to do so would mean ignoring one of the fundamental functions of money as a medium of exchange. It is here that the technological dimension converges on the institutional one: The ability to produce better-quality (that is, less easily falsifiable) domestic coinage at lower cost, and to enforce it *intra vires*, underpinned England (and Spain's) transition from full-bodied to fiduciary coinage in the first instance. It was only then that England (and Spain) could divert Latin American specie to sustain imports from Asia at lower alternative cost. By the mid-eighteenth century, at the latest, it was not just European-conveyed silver bullion that was coveted in sovereign China and Southeast Asia: In fact European-produced silver coinage was more coveted and usually at a premium over silver bullion. In that sense, Latin American silver dollars attained what the Portuguese had not earlier in their foray into the region; due to the fact that silver was not (re-)coined in the commercial heartland of late-imperial China, Europeans could get "more for their buck" there, whereas Mughal India remained more monetarily autonomous.

Notwithstanding the rich literature on New World silver, this aspect of the Divergence received even less attention than the mastery of global bullion flows. Yet the comparative historic analysis offered here presents the mintage patterns leading up to, and following, the "Great Debasement" as crucial to our understanding of the English monetary departure from the European continental (and Chinese) monetary trajectory, beginning as early as the tenth century.

By the early twentieth century, steam-powered mints ultimately proved victorious in uprooting the multiplicity and concurrency of foreign and domestic coinage in favor of standardized national ("territorial") units of payment. That wave of standardization put paid to the "ghost" or "imaginary" units of account that individuals and polities had devised right across Eurasia in order to tackle the uncertainty inherent in the multiplicity and concurrency of money. Yet it would be a grave mistake to merely consider the fledgling European nation-state's takeover of minting as gratuitous provision of public good in return for prestige.

Pointing to the late medieval Great Debasement as the critical juncture in European monetary history, this chapter has argued in fact that European sovereigns' ultimate takeover of minting, including that of subsidiary coinage later in the process, had ensued from novel fiscal thinking that sowed the seeds for the onset of the modern "national debt" economy. Baldly put, the European monetary path was borne out of the late medieval recourse to higher-value gold currencies that allowed at first for greater seigniorage revenue, albeit in a destabilizing manner. But when the limits of coinage-derived seigniorage as a source for sovereign revenue became apparent, English sovereign debt—indeed, money itself—was beginning to grow out of its "premodern" metallic anchorage.

PART II

CHAPTER FOUR

Paper Money in Qing China

*Exactly How Common and Reliable Was It by the
Early Twentieth Century?*

In essence, the Qing monetary system was made up of low-denomination locally cast bronze or brass coins (*tongqian*) widely used in the rural hinterland and in retail. Higher-denomination money was mostly in the form of silver, either ingots known to Westerners as sycee and to Chinese as *yinding* or foreign-minted silver dollar coins (*yinyuan*, meaning round silver). Tax was mostly remitted to imperial coffers in the form of silver ingots, although public wages were often paid out in bronze coinage. Foreign silver dollars, however, became an increasingly common means of payment by 1700, particularly in coastal areas.[1]

The term *sycee* was an English derivative of the Cantonese pronunciation for "pure silk." In South China, a good-quality silver ingot was thought to possess a shiny veneer reminiscent of silk. Customarily, a string (*diao*) of 1,000 Chinese bronze coins was on par with one tael or *liang* of silver (approximately 37.5 grams). In practice, however, the copper–silver exchange rate fluctuated according to the availability of either metal at any point in time. Sycee ingots usually weighed about fifty tael, but there could be considerable variations of ingot weight and fineness even within the same province. These variations gave rise to assaying establishments, mostly of a private-order nature, which guaranteed the quality of sycee used in market transaction and often also in tax remittances.[2]

The net inflow of Spanish-American silver coins into China continued throughout the eighteenth and early nineteenth centuries, until the unraveling of the Canton (Guangzhou) imperially regulated foreign-trade system in the 1830s and the subsequent two Opium Wars (1839–1842 and 1856–1860). Circumstances changed on the other side of the Pacific

Ocean too. In 1821 Mexico formally gained its independence from Spain, and its symbol of sovereignty—the snake-devouring eagle—replaced Spain's Pillars of Hercules on all silver coins exported via Acapulco. U.S. trade surplus with Mexico meant American merchants could at that time lay down their excess silver dollar holdings in China in return for silk, porcelain, and tea—thereby partaking of the British-dominated world trading system. By the early nineteenth century, a number of Western Sinologists and, following them, early twentieth-century visitors to China's treaty ports were already acutely aware of the antecedent use of paper as currency and its pervasiveness there. A few later visitors even alluded, by way of contrast, to the marginality of paper currency in Qing China's traditional largely bimetallic monetary system.[3]

Nonetheless, contemporary Western sources by and large did not provide an incisive answer as to the question of precisely why government and privately-issued paper money went into decline in China through much of the late imperial era: how and precisely when privately issued notes reemerged and how important a component they were within the late imperial monetary system. Neither did they explain in great detail whether the gradual reemergence of privately issued banknotes in China—which could be traced back to the latter part of the eighteenth century at the earliest—had anything to do with global financial stimuli.[4] Some scholars have more recently argued that foreign banks operating in China as of the late 1840s greatly bolstered the reformist monetary discourse there, both within and outside the imperial bureaucracy, and were later subject to emulation by China's home-grown modern banks. Between 1848 and 1945, European, American, and Japanese colonial banks all issued locally denominated notes on Chinese soil, relying on metallic reserve policies and regulatory prescripts derived from the Western and Japanese monetary experience. These foreign financial institutions both challenged and set an example for homegrown financial institutions, laying the foundation for the rise of modern Chinese banks and the popularization of banknotes in China in the early twentieth century.[5]

Other scholars, however, suggest that privately issued banknotes had become a pillar of the late imperial Chinese monetary system (1368–1911 CE) well before the entry of Western banking in the late 1840s. In the alternative narrative these scholars seem to offer, what the Chinese at the time did not trust were government-issued notes. Notes issued by established private financiers were supposedly "well accepted," on the other hand.[6]

These claims underscore what may be a seemingly arcane yet important scholarly debate over the circumstances in which the late Ming and Qing polities were reluctant to issue notes and the circumstances in which *private* banknote issuance spread as of the mid-Qing era. The mainsprings of private banknote issuance entail, in turn, at least five foci of discussion: Why did the Qing court discontinue its first issue not long after it had securely asserted its rule over China (in the 1650s)? Why did the Qing court refrain from engaging in further issues right up until it was hit by financial and political instability in the 1850s? Why was that 1850s issue also discontinued? Finally, and most important, were Chinese privately issued notes considered more reliable, and did they fill the void left by Qing monetary relinquishment?

The following passages will systematically take up this set of questions, as well as the implicit assumptions that trigger them. One might indeed speculate that the issuance of foreign banknotes in China as of the latter part of the nineteenth century mattered much less than is conventionally contended because Chinese privately issued notes had already widely circulated there.

But were these Chinese privately issued notes so "well accepted" that they became a prominent feature of China's monetary system at the time? The answer is an emphatic "yes," at least according to one student of the period:[7]

In market towns and cities, even wage labourers used private notes denominated in copper coins in daily life. In the early 1850s, government officials often referred to the success of private fractional note-issuing banks to urge the Qing court to float government paper money. Nonetheless, safeguarding the value of private banknotes is by nature different from the maintenance of the creditworthiness of government paper notes. The latter is closely related to the government's institutional ability in collecting taxes and managing government spending.

There appears to be a priori a somewhat inconsistent rationale in the foregoing observation: On the one hand, it suggests that Chinese private bank notes were popularly perceived as more reliable than Qing government notes; on the other hand, it might suggest that there was nothing seriously at fault in administering concurrent Qing issues in the 1650s and 1850s. The following passages do not merely offer a counterargument, but they also take issue with the broader vein of literature that might potentially be interpreted as supporting such observations, for if it is found to stand up to close scrutiny, this observation might indeed provide valuable revisionist insights to a fast-growing field of scholarly inquiry.

THE SHUNZHI ISSUE: BACKGROUND AND AFTERMATH

Over the course of its 268 years, the Manchu Qing dynasty (1644–1912) issued traditionally styled (read: vertically printed) paper money only twice. The first issue of Qing notes (*chaoguan*) was ordered by Emperor Shunzhi (r. 1643–1661) not long after the Qing had come to power and amid residual Han resistance to the Manchu invaders. The issue was on a small scale, amounting to 120,000 "strings" per annum, and only lasted from 1651 to 1661. After Shunzhi's demise in 1661, proponents of the resumption of note issuance weakened, although they never completely disappeared.[8]

Peng Xinwei and others have suggested, in that context, that Manchu emperors were historically aware of the inflationary pressure, which had broken out as a result of the abuse of paper money during the era of their forebears, the Jin Dynasty (1115–1234). While Peng deemed the extant historic materials insufficient to assess the volume, metallic reserves, or precise circulation dynamics of the limited Shunzhi issue, he did state that it had been initiated as response to treasury funding shortfalls occasioned by the Qing's expensive expedition to occupy the island of Zhoushan.[9]

The reemergence of Qing issues in the Shunzhi reign (1644–1661) embodied therefore a short-lived monetary policy aberration that ran contrary to the subsequent overarching pattern of Qing statecraft and was born out of military emergency. It was in view of this overarching pattern that scholars have recently made the argument that the Shunzhi issue, while short-lived, probably entrenched the late imperial reluctance to issue notes because it, too, proved inflationary.[10] Li Yu'an's study, which largely relies on Peng but cites additional contemporaneous memorials, came to much the same conclusion: The Qing issued notes in 1651 to defray the costs of quelling insurgencies, as they were asserting their rule over China; this was a form of inflationary government-deficit funding that was discontinued once social order had been restored.[11] Either way, the prosaic fact is that the Qing refrained from issuing notes for nearly 200 years thereafter.

The pertinent scholarly literature is replete with passages that suggest that mid-Qing officialdom was reluctant to issue notes precisely because it was wary of the "weight of history," that is, previous failed episodes of state issuance and their association with sociopolitical instability. That the idea was put into practice on a limited scale in the formative years of the Qing dynasty should be understood against the backdrop of late Ming debates on whether dynastic decline could be turned around through resumption of note issuance. As explained in Chapter Two, late Ming emperors ultimately abstained from that course of action. In 1643, Chongzhen—the last Ming emperor, who was to commit suicide shortly before the Manchu onslaught on Beijing—effectively authorized an unbacked note issue as a desperate measure to replenish imperial coffers. But his directives were stonewalled by officialdom under various pretexts. His treasurer, Ni Yuanlu, sternly warned, for example, of the popular unrest that might follow, and predicted that "merchants would not accept the issue . . . stores would withhold their merchandise rather than take the worthless bills."[12] As it turned out, Ni would commit suicide in 1644 too.

Nevertheless, dissenting late-Ming scholars like Huang Zongxi (1610–1695), who had advocated silver-unit denominated paper money issuance, remained fairly influential in the *early* Qing era. Later, new mid-Qing proponents of note issuance were harshly rebuffed, notwithstanding emergent concerns about the outflow of silver and the spread of imported opium. Prominent supporters of paper money issuance at that time included, for example, Cai Zhiding (1745–1830), whom Emperor Jiaqing demoted in 1814 precisely for that reason, famously dubbing his proposals "preposterous and chaotic" (*wangyan luanzheng*).[13]

Influenced to some extent by Cai and late Ming proponents of paper money, Wang Liu (1786–1843) is another case in point. In his famous essay "Random Thoughts on Currency" (*Qianbi chuyan*), Wang rejected the association between dynastic decline and note issuance by pointing to the fact that late Ming emperors did not resume note issuance despite receiving advice to the contrary. He also invoked the Shunzhi issue as an important exception to conventional dynastic wisdom. At the same time—like Fan Ji of the early Ming—Wang did not balk at citing the cliché about Han Wudi's deer-hide currency as justification for issuing inconvertible paper money.[14]

Concerned by the inroads of foreign silver dollar coins into the Chinese economy, Wang suggested an unusual mix of solutions in 1831: He was in favor of discouraging the use of silver as a medium of payment but called for a stronger state monopoly on copper mining rather than for allowing more private mining ventures by way of stimulating bronze coin output. To further drive foreign silver coinage out, Wang also suggested that higher-value *daqian* and large-denomination bronze-coin notes should be introduced en masse.[15]

Wang Liu's views aroused resistance not only from scholars favoring the status quo but also from leading Daoguang-era officials who were similarly concerned about the inroads of foreign coinage. Wei Yuan (1794–1856) and Lin Zexu (1785–1850), for example, protested that the way to rid China of foreign silver was not primarily through *daqian* or note issuance. Far from being antagonistic to the bimetallic standard as such, they called for invigorated mining through allowing more private enterprise and emphasized the need to issue indigenous silver coinage.[16]

Even some scholars who were not in principle opposed to *convertible* note issuance found Wang Liu's ideas reprehensible. Xu Mei (1787–1862), for example, published in 1846 a searing critique of Wang; Bao Shichen (1775–1855), another prominent critic, attributed to Wang the notion that notes can be issued in an unlimited fashion and resented Wang's defence of the notoriously inflationary *daqian*. Somewhat reminiscent of ideas put forward by Adam Smith and Mollien in Europe a few decades earlier, Bao's model issue was one whereby "real" (that is, bronze) coinage is the foundational driver of "empty" (that is, paper) money (*Yi shi han xu*). He advocated notes that would be denominated and backed by—as well as convertible into—time-honored bronze coinage. In that sense, he differed to some extent from Wei Yuan and Lin Zexu, who stressed the need to issue foreign-style imperial silver dollars. Notably, Bao also implicitly envisioned a metallic reserve ratio of 20 to 30 percent against the circulating volume of notes.[17]

THE XIANFENG RESUMPTION OF PAPER MONEY ISSUES:
BACKGROUND AND CONSEQUENCES

Following Shuzhi's demise, it took another 200 years before supporters of fiduciary currency could muster sufficient clout at court to persuade Emperor Xianfeng to embrace this course of action again. Unusual circumstances made the notion of issuing notes less objectionable: A grave fiscal crisis engulfed Emperor Xianfeng right from the moment he acceded to the throne, a crisis brought about by Opium War indemnities and the onset of the Taiping rebellion. Therefore, Xianfeng notes (*Hubu guanpiao*) were issued on a much larger scale than under Shunzhi 200 years earlier; however, they proved exceedingly inflationary, thereby disrupting the market exchange rate of copper to silver and fueling popular unrest. The Xianfeng issue was finally curtailed in 1861 on the demise of Xianfeng and the accession of Emperor Tongzhi. Nonetheless, during the last year of issue, notes with a total face value of no less than of 60.2 million silver taels had been disbursed, although imperial tax revenue during that time amounted to only 86.6 million taels.[18]

To be sure, note issuance had been experimented with on a very small scale in the waning years of Emperor Daoguang (r. 1820–1850). As early as 1841, an imperial permit was given to five designated semiofficial money shops (*guan yinqian hao*) so that they could engage in the profitable copper-silver exchange business. In addition, these money shops were permitted to issue semiofficial notes denominated in copper cash. But these money shops did not comply with the stipulated one-half metallic-reserve guidelines and often fell prey to officials' embezzlement; their note issue therefore proved inflationary and was retired by 1858.[19]

More important, in 1853, the Qing Treasury (*Hubu*) authorized provincial authorities to *directly* disburse silver- and copper-denominated notes bearing its seal of approval on a much larger scale. These *Hubu* notes were, however, "dumped" (*lanfa*) on purveyors of services and goods to the imperial bureaucracy and were not as readily accepted back in tax payments. Their value depreciated so much that such local issues were discontinued in 1860.[20] In this context, it is worth underscoring Doolittle's contemporary observation—presented at length in the following section—which might suggest that local authorities in Fuzhou also issued and readily converted notes in the Xianfeng era, partly to alleviate cash scarcity. However, debased coins would often be paid in return, to the extent that the metallic reserve backing this issue up lost much of its value, thereby compounding inflationary pressures and the long-standing popular mistrust of paper money.

More recently, Yang Duanliu cited rescripts from the Xianfeng emperor himself in order to show how—despite Xianfeng's original edict to back imperial and *guan yinqian hao* banknote issues with up to 50 percent in silver reserves—the actual reserve ratio varied considerably from province to province. Some provinces did not keep a silver reserve at all. Worse still, several provinces—including Henan, situated not very far from the capital—did not accept its own notes when collecting tax. For Yang, such insubordination to central government edicts was the *main* reason why by 1862 all notes had disappeared, rather than the admission of debased currency into local government coffers.[21] On his part, Jerome Ch'ên suggested in his 1958 study of the Xianfeng-era inflation that the imperial treasury made the situation much worse by insisting that no more than half of individual tax remittance could be made with notes, with the reminder demanded in hard currency.[22]

More generally, the Xianfeng era hyperinflation was not only driven by inadequately backed paper money but was also aggravated by the fact that—after initial hesitation—Xianfeng approved the issue of fiduciary *daqian*. To be sure, as a result of the Opium Wars outlay and the subsequent indemnity imposed by the British, Chinese imperial fiscals had already suffered a 9.2 million tael deficit on the eve of Xianfeng's accession in March 1850. To understand why he eventually changed his mind and resorted to the historically stigmatized *daqian*, it is useful to recall that by December that year a much more ominous threat to Qing suzerainty appeared: the Taiping Rebellion. In that sense, the late Qing bypassing of historical constraints concerning *daqian* and paper money was not so much a policy choice but an emergency measure. Indeed, many of the supporters of note issuance at the Xianfeng court had also been in favor of issuing *daqian* and iron coinage, as a means of alleviating the fiscal crisis and the shortage of copper cash caused by the Taiping inroads in the southeast.[23]

As already indicated, despite the intense backlash against Wang Liu within the imperial bureaucracy, less than a decade after his death his ideas won over the Xianfeng emperor. The official most readily associated with this policy shift, against the backdrop of Western encroachment and Taiping advances, was Wang Maoyin (1798–1865). In fact, Wang was the only Chinese person to be mentioned in name in Marx's *Das Capital*, first published in 1867: In a footnote, Marx equated Wang's putative espousal of inconvertible notes with the failed *assignats* of the French Revolution and speculated that he might have been gravely punished for that reason;[24] Wang himself had of course been oblivious to such analogies. In that sense, Wang can perhaps be seen as the last great Chinese monetary thinker to have advanced the cause of paper money and *daqian* purely based on traditional statecraft argumentation, that is, without reference to the Western or Japanese monetary reform. The nub of his argument was that the Shunzhi issue, albeit short lived, proved that paper money could be sustained. Yet, what he proposed was in fact *not* Wang Liu's idea or Marx's notion of "*assignats*" but a more prudent system whereby the ratio between circulating coinage and total note value would be 4:1. In his memorial of 1851, he also envisioned an upper limit for note issuance at 10 million taels.[25]

Contrary to what Marx believed, therefore, Wang Maoyin could not have been punished for supporting inconvertible notes. Rather, the Xianfeng emperor warmed to his bold ideas in 1851. He fell from grace at court in 1854, only after repeatedly criticizing the overissue of notes and *daqian*, which diverged from his initial policy proposals. Disillusioned with actual Xianfeng policy, he changed his mind in other ways too: In his original proposal, for example, he suggested that it was not up to the government to maintain parity between coinage and paper money, but the role of private-order money shops (*yinhao*). Later on, he argued this had to be done by the government to curb excessive issues.[26]

The last phase of Qing banknote issuance lasted from 1897 right until the dynasty's collapse in 1912. It was substantively different to the two previous phases because, by then, notes were imported from Western printers and were characteristically novel in design (read: horizontal); they were disbursed in the main by Chinese semiofficial modern banks, explicitly modeled on foreign ones rather than by the imperial treasury (*Hubu*) directly.[27]

How British bank note issuance on Chinese soil started informing Chinese monetary thinking later in the nineteenth century and early twentieth century is explained in detail in the next chapter. Suffice it to note at this point that from the 1890s onward the invocation of Western and Japanese monetary history would override, in argumentative terms, Chinese historic precedents in court debates on the viability of paper money. Prominent monarchist, reformer-turned-dissident and intellectual luminary, Liang Qichao (1873–1929), is perhaps the best example: He tirelessly campaigned for China to emulate the West by embracing the gold standard, unify its refractory currencies, and issue state-backed banknotes with a one-third metallic reserve.[28]

Late Qing court memorials did, however, retain a modicum of traditional nomenclature alongside stirrings of modern monetary nationalism. To be sure, preoccupation with Jia Yi's time-honored trope concerning heavy versus light coinage seems to have faded away by then. An imperial compilation on monetary policy from 1909 discussed, for example, familiar Daoguang-era topics like the need to stem the inroads of foreign coinage alongside fairly novel ideas like the need to abolish sycee, that is, measuring silver by weight. The compilation also invoked how monetary sovereignty was vital to China's ability to repay foreign creditors and issue sovereign debt in the future. Notably, one of the key themes broached was also the need to emulate Japan in eradicating the use of "older coinage" (*guqian*), namely coins dating back to previous dynasties, as a prerequisite of monetary sovereignty and modernization.[29]

Another prominent late Qing reformer-turned-dissident who drew inspiration from Japan was Huang Zunxian (1848–1905). Having served at the Qing legation to Tokyo between 1877 and 1882, Huang tried to analyze the complexity of Meiji monetary reforms in his memoirs (*Riben guozhi*), published in 1895. By that time, the Xianfeng experiment with paper money had long been discredited. Nonetheless, Huang argued that China needed to have modern paper money like Japan's. On the other hand, Huang was by no means oblivious to the inflation that government banknote issuance and government bonds had unleashed in Japan in the early 1870s, noting that these issues were meant in principle to be backed by a 40 percent metallic reserve ratio.[30]

FUZHOU AND BEYOND, CIRCA 1850

Scholars by and large agree that a form of private bank note issuance was widespread in busy trading hubs like Fuzhou well before the establishment of British banks in Shanghai, as George Selgin's pioneering study and others have shown. In other words, there is a broad scholarly consensus that, on the eve of British bank entry into China proper, "private moneyshop scrip, remittance drafts and military wage coupons [and] product certificates" had already circulated in different parts of China concurrently.[31]

However, there were to be stark differences between British bank-issued notes in China's treaty ports and the former type of scrip, differences ranging from design layout, print technology, and counterforgery measures right through to the degree of on-demand convertibility or relative issue volumes.[32] I have discussed these differences at length elsewhere. Here I expand on another stark difference that touches right on the matter at heart—popular faith in paper money in Europe versus East Asia around the turn of the nineteenth century. But let me suggest beforehand that it is almost as important to consider what the thrust of Selgin's pioneering work was at the time of its publication (1992). His chapter was published in an edited volume seeking historic rationalization for "free banking" and faulting central banks (a twentieth-century creation for the most part) with intrinsic inflationary proclivities.

In other words, the volume was informed by a Hayekian theoretical framework seeking to establish the ubiquity and reliability of private banknote modalities in the past. That such a research agenda gained credence and proved so prolific in the United States during the mid-1990s may perhaps seem a bit odd in view of the battering that non-state financial institutions have taken of late as a result of the subprime mortgage crisis in the United States. Since 2008, the major theoretical question preoccupying policy makers and economic theorists is of course *not* whether central banks should be replaced by private banks as issuers of currency but to what extent central-government regulatory oversight should actually be strengthened so as to curb private bank imprudence.

Nonetheless, and quite apart from topical media coverage, the free-banking agenda of the 1990s was immensely valuable in that it highlighted important yet hitherto obscure monetary experiences accumulated outside the West. Thus, Selgin's pioneering chapter called attention to the ubiquity of private banknote issuance in early nineteenth-century Fuzhou. But, even if we accept Fuzhou's case as partial historic vindication for "free banking," Selgin was clearly aware this case may have not applied to the rest of China.

This recognition was clearly in line with one of the key witnesses he cited; renowned botanist Robert Fortune (1812–1880) remarked that banking was "carried on to a greater extent in [Fuzhou] that in the other towns which I have visited."[33] Selgin concluded that Fuzhou private notes "circulated at par, and were widely preferred to coin" and that "banking failures were restricted to very small banks." Yet on closer inspection, it immediately becomes apparent to readers that the mostly anecdotal accounts Selgin draws on actually refer to repeated bank failures. Moreover, in data Selgin has painstakingly gleaned from 1932 to 1936, anonymous sources suggest that by then, of the twenty-one private banks (or large money shops) issuing notes in Fuzhou, only four had been established before 1900, with the oldest two dating back to 1877. In other words, none of the note-issuing institutions to which his witnesses had referred to in the 1850s and 1860s seems to have survived long afterwards.[34]

Though somewhat ambivalent, N. B. Dennys's edited account of Fuzhou, published in 1867, sheds valuable light on Fortune's famous travelogue. In a section on the city's currency system, Dennys suggests local private banks of issue were trusted but observes note circulation was "diminishing." At any rate, Dennys, who had visited many other treaty ports but was not much discussed by Selgin, stressed that Fuzhou banking was the exception rather than the norm:[35]

The circulating medium used by Europeans is the Mexican Dollar, which passes current either "chopped" (i.e. with the indented stamps of the shroffs or money-inspectors through whose hands the coin has passed) or plain. No smaller coin exists, with the exception of the Chinese cash, but the deficiency is supplied by notes of the value of 100 cash upwards, which are issued from numerous natives banks established at Foochow [Fuzhou], and which have large, though gradually diminishing, circulation. At no other place in China is banking more extensively practised or notes so largely circulated. No control is exercised by the Chinese government over this issue of paper money, in which, nevertheless, the public has full confidence. The notes are printed from copper plates or wood-blocks on oblong slips of paper, with such artistic design and complicated checks by means of numbering and tallies as to defy the danger of counterfeiting. A Mexican Dollar is exchanged at the average rate of 1,000 to 1,100 cash in currency or paper.

Published more than a decade later, the foreign-run Chinese Imperial Maritime Customs' (IMC) *Decennial Reports* sounded a somewhat less sanguine judgment on the reliability of some of Fuzhou's "cash shops," while oddly accepting regulations to do with local banks' reserve ratios at face value. In addition, the *Reports* suggested that Fuzhou bills were drawn on banks as far away as Beijing and vice versa. Yet the financial institutions engaged in such long-distance transactions were the famous Shanxi banks (*piaohao*), which possessed close links to the imperial bureaucracy, rather than local note-issuing banks:[36]

The business of a cash shop is limited to the exchange of bank notes or silver dollars into copper cash, and its profit depends principally on the number of spurious cash in each string successfully passed on to the public. That these shops used to pay handsomely is proved by the fact that till quite recently they were counted by the dozen in every street. The attention of the authorities, however, having been drawn to the illegal nature of their transactions, a strict watch is now exercised over their doings, and the earnings are therefore considerably curtailed. The capital employed by them is naturally very small, and seldom reaches the sum of $500.

The small banks, numbering about 60, possess larger capitals, varying from $20,000 to $50,000, and their operations are based on sounder principles. They are allowed to issue notes, the lowest specified value of which is limited to 400 cash, and the highest to 500 *tiao* [*diao*], or strings; and the specie in reserve against the paper issue must come up to at least one-half of the total value of the notes in circulation. They also advance money on mortgage, charging interest at the rate of 15 to 30 per cent, a year.

The number of large banks is six, named respectively the Wei Ch'ang Hou, the Wei T'ai Hou, the Hsin T'ai Hou, the Hsieh T'ung Ch'ing, the Hsieh Ho Hsin, and the Yüan Fêng Jun. The five first named are owned by Shansi [Shanxi] bankers, and the last by natives of Chehkiang [Zhejiang]. These banks have business connexions with all the more important commercial centres of China, but the bulk of their exchange transactions is done between Foochow and Peking. Their rates for drafts drawn on non-Treaty ports are, as near as possible, fixed at 5 per cent, premium, and on the open ports, especially where Foreign banks are represented, somewhat below the daily exchange quotation. They do not issue notes of currency, but advance money on merchandise or any other form of acceptable security, and charge interest at a rate varying from 8 to 25 per cent, per annum, according to the soundness of the security. They also assist expectant officials; in this case, however, the rate of interest charged is in proportion to the risk incurred and the prospect of return, within a brief or long interval, of both capital and interest.

That such long-distance "drafts" (*piaotie*) were transacted by institutions, which were staffed by family relatives and fellow townsmen from the north of China with close links to mandarins and that did not engage in impersonal note conversion as such, is instructive. Shanxi banks first appeared as late as the 1820s and were characterized by unlimited liability and relatively small deposit base. Much of their *piaotie* commission business derived from mandarins needing to transfer their wages to family members residing in the capital or vice versa. In addition, the *piaotie* network was used to transfer local tax revenue to the central imperial treasury and vice versa. Notably, such remittances were not handled by more official institutions like the *haiguan* [Haikwan] bank, which was contented with collecting custom duties for the imperial treasury.

Access to the small number of high-ranking officials with such postings required unseemly official patronage as formal charters were not given by the throne as in early modern Europe. These circumstances meant that, once the Qing order collapsed in 1911 and Shanxi banks lost their access to officialdom, they too disappeared from sight.[37]

Of the observations Selgin relies on, the one penned by the Reverend Justus Doolittle is perhaps the most credible because he was not merely a one-off visitor; Doolittle resided in Fuzhou through much of the 1860s. By then, British banks were starting to issue modest amounts of notes in several newly designated "treaty ports," including Fuzhou. Doolittle, however, relates in his account to the immediate past—one that was not "tampered with" by British bank presence. His remarks are therefore highly pertinent to the monetary state of affairs on the eve of contact with European financial institutions.[38]

In fact, Doolittle explicitly recounts that in 1855 an "unusual panic" had broken out in the city, with several smaller money shops failing and unable to redeem their notes. The result was widespread looting of money shop premises by note bearers and an angry mob. He also mentions that frequent runs on local financial institutions occurred thereafter. Concomitantly, against the backdrop of coin scarcity in the city, the Qing local authorities tried to issue convertible notes of their own "a few years ago" (1858?), but these notes were retired soon afterwards because they were often paid for with debased iron and copper cash.[39]

The failure of smaller money shops and the local government issue left the larger and seemingly more solvent money shops (*chupiao dian*) as sole issuer in the city of paper currency that was convertible to "cash" rather than to actual silver coins. From about the 1880s, the latter's notes were mostly denominated in the notional dollar unit current in Fuzhou (the "Dai Fook Dollar" or *Taifu* dollar); they were reportedly first issued by Fuzhou's larger money shops at the instigation of foreign financiers and were modeled on foreign bank notes. Even as late as the 1920s, when one paid a storekeeper with Dai Fook notes, "One [was] always asked to stay in the shop until the notes have been examined and pronounced genuine by an expert."[40]

Of the notes current in Fuzhou as a whole, the smallest denomination was at 400 copper cash (roughly equal to 0.3 silver dollar), and the highest was at "thousands of dollars." Note values can be meaningful in this context: According to Pomeranz's upper-end estimate, the daily income of a Chinese rural cotton-spinner in China's richest provinces was only around 0.1 silver dollar circa 1750.[41] Even if we allow for a tripling of that income level over a century, the smallest note value in 1850s Fuzhou would have still been equivalent to a whole day's wage. This might partially explain why metallic currency was preferred to notes in China's hinterland right up until the middle of the twentieth century.

To be sure, a 1852 treatise by British diplomat Harry Parkes, which Selgin also draws on, did mention that copper-cash-denominated notes in Fuzhou "almost entirely superseded the use of bullion . . . It is adopted by everybody, high or low, to the almost entire rejection of their bulky coins" (p. 180). Yet, a few passages later Parkes somewhat contradictorily stated (p. 186) that dollar notes, which formed the great bulk of Fuzhou's private issue, were in fact "used chiefly by the mercantile or trading community."[42]

That aside, it is the all-important issue of trust where Justus Doolittle's observations are of most value. His account suggests that the dynamic of instilling trust in Fuzhou money shop notes ensued from an intricate *personalized* clearing mechanism:[43]

When a new bank [that is, money shop] is opened [in Fuzhou], custom demands that the proprietors, the head directors or clerks of the principal neighbouring banks, and the principal money go-betweens who are connected with them, shall be invited to a feast at the expense of the proprietors of the new bank. Generally, after this feast, these neighbouring bankers, unless they have especial reason to distrust or be dissatisfied with the new banker, are willing to recognize the new bank, and use its bills according to custom.

The foregoing passage is instructive because it traces out the fine line between personal and institutional trust, which, in turn, informed the reliability of notes in the eyes of fellow bankers and perhaps the public at large.[44] More pertinently, it calls attention to the regionally fragmented nature of private banknote issuance in mid-eighteenth- to late nineteenth-century China. In other words, Doolittle's observations suggest that it was highly unlikely that a note issued by Fuzhou's larger money shops could be redeemed by money shops outside that local financial circle. Incidentally, even within Fuzhou itself, no fewer than five separate clearinghouses were required to deal with the plethora of note-issuing money shops,[45] for personal trust would have by its very nature been harder to maintain across long distances, considering the dialectal barriers and the absence of rail links at the time.

This is perhaps why the very same Doolittle avers toward the end of his book that "in China . . . there is no national currency except the copper cash."[46] Similarly, S. W. Williams's generally less reliable guidebook of 1851 does nonetheless clearly state that "the circulation of promissory notes and letters of credit is very great throughout [China's] provinces, and they are constantly used to facilitate commercial transactions; but this kind of paper hardly comes under the designation of money, as it is not a circulating medium."[47]

Interestingly, Williams then indicates that of the five treaty ports opened up by Europeans along the China coast, it was only in Fuzhou that paper money was widely used, "but we are told that it is also well known in Peking and in some cities in the provinces of Shantung [Shandong] and Honan [Henan]." As for private banks, their banknotes circulated "only as their credit is good, and as far as the bank is known. Consequently, the knowledge of such paper is generally restricted to the immediate region or city where it is issued."[48]

Williams observes later in his article that even within the intimate confines of Fuzhou circulation was regionally prescribed: "The bills of the banks in the Island, in the suburb of Nantai, and those within the city walls, generally circulate in those districts. When a bank fails, the bill-holders rush to the place in crowds, and pull the building down, thus destroying their chances of getting even a percentage for their notes." Curiously enough, another source seventy-five years later suggests not much has changed since Williams's days: Dai-Fook native bank notes "are current only in Foochow city and [the suburb of] Nantai. They hardly ever appear in such neighbouring districts as Mamoi [Mani], and not at all in districts farther away from Foochow."[49]

One of the foreign banks' critical stimuli to China's monetary modernization lies precisely here: Having set up branches in all treaty ports, they could clear each other's notes right across China's principal trading hubs. At the same time, foreign banks astutely took advantage of the country's monetary fragmentation to charge a commission on such simple transactions as clearing their own notes if these were issued at another locality. As explained in the next chapter, British banks, in particular, incrementally instilled impersonal trust in their clientele by adhering to very cautious metallic-reserve guidelines that were regularly revised by Whitehall.

IMC contemporary reports from other treaty ports where *piaohao* were set up confirm the "clannish" nature of their business dealings. All of the sixteen *piaohao* operating in Chongqing (Sichuan province), for example, were run by fellow-townsmen from Pingyao or Qixian in

Shanxi province. Eight of the sixteen had such close affinity with Treasury officials in the capital that the IMC deemed them to be "semigov-
ernment" institutions, although in the same breath the IMC marveled at
their preference for "friendship" over solid collateral or deposits when
issuing and cashing drafts. The interest they charged on short-term
loans made only to "the most reliable of individuals" was considered
low at 10 percent per annum, presumably because this was not their
core business.[50]

Some 200 kilometers due southwest from Fuzhou, along the coast, lay
the treaty port of Xiamen (known to Europeans as Amoy at the time).
Interestingly, the IMC reported that most of the banks there handling
commercial drafts on other ports were in fact run by Fuzhou rather than
Shanxi natives. To be sure, many *piaohao* were operating in Xiamen,
too, and they were considered very reliable. However, they restricted
themselves to official wage remittances. Banks run by Fuzhou natives
had a more varied business than that of the *piaohao*: They made, for
example, advances against cargo and property and collaborated more
closely with foreign bank networks. For these reasons, their notes could
"occasionally" circulate outside the locality. Notably, the annualized
interest rate they charged on commercial loans could reach as high as
25 percent when the collateral presented by the debtor was not considered "strictly reliable." But the IMC hastened to add that "14 of these
establishments have gone into bankruptcy" within a decade because of
their speculative nature. As for the type of banknotes circulating in Xiamen at the time, these were mainly issued by British and Japanese banks
in silver dollar denominations. The main local currency, however, was
bronze coinage, as in much of the rest of China.[51]

In his authoritative 1904 guidebook, Jernigan nevertheless suggested
with an element of hyperbole that Chinese native banks (either *piaohao*
or money shops) were to be found in nearly every "town and village."
He further suggested that many of these banks issued notes of their own
that "materially add to the circulating medium." Nonetheless, he was
quick to add that these notes, unlike foreign bank ones, only circulated
in their "respective localities." As for "native bank" bills and drafts,
some could be cashed in faraway outports, but many were only with
"the street on which the bank is situated."[52]

BIMETALLISM RECONSIDERED

It is worth exhausting the pertinent literature in search of counterfactu-
als, not least because the question at stake has important implications

for the "Great Divergence" debate, which has dominated the field of economic history in recent years: For example, it would be naturally useful to determine how big a role banknote issuance played in China as compared with Europe during the eighteenth and nineteenth centuries before broader inferences can be drawn.

The received wisdom, as postulated in many monographs, is that China's monetary system was "bimetallic" in the late imperial era.[53] In other words, before the rise of modern note-issuing Chinese banks, modeled on their British counterparts, there were only two types of currency in use across the length and breadth of the empire: state-cast copper cash coins and silver sycee or Spanish-American silver dollars.

Chen Chau-nan's influential study, for example, states that China's late imperial monetary system was predicated on a "floating" exchange rate between copper and silver, with both metals largely imported from overseas. As for copper- and silver-denominated private banknote issuance, "Their share in the total money stock remained insignificant . . . as late as 1910, only one-fourth of the total quantity of currency was accounted for by bank notes, foreign as well as Chinese."[54]

Peng Xinwei's monumental study remains the benchmark for research into China's premodern and early modern monetary system. Notably, Peng was also one of very few scholars who—drawing on a broad range of contemporaneous materials—ventured to offer a rough quantitative estimate of various means of payment at the turn of the twentieth century. Summarized in Table 4.1, Peng's findings are highly germane to, but hardly supportive of, the alternative proposition that describes private bank note issuance as a pillar of the late imperial Chinese monetary system.

According to Peng, as late as 1900 the volume of privately issued notes accounted for no more than 3 percent of the Chinese currency stock. Even if we add to the tally silver-denominated notes, which according to Peng were by then mostly issued by state or modern banks, it is highly unlikely that the volume of Chinese privately issued notes surpassed 6 percent of the total. Apart from that, the lack of disclosure by foreign banks as to the volume of their notes outstanding in China proper resulted over the years in inflated estimates thereof. It would thus be implausible to conclude that the ratio of all notes as part of the entire Chinese money stock was—even as late as 1900—much higher than 10 percent.

That said, by the early 1900s, traditionally cast copper "cash" made up only 17.78 percent of the Chinese currency stock and gradually receded from the marketplace thereafter. In that sense, the vitality of copper cash to the Chinese hinterland economy needs to be placed in the

TABLE 4.1.
The stock of currency in the late Qing (c. 1900s).

Type of currency	Total value	Total value in silver (dollars)	Percentage of entire stock
Silver-based		1,297,000,000	61.85
Chinese-minted dollar coins	$200,000,000	200,000,000	9.54
Foreign-minted dollar coins	$500,000,000	500,000,000	23.84
Subsidiary silver coins	$250,000,000	250,000,000	11.92
Sycee (ingots)	Tls. 250,000,000	347,000,000	16.55
Copper-based		522,253,731	24.90
Modern (minted) bronze coins	200,000,000,000 pieces	149,253,731	7.12
Traditionally cast (holed) copper cash	500,000,000,000 *wen*	373,000,000	17.78
Paper money		277,777,777	13.25
Tael-denominated	Tls. 20,000,000	27,777,777	1.33
Silver dollar–denominated (mostly state issued)	$50,000,000	50,000,000	2.38
Copper cash string–denominated (state issued)	54,000,000 *diao*	40,000,000	1.9
Copper cash string–denominated (privately issued)	80,000,000 *diao*	60,000,000	2.86
Foreign banks	$100,000,000	100,000,000	4.77
TOTAL		2,097,031,508	100

SOURCE: Adapted from Peng Xinwei (rev. 1988, third edition), pp. 886–889.

context of Western Europe's monetary systems between the thirteenth and eighteenth centuries, namely, before the universalization of steam-powered mints and nation-state territorial currencies. As indicated in the previous chapter, near-token coinage mostly made of copper re-emerged in Western Europe as of the thirteenth century but—in contrast to China at the time—its circulation was highly localized in nature.

Because it vitally served the needs of local commerce and could not be readily replaced by state coinage due to the high cost of copper coin minting before the invention of steam power, European polities seldom banned such token coinage before the 1900s. Even when they did issue token coinage of their own, it was usually of poorer quality than private-order local fiduciary coinage; neither did European polities much aim at regulating the value of their fiduciary copper coinage against silver and gold currencies.[55]

By contrast, the Chinese late imperial polity was always preoccupied with the value of copper cash against silver and in purchasing grain. Peng estimated that foreign trade dollars—among which the Mexican silver dollar was prominent—had made up nearly a quarter of the Chinese currency stock in the 1900s, considerably above the share of traditional "cash." The trend in Japan and in the Western-dominated world reversed in the meantime: The worldwide introduction of state-issued steam-minted token coinage as of the mid-nineteenth century—as well as the concomitant diffusion of the gold standard and the discovery of extensive silver deposits in Nevada, California, and West Africa—led in fact to a rapid *diminution* in the spread of Mexican-mined silver dollars, particularly in the Americas and the Philippines.[56]

The most authoritative study that might perhaps support the alternative proposition is Wang Yeh-chien's 1981 Chinese-language treatise. In contrast to the received view, Wang wrote there that the significance of privately issued banknotes in China's southeast may have exceeded that of metallic currency transactions by the early nineteenth century. But even according to Wang, private bank note issuance was negligible before the latter part of the eighteenth century.[57]

Wang Yeh-chien had been able to collate an impressive array of positive references to privately issued notes. Notably, however, most of these were made by Qing officials energetically lobbying for the renewal of state issues and are therefore a little suspect. Based on these references, and despite the paucity of available contemporary quantitative data, Wang was convinced that most money shops had kept sound reserves to back up their discrete issues; that such issues became the third pillar of China's monetary system by the early nineteenth century, alongside copper and silver; that they greatly alleviated cash scarcity; and that—contrary to the evidence that will be presented in Chapter Six of this book—they even circulated widely in the then rural backwaters of Taiwan (and Hainan).[58] Yet even the positive references that Wang adduced entertain mention of frequent money shop failures—so much so that the English-language abstract of his treatise passes the following judgment on the period under review:[59]

The issuing of paper notes by private concerns without regulation by the monetary authorities often caused financial crises such as bank runs and suspension of redemption. Worse still was the possible debilitating effect of private notes on the economy.

In addition, the contemporaneous positive references to paper money, which serve Wang, actually suggest that the very officials who made them were mindful of *not* just the existence of money shop notes. Wang Ye-chien mentions that at least one of these officials, Fujian governor Wang Yide, underscored in 1852 *also* the spread of foreign bank notes (*fanpiao*) in China's treaty ports as his rationale for lobbying the court to allow a resumption of note issuance.[60] Wang Yide's call is instructive because it was made merely five years after the Oriental Bank Corporation (OBC), the first foreign-owned bank to operate in China, set up a branch and started issuing notes in Shanghai. The OBC in Shanghai was miniscule at the time, but Wang may have chosen to exaggerate its significance to advance his cause.[61] As for China's vast hinterland, it took three decades after Wang had written his memorial for the IMC to resolutely state that foreign (that is, British) bank notes in Hankou, for example, were being accepted by "native merchants" with "increased confidence."[62]

As already mentioned, the atmosphere at the Xianfeng court was fraught because, by then, the negative effects of opium imports, silver outflow, and the military supremacy of the British had sunk in. Like Wang Yide, Qi Junzao (1793–1866) had also served in Fujian and came to observe the British at close hand. He searched for ways to invigorate the depleted imperial treasury and thus warmed to the idea of issuing *daqian*—an anathema to historically minded conservative officials. Qi tried to persuade the initially reluctant Emperor Xianfeng to resume Qing paper note issuance after a two-centuries' hiatus. Like Wang Yide, Qi's rationale was that foreign and private money shop scrip—denominated as they were in either in silver or cash—had supposedly spread far and wide and were now a common feature in and around all provincial capitals. But he then adduced another interesting justification; following Fan Ji and much like Wang Liu, Qi argued that token money had played a historically important role in alleviating the dearth of cash ever since Emperor Wudi issued deer-hide currency in the Han era.[63]

A BIGGER PICTURE?

The early modern English monetary system was thrown into relief in Chapter Two by way of better demarcating the broader economic "Great Divergence" across Eurasia. Clearly, China's monetary system in 1900 was very different from England's where, by the mid-nineteenth century, coinage accounted for merely 20 percent of the money supply, when bank deposits are included.[64] Peng's data presented in Table 4.1 might suggest that metallic currencies (mainly sycee and "cash") accounted for as much as 86.75 percent of China's money stock circa 1900. However, Peng did not seem to incorporate bank deposits into his tallies. Is Peng's eastimate reliable, and how does it compare with other parts of the world?

To validate Peng's 1900 estimate and correct it for the inclusion of bank deposits, it is useful to cross-reference it with data presented by Rawski for 1910, where the significance of banknote circulation volumes and bank deposits to economic growth is generally stressed. In sum, the two sources seem to correspond quite neatly, allowing for the time lag and differences in measurement methodology. Rawski estimated China's silver stock in China in 1910 at a value of anywhere between 880 million and 1.9 billion silver dollars. Rawski's mean would therefore not be a long way off from Peng's 1.29 billion silver dollars' estimate for China's silver-based currencies in 1900 (look again at Table 4.1). Rawski's estimate for the value of China's monetary copper stock in 1910 is commensurate with 413 million silver dollars, which is again remarkably close to Peng's estimate of 522 million. According to Rawski, neither total bank deposits nor notes in circulation in 1912 much exceeded 101 million silver dollars. This, in turn, might suggest that the lack of data on bank deposits in Peng's 1900 estimate is not a major flaw, considering that he attributed a total value of 277 million silver dollars to banknotes, nearly three times Rawski's figure for a decade later. Either way, both sets of data confirm that metallic currencies accounted for approximately 70 percent of China's money supply in the first decade of the twentieth century.[65]

Late-Qing debates about the viability of paper money can, however, be better appreciated when compared to other "latecomer" economies where paper money and national market integration occurred later than in Britain.[66] In this context, it is also instructive to recall that Western observations of China's monetary system changed considerably in tone between the eighteenth and twentieth centuries. To be sure, in the late eighteenth century a wide variety of metallic and nonmetallic currencies were still concurrent in North America, including tobacco. Through much of the colonial era, North America had suffered a trade deficit with Britain and was therefore short of British-minted cash. On the other hand, local metal deposits had not yet been discovered, and the British authorities otherwise discouraged the issue of local token coinage. The particularities of Chinese assaying and bimetallic exchange did *not* seem exceptionally backward through contemporary American eyes, therefore.[67] However, the advent of steam technology and, by implication, steam minting in the West progressively tarnished China's image.[68] By 1889, the financial expert Joseph Edkins would declare from the pages of the *North-China Herald* that the "chaotic eccentricities" of China's monetary system "would drive any Occidental nation to madness."[69] And William Parsons, an American engineer working in China, would write in his 1900 memoirs:[70]

The Chinese have no equals in their understanding of the use of money . . . Yet they have elaborated a monetary system which, for cumbersomeness and downright wastefulness, is without an equal. The lack of progress is rendered more extraordinary by the fact that bank-notes, one of the greatest steps in the making of financial transactions more convenient, originated in China, where they were known probably as early as A.D. 800, or about eight centuries before the device was reinvented in Europe.

In the eyes of Chinese observers, perhaps the most persuasive testament to China's falling behind was the monetary reform in early Meiji Japan, which bore much more cultural affinity to China than to industrialized England. After all, Chinese coinage played an exceedingly important role in that country's economy well into the fifteenth century. Yet, as Huang Zunxian would relate to his compatriots, by the late nineteenth century Japan's monetary system had unrecognizably changed; though not quite on a gold standard yet, Meiji Japan had demonetized what the Chinese within their setting called *guqian*, namely "older" (read: Tokugawa-era) coinage, as well as demonetizing "foreign" (read: Mexican silver) coinage. Instead, Meiji Japan issued indigenous steam-minted gold, silver, and token coinage and a large volume of government banknotes to the extent that pre-Meiji coinage all but disappeared by 1900.[71]

To be sure, due to a shortage of metallic currencies, various Tokugawa feudatories (*han*) had started issuing banknotes on a large scale for the first time as early as the 1660s, namely, much earlier than the (re)appearance of private-order banknotes in China. For the most part, such *hansatsu* notes circulated fairly stably within their respective *han* and were backed by silver hoarded by the feudal lord through limiting the payment of silver in commercial transactions. They evolved from the first type of Japanese monetary paper instrument, a private-order promissory note (*shisatsu*) that had been in limited use in the early seventeenth century. The Tokugawa shogunate did try to constrain *han* powers by banning the flow of *hansatsu* between 1707 and 1730 but then changed its mind because a deep recession and contraction of the money base ensued. Thus, *hansatsu* totalling 38 million yen were still in circulation on the eve of the Meiji restoration (1868).[72]

Once firmly established, the Meiji authorities strove to retire the hundreds of different *hansatsu* types still in circulation and replace them with stated-backed paper money. Notably, the armed Samurai class, which was seen as a vestige of the feudal era, was, for example, effectively disbanded not with the lure of hard currency but with the promise of interest-bearing, inconvertible government bonds. By 1900, the per-capita stock of money in Japan (excluding bank deposits) was estimated at 6.7 yen, of which no fewer than 5.1 yen were in the form of banknotes.

In other words, up to 76 percent of individual cash holding in Japan at that time was in paper instruments, a much higher figure than Peng's estimate for China at 13.25 percent.[73] Korea's monetary system on the eve of Japanese annexation (1909) was much closer to China's, with just 1.7 yen per person, 76 percent of which in the form of specie or bullion.[74]

Applying Maddison's China population figures for 1820 (that is, 381 million inhabitants) to Peng's 1900 money-stock aggregate (2 billion silver dollars) would yield an upper-bound per capita holding of 5.2 silver dollars.[75] Converted to gold yen based on the 1903 exchange rate Hsiao provides,[76] this would mean every Chinese held on average 4.3 yen. By implication, Korea was in all likelihood much less monetized than China at the turn of the twentieth century. China, in turn, might *not* have been infinitely less monetized than Japan. Yet, in relative terms, the former was much more reliant on metallic currency.

Goldsmith provides a narrow money supply of 2.9 billion rupees for India under British rule in 1900. This estimate is likely lower bound because Goldsmith could not provide data on subsidiary base-metal currencies. Even so, only 8.2 percent of this money supply was made up of banknotes—a lower ratio than the 13.25 percent that Peng imputes to China that year. Aggregate Indian bank deposits were similarly minor in 1900 at 175 million rupees.[77] Maddison estimated India's population at 209 million in 1820. Dividing Goldsmith's narrow money supply by Maddison's population figure would yield an upward-biased estimate of per capita Indian monetization around 1900 of approximately 14 rupees or 9.5 silver dollars.[78] This result, in turn, is nearly double the upper-bound per capita estimate for China that year.

Fragmentary data on the Ottoman narrow money supply is available only for 1914. Pamuk suggests it was around 60 million gold lira. The population effectively under Ottoman rule at the time was 22 million, rendering about 2.8 lira per person. In terms of content, Pamuk also suggests one gold lira was worth 0.9 British pound.[79] Drawing on Hsiao's data, we can conclude that individuals across the Ottoman Empire held on average in 1914 the equivalent of 15.5 Mexican silver dollars or 13.6 gold yen. This 1914 figure is much higher than the one provided for either China or Japan a decade and a half earlier. Yet, in stark contrast to Japan, less than 7 percent of the Ottoman money supply as late as 1914 was made up by banknotes.[80]

In fact, the Ottomans had issued a limited amount of handwritten, interest-bearing treasury notes (*kaime*) as early as 1840. But these inconvertible notes were plagued right from the start by forgery and poor reception, even though they were admissible for tax purposes. Better printing technology and the supply of lower-denomination *kaime* made the notes more popular in the 1850s, to the extent that they could be disseminated at much lower interest rates than in the 1840s. Following the Crimean War, however, the Ottomans resorted to much higher volumes of annual *kaime* issues, resulting in their rapid depreciation against metallic currencies. Faced with popular protests, the Ottoman government decided to retire *kaime* notes altogether in 1862. Another attempt to issue treasury *kaime* in the late 1870s was driven by military exigency but proved equally unsuccessful. From then on note-issue prerogatives were awarded to an Anglo-French consortium, the Imperial Ottoman Bank, which applied a much more prudent metallic-reserve policy, keeping circulation volumes much lower.[81]

Russia was another adjacent "latecomer" economy that moved on the gold standard shortly before Japan. In 1780, it had its first paper money introduced in the form of inconvertible silver ruble–denominated bills. Loosely inferring from Hsiao's exchange rate available for 1912 at the earliest, as well as data provided by Kahan, it may have been the case that the per capita money stock in Russia that year (exclusive of bank deposits) was around the equivalent of 9 yen with banknotes accounting for a *large* share thereof.[82]

Much higher levels of monetization were recorded in Western "latecomers." Across the pre-Zollverein German states, paper money had been known at least since the 1706 Stolberg emergency issue. In 1835, the Bavarian monarchy authorized the first German bank of issue, Bayerische Hypotheken und Wechselbank, to be followed by the more important joint-stock Prussian Bank in 1846 as well as a host of smaller, privately owned note-issuing financial institutions. Concomitantly, governments of other German states issued both convertible and inconvertible paper money directly. By 1913, however, the great bulk of German circulating notes were issued by the unified Reich. According to Sprenger, the total value of notes in circulation that year was 3 billion reichsmarks; and that of coinage, 5.2 billion. Bank deposits against an immobile reserve of 2.1 billion reichsmarks totaled at a whopping 38.4 billion. Based on the exchange rate provided by Hsiao for 1913, it would appear that the narrow money stock in Germany totaled the rough equivalent of 4 billion silver dollars, or twice the China total for 1900, notwithstanding that China was manyfold more populous.[83]

Similarly, in France, where the banknote circulation volume had made up only 5 percent of the money stock as late as 1803, the monetary system radically changed over the course of the nineteenth century. By 1900, of a total money supply of 15.4 billion francs (including deposits), the banknote volume accounted for as much as 4.2 billion. Bank deposits and specie accounted for 5 and 6 billion francs, respectively.[84] The narrow 1900 French money supply, that is, specie and notes (10.2 billion francs), is in absolute terms surprisingly similar to that of Germany. It too would have been tantamount to twice the China total, as estimated by Peng.

In 1860, at the height of America's "free banking" era, some 1,562 banks accounted together for US$ 207 million worth of notes circulation. That total would have been, in turn, commensurate with the same figure in silver (read: Mexican) dollars. Aggregate U.S. money supply (including US$ 254 million in bank deposits and US$ 253 million in specie) amounted to around 714 million silver dollars, or 23 silver dollars per person—a figure more than four times higher than the estimated Chinese per person cash holding forty years later. Although the U.S. *aggregate* money supply in 1860 would have been under half of China's in 1900, and, although North America as a whole had often been associated with cash dearth in European eyes two centuries prior, that part of the world eventually became manyfold more monetized than China thanks to the popularization of banknotes. Concomitantly, as early as 1860, the U.S. monetary system had already been much more geared toward paper money and bank deposits than the Chinese monetary system four decades later, despite occasional bank failures and inflationary "wildcat" practices commonly associated with the "free banking" era.[85]

As previously argued, the variation in the extent to which fiduciary notes and bank deposits complemented metallic currencies in different countries' money stock strongly suggests itself as one of the variations in the cost of capital across Eurasia. The latter factor might plausibly explain why some countries industrialized faster in the twentieth century, alongside other factors that this study mentions in passing, for example the variation in the introduction of joint-stock enterprise. This study does not aim to singularly bear out the linkage among money stock components, interest rates, and economic growth beyond doubt. But it does conclude that the cost of capital in China had been higher than in Europe for a very long time before the twentieth century. In this context, Hao Yen-p'ing showed that, even in the latter part of the nineteenth century, Western financial institutions in China's treaty ports could still charge their Chinese clients well above 10 percent in annualized interest on short-term loans, while paying only 2 percent interest on local deposits. The situation was far worse in the interior, where Western financial institutions rarely operated and where, even in the early twentieth century, a rate of 40 to 80 percent was "common."[86]

CONCLUSIONS

Although this chapter does not present newly mined primary material, it offers a cautious and thorough rereading of the historical sources that are most often cited in the scholarly literature, generally in too cursory a fashion, so as to place the factual record on a sounder footing and to challenge many newly made revisionist propositions. Although the resurgence of private and government banknote issuance in Qing China is certainly a significant historic turnaround that calls for greater scholarly attention, it has been shown here that there is no solid foundation on which to assert that money shop scrip (broadly defined) was "well accepted" in China in the late imperial era. This is because it constituted in all likelihood an insignificant part of China's currency stock prior to 1900 and because the circulation of such scrip was regionally fragmented if not parochial.

Private note issuance did play an exceedingly important role in Fuzhou circa the 1850s, but this setting was clearly not representative of the rest of China. Contrary to what proponents of "free banking" might believe, even within the confines of Fuzhou there had been recorded repeated banking breakdowns in the nineteenth century. On the whole, China's late imperial monetary system remained bimetallic in the nineteenth century, as received wisdom would suggest. Put otherwise, Chinese privately issued notes were *not* considered reliable to the extent that they could compensate for the late imperial relinquishment of monetary reins, primarily the lower levels of "cash" output compared with the Song era, and the reluctance to extensively mint silver coins or countermark foreign imports thereof.

The late Qing court was by and large reluctant to issue notes despite being aware of the emergence of private banknote issuance at the time. This was because of the failure of state issues in previous dynasties and because of the at best inconclusive experience with its own limited Shunzhi-reign issue. The court thus refrained from engaging in further issues right until it was mortally threatened by financial and political instability in 1850s. Yet even this Xianfeng-reign issue proved inflationary for various reasons and was abandoned within a few years. It the late 1890s state issues were resumed. However, from that point on the institutions disbursing Qing notes were joint-stock banks modeled on their foreign competitors. It was well after the fall of the dynasty (1912) that other Chinese modern banks were able to popularize notes deep in the rural interior.

In that sense, one could argue that sediments from China's premodern experience with paper money hindered its economic modernization to the extent that, circa 1900, it was still considerably less monetized than Japan and Western latecomer economies. Both in discourse and in practice, note issuance was strongly associated with social unrest, inflation, and fiscal crises throughout the Qing era. Neither do enduring metallic-reserve principles seem to have been applied. Equally important, the Chinese economy at that time still gravitated toward bullion and specie, in part as a safeguard against monetary excesses. Perhaps for these reasons, modern constituents of the money supply like bank deposits, securities, and other paper-based credit instruments remained underdeveloped in China right up until the 1920s, thereby holding back its financial-system catch-up with other parts of the world and resulting in all likelihood in comparatively high interest rates.

CHAPTER FIVE

British Banknote Issuance in China

Cross-Imperial Connections

BRITISH BANKNOTE ISSUANCE

Family-owned or joint-stock banks issuing notes convertible to bullion and payable on demand were fairly common in Europe at the beginning of the twentieth century. This phenomenon rapidly disappeared during the 1930s when central banks were taking charge of money supply across much of the Western world.[1] In East Asia, the legacy of privately funded European banks entrusted with the supply of currency in colonies and dominions with varying degrees of official approbation continued in a few cases after World War II and is still adhered to in Hong Kong SAR (Special Administrative Region) today.[2] Such banknotes percolated in large numbers into the few interstitial domains that remained outside European metropolitan suzerainty, quite often passing at a premium against local metallic currencies.[3] For example, around the 1900s, Hong Kong dollar banknotes were widely used in South China, while Straits Settlements dollar notes had already spread all over peninsular Malaya.[4]

Monetary links between European colonies and self-governing regions of East Asia were not limited to the inflow of colonial currencies like the Hong Kong or Strait Settlements dollar. One of the least known properties of early European joint-stock overseas banking is the fact that a considerable part of its note issue had been denominated in indigenous units of account and issued intraregionally. This characteristic emerged as a tenet of overseas banking in the early nineteenth century, when private British banks were allowed to issue notes in some of the newly emancipated colonies of Latin America. Similar issues were subsequently introduced in other parts of the world, where Western European banks could enjoy a comparatively free rein—East Asia, the Ottoman Empire, Ethiopia, and for a limited time even in Siberia.[5]

Deprived by the British Treasury of access to retail financial markets at home, British overseas banks tended to specialize geographically through different groups of founding investors who had firsthand knowledge of specific colonial economies and the respective commodity flows emanating therefrom.[6] Although overseas banks could and did solicit deposits in London (and Edinburgh) to finance inbound bills before World War I, Treasury regulations prevented them from granting loans to clients domiciled in the United Kingdom. Until well into the twentieth century, British savings, merchant, and clearing banks found, on the other hand, sufficient outlets for growth in Britain's rapidly expanding retail and industrial sectors, and they kept foreign engagements on the back burner. Consequently, there was little competition between domestic and overseas banks. These two banking communities were far from coterminous in the City of London either in corporate structure or in managerial makeup. Youssef Cassis has, for example, estimated that landed aristocrats and politicians were twice as likely to be found on British overseas bank boards than on savings or clearing bank boards.[7]

In the 1890s, British overseas banks spread over no less than 710 branches around the world, while London's largest domestic clearing banks—for example, Lloyd's and Barclays—operated no branches outside Britain.[8] However, British investors were inclined to consolidate a toehold in secure colonies, and banking was no different. Thus, the largest and longest-standing overseas banks in the mid-nineteenth century were ones strictly associated with colonies and dominions: the Bank of Australasia (est. 1835) and the Union Bank of Australia (est. 1837). It was only when the growth potential in the Antipodes declined that other investment groups shifted their attention to the Americas, India, Africa, continental Europe, and greater China.

The fundamental restrictions on note issuance applicable to British banks in such disparate countries as Brazil, Greece, and mainland China were standardized by the same set of guidelines, dating back to 1830s, that had been devised for the dominions. Drawn up by the British Treasury, these guidelines were commonly referred to as colonial currency regulations.[9] They effectively restricted each bank's geographical branch deployment and ensured the subordination of business practices to colonial authorities. Adherence to these regulations was a prerequisite that competing British groups, bent on investment in far-flung corners of the Empire, had to meet before applying for a Royal Charter that would bestow on them limited liability status.[10] From the perspective of investors, this was a trade-off between acknowledging Treasury supervision and receiving an incentive from the Crown in the form of limited liability to develop banking in remote territories. Notably, the legal precepts of limited liability were introduced to the British domestic financial sector only in 1858. But after limited liability had been introduced domestically, the provision of Royal Charters became a rarity.[11]

These features of early British overseas banks contrasted sharply with economic circumstances in continental Europe. Most nineteenth-century French, Dutch, and German colonial banks had sprung up from initiatives jointly undertaken by well-established domestic banks and the state rather than by ad hoc groups of investors. As a whole, European overseas banks like the Banque de L'Indochine or the Deutsch-Asiatische Bank worked more closely with French and German diplomatic missions around the world and benefited from broader note issue prerogatives and less stringent reserve requirements than those set out by the British Treasury.[12]

Because of its rich natural resources and underdeveloped domestic financial sector, Latin America was one the most attractive regions for European banking ventures in the mid-nineteenth century. British banks took the lead, claiming between a quarter and a third of all banking deposits in Argentina and Brazil at that period.[13] Consequently, Latin America retained one of the biggest amounts of overseas bank notes in circulation outside Asia. But a decade later political unrest cast a pall on financial stability in the region, as foreign banks were progressively ejected from the monetary domain to make way for fledgling national banks. In 1904, for example, the London and River Plate Bank—then the largest British bank in Latin America—was forced to substantially reduce its large banknote issue in Uruguay in favor of the new Banco de la República.[14]

The driving force behind the expansion of early British overseas banks into East Asia—known collectively at the time as the Eastern Exchange Banks—was increasing opposition in early and mid-nineteenth-century England to the tight grip of the East India Company (hereafter, EIC) on the finance of the lucrative opium trade.[15] The monopoly rights that EIC retained in India and China were revoked in 1813 and 1834 respectively, and it was to lose much of the exchange bill traffic between Asia and London soon afterwards.

During 1829 through 1834, leading Calcutta agency houses with which EIC had been associated, such as Palmers, Alexanders, Colvin & Co., and Cruttenden & Co., were succumbing to competition from new smaller trading firms that took advantage of the breakdown of EIC monopoly rights to undercut mercantile banking business.[16] Financiers in the City of London, colonial policy makers, and local Indian mercantile groups then identified exchange banking between India and China as pristine ground for investment. Nevertheless, the absence of effective limited liability laws overseas, as well as persistent EIC obstructionism, frustrated any progress. By the 1850s, small Anglo-Indian copartnerships involved in exchange banking had set up branches in Guangzhou and Hong Kong and operated there without explicit official patronage and, initially, without a charter: the Agra Bank, the North Western Bank of India, and the Bank of Western India.[17]

This fait accompli paralleled initiatives by well-heeled groups in London to lobby the government for a limited liability status in the form of a Royal Charter, which was first given to the Oriental Bank in 1851 (successor of the Bank of Western India) and later to the Chartered Bank of India Australia and China (hereafter, CBIAC), the Mercantile Bank of Bombay, and the Hongkong and Shanghai Banking Corporation (HSBC). Chartered and nonchartered banks alike sought to capitalize on the thriving opium trade between British India and China by selling bills drawn on their Indian branches to China-based importers of the narcotic. The silver proceeds could then be used to purchase discounted sterling bills from exporters of silk and tea, with which the Indian branches could cover their drafts on London.[18]

Yet the first generation of Eastern Exchange Banks disintegrated by the turn of the century. In 1866, there had nominally been eleven foreign banks operating in Hong Kong: the Oriental Bank; HSBC; CBIAC; the Chartered Mercantile Bank of India, London and China (CMBILC); Comptoir d'Escompte; the Agra Bank; the Commercial Bank of India; the Asiatic Bank; the Bank of Hindustan; the Bank of India; and the Central Bank of Western India. Within a year, the last six went into liquidation, leaving behind important client accounts that were quickly taken over by the CMBILC, CBIAC, and above all the newly formed "Hongkong Bank," to be more formally known later as HSBC.[19]

This trail of bankruptcy was largely the result of the Overend Gurney crisis in the City of London. The failure of this pivotal clearing bank was one of the most notorious financial failures in Victorian Britain.[20] It set off a chain reaction right across the City, because Overend Gurney had been one of the most important clearing banks on which financial institutions—including a large number of overseas banks—depended whenever they needed to discount drafts. The clearing bank stopped payment in May only a year after it shed its old Quaker family image to register as a joint-stock firm. The circumstances invited rumors about the founders' motives in floating the bank, while precariously diversifying into long-term investments that were well beyond the core business of discounting exchange bills. Ultimately, the new shareholders acrimoniously dissolved Overend Gurney, having to settle approximately £11 million in debt, owed in part by now-defunct overseas banks.[21]

In 1884, the Oriental Bank failed too. In this case, the prime factor was not a third party but the bank's overambitious distribution of agencies, which aimed to bridge numerous currency zones from Europe to Australasia but thinned out cash reserves in principal branches. One contemporary opined that the Oriental Bank had been "reckless" in its pursuit to pile up business in every corner of the world.[22] The downfall of the Oriental Bank heralded the second phase of exchange banking in East Asia, during which more regional specialization was introduced. From then on, the British Treasury subjected note issues by private British banks in Asia to more scrutiny because, at the height of its payment crisis, the convertibility of the Oriental Bank's notes in Ceylon, Burma, and Mauritius had to be guaranteed by the colonial governments concerned to stave off wider financial implications.[23]

For the exchange banks, mobilizing funds in Asia by issuing notes and accepting deposits was an imperative from the very outset because, as already indicated, their charters precluded similar activities in the United Kingdom. CBIAC, for example, was not permitted to undertake any retail banking activities in London until 1909 and had to refer clients to its acting agent, the City Bank, whenever withdrawals were made from head office current accounts.[24] Worse still was the toll that international currency fluctuations were taking on the Eastern Exchange Banks' stock, which was usually subscribed in gold-based pounds sterling but employed throughout silver-based Asia. While shareholders expected to net a proportionate amount of dividends in pounds, local branch operations and attendant profits were denominated in silver currencies that were rapidly depreciating against gold as from the 1860s.[25]

Note issuance was to complement resource accumulation through local deposit acceptances in the Asian branches of overseas banks and through discounting export drafts flowing along the trade routes among Britain, India, and China. This triangular traffic entrenched Britain's economic supremacy in the later half of the nineteenth century, whereby Chinese silk and tea exports to Britain would be essentially financed by Indian-grown surplus opium or by American-produced bullion.[26] India, in turn, absorbed British manufactured goods, particularly factory-made textiles, to offset British trade deficits with continental Europe and the Americas.

One of the principal attractions of overseas banking in the eyes of financiers in the City of London during the mid-nineteenth century was the comparatively high interest rates prevalent in East Asian entrepôts and the Australasian dominions.[27] Note issuance was arguably one of the most convenient ways of realizing quick gains from such market conditions because note bearers provided the banks with commensurate interest-free bullion that could be turned into high-yield short-term loans. At the same time, banknote issuance was important as a source of working capital for newly established overseas banks because attracting fixed-term deposits in the dominions, colonies, and concession areas took years and was hampered by competition from traditional financial institutions.

In the 1830s banks of issue across the British and French colonial empires were often more profitable than mercantile banks. East Asia was particularly appealing to British bankers because private bank note issuance at home was progressively phased out by the Bank of England and because the semiofficial Presidency Banks were assuming a monopoly on paper money through much of the Indian subcontinent during the 1870s.[28]

Unlike their British counterparts, French overseas banks rarely had to apply for supplemental charter renewal and normally enjoyed monopolistic legal tender benefits in French colonial possessions. However, British and French banks often shared similar charter guidelines relative to their note issues: a minimum of one-third bullion reserve against notes was considered elementary in Europe during much of the nineteenth century.[29] Notably, monetary conventions in Shanghai and other Chinese treaty ports differed from colonial possessions in that many types of quasi-foreign banknotes were circulating there *concomitantly*, and no European power could effectively enforce the paper currency of its preferred banks on local bearers as legal tender.

The British Treasury and Colonial Office were at pains to prevent chartered British banks from forming issue monopolies and made sure that private notes did not attain legal tender status in any single territory across Asia. To protect undiscerning or impecunious bearers, the Treasury often imposed double liability on private bank issues and aimed to confine note values to large denominations.[30] The Treasury's line quite often conflicted with the aims of colonial governors, who were anxious to see money supply in their cash-starved entrepôts increasing without shouldering any of the printing and administrative costs associated therewith.[31]

During the early twentieth century, British overseas banks were stripped of their prerogatives as suppliers of colonial currency in Australasia, Canada, Africa, and other parts of the British Empire, while in Asia the governments of Japan and Siam severely restricted the latitude of foreign banks operating on their soil.[32] Thus, by the 1910s overseas bank notes became a distinct Chinese treaty-port phenomenon, countenanced by the retention of European extraterritorial rights and denominated in either the traditional silver tael or local variations of Mexican dollar units.

BRITISH OVERSEAS BANKING IN CHINA

The first British banks to operate in East Asia during the 1850s had been set up in British India only a decade earlier. It is important to understand that when these banks began issuing notes in East Asia, the notion of fiduciary money—let alone central banking—was still relatively novel in Europe. Like private banks of issue in the metropolis, India-based banks were subject to stringent British Treasury guidelines aimed at protecting uninformed note bearers. The transition in English banking from unlimited to limited liability, which reshaped the regulatory underpinning of London as a global financial center, came into its own only in the late 1870s and was least influential in overseas banking. The practice of overseas banknote issuance remained, therefore, predicated on a nineteenth-century contingency, as central banking was sweeping across Europe in the early twentieth century.

During the early twentieth century, European, American, and Japanese banks also entered the Chinese market. All these entrants—however divergent their backgrounds—cleared each other's banknotes in China; the foreign, non-British sector was, on the other hand, beset by salient bank failures through much the same period. In 1914, the Allies forced the Deutsch-Asiatische Bank branches in China to shut down. The branches were barely able to resume their operation in 1918; the Banque Russo-Asiatique, nominally a Sino–Russian joint venture but effectively a French-owned private firm, had to be reconstituted in the wake of the Bolshevik Revolution in 1917 and ultimately failed in 1925; the Asiatic Banking Corporation, a Sino–American joint venture, was on the brink of failure in 1924 and was eventually sold off to the International Banking Corporation;[33] the Chinese-American Bank of Commerce, another U.S. joint venture, suspended business in 1928;[34] but perhaps the failure most inimical to the reputation of foreign financial institutions occurred in 1921, when the French-owned Banque Industrielle de Chine had to suspend the convertibility of its Shanghai notes until Chinese banks came to its rescue.[35]

Therefore, the rivalry between foreign and domestic banks during the Republican era should not be overstated. As much as Chinese banks benefited from the surge in nationalism after 1919, they seldom agitated against their foreign competitors. The two banking sectors were still interconnected and, for the most part, subscribed to a fundamental division of labor between the finance of international trade (by foreign banks) and business transacted in local currency, like call loans by Chinese modern banks to *qianzhuang* (private money shops). Notably, archival work by Chinese scholars has demonstrated that at least one Chinese modern bank and several *qianzhuang* deposited idle funds with foreign banks on a regular basis.[36]

More generally, British overseas banking could preserve its lead over other foreign banks in Asia until the 1920s largely because of London's preeminence as the number one clearing hub in the world and because U.S. banks had been preoccupied with Latin America until the 1910s; U.S. multinationals were latecomers into Southeast Asia and the Chinese treaty ports. Although they gradually became leading creditors elsewhere in the world, American financial institutions kept a modest regional presence outside the Philippines before World War I.[37]

The early India-based British exchange banks were usually known as "Anglo-Indian." As mentioned, these banks had been set up to cash in on the breakup of the Canton trade system and of the East India Company monopoly on intra-Asian trade and finance in 1833.[38] They discounted exchange bills and converted currencies, but their legal status was vague, and their ties with London's money markets and colonial policy makers remained tenuous. In 1851, a new era began when the Oriental Bank (set up as the Bank of Western India in 1843 and established in Shanghai by 1847) gained a Royal Charter, which enabled it to transfer its headquarters to London, expand its exchange business across Australasia and Africa, and issue banknotes in a large number of British colonies and dependencies. Two years later, CBIAC gained a similar concession and swiftly established branches throughout East and Southeast Asia. In 1865, a portentous Hong Kong Colonial Ordinance gave much the same powers to a bank jointly established by the colony's richest merchants—HSBC.

Together, foreign banks were responsible for a very large inventory of paper currency issued in China and its environs between 1865 and 1935. This is perhaps why the first observers to take keen interest in this prewar monetary phenomenon have been numismatists. Notably, the number of catalogues documenting the different specimens of foreign banknotes in China exceeds by far the number of studies authored by Chinese economic historians or academics generally interested in "free banking."[39]

Foreign banknotes in China embodied influential novel design and advanced print technology, but they were certainly not the only common means of payment current in and around the treaty ports that the European powers had carved up among themselves along the China coast during 1842 through 1914. Neither did they constitute the only form of paper money during that period.

That China did not have a uniform currency during the Ming and Qing dynasties is a well-known historic fact highlighted in the previous chapter. The most ubiquitous form of high-denomination money in the late imperial era was sycee—that is, silver bullion weighing approximately fifty tael with local variations in fineness—or Spanish-American silver dollars; silver bullion as well as traditional bronze coinage was widespread all over China well into the 1930s. From the mid-nineteenth century, successive Chinese governments and warlord regimes had issued various types of paper currency, often imitating foreign designs but with an uneven record of success. In addition, private money shop scrip, remittance drafts, military wage coupons, product certificates, and even, later, underground Communist Party paper currency were circulating in different parts of the country concurrently.[40]

Yet, owing to the extraterritorial setting in which foreign firms operated in the treaty ports, foreign banknotes acquired a contentious characteristic. Unlike Chinese currency, foreign banknote issuance was not regulated in situ by any sovereign government. Although often denominated in traditional Chinese units of account, foreign banknotes were issued at will by private financial institutions operating on Chinese soil yet entirely impervious to Chinese authority.

MONETARY FRAGMENTATION

One of the most vexing problems British businessmen faced as they penetrated deeper into the Chinese mainland from their older strongholds in Hong Kong and Guangzhou in the late 1840s was what they saw as the Chinese mainland's refractory currency system. At first, some tinkered with the idea of proclaiming the sterling standard in Hong Kong as an anchor of monetary stability. But, by the early 1860s, most British imperial policy makers in the region had come to realize that, as complex as China's system was, it was much too entrenched to give way to a uniform currency promoted by a small number of foreigners in a colony perched on "a mere barren rock."[41] Subsequently, the Hong Kong currency was to adapt to the preferred store of value on the mainland:

the silver dollar. The colony's subsidiary coinage, too, largely emulated China's copper cash. While the Hong Kong currency was framed into the Chinese system, it was hoped that it would at least escape the adulteration that its generic equivalents on the mainland suffered from and would gain wide acceptance throughout the Celestial Empire. But the limits of this conjecture soon became apparent: The Hong Kong currency remained at best one of many foreign currencies circulating in littoral China. In Shanghai, where the institutional and cadastral underpinning of British settlement was much more patchy than in Hong Kong, early attempts to introduce Hong Kong minted silver coins denominated in the local tael failed to take root.[42] For the next century or so, the city's foreign concession areas had to rely on Chinese coinage and recast imported bullion for their metallic money supply.

Shanghai initially attracted the British because of its expedient location as a gateway to the Lower Yangzi Basin.[43] The first British bankers to descend on the region in the 1850s realized that the key to success there was mastery of prevailing currency vagaries, and some would later show intimate knowledge thereof. Charles Addis, then a Scottish debutant recruited by the HSBC to be sent East, observed as early as 1886:[44]

The only money which circulates universally throughout the length and breadth of the land is copper cash. With regard to other kinds, an intense provincialism prevails—silver lumps, silver dollars, small silver pieces, and copper cents circulating on their face value only in the province where they are minted, in other provinces at a discount. In the case of foreign [coins], there is some, which circulate throughout the treaty-ports. Some kinds of tael notes, dollar notes, or [copper-denominated] notes, issued by Chinese banks or exchange houses circulate only in the city where they are issued. A traveller when passing from one province to another should be careful to change the money of the former for the latter.

These remarks are revealing because they were made shortly before HSBC launched its banknote issue in Shanghai. Although the passage does not bespeak anticipation of this event, it does demonstrate that British bankers had certainly come to grips with the Chinese monetary system.

What British bankers had to accommodate, though, was the fact that none of the treaties that China had signed with different European powers in the late nineteenth century sanctioned foreign bank presence beyond the designated treaty ports, of which Shanghai became the largest. With the exception of Beijing, British banks could not set up branches in areas under effective Chinese jurisdiction. This meant that the farther one ventured out of Shanghai, the less likely one would be to come across quasi-foreign banknotes in use.[45]

But there was much more to this than jurisdiction because notes were traditionally assessed in the Chinese marketplace based on their place of issue, while particular bank insignia were of less importance. An informed Western testimonial from 1904 described foreign bank practices as follows:[46]

The principal foreign banks [in China] are [HSBC], the Chartered Bank of India Australia and China, the Yokohama Specie Bank, [Banque Russo-Asiatique], [Deutsche-Asiatic Bank], and [Banque de L'Indochine]. These banks do a considerable deposit and discount business . . . [They] do their business in China without any contract with the Chinese government, and with no charter issued by that government. They are there simply on tolerance . . . with the protection of extraterritoriality.

[S]everal of these banks issue bank notes under the authority of their charters from home, but without any charter or other grant of privilege from the Chinese government, either central or provincial. The bank notes form a convenient medium of circulation in some of the treaty-ports and within narrow limits outside of those ports . . .

A Shanghai bank note, for example, is very generally discounted if presented to the Tientsin [Tianjin] or Peking [Beijing] or Hongkong branch of the same [foreign] bank, the discount sometimes being as high as 5 per cent, although the two cities are only some three hours apart by railroad . . .

The [foreign] banks are, generally speaking, known for their accuracy and carefulness in carrying out their contracts and in meeting their obligations. But they occupy a position of such advantage in many ways that it seems likely that their high profits are obtained in part at the expense of the development of trade in other directions in spite of the fact, one may add with even more emphatic truthfulness, without the facilities which they have offered, it would have been utterly impossible for trade to have developed anywhere nearly so well as has been the case.

In a later note on Chinese currency, probably from the early 1910s, Addis made a similar if less critical remark:[47]

Foreign coins circulated widely in all the treaty-ports and in the larger cities of China. But the [foreign] banknotes circulate only in the city where they are issued; for instance, those issued by a bank in Shanghai not being accepted by merchants of Peking [Beijing], or only at a discount.

Monetary fragmentation in China intensified toward the demise of the Qing Dynasty and through the Beiyang period (1912–1927). Though both regimes promulgated countless measures to the contrary, these Beijing-based late imperial and early republican governments had made monetary fragmentation much worse by resorting to debasement to jack up seigniorage revenue from newly founded state mints. Initially, Qing provincial governors purchased European minting machinery to increase the output of bronze coinage, which had been in short supply throughout the late nineteenth century, as Ho Hon-wai has ably shown.[48] Once at work, the governors soon realized that modern technology extended government capacity to reduce the intrinsic value of the coins while passing them off as equivalent to time-honored units of payment. This had far-reaching, often horrendous, effects because low-denomination bronze coinage was the lifeblood of retail in the Chinese premodern economy. While it expedited the recourse to private fiduciary currency in some localities, the debasement resulted in an inflationary spiral and breakdown of trust in metallic money in others.

While the British overseas banks' increasingly potent position as supplier of fiduciary money across East Asia prompted prudence among Treasury regulators in London, it was by no means lost on China's imperial bureaucracy. The growth of foreign banking in Shanghai had generally stimulated late Qing reformers like Zhang Zhidong and Zhang Jian to memorialize the Throne on the acute underdevelopment of China's financial sector.[49] The reformers complained that, without institutions operating on foreign bank principles and comprehensive currency overhaul, China would be unable to sustain a much-needed military and industrial buildup. They noted with chagrin that China's own financial institutions were not cut out for such a task because they were too diffuse. Traditional, privately owned money shops had been regularly issuing paper money in China from at least the late Ming, but its circulation was constricted along regional lines; it was subordinate to wide variations of silver fineness and suffered from mass forgeries.[50]

Structural disparities between the two sectors partly derived from geographical distribution: Chinese banks had, of course, much more leeway to popularize notes in the vast hinterland that stretched beyond the confines of the treaty ports.[51] But the disparities may have also derived from overemphasis late Qing reformers had laid at banknote issuance as a definitive constituent of modern banking. The reformers were quick to note how China's institutional weakness invited foreign banks to recoup profits from note issuance in the treaty ports but failed to heed attendant reserve requirements, which set foreign banks apart from traditional financial institutions. Zheng Guanying epitomized this partiality. As a comprador for Butterfield, Swire and Co., he witnessed foreign business practices from within. Turned an official, he commented with disdain that the proliferation of quasi-foreign notes was merely a result of mercantile inertia and cronyism (*xunqing*) in China's financial sector.[52]

Zheng and others called on the Throne to foster government-run banks to counter foreign economic inroads. Their frame of references and argumentation were not completely different to those of Qing bureaucrats—like Wang Maoyin—who had previously tried to persuade the Manchus to print paper money as panacea for the dynastic decline. Nonetheless, the traditional monetary discourse did change to the extent that the early reformers had been castigated during the 1850s, whereas reformers in the 1890s could make more daring, foreign-sounding suggestions—like the adoption of a gold standard—with impunity.[53]

The most trenchant of Zheng's commentaries on current affairs prescribed concrete measures to stem the Qing's relinquishment of macroeconomic reins. As early as 1873, he suggested for example that Sichuan-grown opium be promoted as substitute for imported opium from India and that imperial consulates be opened in Singapore and San Francisco to tap overseas Chinese wealth.[54] On monetary issues, he was unequivocal: China's monetary fragmentation could be solved only if decisive government action was taken to stamp out debasement and disallow casting by provincial officials or private businessmen.[55] Tellingly, he pinned down HSBC's success in China to its ability to raise capital from both Chinese and foreign shareholders, its strategy to entice petty cash depositors from all walks of life, and the way in which it employed interest-free proceeds from banknote issuance to on-lend.[56]

In the interim, the dilemma for the thinly endowed Throne remained the same: how to retain imperial revenue without unleashing inflation that would provoke popular resistance and without surrendering more central powers. The late imperial body politic was often blighted by indecision and contradictory thrusts that precluded lasting synergy between the state and private spheres in the realm of money. By the mid-nineteenth century, perhaps earlier, this shortfall had opened up a gaping loophole through which privately funded British trading houses and Anglo-Indian financial institutions could thrive on China's coastline.[57] Ultimately, it was the affluent executives of these treaty port firms, the *taipans*, who guaranteed that the eastern thrust of Her Britannic Majesty's gunboats would remain economically sustainable.[58]

Though they benefited from China's economic malaise in the short run, British financiers and their lobbyists in the diplomatic missions had good reason to be wary of a complete monetary nemesis that might eventually project on the prosperity of the treaty ports.[59] In 1908, for example, the British Legation in Beijing informed the Foreign Office that "[the] Shanghae [sic] General Chambers of Commerce has, for some months past, been concerned at the issue of dollar notes by Chinese banks without any restriction or control on the part of the government."[60] The Chambers then approached Shanghai's Taotai [*daotai*], the once all-powerful prefectural commissioner, to clarify the restrictions under which money shops and banks were entitled to issue notes. The Taotai, on his part, was indignant about the fact that foreign banks in the city refused to accept Chinese banknotes of whatever provenance, other than those issued by the Imperial Bank of China. Somewhat confused, he replied that—although unenforced—government regulations restricting unbacked note issues were in effect. Consequently, the British Legation decided to join forces with the foreign banks in applying pressure on Prince Qing and the Board of Finance (*duzhi bu*) to draw up measures for stricter control of China's banks.

In a subsequent statement, the legation did not mince words in an effort to rouse the Board of Finance to action. Observed from the foreign enclaves in the treaty ports, the severity of the situation in the periphery was compelling. It intensified what had already been seen as an intractable currency system:[61]

[It is reported that] the Provincial Bank at Hankow [Hankou], of unknown capital, has a note circulation of over 20 million dollars, that the private bank at Shanghae [*sic*] has issued notes equivalent to its paid-up capital, that another at Hangchow [Hangzhou] has notes of a face value more than three times in excess of its paid-up capital, and that two other institutions at Soochow [Suzhou] and Nanking [Nanjing], with no paid-up capital but with a guarantee from the provincial government, have placed in circulation notes of an aggregate face value of over 2 million.

It should be pointed out that the good reputation that the Imperial Bank of China still enjoyed among foreigners at that stage was due to the fact that the bank's patron, Sheng Xuanhuai, had partly modeled it on the HSBC in 1897, despite concerns raised by Zhang Zhidong and opposition from some *zongli yamen* officials fearing "excessive" private ownership.[62] The Imperial Bank of China was the country's first limited-liability bank, the first to employ foreign staff, and the first of many Chinese banks to order notes from overseas printers.[63] In conformity with early HSBC guidelines, the Imperial Bank of China's total banknote issue was at no time to exceed paid-up capital, and one-third thereof was to be covered by a cash reserve. However, fragmentary

balance-sheet data suggest that this stipulation may not have been enforced after 1906.[64]

Imperial attempts at regulating banks and currency in China came too
little, too late. When financial regulations were finally promulgated, the
survival of the dynasty had already been predicated on synarchic pacts
with the European powers, so that the issue of quasi-foreign money or
restrictions on foreign banking in general were hardly broached.[65] The
Mackay Treaty signed between Britain and China on September 5, 1902
included, for example, an imperial pledge to coin uniform currency
"which shall be legal tender in payment of all duties taxes and other
obligations throughout the Empire by British and Chinese subjects."[66]

By the late 1890s, the protestations of reformers paved the way for
a mushrooming of government-run provincial banks across China.[67]
These banks tried to lay down roots primarily by circulating paper
notes modeled on novel designs and printing technology that were inspired by the foreign bank notes, rather than by China's own traditional
drafts (*piaotie*). Nonetheless, Chinese modern banks often fell prey to
the shortsightedness of their political patrons, who merely harnessed
branch managers to expand their revenue base. Figuratively speaking,
the first Chinese banks were made to jump the queue: They had drawn
on note issuance to attract metallic money long before they could claim
a solid customer base, and their management was dismally interwoven
into that of government ministries.

British banks did not aim at reshaping China's regional monetary
fragmentation. Neither could they command a large portion of China's
money supply from their treaty ports enclaves. In Shanghai, the Western
community relied on the Chinese mercantile caucus just as the latter
counted on foreign judicial and military protection. The period from
1895 to 1914 marked the zenith of European imperialism in China
proper, but even then—with decades of local experience behind them—
British overseas banks could scarcely engage the agrarian interior of the
country without the mediation of local compradors and treaty port mar-
keting guilds.[68] The European colonial powers could break into Chinese
imperial coffers through the imposition of war indemnities and brow-
beat a motley crew of warlord-dominated governments into surrendering custom revenues and railway concessions. However, none of these
factors could fulfil the hyperbole of the propaganda holding out the
prospect of hundreds of millions of consumers in the hinterland eager
for foreign manufactured goods.[69] Therein lay the fabled resilience of
China's preindustrial economy.

THE EVOLUTION OF NOTE RESERVE REQUIREMENTS

Colonial currency regulations imposed in the mid-nineteenth century fairly lenient reserve requirements against note issues by British overseas banks. At times, regulations could be inconsistent and oversight diffuse. In the grand scheme of things, the lords commissioners of the Treasury in Whitehall personified the conventional wisdom of regulatory experience accumulated on the British Isles. Experience in Europe taught that private banks must be forced to keep coin reserve in proportion to the amount of banknotes they issued, and this rule was to be applied to the colonies too. However, quite often, monetary deviations from European norms had to be accommodated. The case for regulatory adjustment was made, in the first instance, by those who were more in tune with local realities—that is, colonial and dominion governments. The secretary of state for the colonies was their effective channel of communication with Treasury regulators. Because the East Asian treaty ports were not strictly under the secretary's jurisdiction, the Foreign Office and diplomatic corps had to be consulted, too, when it came to the issue of quasi-foreign notes in China.

British overseas banks were generally expected to keep a liquid cash reserve on the order of one-third of their notes outstanding in the treaty ports. However, in the absence of widespread telegraph facilities or robust metropolitan inspection, local branches were underregulated until the late 1890s, and this guideline was seldom enforced there.[70] The Hong Kong Ordinances, under which HSBC was incorporated, allowed the Bank to keep a single note reserve in its Hong Kong head office. In theory, therefore, banks headquartered in London were at a disadvantage because they were expected to maintain overlapping reserves to meet contingencies both in Hong Kong and in their other Asian branches.[71]

But when it came to enforcement, the Treasury was sidetracked by minor issues. For example, the Treasury persistently opposed the dissemination of notes in small denominations (under five silver dollars) and subjected note issuance as a whole to double—and in HSBC's case, unlimited—liability, to protect undiscerning bearers of little wealth.[72] This principle was relatively easy to apply in Hong Kong and the Straits Settlements. Yet the Treasury was apparently uninformed as to what was happening in the treaty ports, where British banks violated the stipulation by disseminating one tael and one Mexican dollar notes.

The failure of the Oriental Banking Corporation in 1884—the oldest and hitherto largest British bank in Asia—was an important catalyst for intensifying Treasury regulation of overseas banks during the nineteenth century.[73] OBC left hundreds of clients around the world clamoring for compensation. In Ceylon, where it had a particularly large note circulation, the crisis threatened to destabilize much of the colonial economy. Ceylon's governor therefore decided to guarantee the issue, setting a precedent for official protection of private note issues at which the Treasury fretted.[74]

The Treasury was now compelled to step up its scrutiny of far-flung territories to avoid a repetition of the Ceylon crisis. One upshot was that local coin or bullion reserves to support note issuance overseas were no longer deemed sufficient. When, in 1889, HSBC tried to gain *ex post* recognition from the Treasury of its branches and note issuance outside Hong Kong, the Treasury presented a new condition: From now on the Bank was to deposit with trustees "securities specially appropriated to cover its note issue."[75] In practice, the Treasury's new guidelines entailed an additional note reserve to the metallic one, to be made up of tradable assets under lien to the colonial government. Furthermore, the reserves would now total two-thirds of the circulation volume—almost halving potential profits accruing from the fiduciary (read: uncovered) portion of the issue.[76]

Differences soon emerged between HSBC and the Treasury as to what assets could be designated as security. The Bank was naturally inclined to present idle resources: It offered over $1.1 million of the $2.5 million required in title deeds and private company bonds, which it had received against loans or purchase of branch premises. The remaining $1.5 million were to be covered by Chinese imperial government bonds, which paid relatively high dividends but hinged on the shifting political fortune of the Manchu court. The Treasury was unimpressed: It threatened to have the Colonial Office suspend the Bank's incorporation ordinance unless a different portfolio of securities was presented.[77] Faced with a near ultimatum and potential ramifications in the future, the Bank had to give in. In August 1890, it presented a new portfolio that the Treasury could sanction: Title deeds were to be replaced by Indian government rupee bonds.[78]

Until the twentieth century, the China issue was not specifically addressed by the Treasury because it was still insignificant as a share of the Bank's total issue. This was because of two very different reasons. Primarily, Chinese suspicion of paper notes had roots dating as far back as the fourteenth century and meant that treaty port demand for this medium of payment trailed far behind the vigorous monetization that typified Hong Kong and the Straits Settlements.[79] Apart from that, the British banks operating in East Asia were strategically concerned with the entrepôt trade flowing through the colonies. The banks, therefore, allocated a smaller portion of their global issue quotas, set by the Treasury, to the treaty ports.

The China issue became a strategic factor in British Exchange Bank thinking only in the early twentieth century, when it served as a counterweight to receding circulation volumes in Southeast Asia. In 1902, moves by the Straits Settlements to replace the three private banks of issue—HSBC, CBIAC, and the Mercantile Bank of India (MBI)—with a sterling-pegged governmental currency came to fruition. A gold standard for the Straits had been on the drawing board in conjunction with a government issue a decade before but was stonewalled by these three Eastern Exchange Banks until then.[80] Similar moves to introduce a governmental currency did not materialize in Hong Kong because its economy had been much more intimately linked with the silver-based Chinese economy. But, perhaps more crucially, HSBC executives enjoyed an unusual rapport with many of the Colony's governors—a fact that may have clinched the survival of private banknote issuance there.[81]

To what extent was the loss of the Straits banknote issue a blow to the British banks? A proper answer would require an analysis of the profits accruing from local note issuance. Fortunately, some editions of the *Straits Settlement Government Gazette* recorded the reserves that the banks assigned for their local issue by virtue of an Order-in-Council, whereas reserves against the China issue were never specified in *Hong Kong Blue Book* aggregates. In August 1898, for example, HSBC assigned "unspecified specie and securities" totalling S\$1.6 million against S\$4 million of note circulation in Penang and Singapore.[82] This amounted to a 40 percent cover—26 percent less than the statutory reserve imposed on the Bank's issue in Hong Kong. It is therefore safe to assume that the reserve ratio was much lower in principal branches than in the Bank's Hong Kong headquarters and that local profit margins were similarly wider there.

The point can be further illustrated by using in-house data that are available for CBIAC. In 1898, this bank had a total reserve of S\$1.3 assigned against just under S\$4 million in circulation.[83] This amounted to just 33 percent cover for the local issue, of which only S\$830,000 was metallic. With two-thirds of the issue practically uncovered, and allowing for a moderate interest rate of 2.5 percent, the bank was in a position to garner a gross profit of S\$80,000 annually, if it channelled the fiduciary portion of the proceeds to its borrowing clients. When converted to sterling, profits accruing from the Straits issue alone may well have constituted as much as 5 percent of CBIAC's total profits that year.[84]

Developments in the Straits Settlements at the turn of the century were compounded by the loss of smaller markets for banknotes in Japan and Siam, as governments there decided to revoke foreign bank privileges. HSBC's note circulation in the Japanese treaty ports of Kobe and Yokohama never attained much importance, but Bangkok had held out for some time the potential for large circulation volume. HSBC was the principal European bank entrusted with paper money supply in Siam; the Chartered Bank (CBIAC) and the Saigon-based Banque de L'Indochine played a much more modest role. In July 1902 all three banks were asked to withdraw their issue, which by then had amounted to about 2.5 million tical in total.[85]

The issue quota set by the British banks for China rose immediately after they realized that they were about to lose Southeast Asian note markets. As early as 1899, HSBC head office in Hong Kong informed the Shanghai branch that it had revised the cap placed on the circulation of locally denominated notes in the mainland from $1 million to $1.5 million—two-thirds of which was allocated for Shanghai.[86] But despite the increase in HSBC circulation volumes on the mainland, metallic and bond reserves that were meant to cover the issue remained in Hong Kong. In the absence of specific Treasury guidelines on China, the Bank had simply taken a calculated risk that it would be able to withstand possible redemption waves with minimal reserves.

Toward the end of the nineteenth century there was another important turning point in Treasury policy that would counterweigh the gradual withdrawal of notes in the Straits. In 1898, the Treasury allowed HSBC's note circulation to exceed the Bank's paid-up capital for the first time, if the Bank was prepared to put up 100 percent metallic cover. The concession was made because the Bank and its proponents in the Hong Kong government argued that sudden demand spurts for notes in the Colony shortly before the Lunar New Year could only be met with a special "excess issue."[87] From then on, the Bank's total circulation quota grew according to a set pattern, whereby the "New Year" argument would be used repeatedly to incorporate previous ad hoc excess issues into the authorized one while setting new excess caps for the future. This resulted, as from the end of the imperial era in China, in total circulation levels that were far greater than paid-up capital but backed by a larger metallic reserve.[88]

There had been a steady rise in the global circulation quota that the Treasury sanctioned. However, this rise was accompanied by a narrowing down of the fiduciary (or uncovered) portion of the total issue. In other words, the potential for profit accruing from note issuance wore down over the course of time. Until 1888, the fiduciary ratio stood at 66.6 percent. In other words, as much as two-thirds of the silver bullion or coins that Bank clients paid in over the counter in return for notes could be on-lent without cover. As previously explained, this was the period when Treasury underregulation in China was at its height. Between 1889 and 1897 the fiduciary ratio dropped to one-third. In 1898 it stood at 22 percent and continued to diminish steadily thereafter. The overview suggests that profits accruing from note issuance during the Bank's formative years may have played a significant role in its meteoric rise.

How did the changes in the global issue quota project outside Hong Kong? By 1904, there were definite signs that popular suspicion of notes in China had subsided. In addition, the fact that HSBC's Shanghai branch was not required to hold metallic reserves against treaty port circulation also made local managers keen to issue notes there. These factors were, however, tempered by a head office primarily concerned with money supply in Hong Kong. In November 1904 Head Office informed Shanghai:[89]

We quite appreciate the difficulties you experience in having so limited a circulation, but you know the trouble we have each China New Year now in providing cover for the bank's large banknote circulation [in Hong Kong] at the time . . . [After the] China New Year you may increase your limit to 20 lacs.

In other words, the last tentative China quota set internally in 1899 (1.5 million silver dollars) was to increase by 0.5 million. The circulation grew apace from then on until about 1924. Extant branch records suggest that by 1908 Shanghai notes denominated in Mexican dollars reached a circulation of $1.5 million (about Tls. 1 million), and tael-denominated notes reached a circulation of Tls. 115,000.[90] At the same time, demand in Tianjin and smaller treaty ports perked up. Overall, circulation of HSBC notes in mainland China rose to a peak of $4.3 million circa 1923, by which time tael notes had largely been phased out.

On the eve of the Xinhai revolution (1911), the China issue had already supplanted Southeast Asia as the second most important market for notes in the Bank's strategy. The way in which the head office had come to view the issue of quasi-foreign notes on the mainland was tersely stated in a memorandum it relayed to the Shanghai branch in December:[91]

Your note issue in Shanghai does not embarrass us beyond our having to put up [Hong Kong] dollar for [Mexican] dollar here. So long as you do not object to incurring dollar liabilities at current price of Mexicans, and there should not be much risk in that, you may go on issuing notes moderately, say up to $30 lacs.

The wording inevitably retains some of the Eastern Exchange Bank jargon. Put simply, the head office gave the branch permission to increase its circulation up to 3 million silver dollars (the value of the Hong Kong dollar and Mexican dollar current in Shanghai being similar). Yet, globally, the Bank had a considerable "excess issue" by 1911. Because its first priority was Hong Kong's money supply, and because no note reserves had been kept in China proper at that time, the Bank effectively designated its China issue as part of the "excess issue." Thus, the China issue required full metallic backing: one silver dollar in the Hong Kong central reserve for every dollar note disbursed in Shanghai. More importantly, the memorandum indicates that—even with 100 percent reserve set against it—the Shanghai issue was seen as a generally remunerative pursuit from a head office perspective.

Net profitability of the China issue may have stemmed from a combination of higher market interest rates in Shanghai, coupled with a cross-rate premium on the Mexican dollar against the Hong Kong dollar. Either way, there was another much more prosaic factor that made the China issue attractive: Note issuance was exempt from both Chinese and foreign government tax in the treaty ports, whereas it incurred a 1 percent surcharge in Hong Kong.[92]

Other evidence to support that the China note issue was, on balance, highly profitable is indirect: HSBC archives contain a number of files documenting attempts by con men to make the Bank disburse silver over the counter on presentation of fake notes and the Bank's unstinting investment in improving printing plates and in other preventive measures. The first serious forgery could well have been the one that Charles Addis, then Beijing branch manager, entered into his private diary in 1903: "There has been a forgery of H&S Bank $5 notes, and there is alarm among the Chinese principally. The Bank has been kept open all day."[93]

Notably, this short entry also seems to suggest that most note bearers were Chinese rather than European expatriates. It is therefore plausible to assume that the first forgers were Chinese, and so were their victims. However, the quality of the forged notes was *not* such that the Bank considered forfeiting issuance altogether. At the same time, the Bank seemed to have spared no effort in trying to minimize the risk: In 1901, for example, the Shanghai branch accountant burnt unsigned idle notes to the face value of over SH$1 million.[94]

THE 1925 BOYCOTT OF BRITISH BANKS IN SHANGHAI

The May 30th Incident broke out in 1925 in Shanghai when a labor dispute in a Japanese textile factory situated in a British-policed concession area escalated into a commercial strike and yearlong nationalist boycott against British goods, sweeping across other treaty ports and Hong Kong.[95] The protest movement that the incident sparked off marked a definitive turning point in Sino–foreign relations. Not only did it force the powers to enter negotiations with the Chinese government over treaty revision and the eventual abolition of extraterritoriality, but it also changed long-standing Western perception of the Chinese as servile.

At the height of this conflict, CBIAC was compelled to send Portuguese clerks from Hong Kong to replace large numbers of local staff on the mainland, who had collectively resigned.[96] British firms operating deep in the interior were not spared either: The Peking Syndicate mines at Jiaozuo (Henan Province), for example, had been forced to shut down and did not recover until 1933.[97]

The violent demonstrations rocked British diplomatic legations and militated an increasingly assertive group of Chinese modern banks to fold back cooperation with their foreign counterparts.[98] Despite relative insulation from the hinterland economy and the transient nature of the boycott, banknotes had become by then one of the most tangible aspects of the British banks' presence in the treaty ports and were therefore particularly vulnerable to popular rejection as a means of payment.[99]

The boycott of British bank notes in Shanghai during 1925 has not attracted much scholarly attention, mainly because it had been transpiring backstage and was played down in expatriate press reports.[100] In other words, while the relentless campaign against British consumer goods produced immediate repercussions in bilateral trade statistics and was constantly decried by the British expatriate community in China, accurate information on the extent of British bank note redemption and deposit withdrawals was largely confined to confidential branch correspondence. The Chinese press, on its part, often reported on student activists who—at the height of the conflict—demanded that Shanghai's merchant and banking guilds declare an all-out currency war against quasi-foreign notes, that "wayward" moneychangers who accept quasi-foreign notes be punished, and that all Chinese residents of the city withdraw their deposits from foreign banks.[101] But in the lack of substantive information on the outcome of such calls, Chinese newspapers were more prone to cover the boycott of British-made products, which had readily available—and fairly reliable—local substitutes: cigarettes, kerosene, drugs, and luxury items.

Hong Jiaguan has argued that, perhaps more than any other event in the twentieth century, the May 30th events helped Chinese modern banking flourish, and he has pointed to a 71.4 percent rise in the volume of funds deposited therein through 1925.[102] While such dramatic advances cannot be ruled out offhand, the CBIAC Shanghai branch balance sheet does not indicate a comparable drop in foreign bank deposits.

CBIAC fixed deposits in Shanghai merely dropped from Tls. 7.9 million in December 1924 to Tls. 6.3 million in December 1925, while current accounts actually climbed from Tls. 7.7 million to Tls. 8.5.[103] Considering the fact that the CBIAC note circulation volume in the city was almost halved during the same period, deposit levels clearly show that Chinese response to the antiforeign agitation was by no means uniform. Namely, it seems plausible to assume that Chinese bearers were keen to redeem quasi-foreign banknotes, which were of a highly visible nature, but were less inclined to entrust funds long deposited in foreign banks to Chinese equivalents.

In early June 1925, Shanghai money shops and Chinese-owned banks struck in solidarity with the victims of the May 30th Incident, and an all-out ban on British note clearing was formally declared.[104] The *North-China Herald*, the most influential English-language newspaper in Shanghai, was traditionally dismissive of the ability of student movements and popular discontent to bring about change in Chinese political consciousness. Initially, the general tone taken vis-à-vis the incident was low key. But when it became clear that the disturbances, strike, and boycott would not end soon, as the newspaper's bellicose coverage had first implied, editors shifted attention to physical attacks on British nationals.[105] Runs on British banks were not reported as such, nor was the sensitive issue of how British companies fared through the boycott. Thus, whatever journalistic coverage of massive banknote redemption we have is from the lower rung of the Chinese press in Shanghai, which took a more militant line than established newspapers like *Shenbao* and were therefore less reliable.[106]

Another reason that the boycott of British bank notes in 1925 was less pronounced than the one targeting consumer goods had to do with the fact that the relationship between Chinese and foreign banks at that point in time was not always one of hostility or competition. The Shanghai branch of the Bank of China sought, for example, foreign bank assistance when it experienced a run on its banknotes during the banking coup of 1916.[107] Conversely, Du Xuncheng has shown that the National Commercial Bank (*Zhejiang xingye yinhang*) deposited more than Tls. 300,000 at the HSBC in the course of 1923.[108]

These cross ties may help explain the complex attitude that Chinese business elites took following the May 30th events. In the immediate lead-up to the crisis, Chinese business elites had been incensed by the foreign-run Shanghai Municipal Council's reluctance to grant them more political representation and by attempts to increase wharfage fees and interfere in labor conditions.[109] Chinese industrialists in direct competition with British imports or expatriate firms took advantage of the ensuing political climate to explicitly agitate against their rivals. But

Chinese merchants and bankers were for the most part more hesitant because they often entertained amiable working relations and had inter-meshing interests with British firms.

Advertisements in the Chinese press denigrating rival British con-sumer goods—particularly cigarettes—were very common through 1925. Chinese bank agitation was usually not as extensive and less pro-nounced that the one carried out by students, but notable exceptions can be found. On August 4, 1925, for example, the otherwise conserva-tive *Yinhang zhoubao* (also known as "Bankers' Weekly") carried this Shanghai Commercial & Savings Bank advertisement:[110]

The tragic events following the May Thirtieth iniquity startled the entire na-tion. What has since been uppermost on everyone's mind —apart from protest-ing foreign aggression and bullying—is finding a way to save lives and property. The pursuit of industrial development and the setting up of factories are im-portant collective means of helping the nation cope. Nonetheless, if we are to do that, we must first pool our capital into solid savings. If only each and every one of our four hundred million compatriots opened a savings account—many a little would make a mickle. We will then mutually benefit from enormous re-sources with which to promote industrial development. Nothing will be beyond our reach, and no trade will remain unprofitable.

This bank prides itself on reliability and the ample reserves backing all its business activities. Our service is at its very best when it comes to opening sav-ings accounts, and we offer generous interest rates to clients. We would be hon-oured to answer expressions of interest from patriotic sires, and are able to send printed brochures by mail.

The unprecedented vehemence with which British businesses were at-tacked sounded alarm bells in London and stirred Whitehall to quiz the Eastern Exchange Banks on the viability of their bullion reserves.[111] More important, the Chinese boycott of British goods in 1925 bore on the overall performance of the banks because a large segment of their revenue hinged on the finance of trade between the two countries. In his annual address to shareholders delivered in March 1926, CBIAC's Chairman Sir Montagu Cornish described the situation in blunt terms:[112]

We now come to China, the particular spot which has caused great anxiety both to banks and traders alike. The position in that unfortunate country and the conditions of trade have been most deplorable for some considerable time, but the serious trouble began with the riots in Shanghai in May last. Strikes and boycotting caused a complete collapse of business in Shanghai for a couple of months, and following on this, civil war, suspended for a while, burst out with increased intensity. Naturally, the situation, which has now developed gives cause for much anxiety, and, what it means to Great Britain—the trade figures reveal at a glance. For 1925 we are afraid that the figures will make a poor showing compared with the preceding years.

The tenor of the Chairman's pronouncement was indicative of a substantial diminution of earnings for all the three principal British banks operating in China in 1925. But although CBIAC's total real profits fell by 15.5 percent compared with the previous year, HSBC suffered an overall drop of only 2 percent.[113] The Mercantile Bank of India was even less dependent on the Chinese market. Its returns in South Asia smoothed over poor results in China, with an overall profit hike of 5.8 percent in 1925. However, local statistics available for the Mercantile Bank reveal that its Shanghai branch was incurring heavy losses from 1920 through 1926 and that the bank's note circulation there plummeted from the equivalent of £56,000 to just £19,343 during the same period.[114]

In the mid-1920s, challenges to British economic hegemony in China were palpable in a wide range of sectors. Domestic firms took advantage of the political climate to lure away clients from British multinationals in a wide range of sectors; Nanyang Bros. produced cigarettes in Shanghai that snatched a significant market share from the British American Tobacco Company (BAT); Chinese shippers stung British steam navigation hegemony on the Yangzi; and most Shanghai department stores catering for the masses were dominated by overseas Chinese.[115] In his study of Sino-Foreign corporate rivalry in the treaty ports, Sherman Cochran found that the 1925 boycott had considerably boosted Nanyang's profit margins, but he could not ascertain BAT's performance in China presumably because he had been denied access to the relevant company archives in London.[116] He therefore concluded that the economic effects of the May 30th Incident were "not fully understood, and deserve further research."[117] Based on British consular sources, Richard Rigby has suggested, in turn, that BAT sales in China dropped by as much as 40 percent in mid-July 1925. The psychological impact of this downturn was so dramatic that, by the end of the month, the China Association—a body aligning the biggest British firms operating in the region—had petitioned the Foreign Office to refrain from using military force in Shanghai and to try mollifying student anger with promises of ending extraterritoriality in the distant future.[118]

Although CBIAC Shanghai branch balance sheets fall short of providing a robust estimate of the losses it incurred in 1925, the long-term circulation pattern that they delineate points to the sheer magnitude of the boycott. What available data there is in HSBC's branch ledgers, inspector's reports, and correspondence with Whitehall ministries clearly point to a dramatic drop in mainland banknote circulation volumes in 1925. For Shanghai, they show data that the level of notes outstanding, which had reached $3.6 million by midyear, was more than halved toward the end of the year.[119] Bearing in mind similar findings for CBIAC, these figures leave very little room to doubt the linkage between the May 30th Incident (or the *Wusa* tragedy, as it is known in China) *and* the subsequent winding down of the bank's mainland issue. Whatever ambivalence the head office had expressed about the China issue before 1925, it did *not* arise as a result of disappointing returns or the amorphous legal framework of extraterritoriality but because global Treasury quotas meant that bigger circulation volumes on the mainland offset the bank's ability to issue in Hong Kong, where demand for notes, the premium they carried, and circulation velocity were much higher.[120] Until 1925, therefore, the dynamics between the head office and the China branches allowed the latter to expand their issue to capitalize on the growing demand for reliable media of payments but only within a range that did not imperil the bank's status as the arbiter of the money supply in Hong Kong.

The unprecedented scale of the anti-British demonstration following *Wusa* undermined the very foundations of the treaty port paradigm and put British banks at risk of being literally overrun; for echoes from that momentous year, see Figures 5.1–5.3. HSBC was forced to wind down its China issue between 1925 and 1927, first simply because of redemption waves and later because of fears that similar disturbances might destabilize liquid cash reserves on the mainland. Subsequently, HSBC's role as leading bank of issue in Shanghai was quickly overtaken by a host of Chinese government–backed banks and, to a lesser extent, by an increased CBIAC issue.

Financial signs of distress from China were rapidly translating into turmoil in the stock exchanges, too. Just prior to the May 30th Incident, HSBC shares traded in Shanghai at SH$1300, while fetching £143 in London per unit. By August 29, the share price had fallen by 15 percent and 11 percent in Shanghai and London, respectively.[121] HSBC shares were worst affected in the Hong Kong stock exchange. In early June 1925, the share traded at HK$1,290. By early March 1926, it had dipped as low as HK$1,065, a drop of 17.5 percent.[122]

Recognizing the centrality of *Wusa* to the fate of foreign banking in China is crucial not only because of the drop in HSBC's circulation volumes or share prices but also because the 1925 events are seldom mentioned by name—let alone adequately analyzed—in the literature on overseas banking in Asia.[123] Yet the linkage between foreign note redemption during the anti-British boycott that was championed by the *Wusa* movement, and the subsequent drop in HSBC's mainland circulation figures is clearly mentioned in-house bank correspondence. For example, in a telegram exchange between Barlow at the head office and the new Shanghai branch manager, G. H. Stitt, dated June 19, 1925,

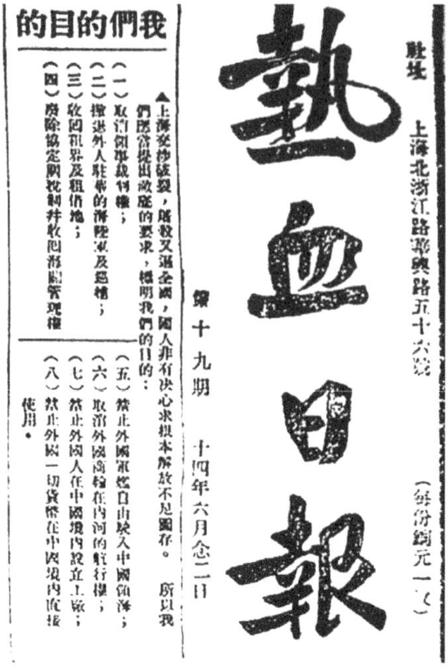

熱血日報

社址 上海北浙江路華興路五十六號

（每份銅元一文）

第十九期 十四年六月念二日

我們的目的

▲上海交涉破裂，屠殺又遍全國，國人非有決心求根本解放不足圖存。所以我們應當提出徹底的要求，標明我們的目的：

（一）取消領事裁判權；

（二）撤退外人駐華的海陸軍及巡捕；

（三）收回租界及租借地；

（四）廢除協定關稅制并收回海關管理權

（五）禁止外國軍艦自由駛入中國領海；

（六）取消外國商輪在內河的航行權；

（七）禁止外國人在中國境內設立工廠；

（八）禁止外國一切貨幣在中國境內流通使用。

FIGURE 5.1. A Shanghai activists' bill explaining the aims of the May 30th Movement.
Aim 8 reads: "To prohibit the use of all foreign banknotes in China."
Source: Reprinted in *Rexue ribao* (Hot-Blooded Daily), June 22, 1925, p. 1.

Stitt warned Barlow that reserves at the branch were "running low" and asked him to intervene with the British consul-general so that the latter would agree to unfreeze immediately the bank's $ 4 million reserve under his custody. Barlow, on his part, advised Stitt to conserve his cash tightly due to the long anti-British strike that he now anticipated.[124]

That the Shanghai consul-general was a custodian of a reserve roughly tantamount to the circulation volume in China did not imply that the mainland issue per se had to be fully backed at that point in time.[125] Attention should be paid to the fact that the bank's head office in Hong Kong had to be called on to contact the Hong Kong authorities, so that they in turn would approve the release of the reserve by the consul-general in Shanghai. This further suggests that the China issue was sim-

A VERY PATIENT BEAST, BUT BETTER NOT ROUSED.

FIGURE 5.2. A caricature capturing the prevailing mood among
British residents of Shanghai soon after the mid-1925 disturbances.
The Chinese activists are depicted as a virulent but small ape that
will surely be crushed if it continues to provoke the ire of stoic
Great Britain ("John Bull").
Source: North-China Herald, July 1, 1925, p. 9.

ply conceived of as part of the bank's general excess issue, which *by
definition* required 100 percent backing in Hong Kong.

The bank managed to have part of the excess reserve placed outside
the central note reserve in Hong Kong no sooner than 1921. This is attested to in an upbeat telegram that Charles Addis sent from London to
Stephen in Shanghai:[126]

Arrangement [is] now concluded with the Colonial Office regarding security of
the Banks' note issue. a) HM Government had no objection to the increase of
the Bank's authorised capital to $50 million. b) An ordinary note issue equal
to issued capital of $20 million shall be one-third fiduciary and the balance of
two thirds covered by coin or approved securities at the Bank's option, while
any excess issue over $20 million shall be fully covered in coin. c) It remained
to be agreed what portions of the security should be held in places other than
Hong Kong.

The conceptual tie-up of the China issue with the excess issue is attested to again in a memorandum sent, on Secretary Winston Churchill's

FIGURE 5.3. An advertisement by the Chinese Patriotic
Tobacco Co. promoting the *Wusa* ("May 30th") cigarette brand
on the heels of antiforeign sentiments.
The caption roughly translates as: "Are you hurting? Our countrymen have
been vanquished, and their human dignity has been shattered. Whither
Truth and Justice? Do not forget *Wusa*, a time when our country has been
humiliated and its sovereignty trampled. Commemorate the dead!
This company and its staff have decided to carry these opening words to
appeal to those who may see them and feel saddened. Lest all people of
conscience forget the shameful atrocity inflicted on us on May 30th—
please smoke *Wusa*-brand cigarettes.
With their unique taste, they will help you remember the dead from
time to time."
Source: *Xinwen bao* ("Sin Wan Pao"), June 13, 1925, p. 2.

instruction, by the undersecretary of state for the colonies to the deputy
of George Curzon, then the British foreign secretary. The memorandum
indicated that HSBC had asked the secretary to allow part of the note
reserves to be kept outside Hong Kong in mainland localities where circulation was increasing.[127] Churchill, the memorandum went on to report, consulted the lord commissioners of the Treasury, who approved
Shanghai and Tianjin as sites accessible enough to house a secondary
reserve. It was, then, HSBC that had suggested that British consuls in
China be appointed as trustees of the said reserve and that they report

from time to time to the Hong Kong government on the amount of securities entrusted to them.

Addis's telegram and the undersecretary's memorandum imply that any mainland note reserve that would have been kept by the bank before 1921 was at the latter's discretion. Until then, any treaty port note reserves could *not* be deducted from the central reserve held against the total global issue in Hong Kong and were certainly not required of the bank by the Treasury or the Foreign Office. Moreover, it was the bank rather than the Treasury that sought to buttress the China reserves by having the mainland issue linked with the global excess issue. This was a measure not only designed to protect the bank from local runs but also to abrogate an onerous overlap between informal local reserves and the formal central reserve.

The regulatory framework underlying HSBC's banknote issuance *after* 1921 is quite complex. In essence, the Bank of England was the ultimate arbiter of British monetary policy and a trustee of HSBC's nonmetallic reserves. Charter guidelines and banknote reserve ratios applicable to all Eastern Exchange Banks, as well as the day-to-day monitoring of financial conditions overseas, were carried out by the Treasury in consultation with the Foreign and Colonial Offices. Colonial governments were then answerable to the Colonial Office insofar as reserve ratio enforcement was concerned. HSBC's bullion and coin reserves were locked up in vaults under the former's jurisdiction. But because Shanghai was nominally a part of the Republic of China, enforcement of HSBC reserve ratios there became the responsibility of the local British consul-general, a Foreign Office employee.

The measure to formalize and buttress the status of the Shanghai reserves in 1921 may have saved the bank's reputation on the mainland from a more severe thrashing during the heady days of mid-1925. Even so, HSBC was hard pressed to meet the redemption wave. The problem was that the Shanghai note reserve held under the consul's trusteeship had been largely made up of precious Mexican dollars. These dollars carried a premium over debased Chinese dollar coinage, and the bank was loath to disburse them. Hence, the bank persuaded Hong Kong's treasurer to allow it to transfer the Mexican dollars to the central reserve in the colony, while replenishing the Shanghai reserves with Chinese dollar coins.[128]

By early July, the enormity of the situation in Shanghai had finally registered with Barlow, who telegramed Stitt: "It looks to me as if this

British Boycott is the most dangerous thing we have been up against for many a long day and will, if it is maintained for any length of time, strain our resources severely."[129]

On July 18, 1925, the *Beijing ribao* reported on a massive run that had occurred on HSBC Shanghai branch:[130]

Since a popular boycott was declared on the British-owned HSBC, Shanghainese depositors in this bank have flocked there to withdraw funds, especially clients elbowing their way to cash paper notes. At the time [of the present run], the Bank had already been squeezed between a rock and a hard place. It scraped through by the skin of its teeth with crucial assistance from a [Chinese] bank related to Yu Xiaqing and from some other avaricious banks, to the extent that it could breathe alive again.

The mainstream Chinese press in Shanghai was conspicuously lacking in reports on any dramatic anti-British bank stampede, and the fact that only a Beijing-based daily raised the allegations against "collaborative" Chinese banks derogates from their reliability. It seems more likely that the pressure on British banks was applied incrementally, as student agitation was gaining ground. A rare local reference to the dynamics of the boycott may be detected in a report carried by the Shanghai students' mouthpiece *Rexue ribao* (Hot-Blooded Daily) on June 7, 1925:

Ever since calls for the boycott of quasi-foreign banknotes spread across Shanghai, there has been unusually heavy traffic of clients wishing to withdraw funds from foreign banks or encash quasi-foreign banknotes. The HSBC was worst affected, [with clients streaming to withdraw funds] . . . from morning to noon without respite. This Bank's predicament is now extremely precarious.[131]

Either way, Barlow was so alarmed at the anti-British wave that he recommended the immediate withdrawal of treaty port issues except in Shanghai. This was because, unlike Shanghai, outport issues had remained covered by the central Hong Kong reserve and because no other local reserve in China was recognized by the Treasury, except Tianjin. The outport issue was therefore "weapons in the hands of agitators." Then, Barlow went on to compare the volatility of the bank's issues in China with the monetary setting in Hong Kong: "In Hong Kong conditions are not the same, as we can always rely on the Hong Kong Government to enact protective legislation in the event of a concerted attack being made on our note issue here."[132]

Barlow knew, of course, what he was talking about. Shortly before the *Wusa* disturbances had spread to the Pearl River Delta, the Hong Kong government had imposed severe caps on note redemption, silver withdrawals, and capital movement between the colony and the mainland. This emergency legislation was a precondition set by the bank and

CBIAC for the grant of a loan on the order of HK$6 million designed to bail out "native banks" in the colony. The new restrictions unleashed a frantic wave of silver smuggling across the border into Guangdong province but may well have saved HSBC and CBIAC from a run on their banknotes within the colony.[133]

Meanwhile, the situation was rapidly deteriorating in Shanghai. On July 2, Stitt telegramed Barlow that local note circulation was already down by $0.5 million since the disturbances started and that Chinese clients were also withdrawing funds from current accounts "rather freely."[134] A week later the circulation volume sank to a record low of $2.7 million in Shanghai and $0.66 million in the outports, whereas total liquid cash reserve (excluding the Mexican dollars entrusted to the consul) stood at only $1.8 million.[135]

The permanent shift in the bank's strategy with regard to its China issue occurred in the course of the following two months. On July 13, Stitt reported that the cash position of the branch was improving and that he might not have to draw on the $4 million consular reserve.[136] Three days later Stitt even thought he detected signs that the vehemence of the boycott against HSBC notes on the mainland was subsiding, with the Shanghai circulation now at $2.4 million—only $0.3 million less than the week before.[137]

Barlow, however, who would have witnessed the spillover of disturbances into South China in late June, remained unconvinced. On August 5, he instructed Stitt to completely stop reissuing redeemed notes in all mainland branches in anticipation of more runs.[138] And on August 17, he imposed a cap of $2 million on the Shanghai circulation volume.[139] Apart from helping to stave off future runs in Shanghai, Barlow also hoped that the decreased circulation volume in China would free up the reserves held against it in Hong Kong to use as cash in claims on the bank in the Colony or, alternatively, underpin an increase of note issuance there.[140]

Ironically, although the *Wusa* disturbances put a downward pressure on the bank's circulation volumes in China, they buoyed up demand for HSBC notes in Hong Kong because the new colonial government restrictions there meant that individuals could not withdraw silver from the banks freely. Receipt of a limited amount of notes was the only way to draw deposits from either Chinese or foreign banks in the colony.[141]

The other factor that stoked up demand for Hong Kong dollar–denominated HSBC notes was the fact that trade between the colony and the wider delta was effectively cut off. This meant that Cantonese silk producers whose goods had been exported via Hong Kong's deepwater port could not use the sales proceeds to purchase imported products for transport upriver because border passages were blocked.

Many, therefore, chose to smuggle the proceeds over the border—and notes were harder to detect than goods.[142]

By mid-1926 the impetus of the disturbances had clearly begun to wane across the mainland. The Maritime Customs report published in 1926, while lamenting the impact of the anti-British boycott, could wishfully point to a silver lining:[143]

The Shanghai incidents of the 30th May, with their counterblast in the South, bade fair to paralyse trade; but the strike and boycott movements were soon restricted to certain centers only, and what could not be shipped or imported through Shanghai or Canton [Guangzhou] found its way in many cases through neighboring ports or through other large seaports such as Tientsin [Tianjin]. Exception being made for the southern and, principally, the West River ports, the Shanghai incidents were but a temporary set-back to trade in general.

The subsequent period saw scattered, intermittent conflicts between locals and expatriates in some of the outports that never degenerated into a countrywide backlash. Nonetheless, the enormity of the past year resonated as far as Whitehall, as a glacial transition in Western attitudes toward China set in. On June 4, 1926, Barlow informed his new branch manager in Shanghai, A. B. Lowson, that the British government was sounding out prominent figures among its nationals in the treaty ports on the future course that its China policy should take.[144]

In the years to come, Whitehall came to question the views of its hard-line expatriates in China—wealthy *taipans* and plebeian Shanghailanders alike. The sheer import of the shift in Britain's China policy sprawls beyond the scope of the present chapter, however. Suffice it to say here that, among other things, the shift ramified into tighter administrative supervision of British banknote issuance in the treaty ports during the late 1920s.

The first harbinger surfaced in August 1926, when the head office informed Lowson that, from then on, the British authorities would require all British banks of issue in China to apply for licence if they wished to continue disbursing notes.[145] But far more stringent demands were to be posed by the new Nationalist government.

CONCLUSION

This chapter has examined in detail the vicissitudes of banknote issuance by the Hongkong and Shanghai Banking Corporation and the Chartered Bank of India Australia and China, particularly through the republican period. In mid-1925, these banks' China issue took a decisive—and entirely *unexpected*—battering as a result of nationalist agitation during the May 30th Movement. HSBC circulation volumes in Shanghai had rebounded briefly by 1927 but operations in China proper progressively diminished sometime after 1927 as a direct consequence of KMT policies and the rise of modern domestic financial institutions.

Because HSBC was by far the most important foreign bank in China, the highs and lows of its note circulation accurately capture not just its own performance but also the transition from intensifying monetary fragmentation in the early republican period to effective central banking reforms during the Nanjing decade.

The perception of Chinese boycotts in the early republican era as ineffectual in the long run—entrenched largely through Remer's early work—is in want of serious revision.[146] This perception should be measured up, with the benefit of hindsight, against the cumulative evidence made available since. One critical source of evidence that Remer neglected was the British Exchange Banks and their changing relationship with Chinese clientele. The case study analyzed in these pages suggests that the ramifications of the *Wusa* movement reached well beyond corporate boardrooms.

The outbreak of intense anti-British sentiments in May 30th 1925 resonated with Whitehall long after bilateral trade, or banknote circulation volumes for that matter, had been shored up. Britain's foreign policy in East Asia in the lead-up to World War II—its repudiation of conservative expatriate views, its reconciliation with the KMT, its growing distrust of Japan, and its endorsement of the *fabi* reform (1935)—cannot be adequately explained without reference to the impact that the May 30th Movement made on Whitehall's perception of Chinese nationalism and its long-term prospects.

Unlike Remer, the great bulk of research subsequently published on antiforeign boycotts and nationalist movements in republican China tended to skirt around thorough economic analysis in favor of the cultural, intellectual, journalistic, organizational, and political dimensions.[147] This is, perhaps, why it is heavily weighted toward the May 4th Movement (1919), which marked a historic turnaround in Chinese sociopolitical consciousness but was—certainly for the Western powers—of much less economic significance than the May 30th Movement six years later. To correct this imbalance, more work in the future seems to be called for.

The failure of late Qing and early republican governments to stem the breakdown of popular trust in state-issued currency was an experience

not entirely removed from that of some European and colonial governments before the consolidation of central banking in the early twentieth
century. But the introduction of central banking in Europe had been
preceded by almost two centuries during which private banknote issuance was receding, while in China the opposite trend persisted. The immediate explanations for the popularity of British bank notes in China
before 1925 lies, of course, in the higher specie reserve ratios adhered
to by British banks, and their immunity to Chinese government diktat
that—when foisted on local banks—often meant expropriation of silver
reserves. But more generally, the Treasury reserve principles that bound
HSBC and CBIAC were just one by-product of institutional innovation,
which had first emerged in London in the sixteenth century and which
eventually transformed the City into the world's largest financial clearing hub. Indeed, much of the legal and regulatory theory underpinning
these two banks carried over from, and was consistently refined by, earlier experience with monopolistic joint-stock trading companies like the
EIC or with failed chartered overseas banks like the OBC.

What this study might also offer, then, is some insight into the factors
that had set the foreign corporate sector in the treaty ports apart from
the domestic sectors. Differences here can be reduced to the use of fungible equity and the provision of limited-liability prerogatives to achieve
economies of scale. Impersonal ownership is, in the final analysis, what
distinguished large, publicly traded corporate entities like HSBC and
CBIAC from Shanghai's diffuse and undercapitalized money shops.

The British Eastern Exchange Banks were predicated on Royal Charter stipulations or Colonial Ordinances. These were enacted only in
the 1850s as rough-and-ready substitute for limited liability. Financial
institutions other than the Bank of England could be bestowed with
statutory limited liability only in the following decade. Looked at from
a purely temporal perspective, therefore, the institutional division between British and Chinese banks in Shanghai may not appear compelling. The crucial point to remember, at the same time, is that what may
seem like a fairly thin difference begot, in fact, one of the root causes for
European economic paramountcy in the early modern age.

CHAPTER SIX

Japanese Colonial Banking and Monetary Reform

China, Korea, and Taiwan, 1879–1937

This chapter seeks to further examine the impact of foreign banking in prewar mainland China, as well as in Taiwan and Korea, by exploring Japanese banks' activities there, with particular emphasis on their role in currency creation and on their changing relationship with the local clientele. While specialized Japanese- and Chinese-language research has tended to focus on Japanese banking activities in the puppet state of "Manchukuo" (ext. 1931–1945), the body of English-language scholarship on foreign banking in prewar China is quite naturally weighted toward British-, American- and European-owned financial institutions.[1] The literature on the rise of Chinese modern banking is, in turn, growing, but the complex nature of the relationship between domestic banks and their foreign counterparts has only recently begun to be explored.[2]

Having surveyed in detail the formative impact British banks had on the Chinese monetary trajectory, it is now crucial to turn to the second most important impact thereon, namely, that of Japanese financial institutions and Japanese colonial policy as of the last decade of the nineteenth century. To be sure, the entry of Japanese financial institutions into China (but *not* into Korea, and to a much lesser extent into Taiwan) followed the lead of their Western European counterparts. Yet Japanese banks preceded by over two decades major American banks' entry. In terms of business volumes, Japanese financial institutions would by the 1920s also rival British banks operating in China proper. And in Taiwan, Korea, and "Manchukuo," these institutions would naturally become predominant as an integral part of Japan's colonial project.

Financial historians broadly agree that the creation of a "gold-yen" bloc in East Asia was one of the centerpieces of Japanese prewar foreign policy between 1897 and 1914. This yen-based gold-exchange bloc was first envisioned by the architect of Japan's informal empire, Gotō Shinpei, in October 1907, ten years after Japan itself had joined the London-centered international gold standard for the first time. However, as Mark Metzler has shown, the implementation of the yen-bloc scheme was staggered over a number of years on account of Japan's shortage of foreign currency reserves and in view of the fact that silver-based units of account had been a deeply engrained feature of China's and Korea's monetary systems. Thus, there would always be tensions in Japanese imperial monetary policy between those who, following Gotō, called for expediting the assimilation of colonial possessions within Japan's gold-exchange standard and those like Baron Sakatani, typically calling for a more cautious approach that would make allowance for varying local conditions and would stop short of alienating other powers.[3]

What remains relatively little studied in this context is precisely how different Japanese colonial banks negotiated these countercurrents of monetary policy in the interwar period. Because Japan, like other powers, suspended the yen's gold convertibility in the wake of World War I and temporarily returned to the international gold standard only in January 1930 and because it virtually refrained from minting coinage in its colonial possessions, the extension and stability of the yen bloc was to rely on minutely aligning domestic and colonial Japanese bank note issuance. Expounding on the technicalities of Japanese colonial bank note issuance from a broad comparative angle might therefore offer valuable insights on the Japanese colonial project as a whole.[4]

Spearheaded by the Yokohama Specie Bank, colonial Japanese banks were latecomers as compared with their Western counterparts, but they quickly caught up in size on the back of Japan's imperialist expansion in the early twentieth century. Chinese-run modern banking also developed apace in that period. The principal institution in that sector—the Bank of China—changed course soon after the breakdown of Yuan Shikai's regime in 1916, steering clear of government intervention, recruiting foreign-trained professionals, and luring treaty port depositors.[5]

Though most Chinese banks cultivated fairly suave working relations with their foreign counterparts, a few prominent local financiers accused foreign banks of unfair competition. The bone of contention was the extraterritorial privileges that foreign banks had enjoyed in Shanghai and the smaller treaty ports ever since the Second Opium War (1856–1860). Extraterritoriality ultimately ensured that foreign banks remained immune to Chinese government taxation, were allowed to print banknotes of their own, and were able to control currency exchange rates. It was against the perceived iniquities of extraterritoriality that foreign banks came increasingly under attack in the 1920s and 1930s.

The following passages will broadly address the pattern of growth of Japanese banks of issue in prewar China and Korea until the watershed year of 1919. We will then move on to explore in much greater detail how these Japanese banks subsequently fared through Japan's severe domestic recession as well as the rise of antiforeign agitation in China proper during the 1920s and 1930s. Indignant at the outcome of the Treaty of Versailles (1919), anti-Japanese protesters rampaged across much of north China, crippling Japanese imports and Japanese local banknote circulation in what became known as the May 4th Movement. Student protests in Shanghai were partly inspired that year by the anti-Japanese March 1st (1919) Movement in Korea, but the longer-term economic effects of the March 1st Movement ultimately proved much less pronounced than those of the May 4th (1919) or May 30th (1925) Movements in China.[6] As Japanese territorial encroachment progressed, more serious anti-Japanese protests spread across the rest of China, seriously hampering Japanese business in the 1920s and 1930s.

Taking account of the broad geopolitical context, the remaining sections are structured as follows: The next section will briefly survey the history of the Yokohama Specie Bank as Japan's first colonial bank and discuss the nature of its note issuance prior to 1919; the following section will then show how this bank fared against the rising tide of anti-Japanese agitation in China after 1919; the fourth and fifth sections will compare the monetary properties of Yokohama Specie Bank with those of the Bank of Chosen and the Bank of Taiwan; the next section after that will analyze the patterns of Japanese bank note issuance right across greater China as a whole, namely, in the colonial settings of Taiwan versus Korea's; in "Manchukuo" as well as in those parts of China that remained nominally sovereign or under Western hegemony; it will then offer comparisons with other foreign financial institutions and discuss the implications for our understanding of the dynamics of nationalist boycotts and of Sino–Japanese economic relations in the period under review.

YOKOHAMA SPECIE BANK BEFORE 1919

Modeled on the British-run HSBC, the Yokohama Specie Bank (*Yokohama shōkin ginkō*) was set up in 1879, three years before the establishment of Japan's lender of last resort, the Bank of Japan (BoJ). In the

1870s, a large number of Japanese joint-stock banks had been authorized to issue notes domestically, but the Japanese government rejected Yokohama Specie Bank's preliminary request to be allowed to issue paper money within Japan itself. Instead, Finance Minister Matsutaka Masayoshi worked to create a central bank (BoJ) modeled on that of Belgium, a European economic latecomer whose specialized bank of issue (Banque Nationale de Belgique, est. 1850) was strictly state run. At the same time, the Yokohama Specie Bank (hereafter YSB) was tasked with banknote issuance in China, which was then one of a few nominally sovereign countries where foreign privately run banks like HSBC could issue notes with their government's approval.[7]

YSB was first endowed with a paid-up capital of ¥3 million, of which ¥1 million was in the form of specie forwarded by the Japanese Treasury, and the other ¥2 million represented private equity. Thus, it was not a state-run colonial bank in the full sense of the word but, rather, a semiofficial bank with a unique mission of facilitating Japan's overseas trade. Implicitly, it was expected to play a pivotal role in Japan's longer-term mercantilist exercise: the accumulation of foreign-currency reserves, which eventually allowed Japan to move off the silver standard and to rebase the yen on the gold standard in 1897. The ability to maintain the yen's convertibility to gold was achieved through the colossal war indemnities Japan had been able to extract from China in 1896 and the floatation of Japanese government bonds in the London stock exchange.[8]

YSB's first China branch was opened in Shanghai as early as 1893, but it was not until 1902 that the bank started issuing notes on the mainland—first in Shanghai, Niuzhuang (Yingkou), and Tianjin. Later, it also started issuing silver-denominated notes in Beijing (1910), Qingdao (1915), Hankou (1917), Jinan (1920), and Harbin (1921). Overall, the bank issued more than eighty-eight different types of notes on Chinese soil primarily in tael and silver-dollar denominations, as well as smaller volumes of gold-yen notes in Dairen, Liaodong peninsula (as of 1913).[9]

As Table 6.1 clearly shows, it was not until the Qing Dynasty's downfall in 1912 and the attendant financial meltdown in the Chinese-run banking sector that YSB's circulation volumes shot up in China proper. Even so, higher demand for YSB notes in China proper through the early 1910s translated into lower circulation volumes in the Japanese sphere of influence across northeast China. This was partly because the YSB total fiduciary issue at the time was capped by the bank's charter, which was similar to the one the British Colonial Office had imposed on HSBC.[10]

Parallel developments are also critical to understanding the spread of YSB notes across China. After Russia's defeat in its war with Japan in

TABLE 6.1.
YSB note circulation in China proper (excluding Manchuria) versus
YSB total note circulation, 1906–1912 year end.

Year	Shanghai	Tianjin	Beijing	TOTAL	China proper as percentage of total YSB circulation
1906	144	41.2	—	752.8	24.6
1907	133.8	42.2	—	619.5	28.4
1908	108.3	49.2	—	417.2	37.7
1909	81	47.1	—	292.8	43.7
1910	75.8	33.6	14	367.4	33.5
1911	66.7	63.9	12	673.7	21.1
1912	152.6	89.1	97.5	657.6	51.5

SOURCE: Adapted from Guo Yuqing (2007) p. 195, Table 3-18; YSB *total* circulation figures in gold-yen terms are derived from *Yokohama shōkin ginkō zenshi* (1984), vol. 6, pp. 399–401. In 1909, the Shanghai branch balance sheet switched from tael totals to local silver dollar totals. Yen and local tael figures have been converted to silver dollar terms based on the exchange-rate data in Hsiao Liang-lin (1974), pp. 190–192; Morse (rep. 1967), pp. 156–173.

NOTE: Unit: 10,000 silver dollars

1905, YSB was asked to convert into its own notes 15 million gold-yen worth of Japanese military coupons that the Japanese Kanto Army had disbursed. In that way, the Japanese government sought to stamp out the use of gold-based rubles along the South Manchuria Railway. Then, in 1916, when the postimperial Chinese government of Yuan Shikai suspended the convertibility of Chinese bank notes, YSB increased its note issue (of both silver and gold denominations) over and above the previous cap, so as to take advantage of the collapse of popular trust in Chinese government-backed banks. Thus, YSB's *total* circulation volume, as measured in Japanese gold yen, more than doubled between 1915 and 1916 from ¥7 million to ¥18 million. Partly to allow the YSB to meet the robust demand for its notes through this period, its paid-up capital—as stipulated in the charter—was consistently lifted from ¥30 million in 1916 to ¥100 million in 1920.[11]

However, in 1917, YSB's stature as a regional bank of issue was set back by the Terauchi government's decision to nominate the Bank of Chosen as its primary bank of issue in northeast China with a view toward narrowing Korea's trade deficit with that region and toward a future monetary unification of Manchuria and Korea. YSB's gold-yen notes subsequently lost legal-tender status in the northeast, but conversely, demand for its silver-denominated notes in China proper continued to rise, to the extent that the overall circulation volume remained at around ¥20 million until mid-1919.[12]

To further understand YSB note circulation patterns, the bank's monetary properties should be placed in the context of other business ends. Notably, the great bulk of YSB activity in China proper, like that of its British competitors, revolved around the finance of intra–treaty port and Sino–Japanese trade through the provision of short-term exchange bills. The bank did attract deposits from Chinese clientele in Tianjin (mainly Qing officials prior to 1912) but—according to Taira Tomoyuki's important study—the proceeds of these deposits were mostly allocated to *foreign* merchants residing in Shanghai. In Taira's view, YSB China branches ran a surplus with the Tokyo head office in those years. In other words, the head office did not seek to employ all China resources locally but to "sacrifice" the surplus there to fund Japan's substantial imports of machinery from Europe and America.[13] Ishii Kanji has similarly shown that during the 1910s YSB relied heavily on deposits by ethnic Chinese and Indians in Shanghai and Bombay, respectively.[14]

Guo Yuqing suggested that, although the Shanghai and Tianjin branches accounted for the great bulk of YSB deposits in China proper (60 percent on average between 1901 and 1913), well under a fourth of its Shanghai deposit base was attributable to ethnic Chinese clients *before* 1900. Notably, in its pre-1900 phase, YSB had not yet set up deposit branches in northeast China. Because YSB was unable to accept deposits within Japan, the vast majority of its deposits at the time were attributable to European (60.4 percent), American (27.3 percent), and Indian (6.4 percent) branches. Yet, by 1913, over a third of YSB's worldwide deposits were attributable to greater China (the northeast alone made up about 9 percent and China proper 15 percent), while the relative significance of American deposits was declining sharply. In other words, by the 1910s, China had become much more vital to the bank's worldwide operations, just when resentment over Japanese expansionism was building up there.[15]

Previous studies' findings on the regional make-up of YSB deposits are aligned in Table 6.2, which clearly shows that YSB's Shanghai deposit base considerably exceeded standard loans between 1906 and 1913. However, until 1910, YSB, like many of the other foreign banks in Shanghai, also advanced a substantial amount in unsecured "chop loans" to local money shops (then known to Chinese as *qianzhuang* and to Westerners as "native banks"). For the most part, the combined value of "chop" and standard loans exceeded the value of deposits in the Shanghai branch prior to 1910, the year in which many of the city's money shops became insolvent.[16] The gap between such liabilities and assets was narrowed down—perhaps strategically—by the issue of notes. Note-bearers could be, for example, depositors who had pledged specie

TABLE 6.2.

YSB deposits and loans versus other banks.

Year	Shanghai deposits	YSB Shanghai standard loans	YSB Shanghai "chop loans"	China proper total deposits	YSB deposit total	YSB total net profit	Bank of Taiwan China proper deposits	The "Ta Ching" Imperial Bank Deposits (renamed "Bank of China" in 1912)	HSBC deposit total
1906	421.4	395.4	761.8	1,752.7	12,431.4	506.6	44.9	1,466.7	19,920
1907	364.0	313.8	406.1	1,482.3	12,350.7	416.4	74	3,066.7	22,410
1908	463.2	137.5	7.2	1,617.0	9,885.3	395.8	127.3	4,897.2	29,860
1909	517.1	129.3	700.2	1,340.6	11,882.1	377.8	111	6,779.2	27,240
1910	650.1	193.6	2.9	1,467.3	10,225.8	361.7	96	7,501.4	26,410
1911	842.4	317.6	220.0	1,775.9	11,972.2	396.5	304.3	8,201.4	29,830
1912	891.7	468.4	0.0	2,117.9	15,992.6	446.8	532.9	313.1	38,840
1913	1,237.1	606.7	0.0	2,627.7	17,834.3	412.8	637.6	2,620.6	29,820

SOURCE: Adapted from Taira (1982) p. 69, Table 2 and p. 71, Table 3; YSB deposit total and profits from *Yokohama shōkin ginkō zenshi* (1984), vol. 6, p. 398, Table 1; Bank of Taiwan, Ta Ching, and HSBC data from Guo Yuqing (2007), p. 190, Table 3-14; silver dollar to yen exchange rate extracted from Hsiao Liang-lin (1974), pp. 190–192; Morse (rep. 1967), pp. 156–173.

NOTE: Unit: 10,000 silver dollars.

over the counter, occasionally withdrawing "cash" from their current accounts in the form of notes. The fiduciary portion of the specie corresponding with the note value could then be on-lent by the bank at higher interest (the notes themselves did not bear any interest).

Equally important, Table 6.2 shows that, in terms of its ability to attract deposits worldwide, YSB did not fall much behind HSBC in the early twentieth century, even though the latter had been established much earlier and was formally endorsed by the British colonial establishment in East Asia. Conversely, the Bank of Taiwan, which also attracted deposits in mainland China (mainly in Xiamen), was no match to YSB there.

But one of the first Chinese-run modern financial institutions, the Ta Ching Imperial Bank (C. *Daqing yinhang*, to be renamed the "Bank of China" after 1912) could by 1907 outpace YSB in terms of deposit mobilization on the mainland. Furthermore, Ta Ching seems to have scraped through the turmoil in Shanghai's domestic financial sector in 1910. However, much of its deposit base was later withdrawn as a consequence of its association with the moribund Qing dynasty.[17]

ANTIFOREIGN BOYCOTTS

Quite apart from the recession that befell Japan in the early 1920s, the May 4th Movement (1919) augured trouble for YSB's note issue in China proper although, nominally, note circulation prevailed there right until 1935—the year in which the KMT government moved China off the silver standard and enforced its *fabi* currency as China's sole legal tender.[18] The May 4th Movement unleashed the first of many anti-Japanese boycotts in the years to come. Despite its formative role in shaping Chinese sociopolitical consciousness, economic research into the May 4th Movement primarily deals with its effects on Sino–foreign trade, to the neglect of the boycott's effects on foreign-run banks and multinationals' local operations.

As explained in the previous chapter, antiforeign boycotts proved equally if not *more* inimical to the interests of British firms operating in China in the mid-1920s. Yet almost all of the Chinese popular ire came to bear on Japan in 1919. It is therefore critical to unearth the Japanese perspective on the events unfolding at the time. To be sure, Takatsuna Hirofumi's recent comprehensive study highlights the extent to which Chinese laborers' agitation in the *Naigai Wata* cotton filatures disquieted the Japanese expatriate community in prewar Shanghai, but it does not address YSB activities at all. Neither does Guo Yuqing's aforementioned study of the YSB go beyond 1919, thereby eliding the implications of the May 4th Movement.[19] Similarly, Kikuchi laconically mentions in his classic study of Chinese nationalism that Chinese clients had withdrawn deposits from Japanese banks in 1919 but is much more preoccupied with the May 4th Movement's effects on the sale of Japanese imports.[20]

Japanese intelligence reports from Shanghai do nonetheless attest at length to the sheer anxiety with which expatriate Japanese financiers and bankers—not just industrialists—viewed the mounting agitation against Japan as of 1919. As part of this agitation, not only were Japanese imported goods boycotted in the 1920s but Chinese-run money shops and modern banks often refused to honor IOUs or notes presented by Japanese firms for encashment.[21]

Although there are numerous intelligence reports detailing such events in the mid-1920s, there are also similar primary materials attesting to the incipient alarm that seeped through the Japanese expatriate community during the formative 1919 boycott. For example, the commercial gazette (*Tsūshō kōhō*) that was published by the Japanese Foreign Ministry frequently contained in its 1919 issues allusions to not only a downturn in the sales of Japanese goods like toothpaste or tires in the Chinese market but also to runs on YSB and Bank of Chosen branches in places as far away from Shanghai as Changchun or Zhifu (Yantai).[22] Likewise, consular reports now held at the Japan Center for Asian Historical Records (JCAHR) suggest that Japanese colonial policy makers were concerned about the implications of the 1919 boycott of Japanese banks in places like Qingdao.[23]

Professor Edmund S. K. Fung has insightfully described the anti-British agitation in South China in the mid-1920s (that is, the *Wusa* Movement recounted in the previous chapter) as the driving force behind the most effective boycott ever carried out by Chinese against foreigners; this agitation sparked a reaction in comparison with which "the anti-Japanese boycott of 1919–1921 pales into insignificance."[24]

Fung's observation is of value precisely because the May 4th Movement (1919), unleashed on the heels of the Versailles Peace Conference and Japanese territorial encroachments in Shandong, has commanded far greater attention from cultural and social historians than from economic historians.[25] Certainly, insofar as the circulation of Japanese banknotes in China is concerned, both periods remain critically understudied. A closer look at YSB indices for 1919 might suggest, however, that the impact of the May 4th boycott on Japanese banks was not trivial.

TABLE 6.3.

Yokohama Specie Bank select midyear balance-sheet entries, 1915–1923.

	1915	1916	1917	1918	1919	1920	1921	1922	1923
Notes in circulation	0.6	1.0	2.3	2.1	1.6	0.7	0.8	0.6	0.3
Cash reserves	2.2	2.4	3.3	4.2	4.1	4.5	3.5	3.6	2.7
Deposits	16.3	25.0	33.7	66.0	53.5	56.4	50.1	50.6	47.9
Balance sheet Total	32.4	42.5	64.3	115.9	124.9	139.0	101.9	99.7	109.3

SOURCE: Bankers' Magazine 1916–1924.

NOTE: Unit: GBP £ million.

On May 17, 1919, Shanghai's money shop guild announced that its members were to halt the clearing of quasi-foreign notes issued by Japanese banks, even though alternative reliable Chinese paper money was hard to find at the time.[26] At that moment, however, the epicenter of anti-Japanese agitation had largely been confined to north China. Japanese reports recount that Chinese student activists had campaigned there for the boycott of Japanese goods, particularly in Beijing and Tianjin. However, silver dollar notes issued in Shanghai by YSB and, to a much lesser extent, the Bank of Taiwan were a highly visible manifestation of Japanese penetration and subsequently became one of the most pronounced targets for agitation by mid-May 1919.[27]

The overall impact of the 1919 boycott of Japanese-issued notes in China proper can be inferred from YSB balance-sheet totals compiled in Table 6.3 in pound-sterling terms. The unit of account is of importance here because, as already indicated, YSB notes were actually denominated in a raft of fairly arcane local Chinese tael and silver-dollar denominations, as well as in gold yen denominations.

YSB was conveying this information in English to an international readership beyond East Asia. In other words, this information was purposefully converted into a familiar unit of account and would have been widely available to political and financial analysts, even though none seem to have publicly associate nationalist sentiments with banknote circulation volumes at the time.

Unlike the Bank of Taiwan or the Bank of Chosen, the YSB was an overseas bank whose note issue at the time was predicated on demand in areas beyond formal Japanese domination: China's northeast, Tianjin, and Shanghai. It is therefore particularly instructive to note that its total circulation volume in pound-sterling terms had peaked in 1917; it had dropped by a whopping 66.6 percent by mid-1920 and waned further between 1922 and 1923. The 1919 setback was much less pronounced when confined to YSB total deposits—those fell by just 28 percent between the 1918 peak and 1923. The anti-Japanese climate in China is still *less* traceable in balance-sheet totals, which ultimately reflected Japan's trade volume with the rest of the world. Here, an increase of 11 percent was recorded in fact between 1919 and 1920. The stark variance between these balance-sheet entries suggests that World War I and the onset of Japan's recession in 1920 were not the only factors at play in explaining YSB performance.

Crucially, China-based British bank figures are indicative of similar dynamics. As the first foreign financial institutions to set up shop in China in the mid-nineteenth century, British banks were also the first to issue banknotes. As previously discussed, the comparative reliability of British banks in Shanghai turned them, from the 1870s, into one of the lynchpins of the expatriate community in this increasingly vital treaty port. British financial institutions in Shanghai were preponderant in the local stock exchange, and stalwarts like the Oriental Bank Corporation, the HSBC, and CBIAC not only funneled a large share of the total foreign investment in the country but also issued a considerable share of the city's fiduciary-money supply. Ultimately, these banks were indispensable to Britain's informal empire in East Asia and to catalyzing the monetary reform of imperial China.[28]

Yet anti-British sentiments had taken over Chinese student agitation in 1925 and 1926, as a result of grievances against the brutality of the British-run Shanghai Municipal Police. These sentiments adversely affected note circulation volumes more than any other balance-sheet entry; British bank fixed-deposit receipts were only temporarily affected by student activists' calls on all Chinese to withdraw funds from British banks.[29]

It would appear that the anti-Japanese student agitation of 1919 ultimately produced a longer-term result in the YSB case than in the British case. After 1919, several contemporary observers noted that the YSB issue in Shanghai had in effect been wiped out by nationalist campaigns.[30] In contrast, the British-run Chartered Bank's note circulation volumes in China recovered swiftly after the 1925 setback. The difference in the durability of the boycott in either case may have stemmed from the turnaround in British policy after 1927—from confronting to appeasing Chinese nationalists—as opposed to intensified Japanese aggression and concomitant Chinese mobilization against Japanese banks in Shanghai.[31] Chinese boycotts proved particularly thorny when directed at one power at a time. Since the early twentieth century, Chinese campaigners had improved their ability to identify cracks in the powers' China policies. At the height of the 1919 anti-Japanese wave, the Western expatriate community largely distanced itself from the fray. But in 1925, the campaigners so adroitly maneuvered Britain into the dock that British expatriates in Shanghai came to believe a Bolshevist conspiracy was afoot to single them out from the French and Japanese.[32]

At the same time, student-led antiforeign campaigns in 1919 and 1925–1926 made the Chinese press turn its attention to foreign bank note issuance as an internationally anomalous monetary phenomenon that must be redressed if China was to rehabilitate the flagging reputation of its financial institutions and achieve respect among the nations of the world. Calls on successive republican Chinese governments to suspend foreign bank privileges began to be heard from 1919, and articles lamenting the considerable discount that Chinese banknotes incurred in the marketplace were not uncommon.[33]

Curiously enough, there is hardly any mention of the effects of these anti-Japanese boycotts on YSB's China operations in the bank's six-volume official history, released from 1980 through 1984. Rather, this official history laconically refers to note forgeries as a factor adversely affecting circulation in inland commercial hubs like Hankou in 1922, as well as to local incidents that are deprived of nationwide political context.[34]

Be that as it may, one of these laconic references cites in passing an internal YSB memorandum of March 1, 1936, that is a memorandum written on the eve of the promulgation of the *fabi* legal tender and the roll-back of foreign bank notes in China; this retrospective memorandum confirmed that the YSB Shanghai issue was valued at 2 million silver dollars at its height, or just under 0.5 million higher than the figure available for mid-1912 (look again at Table 6.1).[35]

Total YSB note circulation for mid-1917 peaked in pound-sterling terms at £2.3 million (look again at Table 6.3), arguably as a result of growing demand in Shanghai. Considering that, by 1912, just over a half of YSB's note circulation could be attributed to demand in China proper, one might plausibly relate the 9 percent drop in mid-1918 (as conveyed in pound-sterling terms) to the loss of legal-tender status that YSB notes had hitherto enjoyed in the northeastern Japanese sphere of influence or to exchange-rate fluctuations (YSB notes were disbursed in both gold- and silver-denominated units of account). On the other hand, the much bigger midyear drop recorded in 1920 (24 percent) was, in view of the qualitative evidence already presented, almost certainly related to the surge in anti-Japanese sentiments in China proper.

In yen terms, finer trends can be observed based on a different *year-end* data set that was compiled *ex post* (see Figure 6.1). Overall, YSB

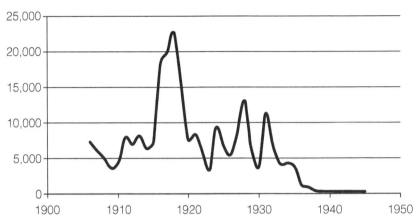

FIGURE 6.1.   YSB total note circulation, 1906-1944 year end.
Note: Unit: thousands of yen.
Source: *Yokohama shōkin ginkō zenshi* (1984), vol. 6, Appendix Table C1, pp. 398–401.

banknote volumes clearly took off on the eve of the Qing dynasty's downfall (1912). This take-off was, however, dramatically accelerated through the ensuing political instability of the early warlord era in China. At play during this period were perhaps not only popular mistrust of Yuan Shikai's interventionist bank reforms (the banking coup of 1916) but also concerns about the solvency of Western banks of issue during World War I.[36] Circulation volumes had started dropping back around 1917 through 1918, at first probably as a result of YSB's loss of note-issue exclusivity in Manchuria. Thereafter, successive waves of anti-Japanese boycotts in China (1919, 1923, 1925, and 1932) seem to have taken their toll on total circulation volumes with partial recovery in the interim.[37]

Notably, there is one difference between the data sets: In yen terms no dip was recorded in December 1917. Rather, circulation peaked in December 1918 (¥22,603,000). Whether this mismatch between the yen and pound-sterling data sets is purely a result of exchange-rate vagaries or perhaps a time lag, the long-term impact of anti-Japanese boycotts on circulation volumes forcefully emerges from both data sets. The yen circulation figure for December 1919 (¥15,154,000) is no less than 33 percent lower on the previous year; the December 1920 figure (¥7,543,000) is more precipitously lower (67 percent) compared with December 1918.

From 1920 right up to the formal banning of foreign bank notes in China proper by the KMT government (1936) a series of less pronounced troughs and peaks can be observed. Total YSB note circulation rebounded noticeably around 1928 and 1931 but never caught up with the 1918 peak. Though I have not found lateral evidence in YSB records to prove this beyond doubt, it is reasonable to suggest that the 1928 and 1931 rebound might also be linked to the concurrent withdrawal of HSBC's China issue, or to the failure of smaller foreign banks during that period, rather than purely a result of specific events or to any putative demand pressures in the northeast, where YSB standing had by then diminished.

It is instructive to use YSB circulation figures as a bellwether for the geopolitics of the Sino–foreign encounter and for variation in economic conditions across greater China. But the vitality of this note issue per se to YSB's worldwide operations in the 1920s should not be grossly overstated. This is because even at its peak (1918) the total note issue did not make up more than 4.2 percent of YSB total deposits and embodied a smaller fraction of the balance-sheet bottom line. Rather, the diminution in note circulation should be seen as compounding the effects of Japan's domestic recession on colonial banks in the 1920s. Smaller circulation volumes overseas meant less ability to offset Japan's current-account deficit at the time with a surplus of silver specie in China.

KOREA AND MANCHURIA

As explained in Chapter Four, Korea's economy was considerably less monetized and more insular than China or Japan's prior to 1882. Much of the commercial activity was performed by a class of approximately 200,000 itinerant merchants (K. *pobusang*), who traveled through villages under government supervision. Commercial practices did not rise much above the level of hawking, and business was conducted mostly by means of barter due to the extensive debasement and dissimilarity of locally available coinage: Three thousand varieties of Korean and numerous foreign currencies proliferated at the time. Villages were mostly self-sufficient, and the volume of traded goods was relatively small.[38]

Beginning in 1882, and against the backdrop of mounting intervention by China and Japan in its internal affairs, the reigning Yi dynasty reluctantly moved to reform Korea's economy. Bumbling attempts were thus made to remedy the chaotic state of affairs in the monetary system by establishing a (short-lived) modern mint, devising annual imperial budgets to replenish specie holdings, and converting in-kind land tax levies to monetary values. The failure to acquire the technological know-how to efficiently operate the mint meant that much seigniorage was lost due to the high cost of production. At the turn of the twentieth century, therefore, Korea was forced to approve Japanese yen coinage for domestic use.[39]

As early as 1878, the Yi court invited one of Japan's first privately run banks, the *Dai'ichi ginkō*, to set up a branch in Pusan to fund the growing trade between the two countries and to disburse its notes on the court's behalf. In 1902, under pressure from Japan, the Yi court further allowed Bank of Japan yen notes to be used within Korea for trade purposes, as well as the issue of silver-yen denominated *Dai'ichi ginkō* notes for exclusive use within Korea.[40] These were the first banknotes disbursed in Korea since the fifteenth century.[41]

In 1904, a formal monetary union between Korean and Japan was announced, and yen coins and notes became legal tender there. Traditional Korean copper and sycee coinage, equivalent in value to ¥9.6 million, was either smelted into bullion or exported overseas. To replace the old metallic currency, *Dai'ichi ginkō* commissioned from the Osaka mint ¥5.9 million worth of new brass coins with Korean inscriptions. The demonetization of traditional currency came as a surprise to many Korean merchants and peasants, and some saw their fortunes written off virtually overnight. However, the colonial government was at pains to attract much of the demonetized silver by continuing to accept it in tax payments. As metropolitan Japan was establishing its new gold-yen currency, the Japanese protectorate of Korea (ext. 1905–1910) was effectively on a silver standard, although Japanese currency was accepted as a matter of course.[42]

Established a year after Japan's annexation of Korea (1910), the colonial Bank of Chosen (*Chōsen ginkō*) was tasked with aligning the local monetary system with Japan's. It took over the note issue prerogative from *Dai'ichi ginkō* and started issuing gold-yen notes backed by BoJ securities. In 1918, the Bank of Chosen was joined by the other Japanese-run semiofficial bank, the Industrial Bank of Chosen (IBC), which was not permitted to issue notes. Rather, IBC specialized in longer-term finance of, for example, the purchase of large tracts of land that were owned diffusely by Korean peasants.

In terms of paid-up capital and deposit receipts, the Bank of Chosen (hereafter, BoCS) and IBC controlled nearly half of the Korean banking system in the pre-war era. The great bulk of their loans and deposits were attributed to monopolistic Japanese corporations (*zaibatsu*).[43]

In 1920, East Asia's wartime boom degenerated into a speculative bubble that soon burst, crippling much of Japan's banking system. The upshot for BoCS was a reduction of its capacity as provider of short-term finance for Korean–Japanese trade and an almost singular preoccupation with note issuance. Because the Bank of Japan played a greater role in underwriting the BoCS issue between 1925 and 1945, and because the use of the former's yen notes and coins had been made legal in Korea, many in Japan called for the revocation of BoCS issue prerogatives at that time. However, BoCS was strongly backed by the Japanese colonial authorities, who argued that Japan had to be buffered from future financial crises in its colonies. BoCS was therefore kept as the sole bank of issue in Korea, as well as one of several banks of issue in the Japanese sphere of influence in northeast China.[44]

Formally, BoCS's charter stipulated strict metallic reserve requirements as well as maximum circulation caps insofar as the banks' note disbursement was concerned. Apart from having to seek advice from the colonial authorities as to the amount of notes needed in the economy, and to relay circulation figures to the authorities on a weekly basis, the BoCS note issue had to be backed by 100 percent securities at least in theory. Securities could be diverse: BoJ gold-yen coins, local silver ingots, local silver and bronze coins, foreign coins, as well as merchants' bills of exchange and interest-bearing Japanese government bonds. However, bonds could not exceed ¥30 (initially ¥100) million as part of the overall reserve. In addition, silver ingots (sycee) were not to exceed one-fourth of the reserve in value, and a 5 percent tax on the volume of notes outstanding was levied by the colonial administration.[45]

Not long after it was established, BoCS gold-denominated yen notes flowed into northeast China. However, the flow was limited at first, and the notes could supplant neither Qing-issued local paper money (C. *guantie*) nor, for that matter, the locally denominated silver-dollar notes that YSB had been disbursing at its branches there.[46] For example, in the environs of the city of Jilin, silver-denominated *guantie* had been used in land-tax payments and in trading agricultural products, while BoCS gold-denominated notes were used mainly in market towns. Due northwest from Jilin, the existing multilayered currency system of Manchuria was not destroyed in the early 1910s but remained largely silver based. Rather, BoCS notes came to be one component of the system (see Figure 6.2).

Since its costly victory in the war against Russia, the Japanese government had aimed at the monetary unification of its spheres of influence in northeast China, but ruble notes continued to flow into the region via Vladivostok right until the Bolshevik Revolution (1917). As Qing-issued *guantie* scrip became worthless after the fall of the dynasty, one principal element of Manchuria's currency system disappeared, partially making way for Chinese warlord-issued currency. Thus, BoCS

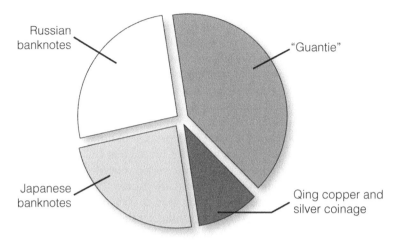

FIGURE 6.2. Estimated distribution of the stock of currency in the environs of Jilin City (approximately 250 km north of the Korean border), 1912.
Total is approximately ¥550,000. Japanese bank notes in Jilin mostly comprised YSB notes and smaller volumes of Band of Chosen and Bank of Japan notes. This estimate appears to exclude Japanese military coupons.
Source: Adapted from Ishikawa (2002), p. 131, Table 2.

gold-denominated notes locally issued at the bank's northeast China branches were proclaimed legal tender in Manchuria alongside YSB notes in 1917. Yet Japanese frustration at the persistent monetary fragmentation meant that by the early 1930s the BoCS's role as bank of issue there was eclipsed by the newly established Central Bank of "Manchukuo" (*Manshū chūō ginkō*).[47]

In the 1920s, a range of banknotes issued by Chinese postimperial provincial authorities predominated at the local level; they were mostly nonconvertible but fluctuated to a large degree in correlation to the price of silver. From an overall monetary standpoint, the 1920s embodied a trilateral battleground in northeast China between YSB-issued notes, BoCS-issued notes, and the Fengtian dollar, the latter having been issued primarily by the Official Bank of the Three Eastern Provinces (C. *Dongsansheng da yinhang*). This bank was amenable to warlord Zhang Zuolin, with whom the Japanese had a checkered relationship. In 1916, for example, when China's President Yuan Shikai suspended the convertibility of Chinese bank notes, Zhang—who often sounded anti-Japanese rhetoric—worked out an agreement with Japanese businessmen to prop up the Fengtian dollar by promising to contract more loans from Japanese creditors. Until Zhang's assassination in 1928, the Fengtian dollar remained fairly stable. But in 1930 the Official Bank, along with other Chinese-run provincial banks of issue, was taken over by the Japanese, and it subsequently merged with the Central Bank of "Manchukuo."[48]

Japanese currencies, both silver- and yen-denominated, were influential mainly in higher-end markets and in the modern sector. In 1921, for example, it was estimated that only 63.9 percent of the BoCS's total issue was circulating in Korea proper; 30.2 percent in northeast China and Manchuria; 4 percent in Siberia, and only 1.7 percent in "China proper" (C. *guannei*). In other words, only about 36 percent of the BoCS's total issue (that is, ¥41 million) circulated outside Korea. Notably, BoCS deposits in China proper amounted that year to ¥11 million, or roughly five times the volume of BoSC notes circulating there. For that reason, it would be a mistake to view BoCS braches in China proper as principally engaged with note issuance in the same way that BoCS's Seoul primary branch was.[49]

Changes in the exchange rate between gold and silver had various effects on the Manchurian economy in the 1920s. After 1932, a new era began when the new "Manchukuo" yuan, which had been initially pegged to the Shanghai silver tael, was put in place. In theory, the yuan contained 23.91 grams of silver like the early Chinese Republican dollar (also known as the Yuan Shikai dollar), but it was mainly disbursed in the form of notes and base-metal subsidiary coins. The "Manchukuo" yuan largely supplanted the Fengtian silver-based dollar prevalent in Manchuria and Japanese bank notes (that is, BoCS yen-denominated and YSB silver-denominated notes), to the extent that Manchuria essentially moved on to a full-fledged silver standard. Critically, YSB supported the "Manchukuo" yuan by accepting it on parity with its own silver-denominated notes, which had been popular in Manchuria much earlier.[50]

Between 1934 and 1936, BoCS yen-denominated notes made a comeback to the region, as the bank became increasingly involved in attempts to rapidly industrialize Manchuria. Reliable data are hard to find, but circumstantial evidence suggests that BoCS's note circulation in Manchuria had reached around ¥85 million in those years. This would have been more than double the 1921 figure. At the same time, the flight of silver from China, as a consequence of the Great Depression, meant that in 1936 the "Manchukuo" yuan had to be rebased on gold in line with Japan, Korea, and the rest of China. The Central Bank of "Manchukuo" ensured the stability of the new gold-based currency by exchanging the yuan with other currencies at a premium to note bearers and by maintaining a 30 percent bullion-reserve backing (the remaining 70 percent was in the form of Japanese government bonds).[51]

Following its adoption of the gold-yen standard, "Manchukuo" decided to redeem BoCS yen-denominated notes with its own new gold-based currency and to pressure Tokyo to order the BoCS to scale down its operations in the puppet state. A new Industrial Bank (C. *Manzhou xingye yinhang*) was eventually set up in December 1936 precisely so as to take over BoCS's role as provider of credit to Japanese firms operating in "Manchukuo." However, BoCS remained the leading creditor in Liaodong.[52]

After the famous Marco Polo Bridge Incident of 1937, Japanese forces began occupying other parts of China proper and issued their inconvertible military coupons on an ad hoc basis. At the same time, the Japanese set up a number of specialized regional banks of issue, modeled on the Central Bank of "Manchukuo." These disbursed wartime paper currencies partially backed against Japanese government bonds right until Japan's surrender in 1945.[53]

A Chinese territorial possession since only 1683, the island of Taiwan had witnessed Japanese, Spanish, and Dutch intervention through much of the early seventeenth century. The Dutch proved most effective and actually occupied part of the island (with Chinese permission) between 1624 and 1655. While this was primarily a strategy to gain access to China, the Dutch also encouraged migration from Fujian and Guangdong to develop an export economy based mainly on sugar. Through the Dutch connection, Taiwan became a regional emporium and part of a worldwide trading network in rice, sugar, and later tea.[54]

Following China's defeat in the first Sino–Japanese war (1894–1895), Taiwan was ceded to Japan, which turned the island into the foundation of its formal colonial empire. Concomitantly, Japan was able to stem Western financial influence on its own soil with the revision of the Ansei Treaties and the reclamation of its tariff autonomy (1894). By the early twentieth century, British banks had been similarly forced to withdraw their small note issues in Japan.[55]

On the eve of the Japanese colonial period, Taiwan's monetary system had been almost entirely metallic, and paper money was virtually unknown to most of the local population. Precious metals in any shape were accepted in maritime trade, but silver was predominantly used—sycee, silver-made ornaments, and Mexican dollar coins.

During the waning years of Qing rule, some ethnic Chinese settlers operated remittance banks linking the island with Xiamen. Pawnshops also provided credit in the tea export business, but indigenous financial networks lost much of their clout once the Japanese had moved in to monopolize the island's foreign trade.[56]

The establishment of the Bank of Taiwan (hereafter BoTW) in 1899 as the island's *exclusive* bank of issue embodied an important difference between Japanese and British colonialism in the region. Unlike the British, who *neither* imposed the pound sterling *nor* set up an exclusive bank of issue in Hong Kong, the Japanese sought to design colonial monetary systems that promoted convergence with the metropolitan system in the long term. The propagation of the Japanese language, Japanese laws, and Japanese monetary units was meant to gradually bring about assimilation of the colonies and the metropole.[57] Compared with the Crown Colony of Hong Kong, colonial Taiwan, or Korea, for that matter, monetary fragmentation and "free banking" persisted to an even greater degree in the British-administered semicolonial treaty port of Shanghai.

On the other hand, the Japanese government did not designate the Bank of Taiwan and the Bank of Chosen as full-fledged state organs (that is, "central banks"). In that sense at least, Japanese colonial monetary regulation seems somewhat more lenient than in the British colonial setting of Singapore, for example, where both metallic and paper money supply were tightly controlled by the colonial authorities in the early twentieth century.[58]

Seven years after it had gone on the gold standard itself, Japan decided to move Taiwan off silver, too. It tried to convert local silver and silver-yen currencies into Bank of Taiwan gold-yen notes, at first without much success. By 1906, four parallel types of money were current on the island: old silver yen coins from Japan; newly minted gold-based yen coins from Japan; Chinese silver currencies notionally denominated in the local Tamsui (Danshui) unit of account, and Bank of Taiwan gold-denominated yen notes replacing its own short-lived silver-yen note issue.[59]

To deal with this monetary fragmentation, the Bank of Taiwan shipped several million newly stamped silver yen coins to back up its new gold-yen note issue and paid out silver against its banknotes at a 10 percent premium. It was only in this way that it was able to begin gaining the confidence of the local population in its notes in the first few years. Fortuitously for BoTW, the introduction of gold-yen notes shortly preceded an upturn in the world price of silver, which tended to drain silver coinage away from Taiwan and facilitated Taiwan's transition to the gold-yen bloc.[60]

The Bank of Taiwan otherwise became famous for its near dissolution during the Japanese financial crisis of the 1920s, but in its early days it was a crucial factor in the growth of the Taiwan economy.[61] World War I was a boon to Taiwan's economy, as it was for much of East and Southeast Asia:[62] During the war years demand for BoTW notes soared. Postwar prosperity ended abruptly with the 1923 Kanto earthquake, which precipitated a looming recession in Japan and its colonies.

In the mid-1920s, BoTW had lent heavily to the sugar exporting business of the *Suzuki shōten* trading company, until the latter went belly up in 1927. The upshot was the temporary closure of BoTW, with the Japanese government as well as YSB being forced to come to its rescue. Many other Japanese banks were similarly crippled by bad debt in the 1920s, and calls for far-reaching financial overhaul in Japan were mounting. In late 1927, new policies were introduced in Japan and its colonies prohibiting bank managers from involvement in other business. Banks with paid-up capital of under ¥1 million were otherwise merged with larger banks. These policies, as well as YSB and Japanese government assistance, alleviated the run on BoTW, so that it recovered by 1928.[63]

Overall, however, Taiwan had achieved significant growth under the Japanese. In half a century it proceeded through a major phase of agricultural development to gain by 1945 a per capita income not far behind that of Japan itself. Though Korea was arguably becoming more industrialized under Japanese rule, the Taiwanese economy harbored a relatively bigger indigenous corporate sector.[64]

The BoTW started issuing silver-dollar denominated notes in south China proper as early as 1905. In 1911, the BoTW established a branch in Shanghai and started issuing silver-dollar denominated notes the following year. As previously mentioned, the bank's early silver-denominated issue in Taiwan itself had been—not long after Japan had moved on the gold standard—effectively retired. By 1906, it was making way for gold-denominated notes.[65]

Because only about 10 percent of the bank's total issue was thought to circulate on the mainland in the 1920s, the great bulk of its issue was tied up to the yen, even though the extensive financial links between the adjacent Fujian province on the mainland and Taiwan meant that the local Chinese population of the island often reverted to silver-denominated currencies.[66] Mainland China, in turn, officially remained on a silver standard up until 1935.

Interestingly, before its move off silver, the BoTW refrained from issuing notes valued under ¥5, a guideline reminiscent of the mid-nineteenth-century British Colonial Currency Regulations. But once gold notes started replacing silver ones in late 1904, a gold-based ¥1 denomination was freely disbursed, much as British colonial banks eventually started issuing $1 notes in China. British and, later, Japanese government concerns about low-denomination notes had generally drawn on the earlier European banking experience but ultimately proved of not much relevance in an East Asian setting, where the lower classes were not as exposed to paper money and, by implication, to paper-money forgeries. Most BoTW notes on the island were of ¥1, ¥5, and ¥10; a ¥50 yen note did not exist before 1921. In the early 1930s, the ¥50 note was still the BoTW's highest, while the BoCS and the Bank of Japan had widely disbursed ¥100 and ¥200 notes by then.[67]

The BoTW was otherwise subject to fewer charter constraints than BoCS with respect to the makeup of its metallic note reserve and the convertibility of its notes, probably because of the difficulties involved in purchasing silver on the mainland to balance off with its head-office gold reserve. Unlike the BoCS, the BoTW could not retain bonds as part of its statutory 100 percent reserve before 1937. Like the BoCS, however, the BoTW was subject to a 5 percent government tax on notes outstanding, so it is plausible that its note issue as a whole proved less profitable than BoCS's.[68]

Published in 1939, the official history of BoTW contains only one allusion to the fact that, as of 1919, its mainland circulation volume dropped sharply. The mainland issue was also adversely affected by the minting of early republican dollars and the rise of modern Chinese banks of issue in south China. However, the quantitative evidence is quite compelling: By 1933 the BoTW mainland issue was virtually defunct, though uncertainty surrounding the proclamation of the *fabi* seems to have temporarily rekindled demand.[69]

Yet, because the mainland issue made up only around 10 percent of BoTW's total issue, the aggregate does not necessarily convey the intensity of the 1919 boycott against Japanese banks on the mainland: Between 1918 and 1921 the total issue dipped only by about ¥5 million or 13.5 percent (see Table 6.4), as compared with 62 percent for the YSB total (look again at Table 6.3) during the same period. Figures are not available for changes in BoCS's total circulation volume during those

TABLE 6.4.
BoTW paid-up capital, year-end balance sheet totals, note circulation
(end-of-month average), and note reserves.

Year	Paid-up capital	Balance sheet total	Circulation average	Bullion reserve	Securities reserve
1899	5,000	10,353	925	925	0
1904	5,000	20,185	4,756	2,586	2,170
1909	5,000	39,952	2,683	5,932	5,781
1914	10,000	104,452	14,200	7,259	6,941
1918	30,000	677,328	40,691	21,275	19,416
1921	60,000	779,488	35,838	22,251	13,587
1923	60,000	917,809	33,656	13,296	20,360
1925	45,000	897,912	47,974	19,727	28,246
1927	15,000	776,334	45,058	19,734	25,323
1929	15,000	491,328	47,277	20,069	27,208
1931	15,000	445,825	37,459	17,499	19,959
1933	15,000	424,568	43,742	23,656	20,086
1935	15,000	414,760	58,423	20,969	37,454
1936	15,000	469,009	64,217	18,484	45,733
1937	15,000	523,981	83,569	28,194	55,374
1938	15,000	556,948	110,854	60,327	50,524

SOURCE: Adapted from *Taiwan ginkō yonjūnen shi* (1939), pp. 54, 69.
NOTE: Unit: thousands of yen.

three years, but it stands to reason it was even less affected than BoTW, as it did not disburse notes at all in China proper and because its clients were mainly Japanese corporations. The dip in the BoTW total from ¥4.7 million to ¥2.6 million between 1904 and 1909 may, in turn, attest to the difficulties in popularizing new gold-yen notes among the ethnic Chinese population of the island.

Taiwanese and Japanese colonists on the island seem to have been more willing to deposit funds in the BoTW than to accept its notes. Right after inauguration, BoTW local deposit receipts stood at only ¥764,000 (see Table 6.5). By 1904, they increased sixfold. Unlike YSB, or the British Eastern Exchange Banks for that matter, the BoTW was allowed to accept deposits within metropolitan Japan, and these grew quickly indeed. However, if the period from 1918 through 1923 saw sustained increase in deposit receipts on the island, in Japan these were halved, and on the Chinese mainland they dropped by 40 percent during the same period. This composite drop is primarily related to the Japanese banking crisis of the 1920s, but the mainland deposit drop may well be linked to the effects of May 4th Movement as well. Either way, only Taiwan deposits had been able to rebound to their pre-1918 level by 1938.

TABLE 6.5.
Bank of Taiwan deposits, regional breakdown

Year	Total deposits	Taiwanese deposits	Japanese deposits	Mainland Chinese deposits
1899	965	764	171	0
1904	6,018	4,804	938	276
1909	17,437	14,351	2,203	883
1914	54,187	24,366	22,600	7,222
1918	389,201	34,341	289,850	65,010
1923	201,905	36,280	126,481	39,144
1929	71,678	39,873	22,636	9,168
1938	186,408	109,105	49,317	27,986

SOURCE: Adapted from *Taiwan ginkō yonjūnenshi* (1939), pp. 58–59.
NOTE: Unit: thousands of yen.

BoTW's mainland deposit base did not constitute more than 20 percent of total deposits. This ratio was not entirely dissimilar to the share
of YSB "China proper" deposits to YSB aggregate deposits before World
War I (look again at Table 6.2). However, the ratio of the BoTW mainland note issue to its total issue was much smaller than either the YSB
or the BoCS "China proper" circulation volume because the latter two
were heavily implicated in the monetary system of the northeast.

CONCLUSIONS

The foregoing passages offered a comparative overview of Japanese colonial banks before World War II with an emphasis on their roles as
banks of issue. Taking account of the geopolitical setting at the time,
the second section surveyed the history of the Yokohama Specie Bank
as Japan's first overseas-geared bank and discussed in more detail the
nature of its note issuance prior to 1919; the third section then decisively
showed that the Yokohama Specie Bank was severely affected by the
rising tide of anti-Japanese agitation in China after 1919, particularly
insofar as its note issue was concerned.

This last finding provides a poignant counterpoint to previous studies, which have tended to focus on the bank's branches in the West and
seem to downplay the rise of Chinese nationalism as one of the key factors that reconfigured the bank's operations in the 1920s and 1930s. To
be sure, the intensification of boycotts in the late 1920s may perhaps
account—beyond domestic factors—for the new strands of belligerence

in Japanese foreign policy at the time; the proposition certainly calls for more research in the future.

The fourth and fifth sections of this chapter have analyzed the monetary properties of the Bank of Chosen and the Bank of Taiwan, offering some tentative comparisons with Yokohama Specie Bank's note issue. These sections pointed to both similarities and differences in the three banks' note circulation patterns; in their note-reserve requirements and their actual application and in their geographical spread and respective colonial mandates. There was some variation in Japanese bank note issuance in the colonial settings of Korea and Taiwan, in "Manchukuo," and in those parts of China that remained nominally sovereign. But all three banks seem, in one way or another, to have astutely adjusted the spread of their note issue in order to control for flagging demand due to nationalist boycotts or to cash in on demand spurts resulting from crises in the indigenous financial sector. All three banks were subject to a 100 percent reserve requirement in theory, but the makeup of their metallic bullion reserve and the degree of their notes' convertibility were dissimilar, reflecting varying local conditions. In terms of both reserve ratios and note denominations, the banks prudently followed charter obligations that were devised by the Japanese Treasury but, at the same time, were reminiscent of the obligations that European overseas banks had to abide by.

Like their British counterparts, Japanese colonial banks seem to have prudently kept a minimum of one-third metallic reserve against their notes outstanding. The Yokohama Specie Bank and the Bank of Chosen were allowed to maintain a considerable share of the reserve in government bonds, while the Bank of Taiwan may have kept in practice a higher metallic ratio (over 50 percent) to tackle the popular mistrust of paper money on the island during the 1900s. It is plausible to conclude, then, that prudent reserve ratios help explain the overall success of Japanese colonial banknote propagation. Yet one would also need to recall that Japanese bank notes in the 1920s were convertible largely by proxy and could therefore better cushion the Taiwanese and Korean colonial economies from financial crises or a breakdown in popular trust. In other words, these colonial notes were backed against metropolitan yen-denominated assets. But the metropolitan yen itself—when convertible into gold—could be converted only in Japan. Token Japanese coinage would, at the same time, help eradicate the everyday use of silver bullion in both cases.

In Taiwan and Korea, the Japanese were slow to standardize local coinage, enforcing gold-yen notes only after a fairly long transition period during which the use of silver currencies was partially tolerated. In Manchuria, moreover, silver-based currencies remained a pivotal medium of exchange right until 1935. China proper, on the other hand, was where YSB was tasked right from its inception with amassing a silver-currency surplus with which to offset Japan's gold-currency reserve deficit. The Yokohama Specie Bank proved indispensable in assisting Japan to move off the silver standard in 1896. The bank's silver-based note issue in China helped deepen YSB local presence. YSB China operations achieved, in turn, a surplus of resources over utilities, which could then be reallocated to cover Japan's trade deficit with gold-based Europe and America. It is this pivotal critical that YSB played in Japan's global trade flows that help explain why calls for the immediate implementation of a gold-yen bloc right across the region did not prevail.

Surprisingly, perhaps, the variability of Japanese colonial monetary policy recalls British attitudes in treaty ports like Shanghai, where monetary fragmentation prevailed, notwithstanding British semicolonial oversight. By the same token, Japanese colonial monetary regulation seems more lenient than in the British colonial setting of Singapore, where all forms of currency were strictly government-issued from the 1910s. In that sense, the analysis provided here might qualify, at least as far as monetary policy goes, interpretations of the Japanese colonial project as unremittingly "assimilationist." Indeed, the overall success of the BoCS and BoTW yen-note issues derived from the astute gradualism with which the construction of the yen bloc was pursued.

By comparison, the YSB note issue per se comes across as a minor factor: It accounted for only 1 to 3 percent of YSB total liabilities in the prewar era, while the Bank of Taiwan and Bank of Chosen respective issues made up 5 to 50 percent of their total liabilities over the same period of time. YSB deposit receipts in China were larger than its note issue there and of more strategic importance. All three Japanese colonial banks were able to attract deposits in China proper, but the Bank of Chosen and Yokohama Specie Bank seem to have contracted twice as much business there than the Bank of Taiwan. Notably, the Yokohama Specie Bank was by far the biggest of the three in terms of balance-sheet totals. Though its note issue had considerably declined by the early 1930s, the Specie Bank was about the size of the two other banks combined in terms of other liabilities, reflecting its vitality to the Japanese economy and international trade as a whole.

The Bank of Chosen total circulation volumes grew progressively larger than those of the Bank of Taiwan, but the latter posted somewhat higher balance sheet totals by the late 1920s, at least in part due to the fact that it did not have strong local contenders in the image of IBC. In that sense, the sources compiled here seem to confirm that in absolute terms Korea had been a more capital-intensive economy than Taiwan during the prewar era, notwithstanding what might have been a slower per capita income growth overall.[70]

This study has also provided insights into the degree to which imperial Japan could be considered as a "statist," bank-centered economy over the prewar era. Certainly, all the three banks of issue studied here were pivotal to the Japanese colonial grand design, but at the same time they were kept semiofficial, critically relying on private shareholders' subscription. They functioned not as full-fledged government central banks, but rather closer to the HSBC model of a dominant note-issuing colonial merchant bank.

Finally, this chapter has argued that the effects of Chinese and, to a much lesser extent, Korean nationalist boycotts on all three Japanese colonial banks call for further scholarly attention. Although the May 4th Movement took a demonstrable toll primarily on the Specie Bank, the Bank of Taiwan's mainland deposit base seem to have been severely affected, too, between 1918 and 1921. In view of gaps in the pertinent literature, the evidence presented above would therefore call for a re-examination of the prewar Sino–Japanese financial matrix across East Asia.

CHAPTER SEVEN

Will the Renminbi Go Global?

Prognoses of China's currency—renminbi, or RMB—going global have become a hotly debated topic in the economic and popular literature of late. While some analysts are tipping a gradual transformation of the RMB into the world's next principal reserve currency in lieu of the U.S. dollar, others contend that the deficiencies of China's financial market will continue to preclude any such transformation for a long time to come. The aim of this conclusive chapter is to survey the arguments put forward by either camp and to weigh into this debate not only through the prism of applied economic theory or political economy but also through the prism of economic history.

The need to approach this issue from fresh perspectives may perhaps be partly vindicated by what Wu, Pan, and Wang identify as the inevitable "paucity" of empirical analyses.[1] Equally compelling, however, is the fact that much of what has already been written on this issue is predicated on the fairly recent historic experience of the onset of the pound sterling and U.S. dollar through the twentieth century, and on the still more recent experience of the euro in the early twenty-first century.[2] Implicitly, therefore, the prospects of RMB internationalization are assessed based on indicators of convergence between the Chinese economy at present and the British, American, Japanese, or European Union (EU) economies in recent decades. But such an analytical framework, when removed from the broader historic context, might of itself rule out a more distinct Chinese path to global economic eminence—one where, for example, the depth of domestic capital markets might not turn out to be as critical a determinant of RMB internationalization as was the case in the Anglo-American development trajectory.

The following historic survey can perhaps shed light on current debates about the future role of RMB in at least one way: They remind us that the prospect of Chinese currency used as international currency may not be entirely new. For even though traditionally cast Chinese bronze coinage was swept aside by Western steam-powered minting technology in the late nineteenth century, it had for a millennium or so prior set the benchmark for East and Southeast Asian monetization. As China was about to phase out traditional bronze coinage—known as *caixa* or "cash" to Europeans—Chinese indentured laborers heading for Australia or the United States were still taking it with them on board British and American ships sailing across the Pacific to serve as token currency for intercommunal gambling and grocery-shopping purposes there.[3]

The analysis offered in the following pages explores what might inspire a geopolitical rally around, and popular trust in, the RMB as alternative or complementary reserve currency in the near future. It aims to revisit the degree to which the well-known and widely discussed imperfections of China's domestic capital markets could hinder currency internationalization. Reliable currency is conventionally understood here as primarily a "store of value," "unit of account," and "medium of exchange."[4]

In this context, economists such as Wu, Pan, and Wang seem to suggest that "highly developed and open capital markets in the home economy, where foreign investors can freely trade the currency-denominated financial instruments and generate profit" is *one* of *eight* important requisites that an "aspirant" international reserve currency must satisfy.[5] The other five important requisites to consider would be China's perceived geopolitical clout; its creditworthiness and the relative size of its economy; the ability of foreigners to obtain and convert RMB notes on demand; low domestic inflation and low exchange rate volatility; and lack of administrative or legal barriers to RMB cross-border mobility. Yet, because they accord great significance to the depth of capital markets—precisely as the Anglo-American experience would warrant—Wu, Pan, and Wang conclude that "it is probably too optimistic . . . to expect the RMB to become a global currency *before* 2025."[6]

THE HISTORICITY OF CHINESE CURRENCY
AS GLOBAL CURRENCY

Economic historians might, on their part, *not* wish to exclusively ponder "China's rise" as a twenty-first-century strategic actuality but also draw insights from China's preponderance in the premodern global economy going as far back as antiquity. As indicated in Chapter One, although

hybrid Sino-Hellenistic copper coins from the first century CE were excavated in Xinjiang, no premodern Chinese (or Indian) coins were ever
found in Western Europe. Similarly, many Sassanid-Iranian (224–651
CE) and some contemporaneous Byzantine gold coins were found much
further east near Huhehot in Inner Mongolia as well as in northwest
China, but only a few Chinese coins of that period were found west of
the Tarim Basin. The Sassanids imported Chinese porcelain en masse
and seem to have paid these off with bullion; there is little evidence of
significant backflow of Chinese coins to Iran before the Song era.[7] Conversely, Roman coins of the republican period were widely excavated in
India but not in China proper, even though Chinese silk was a luxury
commodity imported to Rome.[8]

In light of these findings, it seems that scholars should strive to better
demarcate the supply of various currencies and of currency substitution
across premodern Eurasia. It would appear that the great breakthrough
of Chinese bronze coinage beyond China proper occurred during the
cosmopolitan Tang period (618–907). At that period, Chinese coinage
had served as a model for Japan's first indigenous currencies and was
sought after for the first time in many parts of North and Southeast Asia
where standardized media of exchange were scarcer. Subsequently, Chinese bronze coinage of the Song dynasty (960–1279) was even current,
albeit on a limited scale, in some parts of south India possibly through
trade links with Southeast Asia. Song-style coinage had become so popular that it could serve as the currency of choice well after the Song
dynasty had collapsed in China—either through import or local imitation—in many parts of Southeast Asia. Such coinage thus supplanted by
the thirteenth century Java's original currency system, which had been
predicated as early as the eighth and ninth centuries on south Indian–
inspired silver-gold weights.[9] Moreover, in the mid-twelfth century, Japan imported large amounts of Chinese bronze coins, even though it
was no less abundant in copper and certainly not bereft by then of coin
production or metallurgic know-how.[10]

However, what is not entirely clear is the extent to which the Southern Song's greater reliance on fiduciary currency, or for that matter, the
Yuan's move off copper in favor of effectively a paper money standard,
might have freed up superfluous coinage that flowed across the border to
localities where it could fetch higher returns. It is plausible to assume that
the outflow of coinage from China accelerated remonetization in Japan,
where precisely that form of Song-style coinage was highly prized by
both merchants and the state as of the late Kamakura period (1135–1333
CE). The use of both indigenous and imported coinage seems to have
declined in Japan during the tenth and eleventh centuries. The available

evidence would suggest, at any rate, that the importation of Chinese bronze coinage into Japan grew exponentially during the Southern Song era as a result of more extensive trade links and in the face of opposition from the early Kamakura nobility. Importation may have diminished, in turn, once the Yuan came to power in China and unsuccessfully tried to occupy Japan. Either way, virtually no indigenous Japanese copper "cash" was cast during the Kamakura and Muromachi (1337–1573) eras. But Kamakura coin importation had mostly been in private hands, whereas Muromachi shoguns actively sent tributary mission to Ming China with a view toward obtaining Chinese copper "cash."[11]

The first locally cast Annamese coinage after its independence from China in the tenth century was Chinese style. The Annamese monetary trajectory continued to parallel China's right until 1885, when the French first attempted to introduce their own coinage in the region in lieu of sycee and "cash."[12] Previously, much of the coinage used in the area nowadays occupied by the northern reaches of modern Vietnam was Chinese too, beginning with the Han-era *wuzhu*. Further to the West, the silver-abundant Tibeto-Burman Nanzhao kingdom (eighth–tenth centuries CE), occupying much of the area around modern Yunnan, had in fact been relying on cowrie, as were some polities in the Bay of Bengal at that time. The rest of mainland Southeast Asia, to the extent that it was monetized, mostly resorted to Indian-style silver coinage in the late first millennium of the Common Era. In monetized regions of insular Southeast Asia gold protocoinage was more common, until the Majapahit Empire adopted Chinese bronze coinage in the latter part of the twelfth century.[13]

Chinese premodern bronze coinage reached the apex of its global presence around the fourteenth century, by which time it had been circulating widely in Japan, Korea, Annam, and along the coastal trading hubs of Cambodia, Thailand, and Burma. It was also rapidly gaining popularity in Java and parts of Sumatra, the north Philippines, and Borneo at much the same time. To a lesser extent, Chinese coins could be found along India's Malabar and Cormorandel coasts and in Sri Lanka between the seventh and fourteenth centuries.[14] The famous tributary missions, on which the Yongle emperor sent eunuch Zheng He (1371–1453 CE), even brought Chinese bronze coinage to mainland East Africa, while on Zanzibar Chinese coins may have been first used as early as the seventh century CE. Many fewer premodern Indian coins were, by comparison, excavated in Africa despite the greater geographical proximity.[15]

Though Chinese coin output had been by and large lower after the eleventh century, it was only in 1636 and 1678, respectively, that the new Tokugawa shogunate in Japan and Choson (Yi) dynasty in Korea were able to fully supplant Chinese bronze coins with their own bronze coinage, which was still designed in the traditional Chinese fashion (round with a square hole in the middle). The impetus for issuing indigenous Japanese coinage gradually built up, particularly over the course of the fifteenth century. In response to the diminished supply of Chinese coin, Japan saw the spread of popular shroffing (*erizeni*), whereby authentic full-bodied Song coins were sought out and prized over debased or forged Ming coins when paying out for commodities. Locally made private-order imitations of Chinese coins also became extensive. On the other hand, the Muromachi shogunate had avoided issuing coins of its own, probably due to its perceived high cost and despite the fact that casting technology was widely available locally by then. Chaos and disputes in the market place ensued, and tax collection became thornier due to the influx of forged coinage. In response, the Muromachi *bakufu* as well as local *daimyo*s desperately tried to enforce Chinese coin values from the top down, but without much success.[16]

When the Dutch arrived in Southeast Asia in the seventeenth century, they found that Chinese bronze coinage was still so popular there, too, that they began importing bronze coinage directly from China. Such coins were in high demand in, for example, Annam, and they sold there in return for Annamese raw silk. The Dutch then sold the silk in Japan in return for locally mined silver, which could fetch enormous profits when sold in China.[17]

However, the degree of popularity was uneven across the region. The decline in Chinese coin output and interdiction of foreign trade in the late Ming dynasty did not affect Javanese preferences much but was an important factor in Sumatra and the Philippines. There, on the eve of Dutch and Spanish respective landfall, Islamic variants of ancient Indian coin designs such as the silver *kupang* and gold *masa* surfaced sporadically.[18]

Unlike the English, who generally forbade the export of metropolitan coinage to Asian colonies, the Dutch attempted to introduce their own metropolitan silver coinage (*stuiver, dubbeltjes*) in Java. But this metropolitan coinage proved much less popular than the heavier Spanish-American silver dollars circulating in the region. Therefore, until the eighteenth century, the Dutch East India Company (VOC) relied on the local Chinese community for the supply of *picis*—the Javanese term for imported or locally cast Chinese-style coinage, which served as the colony's main subsidiary currency. It was only in 1724 that the Dutch felt confident enough to reintroduce a European-style copper coin (*duiten*), whereas these had already started taking root in Sri Lanka (Ceylon) in the later half of the seventeenth century. The production of *picis* was finally discontinued as late as 1763, by which time the main high-denomination silver currency in the region was the Carolus dollar (also known as the peso or piece-of-eight). Carolus, and later Mexican dollars, remained an important trade currency in Java and Sumatra right until the turn of the twentieth century.[19]

In 1877, however, the Dutch East Indies were affected by the metropole's decision to switch from a bimetallic to a pure-gold standard, turning along the way its existing stock of *guilder* silver coinage into token currency and abolishing the "free coinage" of silver bullion. By legal extension, the Dutch East Indies thereby went on a colonial gold-exchange standard. Previously, *guilder* coinage did not take root in the region because its intrinsic value was higher locally than its nominal value. Thus, it was taken out of circulation in return for Spanish-American dollars and smelted into sycee. Nevertheless, the Dutch banned the local use of Mexican dollars in 1900 precisely to promote guilders (*gulden*), which did become more widespread in Java afterwards, as did by then Javasche Bank (est. 1828) *gulden*-denominated paper money.[20]

MONETARY GLOBALIZATION *REDUX*

The discovery of abundant silver deposits in Latin America (sixteenth century) reconfigured the premodern Eurasian monetary system, ushering in the first thrust of globalization. On the one hand, this newfound source of silver reinforced the West's comparative advantage in precious-metal supply, and on the other hand it made possible the creation of a truly global currency (the Spanish-American silver dollar) for which the Chinese were willing to sell ever greater quantities of tea and silk.[21]

Latin American silver discoveries dovetailed with Ming China's (1368–1644 CE) sharp reduction of mining and coin production and its growing reliance on external supply of high-denomination currency in the form of silver. To be sure, in absolute terms, the Qing dynasty (1644–1912 CE) revitalized annual coin production almost to the same peak level recorded during the Song five centuries earlier. But China's monetary system had become acutely reliant on imported silver by then, either in coin or ingot form. Silver mainly served as merchants' higher-denomination currency and was by far the preferred means of tax payment, even though its purity and authenticity were assayed privately for the most part. As previously mentioned, for reasons that are still not entirely clear, neither the Ming nor Qing polities opted to enhance domestic silver mine production or introduce silver coinage of its own, right until the late nineteenth century, when European minting technology was universalized.[22]

Archaeological findings confirm that, at least since early modern times, specie (in dollar denominations) flowed on balance from West to East in return for commodities such as silk and tea. At the same time, Chinese copper cash flowed from East to Southeast Asia in return for tropical produce. Economic historians, therefore, might provocatively observe that there is nothing entirely new in the way that modern China is furnishing the United States with manufactured goods in return for U.S. dollar derivatives, while pushing for its own currency zone in Asia. Granted, the reasons behind the undervaluation of the RMB against Western currencies nowadays, which renders Chinese goods so attractive overseas, and the reasons why Western silver currencies were at a premium in early modern China owe to entirely different sets of circumstances; more important, since the collapse of the Bretton Woods accords in the mid-1970s, the U.S. dollar can no longer be counted as a specie substitute. Yet there does seem to be some uncanny resonance between the early modern global monetary system and the contemporary one in that China's net trade surplus with the West is largely funded by U.S. Treasury bonds, which are denominated in an international currency still called the *dollar*.

It is otherwise still not entirely clear why base metals such as copper played a more limited (albeit not entirely unimportant) monetary role in premodern West Asia and Europe compared with East Asia. Perhaps the only exception to this pattern was Japan where, as of the seventeenth century, bronze coinage was supplemented with gold and silver coinage on the back of vigorous domestic mining expansion.[23] In early medieval Europe, silver coinage was predominant, of course, although in Byzantium and the Islamic world both gold and silver flans were used to strike coins. As coins were smelted and often transported from one contiguous currency zone to another, the premodern world was devoid of a truly global currency circulating across *all* zones until the advent of the Spanish-American dollars.

That no single currency circulated right across Eurasia until early modern times was not only a result of the preference for copper in the East or the relative abundance of silver in the West but also the path-dependent monetary structures that obtained in either region. These structures determined, among other prescripts, the production technology used and the modes of coin supply regulation. Hence, Chinese pre-

modern coins of various eras all evince minimalist inscriptions, although
European coinage was largely minted or struck with elaborate imagery;
in premodern Europe "free coinage" was commonly tolerated, whereas
in China coinage and mining were strictly seen as a state prerogative.[24]

Echoing the "oriental despotism" paradigm prevailing in Europe
around his time, Max Weber famously posited that the Chinese preference for base metal coinage had been designed to allow emperors greater
opportunity to extract seigniorage than was possible in Europe.[25] This
preference might also explain why coin-production technology remained
fairly similar in China from the Tang to the Ming eras. In comparative
terms, European feudal lords and West Asian sultans debased the com-
position of their coinage in pursuit of greater seigniorage revenue more
often than could be tolerated in Chinese statecraft. There, the provision
of cheap bronze coinage came to be seen, in the first instance, as a corollary of the Confucian imperial duty to alleviate the needs of the populace rather than a means to generate imperial revenue.[26]

Although subsidiary copper coinage had been issued in republican
Rome, the metal subsequently played a minor role in Europe's disparate
monetary systems and remained rarely coined in much of the medieval
period. It was only in the sixteenth century that alloy copper coinage
respread all over Europe as token currency (billon), but was almost from
the outset subject to heavy debasement.[27] Notably, banknotes had been
invented in China as early as the eleventh century, but came into use
in Europe only in the seventeenth century. It is arguably this temporal
divide that might help explain the different paths by which Chinese emperors and European overlords resorted to enhance seigniorage.

The Mongol Yuan dynasty not only relied on banknote issuance
but radically reduced coin production precisely because it was deemed
unprofitable to the throne. By fiat, therefore, less coin was required in
China per se, and so large quantities continued to flow over the course
of the fourteenth century into Southeast Asia where such standardized
media of exchange were at a premium. Additionally, high-denomination
note issuance made silver ingots less sought after in China, arguably
resulting in outflow of the metal to Europe via West Asia over the course
of the fourteenth century.[28]

In China, therefore, copper cash was less readily debased than European coinage, although banknotes—mostly denominated in strings of
1,000 coins—were ultimately issued without adequate metallic reserve.
Chinese imperially issued notes lost favor among the populace by the fifteenth century precisely because they were overprinted to enhance state
revenue.[29] Initially, Europe's experience with banknotes was uneven

to say the least, but a sounder reserve policy eventually took root in England in the nineteenth century as part of the emergence of the early modern national-debt economy—so much so that, with the suspension of the gold standard in the 1930s, European banknotes were no longer fiduciary but wholly fiat (that is, not partially convertible into bullion), a situation obtaining formally today in most countries of the world following the collapse of Bretton Woods.

Indeed, the nineteenth century was a time when money incrementally shed its universal metallic anchorage with the transition to territorial currencies bound to nation-states' and central banks' "legal tender." Nevertheless, due to political instability and civil war, China was not to have an effective single "legal tender" until 1935.

As China ventured into economic modernity in the early twentieth century, silver dollars, subsidiary coins, and banknotes gradually superseded its bimetallic standard. But for the next three decades, the leaders of the newly established republic were unable to enforce monetary unification on breakaway provinces. An ephemeral turnaround appeared in sight only in late 1935, when an invigorated KMT (Kuomintang or "nationalist") administration took China's currency off the silver standard and proclaimed its first fiat currency in the modern era, the *fabi*. In the lead-up to the *fabi* reform, a large number of regional banks still operated outside of the central government's reach. More often than not, these banks had been amenable to warlords, who did not hesitate to milk the local civilian population through what economists call an "inflation tax." In other words, many regional banks serviced warlord debt with proceeds obtained from banknote disbursement. Still others strove to fend off the unification thrust of the KMT government by maintaining a stable regional currency and securing banknote convertibility to bullion.[30]

The KMT government's intention to trim its large budget deficit helped muster support for the 1935 move off silver. A modest budget surplus, a higher degree of monetary integration, and some improvement in productivity were achieved during 1936 and 1937. However, in the final analysis, unchecked military spending incurred by anti-Communist campaigns and the impending war with Japan did not leave the *fabi* (pegged to U.S. dollar in the main) much chance of retaining its credibility. In 1948, an eleventh-hour attempt to nominally repeg China's nationalist currency to gold failed, unleashing hyperinflation and irreversibly tainting the KMT's reputation in economic management.[31] Today's talk of RMB as future global currency should therefore be placed against the backdrop of China's acute monetary fragmentation in the century or so leading up to the proclamation of the RMB.

Evident throughout both the early modern and modern phases in the evolution of Chinese currency is that having any form of currency widely accepted is contingent on the degree of popular trust in its "store-of-value" and "exchange-medium" properties. Indeed, the pound sterling's supplanting by the U.S. dollar around the mid-twentieth century and the reasons why the renminbi is perceived at present as challenging the viability of the U.S. dollar as global reserve currency may both owe to geopolitical shifts in confidence. And despite the absence of equally detailed records from the eleventh century, circumstantial evidence would indicate that much of Southeast Asia had transitioned from Indian-style coinage to Chinese-style coinage at least in part because of a shift in confidence vis-à-vis Northern Song China (960–1127 CE), which was engendered in turn by the latter's reputation as an exporter of reliable currency and as a powerhouse of economic advancement at the time and by its expanding trade links in the region.[32]

Yet the stature of Chinese government–cast coinage as international currency went into steep decline through the remaining late imperial era, reaching a low-water mark of popular confidence in the republican period. Precisely how the RMB managed to restore faith in Chinese government-issued currency therefore needs to be closely examined in the next section.

THE EVOLUTION OF RMB IN THE ERA OF CENTRAL PLANNING

In the summer of 1947, the People's Liberation Army (PLA) was consolidating its advance across north and eastern China, bringing territorial integrity under Chinese Communist Party rule to many parts of the country. Soon afterwards, trade links between previously cut-off areas were reestablished. But often the currencies used across contiguous areas remained discrete; exchange rates between local currencies proved volatile through the civil war, greatly hampering economic recovery. Carrying over from the late imperial and republican eras, this monetary fragmentation impinged on the momentum gained by PLA ground forces and brought to the fore the need to urgently unify China's currency. From then on, monetary unification became one of the most potent propaganda messages delivered by the Communists, who were well aware of the deep-seated popular disenchantment with KMT monetary reforms in the 1940s.

As the area under Communist control expanded, the CCP leadership therefore had to turn its mind to macroeconomic planning. Later in 1947, it proposed to unify China's disparate currency systems and to work toward a centralized mechanism of banknote issuance. To that end, Dong Biwu was appointed chairman of the Economic Bureau of North China and entrusted with promoting a new "people's" currency—the RMB. Thereafter, currency unification measures progressed incrementally, with local cadres and Dong occasionally publishing official exchange rates between the RMB and currencies issued by erstwhile authorities.

Concomitantly, Dong launched an extensive campaign to rally grassroots support for the RMB. These concerted efforts led to the establishment of the People's Bank of China (PBC) as a singular bank in charge of money supply on behalf of the advancing Communist forces. Gradually, the vestigial note issue prerogatives enjoyed by foreign banks operating on Chinese soil were rescinded, followed by a Communist crackdown on Chinese private bank prerogatives, but disparate currencies issued by the Communist themselves in different parts of the country continued to circulate side by side for another year or so.[33]

On December 1, 1948, the People's Bank of China was formally established in Shijiazhuang, Hebei Province, that is, well before the proclamation of the People's Republic of China itself. On the eve of its establishment, there had been a plethora of currencies circulating side by side in recently "liberated" areas, namely areas taken over by the Communists from retreating nationalist forces. The main Communist currencies at the time had been notes issued by affiliate regional institutions: the Farmers' Bank of Northwest China, the Bank of Southern Hebei; the Bank of Beihai, Zhongzhou Farmers Bank, and the Bank of the Northeast. Over the course of 1949 most of these banknotes had been redeemed in return for new RMB notes at a rate of between 100 and 2,000 units of older currency to 1 RMB.[34]

At the same time, the PBC also enforced measures to strictly regulate China's privately run financial institutions and constrain foreign banks' ability to transact local business. Most KMT-controlled semiofficial banks were dissolved, as was the KMT central bank. Nonetheless, the two largest of these banks were merely reorganized, and their prewar names remained in effect until the 1950s: the Bank of China and the Bank of Communications. Smaller privately run banks and family-run "money shops" were similarly reorganized under CCP oversight or dissolved.[35]

These measures were all carried out with a view toward nominating the PBC as an all-powerful monobank within a few years. To that end, the PBC was allowed to go beyond traditional central-bank roles and provide credit to retail and corporate clients, who were not suspected of KMT sympathies and formed China's shrinking and anxious private sector. Indeed, many such individuals and corporations were experiencing liquidity problems as the economy was gradually transitioning to central planning and collective ownership.[36]

As China emerged from the great destruction of the civil war with a newly proclaimed national currency, severe inflationary pressures came to bear on the real value of the RMB in the early 1950s, as well as on the value of wartime KMT "gold yuan" notes that were now declared legal tender in Taiwan alongside the inconvertible taibi (TW$). These problems were allegedly compounded by the nominally high units of value of non-CCP currencies still unofficially circulating in some regions, by large quantities of forged notes disseminated by Japanese and later by KMT special forces, and by intermittent food shortages.[37] To make matters worse, the official exchange rate between RMB and older currencies often proved confusing because of the different denominations used and due to the low quality of RMB note printing as compared with some of the older currencies, which had been more resistant to wear and tear.[38]

In the face of such problems, the CCP decided to embark on a second currency unification campaign. As of March 1955, the PBC exerted greater efforts to curb money supply and improve RMB note quality, whereby older RMB notes were converted to new ones at a rate of 1:10,000. From 1955 through to the present that newly redenominated RMB has remained legal tender. Concomitantly, the PRC set up in the mid-1950s highly centralized monetary oversight mechanisms. By the late 1950s, all banks had been merged into the PBC, producing a monobank financial system. Under this system, the PBC wielded not only central bank administrative powers but also commercial banking functions; through cash-flow audits, tight credit overhaul, and fiscal restraint on the part of the government, the PBC was eventually able to achieve price and money-supply stability and vest all monetary powers firmly in the hands of the state.[39]

RMB nominal foreign exchange rates during China's monobank era point to two primary development phases before the country opened up to foreign investment: 1955 through 1972 and 1973 through 1979. The first phase parallels the Bretton Woods accords, whereby Western currencies had been pegged to the U.S. dollar at a fixed conversion rate. During that earlier phase the RMB, too, was convertible into U.S. dollars at a fixed rate of 2.46 to US$1 (see Figure 7.1). In practice, however, the RMB was not tradable at all; its availability overseas was dictated by state-controlled trade without any correlation with market demand.

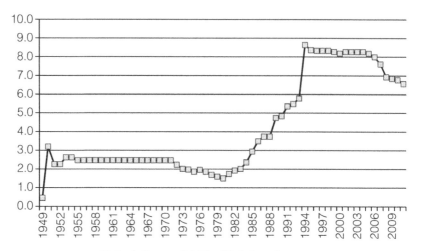

FIGURE 7.1.   U.S. dollar to RMB official exchange rate, 1949–2010.
The figures are corrected for the 1955 issuance of new RMB denominations at
a rate of 1 to 10,000 old RMB.

Sources: Data for 1949 compiled from Li Dongrong (2006). Data for 1950-1978 compiled in the
main from *Geguo huobi huijia tongji shouce* (1979). Data for 1979 to the present mainly compiled
in the main from the State Administration for Foreign Exchange website, retrieved on September
19, 2012, from www.safe.gov.cn/model_safe/tjsj/rmb_list.jsp?id=5&ID=110200000000000000.

During the later phase of 1973 through 1979, the Bretton Woods system collapsed, and Western countries successively went on a floating
exchange rate; the PRC therefore decided to notionally adjust the RMB
exchange rate based on the value of a basket of currencies, while at the
same time aiming to maintain continuity by occasionally *revaluing* the
RMB.[40]

By and large, however, the Nixon Shock with which this book started
off did not affect China, the Soviet Union (USSR), and other Communist countries as much as Western Europe simply because the former
command economies were much more insular, their currencies having
already been delinked from metal and the Bretton Woods system. Yet,
by 1972, most Western experts believed that unbridled Soviet arms expenditure, sluggish industrialization and dependence on Western food
imports nullified any possibility of the ruble, for example, ever becoming a contestant for U.S. dollar dominance.[41]

The gradualist revaluation of the RMB in terms of U.S. dollars between the late 1970s and early 1980s constitutes a little known antecedent to the present era where the devaluation of the same currency
had come to be lamented worldwide. It bespoke to some degree residual

concern for the country's purchase power of food imports like grain, which were vital in the 1970s, rather than the later open-door preoccupation with honing China's comparative advantage as purveyor of cheap labor to foreign manufacturing firms. But, ironically enough, the same measure had adverse effects on Hong Kong, whose currency had by then been effectively pegged to the U.S. dollar albeit being a British colony and that was in fact importing much of its food from the mainland by the early 1980s. The cost of living in Hong Kong experienced upward pressure transmitted by the RMB Hong Kong dollar exchange rate during the first few years of the open-door era.[42]

THE MAKEOVER OF RMB IN THE REFORM ERA

With Mao Zedong's death in 1976, the CCP slowly moved to relax central planning. In 1979, Deng Xiaoping prevailed over Maoist hardliners to embark on a bolder set of economic reforms that came to be known as the Open Door Policy (*gaige kaifang*). The reforms started off by allowing greater freedom to peasant households to retain surpluses above the production quotas set by the state, and to semicollectively operate township and village and enterprises (TVEs). But the focus of policy makers quickly shifted to urban industries, where foreign direct investment in special economic zones was promoted. In the latter part of 1979, the PBC, too, embarked on monetary reform whereby retail credit and deposit functions were localized and the monobank system relaxed. By 1983 China's State Council declared formally that the PBC was to eventually assume central-bank responsibilities only and withdraw from mercantile banking activity.[43]

As a result, the PBC relinquished control of many branches across the country to focus on exercising monetary coordination in pursuit of macroeconomic growth objectives. In order to bolster export manufacturing, in 1981 the RMB was at first devalued in state-controlled foreign trade transactions vis-à-vis the official exchange rate. But in other transactions such as remittances from overseas Chinese to family members on the mainland, the basket-of-currencies peg was still applied. This two-tier approach accentuated China's cheap-labor advantages, while ensuring that other contact between PRC and foreign nationals remained on an even keel (that is, RMB purchasing power in terms of other currencies was not eroded across the board).

To be sure, this two-tier approach remained in effect until 1985 despite criticism from a number of countries as being unfair. But in 1985, the PRC stopped publishing the favorable exchange rates applied to foreign trade (*maoyi neibu*) and nominally returned to single-sheet ex-change rates. These single-sheet rates were nominal because, in effect, the two-tier system was kept unofficially, giving rise to a black market where both Chinese and foreign individuals in possession of foreign cur-rencies aimed to convert their funds underboard, often through trade-licensed companies, for a more favorable exchange rate. During that period, the PRC devalued the RMB single-sheet exchange rate time and again. In 1985 US$1 was worth 2.95 RMB, but by 1993 it was worth 5.76 RMB (look again at Figure 7.1), a measure that clearly boosted China's exports and buildup of inbound FDI.

The next milestone in the evolution of the RMB dates back to De-cember 28, 1993, when the State Council promulgated its intention of reforming the exchange rate mechanism. Aware of the malignant spread of a black market, the PRC undertook to genuinely strive for conver-gence between official and unofficial exchange rates. After an adjust-ment period, it was foreshadowed that the exchange rate would move into a partially floating mode along a band and that a Chinese intrabank market for foreign currency reserves would be established.[44]

As of January 1, 1994, the two-tier system was finally abolished, and the official exchange rate at the time of 5.80 RMB to US$1 was dramati-cally devalued to the swap market rate of 8.70 RMB. At the same time, the foreign exchange retention mechanism was replaced by a compul-sory settlement system, and the PBC was formally enshrined as China's central bank through a law passed by the National People's Congress. From then on, the PBC no longer directly financed government over-drafts and was separated from the Ministry of Finance, even though it was not depoliticized to the extent of focusing on annual inflation tar-gets as did Western central banks.[45]

PBC provincial branches were similarly made fiscally and adminis-tratively dependent on its Beijing headquarters, and overt ties with lo-cal governments were cut off. Instead, China's four state-run commer-cial banks (Agricultural Bank of China, ICBC, Bank of China, China Construction Bank) as well as three "policy" banks (State Development Bank of China, Export-Import Bank of China, Agricultural Develop-ment Bank of China) were tasked with negotiating credit to local infra-structural projects.[46]

The impact of the new policy was felt by tourists later that year: As part of the two-tier rationale foreign visitors had, since the early 1980s, to purchase goods within China at designated venues by using RMB-denominated Foreign Exchange Certificates (FECs). Slightly smaller than RMB notes in design, these certificates were valued in practice above par, partly so as to promote tourist spending on local goods and services and to curb imports. Conversely, Chinese nationals requiring foreign currency for travel abroad were subject to at-par exchange rates and to strict individual quotas; expatriate residents wanting to remit their salaries overseas also had to register with the authorities. But, as of 1994, preferential-rate FECs were abolished following a drastic devaluation of the RMB official exchange rate. Foreigners were expected from then on to purchase RMB at local banks at the same exchange rate that Chinese individuals and firms would convert their foreign currency.[47]

China's financial market reform had gained further momentum as its first two bourses were inaugurated in 1991. More and more foreign banks were otherwise allowed to set up branches in China during the 1990s, although most could provide retail services in local currency only from the mid-2000s onward. Gradually, more and more export businesses were allowed to switch from compulsory handover of foreign currency revenue to voluntary conversion, thereby allowing greater liquidity of foreign assets in the interbank market. Arguably, the thrust toward internationalization of the RMB was held back by the Asian Financial Crisis of 1997 through 1999, when the dangers posed by free capital flows to emerging economies became apparent. Yet, as Liew, Burdekin, and other experts note, although the value of other Asian currencies was plummeting during the crisis, China sought in the main to responsibly stabilize the region through tight monetary policy and a buy-back of its own currency, even at the expense of consequent deflationary pressures within the domestic economy, rather than being dragged into devaluing its currency in a bid to maintain the competitiveness of its export industries.[48] Ultimately, the Asian financial crisis also called into question the desirability for individual Asian countries of maintaining a U.S. dollar peg when much of their trade is intraregional in nature, as Ogawa has persuasively argued.[49]

Following the Chinese economy's swift turnaround between 2001 and 2003, the PBC started amassing billions of U.S. dollars in reserves. Whereas before the Asian financial crisis such reserves embodied an export-led boom on the back of a devalued currency and a flurry of inbound foreign investment in local manufacturing plants, the acceleration in PBC reserve buildup after 2001 represented not just continued FDI inflows or trade surpluses with the United States but *also* the growing attraction of China in the eye of financial speculators. The "hot money" that these speculators channel in is often seen as one of the key factors driving the property price bubble that has developed in China's eastern seaboard cities since the mid-2000s.[50]

Today, despite the accretion of massive foreign currency reserves over more than three decades of export-led economic reform, China may still seem a long way away from a full floatation of the RMB in world financial markets. The RMB does not meet what are widely seen as basic requisites to do with internationalization in terms of financial market openness. As Chen and Cheung have shown, although the use of the RMB in trade financing overseas has increased rapidly in recent years, China still maintains strict capital controls, which render its financial system quite insular from global money markets. Nevertheless, even Chen and Cheung acknowledge that the RMB "has great potential to become an international currency" and that its acceptance in the global economy is affected by *both* economic and *political* factors.[51]

China has not yet reached the stage of unhindered capital account convertibility. On the other hand, the professionalization and depoliticization of the state-owned financial sector has been growing, particularly since Zhu Rongji's tenure as premier (1998–2003). For example, in 2002 the Communist Party's hitherto powerful Central Commission for Financial Affairs was abolished and replaced by a more technocratic Regulatory Commission.[52]

China nowadays enforces greater current account transparency and has been, since 2007, progressively grooming Hong Kong as an "offshore" clearinghouse for the nascent global trade in RMB-denominated financial assets. In 2010, the sanctioning of trade in RMB proper was announced in Hong Kong; and, in January 2011, China for the first time trialed RMB trading even in the United States.[53] Concomitantly, the offshore RMB market has been growing steadily. Due to the U.S. dollar shortage effect on trade experienced in the recent global financial crisis, the People's Bank of China even initiated a scheme to allow in principle settlement of *all* types of cross-border trade in RMB.[54]

To be sure, portentous signs of *politically* induced foreign investor amenability to, if not espousal of, the RMB as imminent global reserve currency may already be found beyond money markets, particularly in countries reliant on trade with China across East Asia, Southeast Asia, and Oceania.[55] Andrew Forrest, CEO of Australian mining giant Fortescue Metals, has recently declared, for example, that his company was "now exploring the possibilities of being paid in renminbi, purchasing equipment in renminbi from our renminbi bank accounts and bringing equipment into Australia and every other type of variety." Forrest's comments came a month after Rio Tinto, a multinational mining and resources group with headquarters in London and Melbourne, had indicated it was considering settling iron ore sales in renminbi because of pressure from Beijing to do so. But, in contrast to Fortescue Metals, Rio Tinto had no initial plans to start trading in renminbi to offset its U.S. dollar transactions.[56]

At the same time, the PRC has been slowly bowing to international pressure to revalue its currency along a narrow band as a means of reducing its trade surplus with the West. In 1994, US$1 was worth 8.6 RMB, but the rate dropped to 6.76 by 2010 (look again at Figure 7.1). Arguably, the greater adjustability of the RMB exchange rate achieved prior to 2008 was one of the factors that helped China weather the global financial crisis better than did the West. That said, many critics of the PRC suggest that this adjustment is too slow to assist Western recovery from the global financial crisis of 2008 and that in the main it reflects the dollar's weakening against other foreign currencies rather that a genuine worsening in Chinese terms of trade (for comparison, see Figures 7.2 and 7.3).[57]

In the second decade of the twenty-first century, the notion of China eventually becoming a dominant economy is seldom disputed. Neither is the notion that China has been one of the most salient beneficiaries of post-1989 globalization.[58] Its growing clout on the world stage is reflected geopolitically in important multilateral organizations such as the WTO and the G20. By now, there seems to be growing recognition on the part of China's leaders of the potential benefits of greater RMB convertibility. Though China faces numerous economic challenges domestically, not least of which are environmental degradation and growing income disparity, there are signs of newfound confidence in China's economic growth model to allow for further internationalization of the RMB. As previously indicated, RMB-denominated bonds have been issued in Hong Kong by PRC state-controlled banks and conglomerates since 2007 ("dim sum bonds"). In recent years, they have been joined by foreign conglomerates with large PRC operations such as McDonald's and Caterpillar. In January 2011, even the World Bank issued a series of "dim sum" bonds in Hong Kong. Within China, too, a select group of multinational nongovernmental organizations (NGOs) and banks have been allowed in recent years to borrow funds on a trial basis from the Chinese public through the floatation of bond in the domestic market ("panda bonds"): These include the United Nations' International Finance Corporation, the Asian Development Bank, and more recently the Bank of Tokyo-Mitsubishi UFJ.[59]

Moreover, experimental payment of RMB for some import goods from Southeast Asia has begun; this would have been next to unthinkable in the 1990s when it was illegal to take RMB out of the country. It

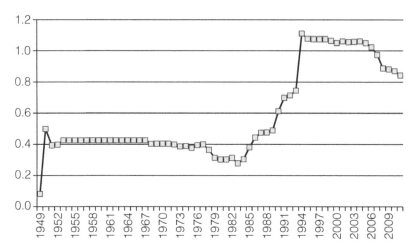

FIGURE 7.2. Hong Kong dollar to RMB official exchange rate, 1949–2010.
The figures are corrected for the 1955 issuance of new RMB denominations
at a rate of 1 to 10,000 old RMB. In 1983 the British colonial authorities in
Hong Kong pledged to peg the Hong Kong dollar to the
U.S. dollar at a rate of 7.8:1.

Sources: Data for 1949 compiled from Li Dongrong (2006). Data for 1950–1978 compiled in the main from *Geguo huobi huijia tongji shouce* (1979). Data for 1979 to the present mainly compiled in the main from the State Administration for Foreign Exchange website, retrieved on September 19, 2012, from www.safe.gov.cn/model_safe/tjsj/rmb_list.jsp?id=5&ID=11020000000000000.

may not be long before the RMB begins to play a significant role as an asset in other countries' sovereign funds and to consolidate its appeal on the cross-rates as a result of *both* trade finance–related and narrower financial demand. In the intermediate range, therefore, the pressure on the People's Bank of China to revalue the renminbi looks set to mount.[60]

THE ADVANTAGES AND DISADVANTAGES OF INTERNATIONALIZING THE RMB

In PBC thinking there is currently a set of quantifiable and intangible advantages associated with potentially allowing the RMB to be freely tradable outside China. The primary quantifiable advantage would be, of course, the ability to enhance "seigniorage" revenue in its abstract modern form (as opposed to the metallic seigniorage of premodern times). In addition, RMB tradability is likely to increase the volume

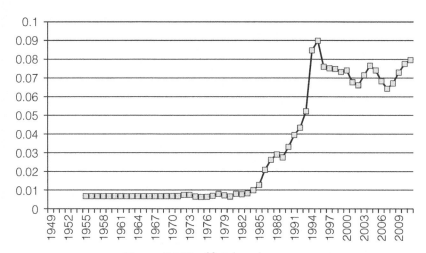

FIGURE 7.3. Yen to RMB official exchange rate, 1949–2010.
Note that the Japanese yen was floated against the U.S. dollar in 1973. Prior
to that, the yen had been pegged to the dollar in line with the Bretton Woods
Accords at 360:1. The figures are corrected for the 1955 issuance of new RMB
denominations at a rate of 1 to 10,000 old RMB.

Sources: Data for 1949 compiled from Li Dongrong (2006). Data for 1950-1978 compiled in the
main from *Geguo huobi huijia tongji shouce* (1979). Data for 1979 to the present mainly compiled
in the main from the State Administration for Foreign Exchange website, retrieved on September
19, 2012, from www.safe.gov.cn/model_safe/tjsj/rmb_list.jsp?id=5&ID=110200000000000000.

of international financial transactions to be cleared in China and thus
hold out the prospect of more premium jobs created locally and greater
financial-services tax revenue. The main intangible advantage would,
according to conventional wisdom, accrue to PRC citizens and firms
rather than to the PRC government, whereby lower exchange commis-
sions would have to be advanced when transacting business overseas.
Yet the PRC government is likely to intangibly benefit from greater "soft
power" if the RMB were internationalized.[61] In this context, it is important to consider some economists' estimates that the United States
derived a compounding windfall of US$953 trillion between 1946 and
2002 purely as a result of the fact that that the dollar was the main
global reserve currency during that period. But the overall benefit to
the U.S. economy could have been manyfold bigger if intangible factors
were factored in.[62]

Economists further suggest that should the RMB become a regional
reserve currency in East and Southeast Asia over the next decade, the
Chinese economy could rake in a windfall of RMB 744 trillion, not to

mention the impact on China's geostrategic clout in multilateral organizations such as the WTO and G20.[63]

The most obvious downside to RMB internationalization is associated in PBC thinking with the potential weakening of macroeconomic levers that have so far stimulated Chinese exports, for example the managed-band exchange rate regime. Internationalization would also pose the risk of Chinese nationals transferring assets overseas on short notice and allow for "hot money" to more easily penetrate the domestic economy and aggravate the already acute property bubble across much of the county's eastern seaboard.[64]

Clearly, China's financial market is not sufficiently open at present to allow comprehensive RMB internationalization. Notably, PRC nationals and firms still cannot independently purchase financial assets denominated in foreign currency. They are able to invest in RMB assets only through a select number of government-accredited foreign financial institutions or buy foreign securities only via a select number of state-controlled financial institutions. There is also lack of sufficient competition in the domestic financial market, with state-owned banks still accounting for the lion's share of retail loans and credit. China's own securities market dates back only to 1990 and is still not easily accessible to private-sector SMEs; credit is therefore skewed in favor of state-controlled large companies, often resulting in low returns to investment and misallocation of resources.[65]

But many of the other preconditions for internationalization have largely been met: China already accounts for large share of the world economy and has until recently been able to overcome inflationary pressures for the most part. Although capital account movements across the border are still restricted, greater current account convertibility is now permitted. In the face of financial market shortfalls, policy makers have of late gingerly moved to bestow on the RMB more international exposure. In June 2007 the first batch of RMB-denominated PRC bonds were floated in Hong Kong; the following month the PBC set up a specialized Exchange Rates Department (*huilüsi*) with a mandate promote the RMB's internationalization as well as its prestige overseas. Furthermore, in March 2010, the State Council approved an experimental global RMB clearing center in Hong Kong that is to be extended into twenty mainland regional centers in the near future. Indeed, in October 2010, the twelfth PRC Five-Year Plan reaffirmed that Hong Kong is to become a test ground for clearing global RMB-denominated transactions. Then, on June 1, 2011, the PRC government announced a new experimental scheme whereby accredited institutions and individuals without domestic representation would be allowed direct purchase of

RMB overseas. Evidently, then, important initial strides toward RMB full convertibility have been completed over the last three years without any major shock recorded on the cross-rates.[66]

Notwithstanding the seemingly slow pace of reform in China's domestic equity markets, and the limited recourse nonstate firms have thereto,[67] Chen and Cheung report that the cumulative volume of nonfinancial trade settled in RMB increased from less than 4 billion RMB at the end of 2009 to 290 billion RMB by November 2010. Similarly, RMB-denominated bank deposits in Hong Kong have experienced exponential growth in recent years; such deposits currently making up around 5 percent of the total volume of Hong Kong bank deposits. It may be the case that RMB-denominated deposits would come close, within a few years, to the 30.8 percent share that U.S. dollar–denominated bank deposits hold in the former Crown Colony.[68]

THE DEBATE AMONG WESTERN AND JAPANESE SCHOLARS

In his classic 1960 study, Robert Triffin suggested that the U.S. dollar morphed into *the* international reserve currency sometime after World War II, namely more than half a century after the United States became the largest economy in the world.[69] But in their more recent important study, Eichengreen and Flandreau have analyzed the makeup of international reserves in the interwar period and found that the U.S. dollar had actually overtaken the pound sterling to become the leading reserve currency as early as the 1920s. During the subsequent decades, despite short-term global currency tribulations arising as a result of U.S. dollar devaluations, the U.S. dollar became all but indispensable to international trade.[70]

Against the backdrop of progressive dollar devaluations and what hitherto seemed like a well-functioning European Monetary Union, Eichengreen and Flandreau concluded that the global monetary system could be remade over a relatively short period of time; they even alluded to the fact that the euro might well be on its way to unseating the greenback as preferred reserve currency. Perhaps more germane to the issue under review, Eichengreen and Flandreau also suggested that network effects and the advantages of incumbency should not be overestimated when weighing up the possibility of an emerging global currency "dethroning" a more established global currency.[71]

Historic experience and economic theory suggest that in order to become global reserve currency a few key preconditions need to be met simultaneously: The home economy of this currency needs to demonstrate stability and low inflation; the volume of the home economy should be the largest in the world; the home country must possess a mature and solvent financial system.[72] The United States was the largest economy in the world throughout the twentieth century and maintained low inflation during that period. At the same time, the U.S. financial system was the most elaborate and invasive as measured, for example, in the ratio of publicly listed equity to GDP. It was the sheer scope and transparency of the New York money market that helped entrench the greenback as global reserve currency.[73]

That said, the domestic subprime crisis of late 2007, which quickly deteriorated into the global financial crisis of 2008, stemmed from regulatory flaws in the very same financial system. The crisis revealed deep structural distortions in the U.S. economy like overconsumption, mammoth government deficit, and distorted risk incentives to corporate executives; these have cast doubts on the dollar as a viable *single* reserve currency, not least among Asian central banks. But talk of the RMB eventually supplanting the dollar in the financial press may not have necessarily emerged as a result. Rather, what triggered speculation of imminent RMB internationalization was the bleak forecast for economic performance in other parts of the developed world: crises in Spain, Ireland, and Greece have weighed heavily on the prospects of the euro complementing the greenback as a more serious reserve currency, while the viability of the Japanese yen—once slated to potentially offset the greenback—has been tarnished since Japan's "Lost Decade" of the 1990s.

With a rapidly industrializing economy that has posted double–digit annual growth rates over the past three decades, China quite obviously attracts more global attention. It would appear that the RMB came to the fore as a future alternative to the greenback mainly as a result of the fact that China's banks seemingly performed much better than Western ones through the global financial crisis. Until not long ago, prominent economists such as Nicholas Lardy had identified China's banking system as the weakest link in its development model.[74] Yet the facts that— contrary to Europe and the United States—no major bank bailouts were reported in China, that a growth rate of over 9 percent was still achieved between 2008 and 2009, and that China has now overtaken Japan as the world's second largest economy may well have psychologically primed Western public opinion to consider more seriously what appears to be a long-term historic shift of power from West to East.

Takatoshi Ito has argued that the PRC economy has proven so resilient because it has benefited from underlying demographic dividend. Based on U.N. demographic statistics, Ito came to the conclusion that

China would become the largest economy in the world no later than 2027. Apart from endogenous factors, Ito believes that the global financial crisis provides the Chinese economy with a golden opportunity to stamp its mark geostrategically. As the United States is coming to the realization that the financial market deregulation it has espoused as part of the so-called Washington Consensus, as well as the neoclassical theory it is underpinned by, irreparably tarnished Wall Street's reputation, more and more commentators are betting on the alternative "Beijing Consensus" as an engine of growth in emerging markets precisely because of its more cautious approach to economic theory and market deregulation.[75]

Zhou Xiaochuan, the PBC governor, has on a number of occasions stated his view that the RMB need not supplant the greenback as global reserve currency. Rather, Zhou supports the creation of a new composite international currency along the lines of the SDR—one that cannot be controlled by a single sovereign state and that would transcend narrow national agendas by factoring in the price of commodities such as gold. Nonetheless, a PBC study group set up by Zhou found that in the intermediate term it might be desirable for China to enhance the role that the RMB plays in trade with neighboring Asian countries as part of an emerging regional trade bloc, whereas today much of that intra-Asian trade is carried out in U.S. dollars even though U.S. firms are scarcely involved therein. Such a regional experiment could help coordinate RMB overseas exposure and help gain experience in averting currency instability in the future.[76]

Within Chinese academe, one can find a wider range of views. Economists are divided on the question of whether RMB internationalization is desirable and, if so, at what pace. Li Daokui of Tsinghua University—arguably the academic whose views have proven most influential in this debate—is in favor of a stalling tactic whereby China would achieve free capital account convertibility over a long period of time. Li advocates a two-track gradualist approach: Domestically, he sees no need to immediately allow full RMB convertibility and instead emphasizes the need to improve the efficacy of China's financial system; on the other hand, Li supports a more rapid expansion of trade in RMB-denominated assets in Honk Kong with more PRC bond issues there and eventually the setting up of a second Hong Kong bourse exclusively dedicated to trade in RMB-denominated equity.[77]

Prominent Hong Kong–born economist Steven Ng-Sheong Cheung (known in China as Zhang Wuchang) has for many years opposed any revaluation of the RMB, believing it would benefit only a small coterie of wealthy PRC nationals who frequently travel overseas. China's most vulnerable population—rural migrants seeking employment in labor-intensive factories—would, according to this theory, be hard hit should foreign investors opt to relocate production lines to other countries as a result of RMB revaluation. In Cheung's typically conservative assessment, exchange rate predictability should firmly remain the anchorage of China's developing economy, although domestic market forces should perhaps be allowed to play a greater role in the PBC interest rate mechanisms. In contrast to Zhou Xiaochuan, Cheung does not believe in promoting a new composite global currency because the value of such a currency might be swayed by the volatile price of global commodities like gold. Instead of the current U.S. dollar peg, Cheung proposes— against the backdrop of rising U.S. indebtedness—to affix the value of the RMB to a basket of thirty foreign currencies and perishable goods, while providing the rural poor with a range of subsidies to alleviate the negative impact of a likely RMB appreciation.[78]

Larry Hsien-Ping Lang (Lang Xianping), a business scholar known for his outspoken opposition to state-owned enterprise reform, weighed into the RMB debate from the opposite direction. Lang pointed out that the problem with likely RMB appreciation as a result of internationalization emanates from the current structure of the Chinese economy, which is fixed-investment driven and export led rather than consumption and services based, as in developed countries. Prior to RMB internationalization, Lang argues that China would have to combat its inadequate domestic consumption rate by laying out more social security nets that would encourage the middle and lower classes to save less of their income. In the short term, however, Lang believes the RMB is too devalued at present because it does not sufficiently factor in U.S.-induced inflation: Although this might seemingly promote employment in China's industrial export sector, the positive effect is *outweighed* by higher imported-food staples (for example, soy) and commodity prices (for example, oil and iron ore). These in turn put upward pressure on the price of essential domestic goods, with a net outcome of making the poor even poorer, constraining consumption, and making industrial inputs more expensive.[79]

Prominent neoliberal economist Chen Zhiwu, now based at Yale University, by and large shares Lang's observations. In Chen's view, the RMB's excessively slow appreciation against the U.S. dollar is accentuating structural imbalances in China's economy, not least of which is loss of government control over the general price level particularly in the property and equity markets. Conversely, China's foreign reserves keep piling up, and hot money pours into the country, fueling a speculative boom that is hurting the country's reputation for stability overseas. Foreign speculators are attracted to China in part because the appreciation pace of the RMB has been made so predictable by government policy over the last decade. Furthermore, according to Chen, the overly devalued RMB is stalling the much-needed transition of Chinese industry to more sophisticated capital-intensive products, while at the same time suppressing income in the bottom percentiles of the socioeconomic ladder.[80]

Returning to the other end on the spectrum of views, Senior Vice President of the World Bank Lin Yifu has recently warned that, in view of the slow pace of the U.S. economic recovery, any further revaluation of the RMB will immediately dampen consumption of Chinese goods in the United States. Because most of these goods are not readily produced within the United States, this will result in a further blow to net consumption there, setting back the recovery. In the longer run, Lin does recognize the need to increase Chinese domestic consumption but adds that a more important means of achieving balanced bilateral trade would be for the United States to trim its government deficit. For Lin, therefore, stability is China is critical to world economic recovery at present, and any experimentation with market forces could jeopardize these aims.[81]

CONCLUSIONS

Amid an emerging debate in the West about the prospects of other currencies or precious metals supplanting or offsetting the U.S. dollar as leading global reserve, this chapter has sought to draw insights from the past in an effort to contextualize China's historic role in international currency provision over the *longue durée*. It has shown that, strictly speaking, there was no truly global currency before the discovery of rich silver deposits in Latin America and the spread of the Spanish-American silver dollar in the seventeenth century.

Nonetheless, well before the discovery of the New World, traditional Chinese copper "cash" had served as a model for Japan and Korea's first indigenous currencies. Copper "cash" was also sought after in many parts of Southeast Asia, where previously South Indian–modeled gold and silver currency had been in use. Notably, in the mid-twelfth century, Japan imported large amounts of Chinese bronze coins, even though copper was more abundant there than in China, and Japan was not be-reft of metallurgic know-how. Invented in China as early as the eleventh century, yet largely phased out by the fourteenth century, banknotes came into use in Europe only in the seventeenth century and spread con-tinuously thereafter. It is arguably this temporal divide that might help explain the varying degree to which Chinese emperors and European monarchs aimed at enhancing seigniorage revenue.

The current preoccupation with RMB as future international cur-rency is not entirely devoid of the historic context of Chinese financial evolution. For even though traditionally cast Chinese bronze coinage started giving way to Western steam-powered minting technology in the late nineteenth century, it had for a millennium or so prior set the benchmark for East and Southeast Asian monetization. Even as China was phasing out traditional bronze coinage at home, Chinese indentured laborers were still taking it with them on board British ships sailing across the South Pacific to serve as community currency for gambling and grocery purposes.

Today, of course, any role that China's currency might play on the world stage would be divorced of the metallic anchorage that typified the monetary development stage prior to 1971. That year, following the breakdown of the Bretton Woods accords, most currencies of the world were beginning to slough off their linkage with gold, thereby circulating as media of exchange purely by state fiat. It would be careless to com-pare the premodern and current phases in the evolution of China's cur-rency without recognizing this ponderous difference. Yet, by the same token, one can still find resonances across these starkly different epochs in that quite often in history financial assets flowed into China from the West to offset surplus Chinese consumable exports.

Faced with a rapidly growing Chinese economy, many pundits are forecasting that the RMB would soon become *the* world's reserve cur-rency in lieu of the U.S. dollar. Such predictions are devoid of a historic context for the most part, nor are these essential in arguing the case. Others contend that the deficiencies of China's financial market would continue to preclude any such transformation for a long time to come. This chapter surveyed the arguments put forward by either camp and weighed into this debate not only through the prism of political econ-omy but also through the prism of economic history. Chinese economist are mostly in favor of RMB gradual revaluation, arguing it would be a boon to Chinese consumers, but some warn a rapid appreciation could risk global recovery. The prevalent view, as well as new policy measures, suggests that, short of imminently floating the RMB, a further revalua-tion is highly likely.

If and how soon the RMB might supplant the greenback as global reserve currency is much harder to predict. Although RMB floatation is likely to benefit the Chinese economy in the long run, it is for now mainly advocated by economists associated with neoliberal views. At the *policy*-making echelons, figures like PBC Governor Zhou Xiao-chuan disapprove of overt challenge to the U.S. dollar as yet. Instead, they ultimately see the RMB as *one* of many monetary and commodity complements to the U.S. dollar in establishing a new global standard. In the broader scheme of things, therefore, the extent to which the RMB would go global in the near future may not be determined solely by domestic financial and equity market reform moves but, more important, by the overall geostrategic posture that China opts to embrace vis-à-vis the IMF, the World Bank and the G20; by the development model it promotes and the shade of hegemony it chooses to exercises, as a resurgent superpower.

The odds for an RMB showdown with the U.S. dollar over global monetary dominance may seem far fetched to many at present. Nonetheless, by designating Hong Kong, with its extensive capital markets, as the RMB's gateway the world, and by laying the groundwork for RMB-denominated bilateral trade agreements across the region, it seems that the government of the People's Republic of China is making quiet yet bold strides toward creating new important functions for its currency than it has ever carried in the past. That the RMB will within a few decades become much more than merely the currency of the people of China is, at any rate, not as far fetched as it may seem at first glance.

Conclusions

Three principal thematic threads have been interwoven in the foregoing chapters. The first sought commonalities between the Chinese monetary trajectory and the Western one over nearly three millennia. This thread was particularly concerned with the question of whether Chinese premodern sources could give evidence with a preoccupation with debasement as was the case in the West. The second thread was concerned with the ways and means whereby fiduciary money underpinned statehood and modern nationalism in East Asia. The last thread sought insights from China's monetary history to contextualize the present debate about the role China might play in the world monetary system in years to come. The following passages will aim at summing up this book's findings along each of these threads. They will both suggest what may be the book's relevance to broader considerations in the field of economic history and point to possible new areas of exploration in the future.

Chapter One set the terms of reference by challenging the perception of the Western and Chinese numismatic worlds as inexorably "separate." While it is still not possible to categorically point to a single common West Asian origin for all types of round coinage in antiquity, evidence to that effect is mounting. The Chinese, at any rate, had been acutely aware of the hallmarks of Western coinage—namely the use of gold and silver as well as anthropomorphic inscriptions—from the first decades of the Common Era at the very latest. They had also used silver and gold monetarily at some moments of their pre- and early imperial history, particularly during the Western Han era. Silver bars (sycee) then became a key component of the Chinese monetary system during the late Ming and Qing eras.

Conversely, base-metal coinage was monetarily used *not* only in China. Copper and copper alloys were a significant element both in the Greco-Roman monetary system and in the early modern Spanish and

Swedish domestic monetary systems. In addition, the global relocation of copper bars from places where they were relatively abundant to places where they had distinct monetary properties was an important element in the making Portuguese and Dutch trading empires.

The case for "separateness" is somewhat more plausible on technological grounds. While bronze metallurgy itself was not developed endogenously in preimperial China, the fact remains that Chinese coinage was cast rather than struck right until the late nineteenth century. Yet the causes for this seem grounded not only in a technological falling behind but are also "institutional" in nature: After all, low-value cast bronze coinage, as well as the strict regulation of copper mining, held a particularly strong appeal in traditional statecraft. In early modern Europe, the use of different precious metal currencies in conjunction with improved minting technology afforded the state greater seigniorage potential, whereas Chinese statecraft arguably entertained a much stronger prejudice against the very notion of the state profiting from currency. Otherwise put, better minting technology was sought by early modern European polities to differentiate sanctioned currencies from forged or foreign ones. In the Chinese setting, however, incentives to improve the quality of coinage were less compelling because bronze coinage possessed a priori lower seigniorage potential.

For these reasons one could plausibly generalize the Chinese premodern economy as one where precious metal coinage was virtually absent and the premodern European economy as one where base metal, state-sanctioned subsidiary coinage was historically in short supply. Yet this is certainly not to say that Chinese bronze coinage was always aplenty. In fact, "coin famines" were quite common across the broader sweep of Chinese history, too. By the same token, ordinary seigniorage revenue—although greater than in China—does not seem to have made up more than a tenth of overall state revenue in early modern Europe.[1]

This book started off with the question of whether the premodern Chinese monetary experience might reveal an equal degree of anxiety concerning debasement or concerning foreign currency substitution, as was the case in the West. Based on the analyses offered subsequently, the answer to the first part of the question would be in the affirmative. However, some of the key modes of debasement clearly diverged across Eurasia, and in that sense there seems to be much value in furthering this line of comparative enquiry in future studies.

The answer appears much less straightforward when it comes to the second part of the question. To be sure, premodern veins of "currency wars" or anxiety about "foreign" currency substitution can certainly be read into the monetary setting of the Five Dynasties era from which the world's first paper money emerged. It might also be read into the way in which the Southern Song polity tried to stem the flow of bronze coinage into the hands of its steppe enemies or how the latter issued paper money of their own. Yet, throughout much of the early and mid-imperial era, Chinese base metal coinage was uniquely welcomed by other polities in East and Southeast Asia that did not wish to issue similar currency of their own even when they had the technology to do so. Whether the benefits of this popularity outweighed the bane of resultant "coin famines" within China itself is questionable, though. Neither is it clear whether these benefits flowed back, on balance, to the state or to maritime traffickers. What is clearer is that, overall, Chinese emperors rarely needed to turn their mind to "foreign coin" substitution of domestic coinage simply because such a problem did not really exist in China before the onset of the Carolus silver dollar. There seems to be, in any event, much room for further exploration here in the future.

One could provisionally speculate that coin "famines" discouraged, over the long run, investment in the production of better-quality bronze coinage, as the latter tended to be taken out of circulation in favor of forged or lighter coinage. The "famines" might also explain why there seems to have been greater de facto tolerance for "older" and forged coinage in late imperial China as compared with early modern Europe even if Chinese de jure treatment of counterfeiting was at least as strict.[2] Quite apart from that, weight and design multiplicity seems to have been well accommodated in premodern China ever since Shan Qi articulated his "light" and "heavy" duality.

To be sure, despite the lure of simply issuing fiduciary currency, late Ming and Qing emperors did try on occasion to raise the market value of their coinage above its intrinsic value through *rebasement* and encouraging the surrender of alternative currency. This was carried out with a view toward repopularizing imperial coinage and eventually stamping out alternative currency. However, Ming and Qing mints did not possess the technology that could effectively ensure that forged coinage would not be mistaken for imperial full-bodied bronze coinage. For this reason, Ming and Qing mints could not decisively realize much profit from increased output other than through coercive means. Sooner or later, the competitive nature of statecraft deliberations within the late imperial bureaucracy would tilt back in favor of those calling for the scaling down of mining and coin production. At the same time, mechanically minted Spanish-American dollars became popular in China during much the same time not merely because they were made of silver but also because they were easier to transact than sycee, readily identifi-able, and harder to forge than copper "cash." All of these were mutually reinforcing qualities.

Insofar as the divergent modes of debasement across Eurasia are con-cerned, there has not been to my knowledge a comprehensive study based on chemical analysis. Yet a cursory look at any catalogue of Western or Chinese coinage spanning longer stretches of time would reveal remark-able permutation. In the Western setting, debasement often entailed the introduction of *smaller*-size coins or greater use of alloys. These pat-terns of debasement can certainly be observed in China, too, particu-larly in the Eastern Han and late Ming eras. However, in the Chinese setting, debasement seems to have been at least as closely linked with the issuance of *bigger* fiduciary coinage from bronze (*daqian*). Moreover, the negative impact of *daqian* on peasants' livelihood was frequently in-voked in traditional statecraft right alongside the perceived scourges of unbacked paper money. In that sense, China's earlier use of paper money has an important institutional dimension; it does not simplistically en-sue from the invention and earlier use of paper, as token currency is known to have historically assumed other ancient forms too. Rather, it may have been the case that the path-dependent focus on bronze coinage as the corollary of an ideal agrarian society induced Chinese rulers to seek seigniorage in the form of *daqian* to the neglect of other possibili-ties. Its negative popular connotations aside, *daqian* paved the way to the introduction of convertible paper money during the Song era since the fiduciary principles it embodies had become well known by then; judicious state backing then assuaged fears of overprinting and forgery during much of the Yuan era.

By way of contrast, paper money spread around Europe long after paper itself had been used for writing. The fear of note forgery had probably impeded its uptake beforehand, but here, too, there were at least two more institutional dimensions at play. Firstly, the concurrent use of higher-value metals in European coinage had presented suffi-cient debasement potential without resorting to more fiduciary forms of currency like *daqian*. Apart from simply reducing the metal content of coins or alloying it, early modern European sovereigns could *also* ma-nipulate the decreed exchange rate between domestic coins made of dif-ferent precious metals so that it diverged from the coins' intrinsic value. But, at the same time, these sovereigns had to work harder and often constrain themselves in order to prevent the *outflow* of either silver or gold coins to regions outside their own polities where they might be valued higher relative to the other metal. The flipside of this state of af-fairs was toleration of the *inflow* and usage of some foreign coinage, not least because European sovereigns often depended on *voluntary* rendition of metal to their mints and could otherwise benefit from expanding cross-border trade. Secondly, when paper money use did start spreading across eighteenth-century Europe, it was accompanied by the diffusion and implementation of more *concrete* metallic-reserve principles. These were first applied in England, where metallic debasement had notably been more moderate compared with the Continent and where the stirrings toward "territorial money" had occurred first.

Scholars studying the emergence of paper money in Europe without reference to the Chinese experience quite often come to the conclusion that it was definitive improvement to, and acceleration of, the flow of public information that allowed fiat currency to eventually take root. In their view, fiat money could not take root before the 1800s because state excesses in the form of overprinting could not be picked up by the populace quickly enough.[3] Yet, in comparative terms, the Chinese experience might qualify the significance of information or technological gains in that regard. That fiduciary paper money could be introduced on a large scale by the Northern Song, and then reintroduced time and again by Yuan and early Ming emperors despite lingering memories of abuse by previous emperors, owed *less* to technological advancement or information gains than to the cachet that new dynasties could conjure up. In that sense, political clout may be said to have instilled popular faith just as much as the perception of metallic reserve violability could stir up panic in the marketplace.

And although this book is framed by world monetary history, it reaches the conclusion—across several key junctures—that monetary history cannot of itself account for the "Great Divergence" between East and West. To be sure, more flexible mining regulation and better protection for individual mineral wealth may explain why, on a per capita basis, European precious metal output was probably higher than China's during the Greco-Roman and early modern eras. The post-Roman hiatus aside, it similarly stands to reason that Europe was more monetized than China at least from the Yuan period on. Nonetheless, the great technological breakthroughs in East and West correspond with broader societal and fiscal factors. Thus, the Song premodern "Industrial Revolution" saw a sweeping transition from corvée to remunerated labor and from grain-based tribute to monetized commercial taxes, even if a proportion of tax receipts was levied in grain for consumption in the capital right until the twentieth century. Similarly, England's modern "Industrial Revolution" had been long preceded by a dramatic growth and recomposition of the tax base and a newly acquired state capacity to leverage itself through "national debt." The latter funded the creation of

a great naval power, which could then extend a modest trading empire
to the furthest corners of the globe well before steam engines came on
stream.

Compared with the Portuguese, Spanish, French, and Dutch trading
empires, the British lead lasted longer because it came to be based not
only on naked military power but also on institutions adept at maximizing returns from the expansion of unhindered global trade. Britain
therefore promoted "free" trade on the back of gunboats but propagated individual property rights at the same time. Its colonial monetary
policy came to be geared toward furthering trade rather than enforcing
its domestic coinage overseas. Quite to the contrary, insulating domestic
currency from global bullion flows was one of the hallmarks of British imperial policy, even as it pushed for a level monetary playing field
outside the metropole. Neither was royal income from debasement or
seigniorage very significant in early modern British national accounts, as
compared with other sources of revenue.

One of the key differences between the Song economic ascendancy
and the British one was therefore the fact that the former did not seek
to expand trade to the same degree. The Song polity contented itself
with some foreign trade but did not vigorously pursue it. By implication, one might add, Southern Song, and late Ming debasements seem
"defensive" in nature; namely, they were aimed at defraying the cost of
fending off steppe invaders and offset the outflow of full-bodied bronze
coinage across the border. Mongol paper money abuses may be partly
linked with attempts at occupying Japan, but late Qing debasement is
more closely associated with the costs of quelling rebellions at home.

Early modern European debasement seems, however, somewhat
more "offensive" in nature in that it was more often aimed at defraying
expansionist warfare. The Song era apart, it would be hard to find a
Chinese historic parallel to the pattern whereby the city-state of Venice
could foist, for example, debased coinage on its Greek colonies during
the fourteenth century, while denying it legal-tender status elsewhere.
That Venetian pattern, which was first mentioned in Chapter Three, un-
cannily echoes the later Japanese imperialist monetary project in Taiwan and Korea. This project, in turn, constitutes an important episode
in the global transition from fiduciary to fiat currency over the course
of the twentieth century—one that would hopefully fuse in the future
with the growing body of literature on the stability of paper currencies in other "latecomer" economies, for example, pre-1914 Russia and
Austro-Hungary.[4]

On their part, the particularities of Japanese colonial bank note issuance do not lend themselves all too easily to "statist" stereotypes.

As discussed in Chapter Six, Japanese colonial banks of issue were not "central," strictly speaking, but publically listed, notwithstanding their singular role in empire building. Their reserve requirements varied according to local conditions and at the same time drew much on the nineteenth-century British banking experience in both implicit and explicit manners. Notably, although Japanese monetary reform measures met with relatively little popular resistance in Korea and Taiwan, the Yokohama Specie Bank bore the brunt of nationalist boycotts on mainland China. Largely neglected by the pertinent literature, these historic boycotts are important *not* only because of their lurid antiforeign rhetoric, which quite readily brings to mind today's boycott against Japanese carmakers in China following the dispute over the Senkaku/Diaoyu islets; or only because they eroded foreign bank profitability. After all, bank note issuance constituted a relatively minor business end in either Japanese or British bank operations on Chinese soil.

Rather, the significance of these boycotts *also* lies in how they stimulated the rise of modern Chinese banking and the diffusion of Chinese bank notes, for, as I have argued throughout this book, bank-deposit agglomeration and the buildup of an intangible "national debt" are critical to our understanding of the process of economic modernization. These factors are of course linked up with modern bank note issuance, with the diffusion of metallic reserve principles and with the receptivity toward paper-based financial instruments in the marketplace, but, ultimately, they are more important.

In other words, the stabilization of fiduciary banknote issuance was historically significant in that it paved the way—first in the preindustrial English setting—to an explosion in public borrowing and lower interest rates. After all, the value of tangible banknotes in circulation makes for a small share of the money supply in our twenty-first-century economies and pales in comparison with the size of long-term government debt. It is thus hardly surprising that Chinese governments had more difficulty floating public debt in the prewar era than foreign banks had in disbursing paper money to Chinese clients. In monetary terms, where China stood out circa 1900—as compared with other latecomer economies—was not necessarily in its undermonetization. More compelling in this context is the degree to which the Chinese money supply at that time was grounded in metallic currency and the low magnitude of bank deposits and public debt.

Viewed with the benefit of hindsight, there seems to be a big difference between these prewar Chinese boycotts and the dynamics of monetary nationalism (read: mercantilism) in our twenty-first-century, postmetallic setting. Although express preference for locally manufactured goods is still an obvious facet of modern nationalism, monetary overtones are harder to find nowadays. Thus, for example, East Asian central banks increasingly rely on U.S. Treasury bonds and other U.S. dollar–denominated assets to offset trade surpluses even if U.S. geostrategic hegemony is resented by some. And while self-imposed de jure dollarization still arouses popular resistance in Central America, many Quebecers actually support a North American monetary union over a separate regional currency. Likewise, calls for a greater role to be played by the RMB in settling international accounts are made not just within China but by foreign business people as well.[5]

On the other hand, the delinking of "territorial currency" from metal has not mollified calls for the abandonment of central banking in favor of a more competitive, private-order "free banking" within the "territory." On the contrary, libertarians are nowadays so alarmed at the rising debt level of the U.S. government that a return to "free banking" and an international gold standard of sorts may not sound so far fetched in their ears. There is in that sense uncanny resonance between Zhou Xiaochuan's call, mentioned in the previous chapter, and the position advanced by GOP figures like Ron Paul or Robert Zoellick for gold to be given greater weight in settling international accounts. Influential columnists like *The Economist*'s Philip Coggan have, moreover, diagnosed the Nixon Shock, namely the abandonment of the postwar gold-exchange standard, as the original sin that has led to the current global financial crisis.[6]

This book does not aim to prophesy whether or not gold will "come back" with a vengeance. But it does suggest that if (Chinese) history is anything to go by, then a lapse back to commodity money may be somewhat less implausible than it currently sounds. On the other hand, recourse to "free banking" is a cause that historians might find exceedingly hard to defend, particularly in view of the late-imperial Chinese experience. A more likely scenario still would be for the RMB to assume global reserve properties over several decades, including greater convertibility overseas and looser cross-border capital flows. If and when this transpires, the RMB will be the first global reserve currency issued by a state *never* to have been meaningfully linked to metal. Equally significantly, the RMB may blaze a trail to global prominence different to the one charted by the pound sterling and incumbent U.S. dollar, namely, one that would be driven by bilateral trade agreements to a greater degree than by capital market liquidity.

But, for this to happen, those favoring a low international profile in Chinese circles of power would need to be disabused of the notion that subsequent RMB appreciation would ruin China's manufacturing industries. Domestic forces opposing future RMB internationalization are, in that sense, almost as strident as Western criticism of the RMB's devaluation at present. All of this suggests that the question of "what's in it for China?" is far from resolved. As mentioned in the Introduction, the global reserve properties that the pound sterling had acquired in the nineteenth century are thought to have prolonged British imperial reach even as British industries were becoming increasingly uncompetitive at the turn of the twentieth century. Britain ultimately remained the dominant global power until World War II although America's GDP may have overtaken Britain's as early as 1860 and although American per capita income edged higher by 1914.[7]

The creation of a "sterling area" in the late 1930s may have eventually allowed Britain to mobilize crucial resources to fight World War II, and the existence of a "sterling block" in the early postwar era helped sustain London's vital financial industry alive in the face of competition from New York. Current U.S. dollar dominance in the world monetary system is similarly thought to be funding U.S. geostrategic hegemony at a low cost, even as U.S. manufacturing industries are languishing.

The PRC casts its rise as uniquely "peaceful," however. Supporters of RMB internationalization might therefore wish to eschew associating the latter with the foregoing notions of "hegemony" or "war" and might raise instead innocuous arguments about cutting transaction costs.

A decade ago, economists predicting that the euro would one day supplant the U.S. dollar as the preferred global reserve currency were not uncommon. In fact, today's talk of RMB internationalization owes much to Eurozone disillusionment. But is today's talk of RMB internationalization *not* premature and misguided to the same degree? Awareness of the competent manner in which the RMB was propagated and stabilized in the 1950s might perhaps make one a fraction less sceptical of that currency's potential to play a greater international role. Ironically, with the RMB managed by a party-state credited with three decades of breakneck economic growth rather than by a monetary union of fractious, developed nation-states might also be more reassuring to financiers.

Not necessarily a guide to the future, Chinese history is nevertheless replete with episodes of failed currencies and haunting inflation. Would these bitter sediments from times past make the leaders of modern China steer clear of Nixon-like "shocks," or is history doomed to repeat itself if and when the RMB does become a global reserve currency? Would China—in view of more recent lessons from Britain's imperial decline or America's ballooning sovereign debt—seek to chart a path to modern superpowerdom that right from the start eschews substantive public indebtedness?

This book has aimed to strike a balance between various notions of Chinese and Western exceptionalism. History's message here seems to be that debasement and inflation are inherent to human society even if they took slightly different forms and were discussed with distinct vocabularies across premodern Eurasia.

Reference Matter

Notes

1. On the notion of Chinese currency being "entirely separate development," see for example Howgego (1995), p. 1.

2. On the Bretton Woods system and Nixon's "destruction" thereof, see for example Block (1977); Zimmerman (2002); Gavin (2003); and Schenk (2010), pp. 315–347.

3. Drawing on Pigou's (1979, pp. 18–27) parlance, one might perhaps conceive of money as both the "veil" behind which the nation-state aims to assert its authority and the very substance that animates the nation-state.

4. Fisher (1929), p. 131; on stable fiat money as a novel twentieth-century phenomenon, see Friedman and Schwartz (1986). Cf. Ritter (1995) and Levintal and Zeira (2009). For two different translations of Marco Polo's impressions, see Yule (Polo, 1903), and Latham (Polo, 1987); see also Ibn Battuta (2009), p. 209. Notably, mention of China's earlier experiment with "token" paper money resurfaced on occasion in early modern Europe. See for example Sargent and Velde (2003), p. 111.

5. See for example Glasner (1998), pp. 22–27. Cf. Kindleberger (1984), pp. 30–31.

6. On the circumstances leading to the emergence of coinage in Lydia, see Ederer (1964, pp. 1–7, 75) as well as the debate between Schaps (2001) and Kroll (2001). In essence, Schaps argues that Lydian round coinage, which was stamped with kingly insignia, embodied a new monetary development stage because, prior to that, randomly shaped silver bars (*hacksilber*) had not been used in the Hellenic world, as in Babylon. Rather, irregular "utensil money" (for example, iron splits and bronze cauldrons) was the norm. Kroll, however, believes that Hellenic world had gone through an intermediate development stage whereby silver weights did function as money, much as they did across the Levant.

7. In this context, it is worth noting that Hu's (1988) translated work seems to be the only comprehensive study available in English about the 2,700-year history of Chinese economic thought. Cf. Chang (1987); Ma Debin (2013).

8. On Oresme and Bodin, see for example Spooner (1972), pp. 88–89; Spiegel (1991), pp. 69–74, 89–92; Wood (2002), chapter 4; and Sargent and Velde (2003), p. 98.

9. On Thomas Mun and the fizzling out of mercantilism, see for example Kindleberger (1989), pp. 10–14.

10. Chown (1994), chapter 6.

11. See Chapter Three.

12. Arnon (2011), chapters 1–4.

13. For a classic near-contemporaneous account of the rise and fall of *assignats*, see Smith (1805, rep. 1952), supplementary vol., pp. 494–513.

14. Arnon (2011), chapters 5–13. Cf. Galbraith (1975), pp. 33–49, and Rowlinson (1999).

15. Efforts at reestablishing an internationally convertible gold standard were made throughout the interwar period. But the failure of the World Economic Conference in 1933 to bring these efforts to fruition unsettled money markets and drove the United States on an isolationist path whereby gold exports were rejected and Senator Pittman's calls for a partly silver-based devalued dollar were largely accepted. See Ashworth (2006), pp. 163–189, 265–324; and Kindleberger (1986), *passim*.

16. Gresham was certainly not the first Westerner to recognize this monetary principle, but his articulation thereof later prompted H. D. Macleod (1821–1902) to coin the term "Gresham's Law." See Selgin (1996).

17. Helleiner (2003), passim. See also Gilbert and Helleiner (1999). Cf. Van Dormael (1997, p. 63) who opines, for example, that the establishment of such critical postwar financial pillar as the International Monetary Fund (IMF) also represented the triumph of prolonged efforts by Treasury Secretary Morganthau to exclude Wall Street from intergovernmental macroeconomic consultation and decision making.

18. See for example Flandreau and Zumer (2003).

19. Eichengreen (2008), p. 15. Cf. Craig (1953), pp. 154–155, and Sargent and Velde (2002), p. 206.

20. Eichengreen (2008), pp. 20–21. Cf. De Cecco (1975). There had been correlation between the late-nineteenth-century establishment of the international gold standard and the spread of state-issued token coinage (mostly made of silver) in Germany and the United States. In that sense, the modern formalization of the gold standard that was generally espoused by liberal theoreticians dialectically embodied one step further in disabusing currency from its age-old metallic anchorage. For a more comprehensive discussion, see Helleiner (1999) and Helleiner (2003), p. 33–34.

21. Cassis (1994), pp. 229–231. For two somewhat different interpretations of the bimetallists' political agenda, see Green (1988) and Howe (1990).

22. Triffin (1985); and Schiltz (2012b)

23. Friedrich Hayek (1899–1992) was perhaps the best known modern proponent of "free banking," a school of thought that posits that money must not be issued by governments as the latter are prone to inflationary abuse. Georg Knapp (1842–1926) is considered the main proponent of modern Chartalism, a

school of thought that posits that money should be issued only by governments and possesses no other intrinsic value of itself.

24. On the Aristotelian conception of money, see for example Ederer (1964), pp. 7–8.

25. Horesh (2009a).

26. Bernholz (1997). It is interesting in this context that Bordo's excellent survey of the English-language literature on monetary history (1986) touches on Bernholz's work but is devoid of any reference to China.

27. Galbraith (1975), p. 13.

28. Spence, quoted in Lu (2004), p. 141.

29. Greif (2006), pp. 379–380. Douglass C. North is considered the founder of NIE. See North's by-now classic work (1973), coauthored with Robert Thomas.

30. For an authoritative survey of the latest studies of the economic impact of the plague, see for example Pamuk (2007).

31. Kehoe (2007), pp. 566–568.

32. Lo Cascio (2007), pp. 643–646.

33. For an overview of European metallic-reserve principles, see for example Nicholson (1893), vol. 2.3, pp. 164–196; and Kindleberger (2000), pp. 334–336. The Bank of England Act of 1844 required 100 percent metallic reserve to be set aside for any amount of notes issued *above* the fiduciary quota. However, the Bank of France adhered de facto to a ratio of only one-third metallic reserves against notes issued during the latter part of the nineteenth century.

34. Needham (1974) vol. 5, pp. 188–281.

35. Bretton (1980); Van Dormael (1997); and Figueira (1998).

36. These foreign advisers left behind a fairly large body of literature on China's economic problems. The principal foreign adviser to the Qing was Jeremiah Jenks; for details on his mission, see Wagel (1915), p. 86, and Hanna, Conant, and Jenks (1904). Another principal adviser, Dutchman G. Vissering, completed his work on China after the fall of the Qing; see Vissering (1914) and Wagel (1915), pp. 111–112, 124–126. In 1928, the KMT government invited E. W. Kemmerer, a Princeton University professor, to overhaul China's silver currencies; for details on his mission see Ji Zhaojin (2002), p. 171. Toward the end of the Nanjing Decade, Sir Frederick Leith-Ross and American envoy Arthur Young were intimately involved in Chinese monetary reforms. For background details on their mission, see Ji Zhaojin (2003), pp. 190–194, and Young (1971); cf. Spalding (1924).

37. For a useful overview of this symbolism, see for example Wilkinson (2000), pp. 247–252.

38. Bentley (2006).

39. Kirshner (1995), pp. 140–148.

CHAPTER ONE

1. See, for example, Flynn and Giráldez (2010); Rajan and Zingales (2003); and Friedman (2003).

2. For pathbreaking studies in medieval and early modern global monetary history, see Quan Hansheng (1972); Vogel (1987, 1993a,b); Von Glahn (1996a,b, 2007); Flynn and Giráldez (2002); Helleiner (2003); and Kuroda (2003, 2008, 2009).

3. Hobson (2004) and Frank (1998).

4. Lacouperie (1894).

5. Lacouperie (1894), pp. 89, 118, 191, 217. Curiously, Macdonald (1916, p. 9) reached the opposite conclusion: "All the evidence from native writers goes to indicate that coins were in use in China . . . as far back as 1091 BC." On the Han monopoly of coinage production, see for example Wagner (2008), pp. 171–248, and Kakinuma (2011), pp. 309–350.

6. Golas (1999), pp. 69–78; and De Ryck, Adriaenes, and Adams (2005).

7. Bronze coinage in Mesopotamia appeared much earlier than in China. See Xu Jinxiong (1988), pp. 121–123.

8. Although scholarly doubts have recently emerged as to whether cowrie served as protocurrency in ancient China beyond its mortuary and sumptuary purpose, it is recognized that cowrie had been current over an expanse matched by no other single metallic currency in the ancient world (Oceania, Africa, Middle East, and Far East). See Cook (1997); Li Yung-ti (2006); and Kakinuma (2011), pp. 73–104. Interestingly, the Chinese radical for *cowrie* (*bei* 貝) has been preserved in scores of monetary terms, including the modern composite for currency (*huobi* 貨). See Xu Jinxiong (1988), pp. 360–366, and Wang Yü-ch'üan (1951), pp. 83–89. Cf. Davies (1994), pp. 1–35.

9. Wagner (2008), pp. 83–89.

10. On Chu currency, see for example Zhao Dexin (1996). Chu first cast bronze cowrie around 600 BCE, while the spread of natural cowrie in the Chu had predated the establishment of the Chu kingdom, arguably as early as 1600 BCE. Notably, *Guanzi* ("Qingzhong" 1) refers to Chu as a kingdom more abundant in gold deposits than other kingdoms to the north.

11. Miyazaki Ichisada (1977), vol. 1, pp. 50, 126, 184, 220; and Xu Jinxiong (1988), pp. 360–366.

12. Wang Xipeng (2009). Animal hide had already been used monetarily in the preimperial era but did not serve as main currency.

13. Von Glahn (1996a), pp. 35–36, 43. On Wang Mang's coinage reforms, see for example Xiao Maosheng and Yang Ming (2005). On bronze vessels for cowrie storage, see for example Li Jinlian (2005). Another important stage in the standardization process that occurred only much later in the Tang era was the inscription of round coinage with reign names (*nianhao*) rather than with their weight units (such as 兩 *liang* for the Qin and early Western Han and *zhu* 銖 for Western Han coinage as of 118 BCE).

14. For a diachronic overview of Chinese coinage, see Peng Xinwei's classic (1958); see also *Zhongguo lidai huobi* (1999); for an evaluation of the early Han permutations of *banliang*, see Katō Shigeru (1963), vol. 1, pp. 147–148.

15. Snodgrass (2003), pp. 8–11; Lowick (1970); and Husain (1967). On cowrie as global currency, see Einzig (1966); Johnson (1970); Hogendorn and Johnson (1986); and Yang Bin (2004).

16. See, for example, Burnett's concise history of coinage (1991), p. 9.

17. See, for example, Sellwood's (1976) detailed illustration of Roman minting techniques.

18. One of the most compelling aspects of this uncertainty as regards the scope of intercivilizational contact in antiquity is, of course, the fact that scholars are still far from agreement on precisely when Chinese silk was first traded along the Silk Road. Herodotus may have alluded to the availability of silk in Greece. Moreover, relics of what may be Chinese (or wild) silk—long predating the Han Dynasty—have been found in Siberia, India, and even Egypt. However, Good (1995) suggests that chemical identification techniques are not yet sufficiently advanced to allow for categorical conclusions to be drawn from these findings.

19. Bronze had been considered, of course, an auspicious metal (*jijin* 吉金) in preimperial China, which might possibly explain at least in part why it remained the mainstay of Chinese coinage until the nineteenth century, as opposed to gold and silver in the West. See Wagner (2008), pp. 83–91.

20. Notably, gold and silver ingots were a fairly common store of value during the Han era; see, for example, Peng Xinwei (2007), vol. 1, pp. 137–139. Round cast-iron coinage was current in some parts of China as early as the Han era, and its use continued sporadically right until the nineteenth century. However, it was always deemed inferior to standard bronze coinage; it made for a significant constituent of the money stock only during the Five Dynasties and Song era (particularly in Sichuan), and otherwise never reached the pervasiveness of standard bronze coinage. See Wagner (2008), pp. 286–289. On preimperial, spade-shaped iron coinage, see for example Zou Guishan (2011).

21. On the significance of copper coinage within the Roman world, see for example Katsari (2011), pp. 209–243. On fifth and fourth century Athenian bronze coinage, see Gardner (rep. 1974), pp. 295–297.

22. For an analysis of Aristophanes' views on debasement, see, for example, Bernholz (2003), pp. 24–29.

23. See *Guoyu*, "Zhouyu xia." For an analysis of Shan Qi's views and their impact on premodern Chinese statecraft, see for example Hu Jichuang (1988), pp. 24–29, 119–131; Von Glahn (1996a), pp. 43–44; and Ye Shichang (2003), pp. 32–33.

24. Cited in *Qin Han jingji sixiang shi* (1989), p. 61. Jia Yi's ideas on money are compiled in his *Jia Yi Xinshu*, Chapter 4.5.

25. Xiao Qing (1984), pp. 15–21. Cf. Pines (2009), pp. 198–217.

26. Ma Tao and Song Dan (2009), passim.

27. See in particular statist passages attributed to statesman Sang Hongyang 桑弘羊 (ca. 152–80 BCE) in *Yantielun*. Jia Yi was arguably the most prominent official citing the *Guanzi* to advance statist views. On the reunification of China under the Tang dynasty, Sang and Jia's views were famously reaffirmed by Liu Zhi 劉秩 (born ca. 730 BCE). See Von Glahn (1996a), pp. 34–39; Golas (1999), pp. 416–417; and Ye Shichang (2003), pp. 165–166. On India, see, for example, Sihag (2009). On monopolies in the ancient world more generally, see Finley's classic (1973), pp. 166–170.

28. See Shaughnessy (1988) and Kuz'mina (2008, pp. 39–70). Cf. Loehr (1949); Forbes (1950), pp. 4–40; and Beckwith (2011), pp. 43–46. On the fifth to second century BCE diffusion of the Bronze Age from Mesopotamia across Eurasia, see Chernykh (1992). Barnard's minority view (1983) is that ancient Chinese metallurgy was developed indigenously, though he does acknowledge that Mesopotamian bronze casting was earlier.

29. Maspéro (1955), pp. 505–515); and Rawson (1989); cf. Tylecote's 1976 classic work on metallurgy, pp. 1–25. For a more comprehensive overview of China's Bronze Age, see Von Falkenhausen (1999).

30. Xiao Qing (1984), pp. 4, 72–74. By way of contrast, Hua Jueming (1999, pp. 468–471) suggested that Chinese knife and spade-shaped coinage had emerged no earlier than the fifth century BCE. Hua further believed that raw copper weights (10 grams to around 1 kilo) had served as protocurrency beforehand, much like the function of silver weights in Mesopotamia and the Levant. Coole (1981) seems to be the only English-language monograph dedicated to preimperial Chinese round coinage, but it does not discuss the provenance of *yuanqian* or why it supplanted knife and spade currency. On the provenance, great originality, and dating of early Lydian coinage, see, for example, Thompson (2003) and Bresson (2009). For more recent studies reasserting the older origins of Chinese coinage see, for example, *Zhongguo jinrong baike quanshu* (1990), vol. 1, pp. 15–16.

31. Hua Jueming (2000).

32. Wang Yü-ch'üan [Wang Yuquan] (1957), pp. 116–125.

33. Peng Xinwei (2007), pp. 9, 39–42. The doyen of Chinese numismatics in Japan, Katō Shigeru (1991, pp. 107–109, 121–125), believed the transition from spadelike to round coinage was primarily driven by smaller size and simpler casting considerations. However, he did accord jade discs some role in the process.

34. Dai Zhiqiang and Zhou Weirong (1993).

35. *Erya zhushu* [*Erya* Commentaries], Ch. 5 and 6.

36. *Lüshi chunqiu*, Chapter 15 ("Huandao"). Cf. Hua Jueming (1999), pp. 468–510.

37. Kakinuma (2011), pp. 73–104.

38. Such views largely follow Peng (2007, p. 40) who explained that the first *yuanqian* coins carried the homophone 垣 *yuan*, a Wei 魏 locality.

39. Scheidel (2009b, p. 140) presumes that the *yuanqian*, which emerged for the first time around 350 BCE, was inspired by earlier Chinese jade disc designs and had nothing to do with contemporaneous round Greek coinage. As previously indicated, this is a fairly common view among Chinese scholars as well. Cf. Chen Longwen's revisionist overview (2006); on the plausibility of Greek coinage reaching preimperial China, see for example Harl (1996), pp. 302–303; cf. Lewis (2007), pp. 115–117. For an overview of Greek coin design, see Kraay (1976).

40. Edmondson (1987) and Healy (1978).

41. Badian (1972); Love (1991), pp. 175–189; and Malmendier (2005).

42. Cooper (1988).

43. Bivar (1971) and Stronach et al. (1978).
44. Bivar (1985).
45. See "Siglos Coins Found in Taxila" (1934).
46. Bivar (1985).
47. Bivar (1971).
48. Schaps (2006). See also Schaps (2004), p. 235, and Maity (1970).
49. See Decourdemanche (1913), Dhavalikar (1975), and Kennedy (1898). The earliest Persian coins excavated in China proper are from the Sassanid era (224–651 CE). On these findings see "Huhehaoteshi fujin chutu de waiguo jin-yin bi" (1975). For a comparative overview of the evolution of Indian minting techniques and late imperial coinage, see Om Prakash (1988) and Kuppuram and Kumudamani (1990), vol. 8.
50. Carradice (1987), pp. 89–90. See also Schlumberger (1953); Farrokh (2007), pp. 65–66; Mitchiner (1977); and Jackson (1922), pp. 341–344.
51. Gupta and Hardaker (1985).
52. Bopearachchi and Rahman's catalogue of recently discovered hoards in Afghanistan and Pakistan (1995) is arguably one of the best indicators of the impact of Achaemenid and, more clearly, Greco-Bactrian coinage on the transition of Indian currency into round shapes and anthropogenic motifs.
53. Brown (1967) and Kosambi (1981).
54. Krishnamurthy (2000) and Sagar (1992), p. 48. Cf. Kim Hyun Jin (2009), p. 148, and Yang Bin (2009), pp. 33–34. Roman gold and silver coins are otherwise known to have circulated in South India alongside local copper coinage well before the Common Era. See, for example, Hall (1999).
55. Narain (1990), p. 161. See also Yu Taishan (2006), pp. 165–166.
56. For an overview of the Yuezhi conquest of Daxia (Bactria), see Yu Taishan (2006), pp. 12–14.
57. The name Yuezhi was pronounced at the time as *zguja*, that is, Scythians; see Enoki, Koshelenko, and Haidary (1994), p. 172.
58. Narain (1990), p. 155, and Hill (2009), pp. 312–318.
59. For discussion on this identification see Hill (2009), p. 537.
60. Possibly these Saka were the Yuezhi or included the Yuezhi. See Czeglédy (1983), p. 28, and Van Wickevoort Crommelin (1998), p. 270.
61. For the later collisions between the Parthians and the "Scythians," probably the Yuezhi, see Enoki, Koshelenko, and Haidary (1994), pp. 181–182.
62. *Hou Hanshu* 118.0905. 1. See also Hill (2009), p. 29.
63. See Puri (1994), pp. 248–249, and Hill (2009), pp. 29, 329–332.
64. See Narain (1990), p. 165; and Pugachenkova, Dar, Sharma, Joyenda, and Siddiqi (1994), p. 372. See also Wink (2001), p. 221.
65. See Harmatta (1994), pp. 422–433; Mukhamedjanov (1994), pp. 280, 286; and and Puri (1994), pp. 257–258.
66. Pugachenkova et al. (1994), pp. 333, 348, 367, and 372. See also Puri (1994), p. 258.
67. Grayson (1985), pp. 43–44.
68. For a general introduction on the Wusun, see Yu Taishan (2006), pp. 25–32.

69. *Shiji* vol. 43 and Crump, trans., *Zhanguo Ce* [*Zhangguo ce*] (1979), pp. 299, 302–303. Cf. Pines (2005).

70. *Hanshu*, "Liezhuan" 70.96, "Xiyu" 66.

71. Di Cosmo (2002), pp. 71–78.

72. Higuchi (1992).

73. Xia Nai (1966).

74. Whitfield (2004), pp. 27–30. See also Wang (2004).

75. Whaley (2009).

76. Redish (2000), pp. 54–61.

77. See, for example, Becker (1969), p. 115.

CHAPTER TWO

1. Crawford (1985), pp. 9–17; cf. Bolin (1958), pp. 41–46.

2. Crawford (1985), pp. 29–30, 41–72, 116.

3. Crawford (1985), pp. 143–146, 175, 256–257; cf. Bolin (1958), pp. 47–50.

4. Sawyer (1982), p. 33. Scandinavian coinage was first struck in the ninth century. Coin hoards found in England and the Baltic region point to extensive Viking fur trade, largely transacted in Arab silver dirhems.

5. Davies (2002), pp. 125–128. Cf. Metcalf (1980–1981).

6. Sang Hongyang's (d. 80 BCE) short-lived interventionist economic policies included what was probably the most serious attempt at introducing silver as standard currency during the early imperial era; see Miyazaki Ichisada (1977), p. 185; cf. Davies (1994), pp. 60–87, and Baskin and Miranti (1997), pp. 315–316. Monetary uses of silver and iron occurred somewhat more frequently during the early Eastern Han era, as monetary gold became increasingly rare. See Qian Jiaju and Guo Yangang (2005), pp. 114–129. However, in China proper, gold coinage was virtually defunct later in the imperial era with the brief exception of the Song-era *Taiping tongbao*. See for example Peng Xinwei (2007), vol. 1, pp. 364–366. Cf. Hozumi Fumio (1944), pp. 25–33.

7. On Dong Zhuo's clipped coinage, see for example Dai Hongjia (1988). On Sun Quan's "thousand cash" coinage, see for example Peng Xinwei (2007), pp. 139–144.

8. Peng Xinwei (1994), vol. 1, pp. 214–215; and Zhou Weirong (2009).

9. Xiao Qing (1984), pp. 94–120.

10. Lewis (2007), pp. 6–7.

11. Lewis (2007), pp. 80, 100–101.

12. Scheidel (2009a).

13. Scheidel (2009b).

14. On papermaking, literacy, and the later appearance of paper currency in Europe, see Robinson (2004, vol. 7.2, pp. 56–58, 188)

15. Twitchett (1970), pp. 73–74.

16. Katō Shigeru (1963), vol. 1, pp. 395–411; and Twitchett (1970), pp. 72–73.

17. See Katō Shigeru (1963), vol. 2, pp. 1–11, 56.

18. Elvin (1973), pp. 150–161, and Schifferli (1986), passim; cf. Peng Xinwei (1958), pp. 280–291.

19. Jia Daquan (1994a,b); Xu Ping'an (2000); and Von Glahn (2005), pp. 67–69. Unlike today's banknotes, premodern Chinese banknotes were printed vertically.

20. Jia Daquan (1994a,b); Xu Ping'an (2000); and Von Glahn (2005), pp. 67–69.

21. Smith (1991), pp. 93–108. The leader of the anti-Song rebellion that broke out in 993 was Wang Xiaobo 王小波, who actually descended from a family of tea merchants.

22. Jia Daquan (1994a,b); Xu Ping'an (2000); and Von Glahn (2005), pp. 67–69.

23. Wang Shengduo (2003), vol. 2, pp. 610–625.

24. Jia Daquan (1994a,b); Xu Ping'an (2000); and Von Glahn (2005), pp. 67–69. Cf. *Songshi* 181.134 "Shihuoxia" 3.

25. Elvin (1973), pp. 164–199; cf. Deng Gang (1999), pp. 301–324.

26. Quan Hansheng (1972), vol. 1, pp. 355–416; and Wang Wencheng (2000). During much of the preceding Tang era, payment of silver was common in the Lingnan area, but it was otherwise quite restricted to ceremonial purposes. It was very rarely levied in land tax. See Katō Shigeru (rep. 1970), vol. 1, pp. 47–82.

27. Zelin (1984, p. 28, table 2.1, 43) estimates Qing central land-tax revenue in 1685 at the "cash" equivalent of just 23 million strings, and overall land-tax revenue at 30 million. In practice, however, well over 80 percent of all land taxes collected in the provinces ended up in central government coffers. Ji Zhaojin (2002, p. 69) estimates Qing central revenue from both land and commercial taxes in 1895 at the "cash" equivalent of 89 million strings.

28. Elvin (1973), p. 149; see also Gao Congming (1999), pp. 16–20; and Bol (2010), p. 25.

29. Andréadès (rep. 1966), pp. 54–56, 85–89, 192. Cf. Ferguson (2001). Notably, monarchist Tories had initially opposed the creation of the Bank of England because they believed it would advance the republican cause.

30. Webber and Wildavsky (1986), pp. 262–355. Huang (1974, pp. 46–50) estimated Chinese annual imperial revenue in the early sixteenth century at only 26.7 million strings of cash, 75 percent of which derived from land taxes.

31. Qi Xia (1987), vol. 2, pp. 576–587; and Wang Shengduo (2003), vol. 1, pp. 71–78.

32. Hartwell (1967); Qi Xia (1987), vol. 2, pp. 557–565; and Von Glahn (1996a), pp. 48–50. "Coin famine" or *qianhuang* continued to haunt policy makers in late imperial China. For an illuminating description of how mid-Qing administrators perceived of the flight of bronze coins, see for example Dunstan (1996b). For London Mint output estimates, see Craig (1953), p. 39–40, 52, 84. Although these figures are impressive for their time, it is worth recalling that according to Nef (1941, p. 581) copper produced as a by-product of silver mining in Mansfeld alone had reached 2,000 tons annually by the mid-sixteenth century.

33. Elvin (1973), pp. 147–149.

34. Xiao Qing (1984), 162–171. The trope "cannot be fed on when starving" was first invoked in the *Guanzi* and often paraphrased in subsequent currency debates. See Herbert (1976), pp. 266–268, 278–279 footnote 86.

35. Zhao Jing (1997), vol. 3, pp. 272–281; and Zhang Jiaxiang (2001), p. 19.

36. For an overview of Anastaius's nummi coinage and its subsequent evolution, see Grierson (1999), pp. 17–22.

37. Xiao Qing (1984), pp. 154–162. Notably, salt *slabs* literally functioned as money at various moments in history across Africa, Southeas Asia, and Yunnan. See Vogel (2013), pp. 286–287.

38. Xiao Qing (1984), pp. 148–154; and Bol (2010), pp. 14, 41–42.

39. Elvin (1973), p. 147; Xiao Qing (1984), pp. 148–154; and Wang Shengduo (2003), vol. 1, pp. 137–171, 300–303, 354–386. On *duanmo*, see also Hartwell (1967), pp. 280–289; Von Glahn (1996a), pp. 21–23; and Von Glahn (2005), pp. 65–69.

40. *Shiji* 30, "Pingzhunshu" 8.

41. Tao Jing-Shen (1983), pp. 76, 81; Qi Xia (1987), vol. 2, pp. 576–587; Levine (2008), pp. 72–90, 159; Bol (2010), pp. 86–89, 103–105, 120–138, 220–222; and Pines (2012), pp. 40, 119–120. The neo-Confucian tendency of sanctifying emperors and hollowing them out at the same time ("omnipotent rubber stamps") might in fact have drawn on heterodox pre-Qin thought, as Pines (2009, pp. 82–113) suggested. On Wang Anshi's role in reforming the Song imperial examination system, see Elman (2000), pp. 15–43.

42. *Songshi*, 255.314 "Liezhuan" 73.

43. On *fukoku kyōhei* as the rallying cry of the Meiji reform, see, for example, Morris-Suzuki (1989), pp. 34, 56–58; and Samuels (1994), Chapter 2.

44. Gao Congming (1999), pp. 43–44.

45. Gao Congming (1999), pp. 50–66.

46. Katō Shigeru (1963), vol. 2, pp. 86–138; Wang Wencheng (2000) suggests the demand for Chinese bronze coinage outside China had been the main catalyst for the spread of both Tang-era "flying cash" and Song-era *jiaozi*.

47. Takahashi Hiro'omi (2002), p. 142, footnote 16 Cf. Wang Shengduo (2003), vol. 2, pp. 619–625, 701–703; and Miao Mingyang (1995).

48. Ma Tao and Song Dan (2009). Cf. Xiao Qing (1984), pp. 183–187; and Von Glahn (1996a), p. 44.

49. Von Glahn (2005), p. 75.

50. See, for example, Ye Ziqi's 葉子奇 (1327–1390 CE) observation in his *Caomuzi*, vol. 3b, "Zazhi": "當其盛時皆用鈔以權錢. 及當衰叔, 財貨不足, 止廣造楮幣以為費" ("When the Song and Yuan were in their golden age, they both used paper money to support bronze coinage. But once in decline, and as material goods and metallic money became scarcer, they increasingly resorted to paper money for imperial outlay.") Notably, Ye was *not* against paper money in principle; he supported the early Ming issue but suggested sound metallic reserves must be kept.

51. Yuan Yu's original passage is cited by Xiao Qing (1984, pp. 248–257) as: "楮之為物也, 多則賤, 少則貴, 收之則貴矣;賤則壅,貴則通,收之則通矣."

52. Qi Xia (1987), vol. 2, pp. 1188–1194; and Von Glahn (1996a), pp. 51–56.

53. Franke (1992); and Yao Shuomin (2003).
54. Franke (1992); Yao Shuomin (2003).
55. See Franke's pioneering study (1949).
56. Von Glahn (1996a), pp. 56–59.
57. Rossabi (1989), pp. 123–124, 186–187.
58. Miyazaki Ichisada (1977), vol. 2, pp. 418–422.
59. Von Glahn (2005), p. 84.
60. Li Gan (1985b), pp. 384–411; and Von Glahn (2010), passim.
61. Wang Shengduo (2003), vol. 1 pp. 24–27.
62. *Yuanshi*, vol. 93, "Qianfa." Cf. Von Glahn (2005), p. 73, 86 bottom caption; Vogel (2013), pp. 96–101
63. Rossabi (1994), vol. 6, pp. 449–488. In 1309, the Yuan briefly experimented with notes purely denominated in silver rather than in *guan* (*Zhida yinchao* 至大銀鈔).
64. Schurmann (1967), pp. 131–137; and Hsiao Ch'i-Ch'ing (1994), vol. 6, pp. 500–501.
65. Li Gan (1985b), pp. 413–417; Dardess (1994), pp. 575–578; and Tang Jing (2009).
66. Von Glahn (1996a), pp. 62–64; and Ma Tao and Song Dan (2009).
67. Xiao Qing (1984), pp. 200–247.
68. Xiao Qing (1984), pp. 212–215.
69. Xiao Qing (1984), pp. 247–249.
70. Ye Shichang (1996); and Zou Jinwen and Huang Ailan (2010).
71. Liu Sen (2007). Cf. Xiao Qing (1984), pp. 221–223.
72. The Ming launched a rearguard attempt to revive note issuance between 1629 and 1644 but met with resounding failure. The large-scale issuance of notes was abandoned subsequently by imperial governments until the late Qing. See Von Glahn (1996a), pp. 197–206; cf. Tullock (1958) and Chen Chau-nan et al. (1995), pp. 273–279. On intellectual debate among Yuan officials as to whether notes can be redeemed with more fiduciary or completely fiat note, see Xiao Qing (1984), pp. 219–249.
73. Laufer (rep. 1967), p. 560. On paper money in Mongol-ruled Iran, see also Allsen (2001), pp. 176–199.
74. Jahn (2009); See also information on sources retrieved on July 11, 2012, from www.iranicaonline.org/articles/cav-cao-from-chinese-chao-paper-money-assignat-mathews-chinese-english-dictionary-no.
75. Li Gan (1985), p. 52; for more such erroneous observations, see, for example, Yuan Shuiqing (2003), p. 64.
76. Chaudhuri (1990), p. 83.
77. On *baochao* issuance and the ensuing inflation, see for example Tsai Shih-shan (1996), pp. 172–173; and Brook (1999), pp. 68–71.
78. Von Glahn (1996a), p. 156, citing the eminent Ming official Guo Zizhang 郭子章 (1543–1618).
79. Huang (1974), pp. 36–43, 118–122. The effects of the *lijia* reform have also been explained in detail by Yamane Yukio (1984). According to Quan Hansheng (1972, vol. 1, pp. 355–416), Song central government revenue in 997 was just

12,325,000 strings of cash as well as Tls 376,000 in silver. In other words, only 2.4 percent of Song revenue at the time was received in silver. By way of contrast, Quan estimates Ming imperial revenue in 1573 was just Tls. 2,819,153 in silver as well as only 2,678 strings of cash. In other words, bronze coinage made only 0.095 percent of imperial revenue under Ming Emperor Wanli.

80. Dunstan (2006), pp. 233–243.

81. Flynn and Giráldez (1994), pp. 79–83; one source put the amount of silver dollars transported by the Spanish across the Pacific between 1571 and 1821 at 400 million; see Quan Hansheng (1972), p. 439. See also Schurtz (1959), pp. 1–32; and Kazui Tashihiro (1991).

82. Japanese topsoil metal deposits had already been depleting during the late Muromachi era, thus possibly contributing to the Tokugawa shogunate's decision to curb silver exports. Deeper deposits were not tapped into partly because local miners did not employ drainage pipes, a technology that had become available by that time in Europe. Concomitantly, the Tokugawa shogunate cracked down on private mining, thus further reducing metal output. Domestic demand for silver rose at much the same time because the Tokugawa shugunate unified Japan's monetary system and increased coin output. In other words, by the eighteenth century Japan produced less silver and copper overall, although its monetary demand for these very same metals grew. See *Meiji-zen Nihon kōgyō gijutsu hattatsushi* (1982), pp. 207–273; Kobata Atsushi (1969), pp. 368–374; Lin Man-houng (2006), p. 59–63; and Shimada Ryuto (2006), pp. 52–67. Cf. Sakurai (2008).

83. For respective historic overviews of the Chinese and Western monetary systems, see Peng Xinwei (1958), Helleiner (2003), and Davies (1994).

84. The Ming tried to reintroduce paper money in the fourteenth century, but popular rejection of government notes at that stage was too difficult to overcome. Ming officials occasionally revived the idea of paper money in various memorials to the Throne thereafter, but a new issue was not implemented. See Peng Xinwei (1958), pp. 429–433, 506–509; and Yang Lien-sheng (1952), pp. 67–68.

85. Wang Yeh-chien (1973), pp. 59–61; for an overview of bimetallism in the late imperial era, see Kann (1927).

86. This custom may have evolved from the burning of mock metallic coins in pre-Han burial rites. See Hou Ching-Lang (1975); Chen Qixin (1996).

87. Peng Xinwei (1994), pp. 574–576; and Von Glahn (1996a), pp. 74–77.

88. Von Glahn (1996a), pp. 161–166.

89. Von Glahn (2005), p. 85–88, 156, 188–189. Attempts at culling and recasting all Song-era coinage (*gua guqian* 括古錢) were made again under Emperor Tianqi (r. 1621–1627).

90. Golas (1999), pp. 417–427. An abatement of antimining sentiments can perhaps be traced back to statecraft treatises written during the Min-Qing transition. Cai Yurong 蔡毓荣 (?–1699), for example, who served as an official during the late Ming as well as under Qing Emperor Kangxi, suggested that allowing more private mining ventures could help enhance imperial revenue. See *Ming shilu leizhuan* (1993), "Jingji shiliao juan," pp. 118–136.

91. *Ming jingshi wenbian*, vol. 29: "華夷諸國莫不奉行."
92. Wu Baosan (1990), vol. "Ming-Qing," pp. 1–4.
93. *Zhongguo guchao tuji* (1987), passim. Cf. Vogel (2013), pp. 173–174.
94. The original passage is cited by Xiao Qing (1984, pp. 256–257) as: "多造之則鈔賤；而過多則不可以行，必也."
95. Xiao Qing (1984), pp. 257–262; Zhao Jing (1997), vol. 4, pp. 1719–1725; and Ye Shichang (2003), pp. 349–352. See also Cobbett (1820); cf. Von Glahn (1996a), pp. 80–82; and Kindleberger (2000), p. 351.
96. Von Glahn (1996a), pp. 186–189.
97. Xiao Qing (1984), pp. 269–279; and Hu Jichuang (1998), vol. 2, pp. 434–437. Notably, Jiang Chen envisioned notes convertible into silver, while Qian Bingdeng dared propose inconvertible notes.
98. Von Glahn (1996a), pp. 154–155. Cf. Zhang Jiaxiang (2001), vol. 1, 27–29.
99. Zhang Jiaxiang (2001), vol. 1, pp. 636–644. Cf. Xiao Qing (1984), pp. 285–290.
100. Zhang Jiaxiang (2001), vol. 1, 622–629; Zhao Jing (1997), vol. 4, pp. 1881–1187; and Liu Hengwu and Yang Xinmin (2010).
101. Xiao Qing (1984), pp. 280–290; Zhang Jiaxiang (2001), vol. 1, pp. 629–629; and Rowe (2010).
102. See Gu's treatise "Qianbi" in *Huangchao jingshi wen tongbian*, section 59, "Licai."
103. Faure (2006), passim; and Puk Wing-kin (2010). Cf. Zelin (1984), p. 283.
104. Government borrowing through bonds in all medieval Italian city-states was more coercive and short-term in nature that later English patterns. See, for example, Pezzolo (2005). Cf. Braudel (1992), vol. 2, pp. 519–522.
105. Hargreaves (1930), passim; Braudel (1992), vol. 2, pp. 375–379.
106. O'Brien and Hunt (1999), pp. 56–57.
107. Cassis (2006), p. 17.
108. Usher (1914) suggests that *lettres de foire* and promissory notes were employed in Crusader trade between the Italian city-states and the Levant as early as 1156, but these seem *not* to have been of impersonal, public-order nature; Andréadès (rep. 1966), pp. 45–46; De Roover (1999), pp. 104–106; and Homer and Sylla (2005), pp. 124–159.
109. Smith (rep. 1952), pp. 30–31, 82–83, 90, 318. For a groundbreaking econometric reassessment of this particular claim, see Allen et al. (2011). Notably, Allen and his coauthors (2011) support the view that the Chinese standard of living had already been much lower than in northwestern Europe on the eve of the Industrial Revolution. Their view is much more in line with Staunton's account (1799, passim), which—contrary to the Jesuit sources earlier in the eighteenth century—stresses the poverty and shorter life span of ordinary Chinese, as compared with Europeans.
110. Smith (rep. 1952), pp. 40, 159, 212.
111. Smith (rep. 1952), p. 55.

112. Smith (rep. 1952), p. 298, 318, 367–368. Smith estimated the mainly land-derived tax revenue in Mughal-ruled Bengal at a fifth of all produce. This is, however, *not* to suggest that the actual total tax burden on Chinese peasants everywhere was necessarily and invariably low. Here, arbitrary exactions and corruption by local officialdom could make a big difference. For a discussion of the actual tax burden, see for example Elvin (2009).

113. Labib (1969); Pamuk (2000), p. 6; Khan (2003), p. 74, 174; and Banaji (2007). Cf. Denzel (2010), Introduction.

114. Wagel (1915), p. 240; and Brown (1994), pp. 158–159, 188.

115. See Brewer (1988), passim.

116. Davies (1994), pp. 278–282; Rondo Cameron proposed a more conservative estimate with specie still constituting half of Britain's means of payments in 1688–1689. See Cameron (1967a), Table II.2, pp. 42–46; for France, see also Cameron (1967b), p. 116.

117. Sherman (1996), p. 5; cf. Chamley (2011).

118. Clapham (1944), vol. 1, pp. 21–23; and Neal (1993), pp. 203–207.

119. Glasner (1989), pp. 75–81.

120. This paragraph is based on data presented in Clapham (1944), vol. 1, pp. 295–298, Appendix C.

121. Andréadès (rep. 1966), p. 257.

122. Tennant (1866), p. 354.

123. Faulkner (2004).

124. Irigoin (2009), pp. 226–229.

125. Mira and Noble (1988), pp. 5–6; cf. Teare (1926).

126. Clark (2008); Allen (2011).

127. See, for example, Liu Qiugen (2000); cf. Pan Ming-te (1996); and Homer and Sylla (2005), pp. 124–159. Rural short-term loans in late imperial China could often entail an implicit interest rate exceeding 50 percent per annum.

128. Cibot (c. 1776), pp. 336, 368–372, 385–386. On the Jesuit's view of the Chinese economy, more generally, see also Huey (1985). Notably, Cibot suggests the statutory interest rate limit in China was around 30 percent, whereas the statutory cap was just 5 percent in 1714 England. English usury laws were abolished in 1833. See also Temin and Voth (2008); Wennerlind (2010).

129. Baskin and Miranti (1997), pp. 34–63.

130. Magnusson (2000), pp. 72–103.

131. Goudsmit (2004), p. 159.

132. Heckscher (1954), p. 9–92; and Dewey (2007).

133. Heckscher (1954), pp. 252–253; and Bernholz (2003), pp. 41–45. Note that Sweden had already temporarily been on a silver standard of sorts and partially retired banknotes between 1776 and 1789, so as to fight inflation. See Eagly (1971), "Introduction" and Figure 3.

134. Neal (1993), pp. 14–16. English state annuities were modeled on the Dutch equivalent, yet there had not yet been extensive banknote circulation in the Netherlands at that time. In fact, until the issuance of "consols" around the mid-eighteenth century, English state annuities did not prove exceedingly popular. Notably, Dutch public debt in the early eighteenth century was almost twice

as high as that of either England or France on per capita basis. See, for example, Hargreaves (1930), pp. 1–46, 56–59; and Gorski (2003), p. 50.

135. Engdahl and Ögren. (2008).

136. Magnusson (2000), p. 181.

137. Heckscher (1954), p. 20–23. Swedish copper output peaked around 1650 at 3,000 tons annually, or around one-third of the output level achieved by Wang Anshi in China six centuries earlier.

138. Mackenzie (1953), pp. 24–35; Schuler (1992); and Mokyr (2009), pp. 220–254.

139. Goudsmit (2004), pp. 156–157; Quinn and Roberds (2005); and French (2006).

140. Heal (rep. 1972), "Introduction"; White (1984), pp. 38–33; Van der Wee (1977), pp. 350–355; and Goudsmit (2004), pp. 161–164.

141. Helleiner (2003), pp. 58–59, 103.

142. Taylor (2006); on joint-stock banks, see also Griffiths (1974); Cameron (1967a), pp. 27–29; and Michie (2006), pp. 52–53.

CHAPTER THREE

1. Schaps (2006); and Scheidel (2008).

2. For recent studies of the Great Divergence in this vein, see for example O'Rourke and Williamson (2004); Williamson (2008); Galor, Moav, and Vollrath (2009); and De Vries (2010). Notable studies in monetary history that do consider to some extent a Great Divergence include Peng Xinwei (1958); Perlin (1993); Von Glahn (1996a); Kuroda (2009); and Mark Elvin (forthcoming).

3. Helleiner (2003), passim.

4. Kuroda (2009), pp. 268–269.

5. Carson (1970), pp. 242, 563–569; Doty (1990); Sargent and Velde (2002); Helleiner (2003), pp. 46–53; and Selgin (2008).

6. For a survey of "cash" taxonomy in late-imperial China, see for example King (1965). The origin of the English term *cash* as distinctly denoting Asian copper coinage is the Sanskrit silver and gold weight unit "karsa." The latter evolved into the Tamil word *kaasu*, denoting low-value coinage. It entered the English language via the Portuguese variants for *kaasu, caixa*. This is not to be confused with the primary (and older) instruction of *cash* in the English language, which derives from the medieval Italian *cassa*.

7. Kann (1927), pp. 41–44, 149–157, 443–445.

8. Quan Hansheng (1941); He Ziquan (1949); and Xiao Qing (1984), pp. 94–120.

9. Blackburn (2005), pp. 660–675.

10. Del Mar (2004), p. 34. Diodorus of Sicily, who lived in the first century BCE, was the first to discuss in detail the importance of slave labor in the gold mines of Nubia.

11. Pirenne and Clegg (2006), p. 100; and Kuroda (2009).

12. Pirenne and Clegg (2006), pp. 115–120.

13. Grierson (1960); and *Umayyads* (2000), pp. 173–180. On Byzantine coinage, see Hendy (2008).

14. On early Islamic monetary reform, see for example El-Hibri (1993). For an overview of later Arab and Ottoman monetary evolution see for example Carson (1970), pp. 478–490; Ehrenkreutz (1970); and Inalcik (1970).

15. Pamuk (2000), passim.

16. Ironically, though, the Arabic gold dinar was etymologically derived from the Roman silver denarius, while silver dirham arose from the Sassanid permutation of the sound of the ancient Greek silver drachmas. Trade could explain bullion traffic in that era to a considerable extent, given the almost synchronic abandonment of the post-Roman gold standard in Western Europe and the upturn of gold coinage in Arabia and Byzantium. Islamic gold coinage seems to have flowed en masse into Europe as of 'Abd al-Malik's time, suggestive of a trade deficit for Arabs with a politically fractured Western Europe at least initially. Muslim silver dirhams, in turn, reached Eastern and Northern Europe especially as a result of the extensive fur and slave trade of Arabs with the Baltic. Yet, on balance, it is probably the low mining and minting activity in feudal Europe that accounts for the demand for Arab coinage. For a more detailed discussion, see Spufford (1988a), chapter 2.

17. Grierson (1960), pp. 263–264.

18. Lopez (1951); and Kaplanis (2003). It is worth mentioning in this context that the Crusaders issued gold dinars in the Levant, imitating Egypt's fatimid gold coinage, even though Western Europe was still on a silver standard at the time. Fatimid coinage was a state prerogative, much as in Byzantium and China.

19. Tylecote (1976), p. 77; and Allen (2012), pp. 35–40, 372.

20. Miskimin (1984); Sussman (1998); Ormond (1999); and Allen (2012), p. 364.

21. Gould (1970); Glassman and Redish (1988); and Rolnick, Velde, and Weber (1996), pp. 789–808.

22. Li Ming-Hsun (1963), passim; Carson (1970), pp. 238–241; and Andréadès (rep. 1966), pp. 90–100.

23. Braudel (1992), vol. 2, 423–428; and Sargent and Velde (2002), pp. 208–213. On European early modern assaying techniques, see Agricola's classic (rep. 1950), Book 7.

24. Kuroda (1987) and Dunstan (2006), pp. 60–61, 431–433. Cf. Vogel (1987) and Wang Hongbin (1987). The linkages in Chinese late imperial statecraft between increased output of coinage (*guzhu* 鼓鑄) and tax remission or cash distribution (*juanzhen* 蠲賑) were mutually reinforcing. Both were often measures jointly designed to alleviate famine suffering and avert rebellions. See for example the memorial to the Ming throne by Wang Ji 王紀, advocating these two measures in tandem; in *Ming jingshi wenbian*, section 473. On the linkages among Qing granaries, cash distribution, and famine relief policy see also Will (1990) and Will and Wong (1991).

25. Li Ming-Hsun (1963), pp. 147–150; and Deng (2011), ff. Chapter 6. Cf. Snelling (1762), passim; Brooke (1950), pp. 174–231; Peters (2002), p. 87–115; Sargent and Velde (2002), p. 31, 132–135; and Allen (2012), p. 77. Throughout

the course of the eighteenth century, foreign coins found in England were seen as legitimate only when countermarked.

26. For seminal comparative studies of world taxation history see Goldstone (1983) and Webber and Wildavsky (1986).

27. Herbert (1976); cf. Von Glahn (1996a), pp. 41–42.

28. Franke (1949). Cf. Huang (1990) and Von Glanh (1996a).

29. Song Yingxing (rep. 1987), pp. 184–189; and Zheng Jin (2007), pp. 207–213. Redish's (2000, pp. 24–26, 109–112) work on early modern Europe would, indeed, suggest that the higher a coin's nominal value was the more attractive target it became for counterfeiting. Much like Song Yingxing, many early modern European economists knew that. This is why, when banknotes emerged in Europe in the late seventeenth century, those economists insisted that banknotes could potentially serve as an even easier target for forgers. Therefore, European banknotes at first were of high denominations: The idea here was that undiscerning commoners would not likely use them and that merchants would by necessity carefully double-check their authenticity.

30. Spufford (1988a), pp. 320–330; Chown (1994), pp. 31–32; Stahl (2000), pp. 16–27; and Sargent and Velde (2003), p. 79. Cf. Lin man-houng (2006), pp. 29–30.

31. On Qianlong's coinage invigoration efforts, see for example Wang Xianguo (2006) and Adachi (2012), pp. 463–482. For a passing observation of Qianlong-era efforts at recasting "old" (that is, counterfeit) coinage see, for example, Mark Elvin's (2013) discussion of Zhu Tingzhang 褚廷璋 in "Cash and Commerce in the Poems of Qing China."

32. Wang Hongbin (1987).

33. Von Glahn (1996a), pp. 111–112. See also Kishimoto (1997), pp. 329–332.

34. Von Glahn (1996a), pp. 93–94, 142–187; and Zheng Jin (2007), pp. 78–85.

35. Du Halde (c.1741), p. 330.

36. Du Halde (c. 1741), p. 333. Counterfeiting coins incurred the death penalty until the fifteenth century in Europe, too. But punishments became somewhat lighter following the Enlightenment. See for example Spooner (1972), pp. 105–107, and Allen (2012), p. 373.

37. Zelin (1984, p. 48) suggests that, as of the early Qing era, peasants were allowed the convenience of paying their taxes in bronze coins instead of silver. But the exchange rate they were charged was higher than the prevailing market rate.

38. Liang Fangzhong (1989), pp. 572–573.

39. Lin Man-houng (2006), pp. 68–71, 294. Kuroda (2003, pp. 137–140) cites a report by a fifteenth-century Korean envoy to Japan, who was impressed with the extent to which bronze coinage was current there whereas commodity moneys like cloth and grain were still the mainstay of the Korean monetary system at the time.

40. Vogel and Theisen-Vogel (1989), p. 147. The cost of transporting copper from Yunnan as a cause for dearer "cash" is also attested to in the Qing Imperial Treasury compilation *Qinding Hubu zeli*, vols. 6.36–6.39.

41. Zelin (1984), pp. 264–301; and Lin Man-houng (2006), pp. 29–30. Cf. Rowe (2005).

42. Xia Xiangrong et al. (1980). Zhu Yuanzhang, the Ming founder, is particularly well known for his antimining exhortations. Cf. King (1965), pp. 3–5; Dunstan (1996a), pp. 164–167; Vogel (2006), p. 177; and Elvin (2006), pp. 341, 441–2. Notably, the Yongzheng Emperor (r. 1722–1735) was one of few who tolerated greater private mining ventures, combined with lower output imposts, as a way of stimulating and tapping into the expansion of mining. Net gains in mining tax were aimed at bolstering provincial revenue and combating corruption by petty officials through salary increases (*yanglian* 養廉). See Zelin (1984), pp. 141–148.

43. Vogel and Theisen-Vogel (1989), pp. 170–178. Cf. Stahl (2000), pp. 226–242; and Golas (1999). Notably, gunpowder—though a Chinese invention—was first operationalized in mining in Venice as early as 1574. Similarly, compasses were first used in mining in sixteenth-century Europe. See also Horesh (2009b).

44. See Agricola (rep. 1950), Book 4, pp. 89–100.

45. Kobata (1965). Cf. Morelli (1976); Molenda (1976); Totman (1993), pp. 69–70; and Farris (2009), pp. 176–180. Cf. Vogel and Theisen-Vogel (1989).

46. Interestingly, Mattingly (1960, pp. 252–253) suggested that copper and alloy coinage was the one most prone to counterfeiting in the Roman Empire. On clipping, see also Spufford (1988a), Chapter 3; on the historic circumstances surrounding the establishment of the Bank of England as a bank of issue, see Andréadès (rep. 1966), pp. 14–67.

47. Einaudi (1953).

48. Cipolla (1967), pp. 14–16.

49. Postan (1987), pp. 168–305, ff. 212–214.

50. Walker (1983).

51. Stahl (2000), pp. 61–63, 81–86, 99–102, 117, 127–128; and Sargent and Velde (2002), pp. 173–181.

52. Vilar (1976), pp. 30–36, 66–69, 93–94, 108–109.

53. Prakash (1998), pp. 30–31, 83–84.

54. Hamilton (1943); Carothers (rep. 1967), p. 11; Sprenger (1991), pp. 111–116; and Motomura (1994).

55. Walker (1983).

56. Spufford (1988a). Cf. Allen (2012), pp. 246–259.

57. Nef (1941) and Munro (1983), p. 99. Cf. Agricola (rep. 1950), Book 6, pp. 171–200.

58. Cooper (1988), pp. 39–51; Snodgrass (2003), p. 53; and Challis (1978), p. 37. Cf. Becker (1969), pp. 111–157.

59. Snodgrass (2003), p. 12.

60. The Kilwa sultanate was the only other part of sub-Saharan Africa that issued its own distinctive coinage at the time. See for example Freeman-Grenville (1960).

61. Tschoegl (2001), p. 443–448, and Lane (2008), pp. 204–206. On the subsequent history of the MMT, see Kuroda (2007).

62. Robbert (1983), pp. 60–62.

63. Miskimin (1983), p. 82; Allen (2012), pp. 1–22, 41–72, 115–117, explains that by the fourteenth century English minting was much more centralized in London than in the Anglo-Saxon era. To be sure, between 970 and 1278, moneyers' names appeared on English coinage, but these were removed in 1279. Similarly, English monarchs cracked down on ecclesiastic minting rights by the fourteenth century.

64. Lopez (1953). On the hereditary moneyer caste in Rome, see for example Mattingly (1960), pp. 254–255; on moneyer guilds in medieval Europe, see for example Spufford (1988b, pp. 15–17). Spufford further suggests (1988b, p. 17) that early medieval European principalities often farmed local minting rights to the highest bidder. In fact, until the early fifteenth century, many European mints—including the one in London—often entrusted management to foreigners, usually financiers from the Italian city-states.

65. Calculated based on data provided in passim in Von Glahn (1996a), Blanchard (2005), and Vogel (1987). Cf. Lucassen (2005).

66. Tylecote (1976), pp. 48, 65–69; and Hua Jueming (2008).

67. Tylecote (1976), pp. 81–83. On Ming-era metallurgy, monetary cycles, and urbanization, see also Zhou Weirong (2004) and Tanaka, Kominami, and Shiba (2009).

68. Tylecote (1976), pp. 105–143.

69. Ling Yeqin (1987), pp. 318–343. Cf. Hill (1922).

70. For a contemporaneous notation of ubiquity of Spanish-American dollars across eighteenth-century Asia, see Staunton (1799), pp. 9–11. See also King (1965), pp. 37, 46, 174–175; and Hao Yen-p'ing (1986), pp. 34–36.

71. Hao Yen-p'ing (1986), pp. 40–42; Lin man-houng (2006), pp. 46–47; Von Glahn (2007); Burger (2008); and Giráldez (2008). For a contemporaneous observation of the Carolus-dollar premium and local attempts to forge it in China, see for example Morrison (1848), pp. 234–237.

72. Pamuk (1997). On European coinage across the sixteenth and seventeenth century Ottoman Empire, see also Masters (1988), pp. 148–149. Within Europe, too, better-quality mass-produced coinage also carried a premium over lesser-known manually produced coinage; see for example Stahl (2000), p. 47; and Chilosi and Volckart (2011). Notably, English coins were much less common across Asia at the time because London burghers and politicians often blamed the East India Company for draining the country of coinage. As a result, until the eighteenth century, it was forbidden to take English specie overseas. See for example Chaudhuri (1975), pp. 160–174.

73. Chaudhuri (1985). The Gupta currency was largely gold based, but between 600 and 1300 CE hardly any gold coinage was minted in North India, silver coinage being the mainstay. South Indian currency was, on the other hand, gold and copper based during that era. The Mughals did mint gold but largely relied on silver coinage.

74. Kuroda (2009). Cf. Blake (1937); Watson (1967); and Lane and Mueller (1985), , p. 539.

75. See for example Franke (1949). Cf. Carson (1970), pp. 485–487.

76. See for example Spufford (1988a), pp. 109–115, 146–147, 267, 282; Blanchard (2005); and Munro (2007).

77. Vogel (1993a,b). See also Heimann (1980); Deyell (1994); and Yang (2004), pp. 301–304. For a comprehensive survey of Yunnan's integration into the Chinese imperial system, see, for example, Fang Guoyu (2001).

78. Von Glahn (1996a), Chapters 2–3.

79. See for example Flynn and Giráldez (2010); cf. Atwell (1982), p. 81; Flynn and Giráldez (1995a, 1995b, 2004)

80. Shimada (2006).

81. Vogel (1987).

82. Bloch (1935), p. 623; T'ang Leang-Li (1936), pp. 8–19; Yang Duanliu (1962), pp. 22–23, 44–45; Ho Hon-wai (1993); and Zheng Jin (2007), pp. 218–220.

83. Huang (1974), pp. 60–70.

84. Sahillioglu (1983), pp. 287–288, and Walker (1983), p. 18; see also Pamuk (2004). It has to be noted, however, that the decreed value of Ottoman copper coinage was well above its intrinsic value. Another caveat is that aksum silver content was drastically reduced during the seventeenth century, but debasement was not always recorded.

85. Markley (2003) p. 516; for a very similar argument see also Porter (2002), pp. 400–401.

86. Defoe (rep. 1989), chapter 26, p. 184.

87. Tavernier (1677), segment entitled "The Money Currant under the Dominions of the Great Mogul."

88. Richards (1987), p. 2.

89. Hasan (1969) and Om Prakash (1988).

90. Om Prakash (1987), p. 175.

91. Shimada (2006), pp. 91–97.

92. Headrick (2010), pp. 139–176.

93. Om Prakash (1987), pp. 171–174. Cf. Carson (1970), pp. 521–525.

94. Ferguson (2008), pp. 48–52.

95. Hogendorn and Johnson (2003); and Yang Bin (2009), p. 207.

96. Lin Man-houng (2006), pp. 107–114.

97. Curtin (1983), p. 260–263.

98. On wampum, see for example Davies (2002), pp. 40–42.

99. Hogendorn and Johnson (2003). See also Vogel (1993b), pp. 225–226; cf. Dunstan (1992).

100. Devell (1994), p. 128; there is a debate among Chinese scholars over the extent to which cowrie served as everyday "money" before the second century BCE. See Yang Bin (2011).

101. Sundström (1974); Curtin (1975), p. 313; and Curtin (1983), pp. 255–259.

CHAPTER FOUR

1. Lin Man-houng (2006), p. 43.

2. For an overview of late imperial Chinese metallic weights and standards, see Kann (1927); Cribb (1992); and Rang Huey-shin (1988).

3. Klaproth (1823); Chaudoir (1842); Doolittle (1868), vol. 2, p. 139; and Edkins (1905), pp. 106–107. Cf. Jernigan (1904, pp. 77–91), who went as far as erroneously stating: "It appears to be quite authentic that there was paper money in China as early as the year BC 119"; Wagel (1914, 1915).

4. Lin Man-houng (2006, pp. 36–37) suggested, for example, that premodern Chinese money shops did not start issuing notes until very late in the Qianlong reign; these shops were probably more developed in the north of China, where they mostly issued bronze coin–denominated notes. Notes issued by southern money shops were denominated in silver taels. Hou Houji and Wu Qijing (1982, vol. 1, p. 11), on the other hand, suggest private-order notes might have emerged earlier in the eighteenth century and that they were very common by the 1820s.

5. See for example Cheng Linsun (2003); cf. Horesh (2009a).

6. He Wenkai (2010). See also Wang Yeh-chien (1981) and Hao Yen-p'ing (1986), pp. 47–50.

7. He Wenkai (2010).

8. *Qingchao wenxian tongkao*, vol. 13.1; Xiao Qing (1984), pp. 292–294; and Lin Man-houng (2006), p. 40.

9. Peng Xinwei (1958), pp. 807–808. See also Yang Lien-sheng (1952), p. 68; and Shi Yufu (1984), pp. 109–111.

10. Horesh (2009a), p. 63. For a similar view, see Wei Jianyou (1986), p. 83; cf. Peng Xinwei (1958), pp. 556–559.

11. Li Yu'an (1996).

12. Wakeman (1985), vol. 1, pp. 13–14, particularly footnote 32, pp. 238–240, particularly footnote 36; and Von Glahn (1996a), pp. 205–206.

13. Yang Duanliu (1962), pp. 104–113.

14. *Huangchao jingshi wen tongbian*, "Licai," section 59, memorial entitled "Chaobiyi" 鈔幣議.

15. See Xiao Qing (1984), pp. 320–332; Hou Houji and Wu Qijing (1982, vol. 1, pp. 212–225) suggests Wang Liu was particularly influenced by late Ming officials Ni Yuanlu 倪元璐 (1593–1644) and Jiang Chen 蔣臣 (in office c. 1636).

16. Xiao Qing (1984), pp. 309–318; and Lin Man-houng (2006), pp. 1–35.

17. Hou Houji and Wu Qijing (1982), vol. 1, pp. 90–96, 108–113, 143–149; Xiao Qing (1984), pp. 332–348; and Rowe (2010). On Adam Smith and Mollien's objection to inconvertible paper money, see for example Jacoud (2001).

18. Ji Zhaojin (2002), pp. 30–32.

19. Li Yu'an (1996); and Huang Hengjun (2001), passim.

20. *Zhongguo jindai zhibishi* (2001), p. 6. For a detailed analysis of Xianfeng monetary policies, see also Hamashita (1989), pp. 57–61.

21. Yang Duanliu (1962), pp. 112–113.

22. Ch'ên, (1958).

23. Ch'ên (1958).

24. Marx (rep. 1967), vol. 1, p. 141 footnote 83; for the English translation, see Marx (rep. 1990), vol. 1, p. 224, footnote 34.

25. Hou Houji and Wu Qijing (1982), vol. 1, pp. 401–414; and Xiao Qing (1984), pp. 348–358.

26. Hou Houji and Wu Qijing (1982), vol. 1, pp. 401–414; and Xiao Qing (1984), pp. 348–358.

27. For a survey of the first modern Chinese banks, see for example Ji Zhaojin (2002), pp. 80–89; and Cheng Linsun (2003), pp. 10–36. Cf. Sheehan (2003), pp. 1–44.

28. Hou Houji and Wu Qijing (1982), vol. 3, pp. 322–339.

29. The compilation is entitled *Huozhishuotie jianming zongyao* (貨制說帖簡明總要), dated Gaunxu 34.3.23. It is preserved in the Palace Museum Archive in Beijing, "Shangyudang" 上諭檔 (digitised version), "Tiao" 1, Box no. 1510, "Ce" 3.

30. Hou Houji and Wu Qijing (1982), vol. 2, pp. 292–298.

31. Selgin (1992). Cf. Horesh (2009a), p. 13.

32. "Convertibility" here refers to the time required to encash notes. Shanghai's money shops, for example, lent funds and issued scrip against individual deposits called *zhuangpiao* 莊票 (shop coupon), but this could be cashed by proximate shops only after ten to fifteen days during which couriers would liaise with the issuing shop to rule out fraud. See McElderry's classic study (1976).

33. Fortune (1847), p. 376. The absence of paper money use in the immediate rural surroundings of Fuzhou—which were renowned for the quality of tea grown there—can be inferred from another observation by Fortune (p. 207):

> When the teas are ready for sale, the large tea merchants or their servants come out from the principal towns of the district, and take up their quarters in all the little inns or eating houses, which are very numerous in every part of the country. They also bring coolies loaded with the copper coin of the country, with which they pay for their purchases.

34. See Selgin (1992), pp. 104, 109, Table 6.1; cf. "Native Banks in Fuchow" (1932).

35. Dennys, Mayers, and King (1867), p. 285.

36. Archive of the School of Oriental and African Studies (hereafter, SOAS), London, Imperial Maritime Customs Collection, *Decennial Reports* (1882–1891), "Foochow," p. 427.

37. On the Shanxi *piaohao*, see for example King (1965), pp. 94–96; *Shanxi piaohao shiliao* (1990), ff. 132, 742–751; and Huang Jianhui (1992), passim.

38. Doolittle (1868), vol. 2, pp. 138–147.

39. Doolittle (1868), vol. 2, pp. 138–147. Parkes's earlier observation (1852, p. 184) confirms that "a run is made upon these small [Fuzhou] banks at the close of the year, when specie is mostly required; and, at this crisis, one or two failures among them gradually occur."

40. "The Dai Fook Dollar" (1927), pp. 129–131. Bloch (1935, p. 618) suggests that one Dai Fook dollar was notionally equal to 1,000 standard bronze coins.

41. Adapted from Pomeranz (2001), pp. 102, 122; based on contemporaneous sources, Hao Yen-p'ing (1986, p. 272) suggests the average daily income of a Chinese peasant in 1883 was around 0.4 silver dollar. Cf. Fortune (1847), p. 376, who also attests to the smallest note value being 400 cash or "about eighteen pence English money."

42. Parkes (1852).

43. Doolittle (1868), vol. 2, p. 141.

44. For a meticulous study of the post-Qing emergence of impersonal trust in Chinese modern banks, see Sheehan (2003).

45. Selgin (1992, p. 112), citing "The Dai Fook Dollar" (1927).

46. Doolittle (1868), vol. 2, p. 365.

47. Williams (1851) believed that Chinese paper notes were made of bamboo (p. 292). He also exclaimed in a bigoted fashion not uncharacteristic of European expatriates at the time (p. 289):

> The convenience of notes instead of coin in the common transactions of life is, however, as well understood among the Chinese as in any country of Christendom; and if it were not for the trickery which forms a prominent feature in their character, and leads everyone to mistrust his neighbour, the use of paper money would doubtless be general.

48. Williams (1851), p. 289. On the other hand, Hao Yen-p'ing has shown (1986, p. 49)—based on *North-China Herald* contemporary articles—that privately issued Chinese drafts had probably become common in Shanghai, too, by 1859. The trading house of David Sassoon & Co. used them to purchase gold from locals. Another foreign insurance company was willing to accept such drafts in 1862 when issuing policies. Hao even suggests such "native drafts" often commanded a premium over coins. However, it is useful to recall that Shanghai's foreign banks in fact helped popularize drafts by laying down "chop loans" to local money shops ("native banks") against draft security and their comprador's personal guarantee.

49. Williams (1851), p. 292, and "The Dai Fook Dollar" (1927), p. 133.

50. SOAS, Imperial Maritime Customs Collection, *Decennial Reports* (1882–1891), "Chungking," pp. 115–116. See also Jernigan (1904), pp. 93–95:

> The bankers, themselves, being Shan-si men, always aim to employ only native of the province of Shan-si, and when possible, select men of their own village . . . Each [Shanxi] bank issues its own bills, which are made payable to bearer, and customarily on demand, but sometimes are payable so many days after being issued.

51. SOAS, Imperial Maritime Customs Collection, *Decennial Reports* (1882–1891), "Amoy," pp. 516–518.

52. Jernigan (1904), p. 84.

53. See for example Wagel (1914); Kann (1927); and Von Glahn (1996a,b).

54. Chen (1975), p. 361. In "The Dai Fook Dollar" (1927, p. 132–133) it is estimated that the value of notes outstanding that were issued by all Fuzhou financial institutions was $10 million, including $100,000 issued by the foreign-run American-Oriental Bank. In "Native Banks in Foochow" (1932, p. 447) it is estimated that the value of notes outstanding that were issued by "native banks" in Fuzhou was just $4 million.

55. Carothers (1930); Kuroda (2003), chapters 1–2; and Helleiner (2003), pp. 23–24, 37.

56. Triffin (1985) and Helleiner (2003), p. 38.

57. Wang Yeh-chien (1981, p. 5, 16) suggested that copper-denominated notes were dominant in Northeast China, while in the southeast silver-denominated notes prevailed.

58. See for example Wang Yeh-chien (1981), p. 19, map on p. 21.

59. Wang Yeh-chien (1981), p. 102.

60. Wang Yeh-chien (1981), p. 16. On Wang Yide, see also Peng (1958) p. 708, 809, 817 footnote 11; and *Zhongguo jindai huobi shi ziliao* (1964), vol. 1, p. 237, 458–460.

61. On the Oriental Bank Corporation's China business, see Wang Jingyu (1983).

62. SOAS, Imperial Maritime Customs Collection, *Decennial Reports* (1882–1891), "Hankow," pp. 177–178.

63. See memorial from Qi Junzao to Emperor Xianfeng, dated 1852 (r. 2nd.6.12), preserved in the Palace Museum Archive in Beijing ["Shangdangyu" 上諭檔, Tiao 3, Box 1169, Ce 3]: "省城以及外府州縣所用銀票或錢票或番票處處皆然". Cf. Yang Duanliu (1962), pp. 94–97.

64. Capie and Webber (1983).

65. Rawski (1989), p. 135, table 3.1; p. 157, table 3.4; pp. 364–394, Appendix C.

66. On the emergence of modern national markets and economic nationalism in the West, see for example Polanyi (1944); Braudel (1992); Heilperin (1960); and Helleiner (2003), chapter 3.

67. Galbraith (1975), p. 48; and Davies (2002), pp. 459–462. Cf. Mihm (2007), Introduction.

68. King (1965), p. 25.

69. Cited in Burger (2008), p. 177.

70. Parsons (1900), p. 181.

71. Kuroda (2003), pp. 137–140, 155–164. Cf. Frost (1970), Hirokichi (1980), and Hanashiro (1999).

72. Maruyama (1999). Segal (2011, pp. 169–179) suggests that the use of land-tax remittance paper certificates (*kawase* 為替 or *warifu* 割符) was common in Japan as of the fourteenth century.

73. *Meiji taishō zaisei shi* (1955), p. 133, Table 156; p. 144, Table 173.

74. Per capita data compiled from *Meiji taishō kokusei sōran* (1975), p. 144, Table 173.

75. Maddison (2007), p. 24.

76. Hsiao Liang-lin (1974), p. 191.

77. Goldsmith (1983), p. 13, Table 1-6.

78. Maddison (2007), p. 24. The result is upper-bound because Indian population in 1900 was considerably higher than in 1820. The exchange rate between the rupee and the Mexican silver dollar is based on Hsiao Liang-lin (1974), p. 191.

79. Pamuk (2000), pp. 241–242.

80. Inferred from Pamuk (2000), p. 218.

81. Pamuk (2000), pp. 210–213.

82. Kahan (1989), pp. 48–52, Table 1.24. Because Russia went on a gold standard at the turn of the twentieth century, inconvertible notes were redeemed for gold-denominated notes by the Russian State Bank (est. 1860). See Olga Crisp (1967), p. 198. On the start of redemption, the value of inconvertible ruble notes in circulation totaled 1,131.7 million.

83. Sprenger (1991), p. 201, Table 28. On the money supply before prewar German unification, see Tilly (1967).

84. Cameron (1967b), p. 116, Table IV.3.

85. Davies (2002), p. 484, Table 9.1. Cf. Friedman and Schwartz (1963), p. 30, Table 5; and Martin (1977). For an authoritative literature review on "free banking," see Briones and Rockoff (2005).

86. Hao Yen-p'ing (1986), pp. 107–111. Cf. Tawney (rep. 1972), pp. 58–62.

CHAPTER FIVE

1. Notable examples of countries that retained private bank note issues in the early twentieth century include Switzerland and Greece. Banknotes in Scotland are still issued by commercial banks. See Schuler (1992).

2. On the evolution of Hong Kong's unique monetary system, see Jao and King (1990).

3. Spalding (1924), pp. 272–273.

4. For currency substitution between local currency and HK$ in South China, see Li Taichu (1936), pp. 3–21; and Schenk (2000), passim. Banknotes issued by the British Chartered Mercantile Bank in Malacca, which amounted to Straits Settlement $70,000 in 1882, were crucial for the survival of its branch there. These banknotes were commonly used in neighboring Malay states; see Muirhead (1996), pp. 224–225.

5. France's predominant financial organ in East Asia, the Banque de L'Indochine, issued ruble notes with Cyrillic script in Vladivostok between 1919 and 1920; see Kolsky and Muszynski (1996), pp. 303–306. The Bank of Abyssinia, a subsidiary of the British-owned National Bank of Egypt, opened its first offices in Addis Ababa and Harare on February 15, 1906. It had pioneered banknotes in Ethiopia in 1915 and was subsequently nationalized by Haile Selassie in 1931; see Marcus (2002), p. 130–146. On the notes issued by the Franco-British owned Imperial Ottoman Bank, see Eldem (1998), pp. 75–110.

6. Bowen and Cottrell (1997), pp. 107–108.

7. Cassis (1994), p. 78.

8. Jones (1990), pp. 33–34.

9. On the evolution of British legislation as regards overseas note issues by private banks, see Chalmers (1893), pp. 27–32.

10. Grossman (2001), p. 111.

11. Jones (1990), p. 40.

12. See Gonjō (1993), pp. 178–182, 267–271; and Müller-Jabusch (1940), pp. 215–219.

13. Jones (1990), p. 36.

14. Joslin (1963), pp. 137–138. Private note issuance in Latin America was ultimately phased out through government-backed issues in the early 1920s; see Bulmer-Thomas (1994), pp. 179–180.

15. Greenberg (1951), pp. 179–184; and Philips (1961), pp. 276-280. Cf. Kawamura (2005), pp. 25–39.

16. Baster (1934), pp. 140–141; and Jain (1929), pp. 140–142. Cf. McGuire (2004), pp. 2–4.

17. Limited liability provisions were enacted in India only in 1860; see Jain (1929), pp. 142–146. On the evolution of the Agra Bank's legal status, see summary by Orbell and Turton (2001), pp. 48–49. The Bank of Western India opened its Hong Kong and Guangzhou branches as early as 1845, closely followed by its Shanghai branch (est. 1847); see Ding Richu (1994), vol. 2, p. 62.

18. Baster (1934), pp. 143–145; and Davenport-Hines and Jones (1989), pp. 11–12.

19. Baster (1934), p. 147. The Bank of India may not have actually commenced business; see Orbell and Turton (2001), pp. 70–71.

20. Jones (1993), pp. 23–24.

21. On the liquidation proceedings of Overend Gurney, see the *Bankers' Magazine* vol. 26 no. 2 (1866), pp. 848–863, 1132–1138; and King (1936), pp. 238–256.

22. For a somewhat different analysis for the reasons behind the Oriental Bank's failure, see McGuire (2004), pp. 14–15.

23. The Oriental Bank's total liabilities in December 1883 amounted to £11,250,000, of which the note issue made up more than 6 percent; see *Bankers' Magazine*, vol. 44 (1884), pp. 664–670.

24. Mackenzie (1954), p. 146.

25. Triffin (1985); Van der Eng (1999); and Yokouchi (1996), pp. 171–173.

26. Davenport-Hines and Jones (1989), pp. 1–4.

27. Short-term interest rates in Europe at the time were close to 8 percent per annum, whereas call loans in East Asia could fetch upwards of 10 percent. See for example Baster (1929), pp. 10–13; on the lucrative credit market in Guangzhou (Canton) shortly before the onset of overseas banking, see Greenberg (1951), pp. 152–156, and Van Dyke (2005), pp. 97–99, 150–160.

28. The Presidency Banks were closely aligned with the colonial government of British India. They enjoyed exclusive custody of government balances but, unlike the Eastern Exchange Banks, were denied the right to raise capital in London. On their note issue, see Bagchi (1989), pp. 96–98.

29. Baster (1929), pp. 46–48, and Hickson and Turner (2004), passim.

30. Baster (1929), pp. 23–24; see also Grossman (2001), passim.

31. A colonial issue was initially considered less desirable than a private one because it entailed higher reserve requirements by law; see for example King (1987), vol. 1, pp. 374–376.

32. The Siamese government decided to replace HSBC, Chartered Bank of India Australia and China, and Banque de L'Indochine notes circulating in Bangkok with an issue of its own in 1902; see Ingram (1971), pp. 150–155. Between 1889 and 1894 HSBC's circulation in Yokohama and Kobe slumped from

the yen equivalent of HK$86,517 to HK$5,675. Japan's share of the Bank's total circulation volume thereby dropped from approximately 1.5 percent to 0.057 percent; see King (1987), vol. 1, p. 39, 485.

33. Xu Jiqing (rep. 1970), pp. 138–140, and Ding Richu (1994), vol. 2, pp. 67–68, 101.

34. On the Chinese-American Bank of Commerce, see Pugach (1997).

35. Chen Shao-teh (rep. 1982), pp. 293–296; see also contemporary observations quoted in *Zhonghua minguo huobishi ziliao* (1989), vol. 1, pp. 894–897.

36. Du Xuncheng (2002), pp. 82–83, and Cheng Linsun (2003), p. 75.

37. U.S. overseas banking was effectively blocked by senate legislation before the 1920s; see Cleveland and Huertas (1985), pp. 76–79; Dayer (1981), pp. 1–3; Jones (1990), pp. 33–34; Pugach (1997), pp. 32–33; and Wilkins (1986), pp. 281–282.

38. Because of their lead position in issuing exchange bills, the larger British trading houses—headed by Jardine, Matheson & Co.—tried to resist the establishment of Anglo-Indian banks in Guangzhou (Canton) and Shanghai. When the transition to specialized banking appeared unstoppable, Jardine, Matheson & Co. worked in conjunction with other merchant groups to set up their own bank, that is, the Hongkong and Shanghai Banking Corporation (est. 1865). See Checkland (1953), passim.

39. For few of the most comprehensive numismatic listings, see Pick (1990), vol. 1, pp. 253–288; Huang and Wang (2004), vol. 1, pp. 14–54; Mao King On (1977), vol. 2; Ma Chuande et al. (2000), pp. 23–60; *Zhongguo zhibi biaozhun tulu* (1994), pp. 567–644 ; *Ziben zhuyi guojia zai jiu Zhongguo faxing he liutong de huobi* (1992); and Cribb (1987). On "free banking," see for example Dowd (1992), passim.

40. For an overview of Qing and early republican monetary fragmentation, and of how novel foreign banknote designs were emulated by Chinese financial institutions, see *Zhongguo jindai zhibi shi* (2001), passim; Hsu Yih-tzong (1997, 1998), passim; and Zhang Zhizhong (1997), passim. On "underground" Communist currency, see for example Wu Ping (1994) and Ding Guoliang and Zhang Yuncai (1993).

41. See a copy of the despatch from Hong Kong's Governor, Sir Hercules Robinson, to the Duke of Newcastle dated March 9, 1861, in *Hong Kong: Copy of Correspondence between the Secretary of State for the Colonies and the Governor of Hong Kong upon the Subject of the Currency of the Colony* (1863).

42. The British contemplated minting tael coinage in 1867 specifically for use in Shanghai, but the plan fell through due to Chinese suspicion. See, for example, Cribb (1987), p. 11; in 1925, another attempt to introduce municipal subsidiary coinage was similarly aborted. See the notes on currency in *Gongbuju dongshihui huiyilu*, vol. 23–24 (1925–1926); cf. *Dongfang zazhi*, vol. 22 no. 12, June 25, 1925, pp. 46–51; *Shenbao*, April 11, 1925, p. 14; *Shenbao*, September 6, 1925, p. 15; *Shenbao*, December 2, 1926, p. 10; and Xu Jiqing (rep. 1970), pp. 233. On the import of Hong Kong currency in Shanghai, see for example Goodman (1995), pp. 241–242; on the incremental geographical character of the British Settlement, see Kotenev (1927), pp. 27–71; Bickers (1999),

pp. 123–131; Takahashi and Furumaya (1995), pp. 79–85; and Osterhammel (1999), pp. 146–15. For a perspective on the institutional underpinning of the neighboring French concession, see Marybon (1929), passim.

43. Murphey (1953), pp. 57–61.

44. See "Notes on Chinese Currency," dated March 22, 1866. In SOAS, Charles Addis Papers, PP MS 14/380.

45. Yang Yinpu (rep. 1972), pp. 194–195; Lee (rep. 1982), p. 32; Baba (1922), vol. 2, pp. 1432–1433; and Chen Shao-teh (rep.1982), pp. 292, 300–301.

46. Hanna, Conant, and Jenks (1904), pp. 47–49. These paragraphs were part of the report submitted by the Jenks advisory mission to China, referred to in the following pages.

47. In SOAS, Charles Addis Papers, PP MS 14/380. This subsequent memorandum is not dated but reference to "the late Manchu Dynasty" suggests that it was entered not long after the 1911 Revolution; for near-contemporary surveys that reached much the same conclusion, see Wei Wen Pin (1914), p. 50, and Arnold (1919), p. 591.

48. Ho Hon-wai (1993), pp. 389–391.

49. For a general survey of late Qing economic reforms, see Ch'en, Jerome (1980), pp. 120–123; on Zhang Zhidong's economic standpoint, see Li Xizhu (2003), pp. 176–192. One of Zhang Jian's most formative experiences as an entrepreneur was his inability to raise sufficient capital for his first textile mill in 1898, which persuaded him of the urgent need to set up new financial institutions; see Zhu Zhijian (1972), pp. 20–23.

50. Ye Shichang (2002), pp. 599–604.

51. In the treaty ports, foreign banks were protected from Chinese government intervention by virtue of their extraterritorial status. Foreign banks rarely opened branches elsewhere, with the exception of politically sensitive Beijing.

52. Xia Dongyuan (1981), pp. 73–75; and Zheng Guanying (1982), vol. 1, p. 685.

53. By the turn of the century, Zheng Guanying and several other Qing officials argued that China needed to abandon the silver standard in favour of a more stable gold-pegged currency; see for example Zheng Guanying (rep. 1969), pp. 921–927; and Huang Jianhui (1994), pp. 90–91.

54. Zheng Guanying (rep. 1982), vol. 1, pp. 19–22, 71–75.

55. Zheng Guanying (rep. 1982), vol. 1, pp. 192–193.

56. Zheng Guanying (rep. 1982), vol. 1, pp. 680–681, 683–690.

57. See Elvin (1999), passim.

58. McLean (1976), pp. 292–293, 300–304.

59. Foreign banks in China habitually complained about the chaotic state of China's currency, but the silver-convertible notes they issued were nothing more than a palliative designed for use within specific treaty ports and *not* between them. That the foreign banks were in fact ambivalent about monetary unification is evidenced by the fact that they used to discount their own notes by 5 percent when presented for encashment in another treaty port. See for example Conant (1927), pp. 598–599.

60. See the classified report from Jordan to Grey, dated December 11, 1908, in United Kingdom National Archives (formerly Public Records Office), London (hereafter PRO), FO 371/435, ff. 561–562, 570; cf. Cheng Linsun (2003), pp. 162, 168.

61. Jordan to Grey, dated December 11, 1908, in PRO FO 371/435, ff. 561–562, 570.

62. See Feuerwerker (1958), pp. 228, 232; and Chen Limao (2003); cf. Hamashita (1980), p. 459.

63. *Zhongguo di yi jia yinhang* (1982), p. 157; on Chinese bank notes produced by foreign printers, see for example Huang and Wang (2004).

64. Feuerwerker (1958), pp. 230–231, 233, 240 (Table 24); and *Zhongguo di yi jia yinhang* (1982), pp. 28–29.

65. Huang Jianhui (1994), pp. 100–104.

66. Wagel (1915), p. 83; and Hall (1921), pp. 20–23.

67. Jiang Hongye (1991), pp. 3–17; and Huang Jianhui (1994), pp. 96–104.

68. Hao Yen-p'ing (1970), p. 109–112.

69. Feuerwerker (1958), pp. 54–56. British foreign policy makers were, in fact, averse to calls by the expatriate mercantile community in the treaty ports to use military force to establish effective control over the Chinese hinterland. As was precociously stated in the Mitchell Report (1852), the Foreign Office could not be led to believe that military intervention would make appreciable headway for British exports because it perceived the Chinese economy as self-sufficient. See Pelcovits (1948), pp. 15–18; and Moulder (1977), pp. 107–109.

70. CBIAC, for example, designated a note reserve in Shanghai only in 1928. Until then, there was only one metallic reserve to support local liabilities, but its ratio was effectively at the branch managers' discretion; see Hongkong and Shanghai Banking Corporation—Group Archives, London (Hereafter, HSBC GA), Ms 31519/1–101. Neither do early HSBC records from Shanghai attest to the existence of a special note reserve. By the same token, the overall metallic branch reserve was not to fall below one-third of the value of local current accounts; see for example Allen and Donnithorne (1954), p. 112. The CBIAC Shanghai balance sheets suggest, however, that this guideline was not applied uniformly. On underregulation, see also King (1987), vol. 4, Preface, ff. xl–xli.

71. Treaty port notes had to be readily redeemable in Hong Kong, too, hence the implicit overlap relative to all British banks except HSBC; figures published in the *Straits Settlements Government Gazette*, vol. 32 no. 33, June 10, 1898, p. 665, suggest that, at least until the turn of the century, CBIAC was expected to maintain locally a bullion reserve of up to one-quarter of its notes outstanding in Singapore and Penang, while HSBC drew on its Hong Kong reserve to cover its note issue there; cf. King (1987), vol. 1, pp. 120–122.

72. Double and unlimited liability meant that note bearers were to receive preferential treatment, compared with other debtors, should the issuing bank fail. Thus, bearers could make a commensurate or unlimited claim against stakeholders' private property, if the bank was stripped of all its assets and unable to redeem notes.

73. On the collapse of Ceylon's coffee plantations, which brought down the Oriental Banking Corporation, see Bandarage (1983), pp. 77–79.

74. Chiang Hai Ding (1963), pp. 356–360.

75. See HSBC Chief Manager G. E. Noble to J. Stewart the Hong Kong Colonial Secretary, dated June 8, 1889, in PRO CO 129/241, ff. 621–624.

76. See Treasury letter to Under Secretary of State for the Colonies, dated February 22, 1890, in PRO CO 129/248, f. 273; as from the 1900s, similar bond purchases were imposed to secure the note issues of all the other British banks in Asia. Nonetheless, because the bonds bore interest, the new reserve of securities was different to the unremunerative metallic one.

77. See Treasury to Under Secretary of State for the Colonies, dated July 18, 1890, in PRO CO 129/248, ff. 295–296.

78. See Treasury to Under Secretary of State for the Colonies, dated August 4, 1890, in PRO CO 129/248, ff. 299–300.

79. Nelson (1984), pp. 157–159; and Tom (1964), pp. 50–56. On the deep-seated suspicion of paper money in late imperial China, see for example Cheng Linsun (2003), pp. 160–161.

80. Frank King has argued that HSBC had opposed the introduction of the Straits legal tender due to concerns that its notes could not be withdrawn quickly enough there to satisfy the demand for notes in greater China; see King (1987), vol. 1, p. 487. This explanation overlooks the considerable profits made by HSBC on the Straits issue, as well as its proportionate volume, as compared with the transient Lunar New Year demand for notes in Hong Kong. The opposite may have been true: The HSBC worried that slack demand in Hong Kong and the Chinese treaty ports might not be appropriate recompense for the loss of its Straits issue; for a detailed analysis of the Eastern Exchange Banks' opposition to the monetary reforms in Straits, see Chiang Hai Ding (1963), pp. 355–357, and Nelson (1984), pp. 190–197, 223–229.

81. Exactly how the different shades of governance in Hong Kong and the Straits Settlements played out in the monetary sphere is an understudied question.

82. See *Straits Settlements Government Gazette*, vol. 32 no. 33, August 10, 1898, p. 665.

83. Ibid.; for CBIAC, the *Gazette* provides a breakdown of the reserve: S$830,000 in silver dollars deposited with the Straits government, S$237,000 worth of Japanese government bonds at 5 percent per annum stored in Singapore, and S$266,000 worth of British dominion bonds at 2.5 percent per annum held by Crown Agents in London.

84. CBIAC's net published profits are listed chronologically in Jones (1993), Table A5.I.

85. See laconic reference to the Bank's Bangkok notes in HSBC GA F1.1, "The Note Issue"; CBIAC notes in Bangkok were first introduced in 1898, and this bank's local circulation volume was about Ticals 400,000 by 1902. See Archive of the Chartered Bank of India Australia and China, Guildhall Library, London (hereafter, CBIAC GL) Ms 31519/15; the substantial issue of Banque de L'Indochine in the city began a year later but declined immediately thereafter.

Local circulation figures in 1902 were given as FF 865,000, which were then equivalent to about Ticals 430,000. See Gonjō (1993), pp. 181–182.

86. See S/O ("semiofficial") memorandum from Head Office to Shanghai, dated November 3, 1899, in HSBC GA SHG I-51.

87. The Cantonese population in the colony increasingly resorted to notes rather than traditional silver ingots for the traditional debt settlement that accompanied the Lunar New Year.

88. See for example King (1987), vol. 1, p. 68.

89. S/O from Head Office to Shanghai, dated November 17, 1904, in HSBC GA SHG I-51.

90. See Shanghai branch to Peter Smith in Head Office, dated March 12, 1908, in HSBC GA London II-670; "Notes Outstanding" in HSBC GA SHG I-51.

91. See S/O from Head Office to Shanghai Branch, dated December 30, 1911, in HSBC GA SHG I-51.

92. See S/O from Head Office to Shanghai Branch, dated December 30, 1911, in HSBC GA SHG I-51; notably, private bank note issuance in Australia incurred a state tax of 2 percent before 1910. Yet banks of issue were still thought to have enjoyed a 2.5 to 3 percent margin of profit there. See Vort-Ronald (1982), pp. 35, 253.

93. See SOAS, Charles Addis Papers, PP MS 14/21 dated March 7, 1903.

94. See entry in "Notes Received and Issued," HSBC GA SHG I-51, dated October 24, 1901; the increasing number of attempted forgeries of foreign bank notes in China is also attested to in a short reference by the *Times* correspondent (September 22, 1908, p. 6): "Of trade questions with Japan, the most important for foreigners in China is the infringement of trade-marks, the forgery of foreign bank-notes, and the importation into China of Japanese imitations of Chinese provincial notes."

95. On the antiforeign flux unleashed in 1925, see primarily Rigby (1980), pp. 38–56; cf. Borg (1947), pp. 39–40; and Waldron (1995), pp. 241–244, 255–256.

96. Mackenzie (1954), p. 236–237; the *China Press* reported on June 25, 1925 (p. 1) that "some of the office-boys of the Hongkong and Shanghai bank have walked out."

97. Wright (1984), p. 130.

98. Some Chinese bankers demanded, for example, that customs surplus be deposited only with Chinese banks; see for example *North-China Herald*, September 19, 1925, p. 338.

99. In the long haul, "invisible" CBIAC liabilities in Shanghai, like fixed deposits, were not as vulnerable to antiforeign agitation as to the bank's local note circulation. In fact, total liabilities grew from Tls. 16.2 million in June 1925 to 18.3 million in June 1926. See CBIAC GL Ms 31519/83 and 86.

100. The first issue of the *North-China Herald* to report the disturbances appeared only on June 6, 1925 (see pp. 414, 416–417). The *Herald* then had to concede that the strike had brought the city to a standstill and that one of the alarming goals that students in Shanghai and Beijing agitated for with some degree of success was a ban on British banks. However, British executives and

company managers were not asked to comment on the severity of the boycott; for expatriate press reports on the Chinese student campaign in Shanghai and Beijing to boycott quasi-foreign banknotes and to withdraw deposits from foreign banks, see also *South China Morning Post*, June 2, 1925, p. 8; and June 6, 1925, p. 12.

101. See report in *Minguo ribao*, June 3, 1925, quoted in *Wusa yundong shiliao* (1981), p. 214.

102. Hong Jiaguan (1989, pp. 18–19) estimated total deposits in principal Chinese banks at 1.4 billion silver dollars in late 1924. By late 1926 the total is said to have reached 2.4 billion silver dollars.

103. See CBIAC GL Ms 31519/78 to 83.

104. See report in *Shishi xinbao* 时事新报, June 4, 1925, quoted in *Wusa yundong shiliao* (1981), p. 199.

105. On the *Herald* as mouthpiece of expatriate disdain for Chinese national aspirations and for racialist commentary on the "Chinese character," see Clifford (1991), pp. 117–118, 241, 278–279.

106. On June 8, 1925, the *Gongli ribao* 公理日报 reported that a sudden run on HSBC in Shanghai exhausted its cash reserves and that Chinese bearers of CBIAC notes were now anxious to redeem them. The two British banks were allegedly saved from collapse only when two money shops secretly decided to honor their notes for an exorbitant commission; quoted in *Wusa yundong shiliao* (1981), pp. 200–201. Although front page advertisement promoting substitutes for British cigarette brands and reports on student demands for the boycott of quasi-foreign notes started appearing in the *Shenbao* as early as June 4, 1925 (pp. 2–4, 13–15), the newspaper's editorial line remained relatively subdued.

107. *Zhongguo yinhang hangshi* (1995), p. 78.

108. Du Xuncheng (2002), pp. 83–84; cf. Du Xuncheng (2003), pp. 81–89.

109. Fewsmith (1985), p. 65.

110. *Yinhang zhoubao* vol. 9, no. 29, August 4, 1925, p. 410; for background information on the Shanghai Commercial & Savings Bank in the 1920s, see Zeng Xianming (2000).

111. See extensive correspondence between the Colonial Office and the Eastern Exchange Banks through 1925–1926 in PRO CO 129/510/1.

112. Cornish was quoted in "Chartered Bank of India, Australia & China: Conditions in Eastern Markets" (1926).

113. Calculated from Jones (1993), Table A5.1. Based on the adjusting account entry in the Shanghai balance sheet, it can be plausibly inferred that at least 30 percent of the drop in overall CBIAC profits during 1925 was attributable to underperformance at this branch; see CBIAC GL Ms 31519/83. Despite the superior performance of HSBC in 1925, its executives were equally alarmed by the long-term implications of the boycott; see report in *The Economist*, April 17, 1926, pp. 791–792.

114. Calculated from Green and Kinsey (1999), pp. 199–212.

115. Osterhammel (1989), pp. 193–194; British-owned department stores in Shanghai's International Concession catered almost exclusively for the foreign community. The leading Chinese chains, Wing On and Sincere, had been set up

with overseas Chinese joint-stock capital. They do not seem to have borrowed foreign bank capital on a large scale until the 1930s; see Chan (1977), passim.

116. Cochran (1980), pp. 177–178; cf. Remer (1933), pp. 101–112, 121.

117. Cochran (1980), pp. 182, 230. Nicholas Clifford reached a similar conclusion; see Clifford (1991), p. 132.

118. Rigby (1980), pp. 142–146; see also Clifford (1991), pp. 137.

119. Aggregated from HSBC GA files: SHG II–1023; SHG 343.1–5; SHG II 1044; London II–Box 8 Item 127 (Inspector's Report on Shanghai; GHO 96.2; GHO 13.2; SHG LEDG 294; PRO files: FO 371/13193; FO 371/18130; year-end 1935 based on King (1987), vol. 3, p. 247.

120. This point is made eminently clear in a letter, entitled "Peking Agency Note Issue," that A. H. Barlow sent to A. E. Baker of the Shanghai branch on April 16, 1924, in HSBC GA SHG II 576; in essence, Barlow explained to Baker how the mainland issue offset the bank's issue capacity in Hong Kong. He then told Baker that it was "unadvisable" for the bank to increase its Beijing issue beyond $600,000 because the prevailing political uncertainty in the capital made HSBC notes extremely popular to the extent that additional issues would be immediately hoarded, thus narrowing the bank's ability to balance off circulation volumes between the mainland and the colony; the premium on HSBC notes in Hong Kong was often the theme of discussions between the Colony's government and the Treasury in London during the 1920s and 1930s, but there are many fewer references to a similar premium over metallic currencies on the mainland. See for example Barlow to Hillier, dated January 6, 1922, in HSBC GA SHG II 576. In that correspondence, Barlow recounted en passant that many deposits had been withdrawn from the bank's mainland branches on the outbreak of World War I but that often the clients insisted on payment in HSBC notes rather than in silver.

121. Share prices in Shanghai and London are based on the *North-China Herald* and the *Financial Times* respectively; interestingly, CBIAC and MBI shares, which traded exclusively in London, sustained a smaller price decline during the same period.

122. Hong Kong Share prices are based on the *South China Morning Post*. Trading in the colony was suspended between July and November 1925 as a result of the spreading disturbances; cf. Ku Hung-ting (1983), pp. 863.

123. See for example King (1987), vol. 3, pp. 62–63; surprisingly enough, the May 30th Incident does not appear in the index to volume 3 of this work. Similarly, volume 3 does not discuss the evolution of circulation volumes in China before 1927.

124. Barlow to Stitt, dated June 19, 1925 in HSBC GA GHO 13.2, folio 28. Stitt resigned from the Bank in 1926 after thirty-six years of service; see King (1987), vol. 3, p. 300. The lack of reliable data on the foreign financial sector obscured the few contemporary reports that emerged in the Chinese press on the impact of the boycott of quasi-foreign notes. On October 10, 1926, the *Jingji xuebao* (Journal of Economics) briefly addressed the issue with these words (vol. 2, no. 2, p. 271):

HSBC banknotes had been popular in China ever since the use of paper money was [reintroduced] to the country. Following the tragic events of *Wusa* last year, Chinese [activists] have called for the severing of economic ties [with Britain]. The circulation of HSBC notes in the Chinese sector [diminished] somewhat thereafter, but was entirely unfazed in the foreign sector.

125. For this view, see King (1987), vol. 3, pp. 62–63.

126. Addis to Stephen, dated June 15, 1921, in HSBC GA F1.1 ("The Note Issue/Extracts from Sundries File Kept in the Chief Accountant's Office").

127. Undersecretary of State at Colonial Office to the Foreign Office, dated June 2, 1921, in PRO FO 371/6650, f. 154.

128. Hong Kong Colonial Treasurer to Barlow, dated June 25, 1925, in HSBC GA GHO 13.2 f. 45; Stitt to Barlow, dated June 30, 1925, in HSBC GA GHO 13.2 folio 52.

129. Barlow to Stitt, dated July 3, 1925, in GHO 13.2 folio 50.

130. Cited in Pan Liangui (2004), pp. 126–127. The Chinese bank implicated was rumored to be Yu's *Siming yinhang* 四明銀行, but it promptly denied the allegations; see Du Xuncheng (2002), p. 84; cf. Du Xuncheng (2003), pp. 85–86.

131. See *Rexue ribao*, June 7, 1925, p. 2.

132. Barlow to Stitt, dated July 3, 1925, in HSBC GA GHO 13.2 folio 50.

133. In fact, the Bank's Hong Kong dollar circulation volume rose through 1925 and 1926 because of the moratorium on coin withdrawals and concurrent run on "native" banks. For background details, see *South China Morning Post*, July 2, 1925, p. 2.

134. Stitt to Barlow, 2 July 2, 25, in HSBC GA GHO 13.2, f. 54; the wording of Stitt's telegram suggests that notes were more vulnerable to popular runs than current accounts or fixed deposits because they were redeemable on demand.

135. Stitt to Barlow, July 8–9, 1925, in HSBC GA GHO 13.2, f. 69.

136. Stitt to Barlow, July 13, 1925, in HSBC GA GHO 13.2, f. 71.

137. Stitt to Barlow, July 16, 1925, in HSBC GA GHO 13.2, f. 81.

138. Barlow to Stitt, August 5, 1925, in HSBC GA GHO 13.2, f. 111.

139. Barlow to Stitt, August 17, 1925, in HSBC GA GHO 13.2, ff. 121–122.

140. Barlow to Stitt, July 24, 1925, in HSBC GA GHO 13.2, f. 83.

141. Barlow to Stitt, June 23, 1925 in HSBC GA GHO 13.2, f. 43; in this telegram, Barlow indicated, among other things, that "Head Office note issue [in Hong Kong] has so heavily increased that it is probable we shall require at least $2 million of our [consular note reserve] deposit in Shanghai retained as cover"; for background details on the situation in Hong Kong and unusual demand for Hong Kong dollar notes at that time, see the *Times*, June 23, 1925, p. 16; see also Sinn (1994), pp. 33–35. In all, however, HSBC's global circulation volume fell from the equivalent of HK$49.6 million in December 1924 to HK$45.2 million in December 1925; see *Bankers' Magazine*, vol. 121, pp. 643–644, for 1924; vol. 121, pp. 768–777, for 1925. CBIAC circulation patterns in Shanghai and Hong Kong through 1925 and 1926 are negatively correlated in much the same way.

142. Barlow to Stitt, dated October 5, 1925, in HSBC GA GHO 13.2, ff. 225–226.

143. *The Foreign Trade of China* (1926), p. 1; The China Association Annual Report for 1925–1926 also noted anti-British sentiments were largely "abating"; see SOAS CHAS/A8.

144. Barlow to Lowson, June 4, 1926, in HSBC GA GHO 13.3.

145. Head Office to Lowson, August 24, 1926, in HSBC GA GHO 13.3.

146. See Remer (1933), passim.

147. See for example Chen (1971).

CHAPTER SIX

1. Tamagna (1942); King (1965, 1987); and Jones (1993).

2. See for example Cheng Linsun (2003), Sheehan (2003), and Horesh (2009a).

3. See Metzler (2006), pp. 57, 108. See also Schiltz (2012a), passim. On Japan's posture within the international gold standard before World War II, see Eichengreen and Flandreau's classic (1997, p. 5).

4. Tamaki (1995), pp. 111–168, and Metzler (2006), pp. 199–217.

5. Many Chinese modern banks employed Western advisors. See *Shina kinyu kikan* (1919), pp. 101–102. In this chapter, I do not aim to discuss in detail Sino–foreign joint-venture banks that issued notes with Chinese government approval. It is nonetheless worth recalling in this context that the Exchange Bank of China (est. 1918) was one such prominent Sino–Japanese bank. It similarly issued notes in China but was beset by anti-Japanese agitation in 1928.

6. Eckert (1996), Manela (2007), and Wells (1985).

7. *Yokohama shōkin ginkō zenshi*, vol. 2, p. 32, 144; and *Meiji taisho zaisei shi* (1955), vol. 14–16. On Japanese early modern monetary and banking history more generally, see also Noda (1980); Tamaki (1995); Kuroda (2006); and Ishii (2007). On Taiwan's colonial economy, see Ho (1978), chapter 3. On Matsukata's adoption of the Banque Nationale de Belgique model, see Schiltz (2006). In 1947, the Supreme Command of the Allied Powers (SCAP) restructured YSB into the Bank of Tokyo, which has more recently evolved into the Mitsubishi Tokyo Bank. After World War II, SCAP similarly restructured other long-standing Japanese semiofficial banks (*Tokushu ginkō* 特殊銀行)—which had been initially chartered on the German and French model—into purely privately run banks. These banks had often incorporated with large private share subscription, but they won active Japanese government endorsement and proved pivotal to the country's military and industrial modernization.

8. Tamaki (1995), pp. 69–73.

9. Wu Chouzhong (1989); and *Ziben zhuyi guojia* (1992), pp. 27–35. Cf. Pick (1990), vol. 1, pp. 285–288.

10. *Yokohama shōkin ginkō zenshi* (1984), vol. 2, p. 144.

11. *Yokohama shōkin ginkō zenshi* (1984), vol. 6, pp. 399–401; for YSB paid-up capital figures, see *Hundred-Year Statistics of the Japanese Economy* (1966), pp. 166–167. The ¥100 million cap subsequently remained intact until 1945.

12. Wray (1989), p. 61; Deng (1995); Metzler (2006), p. 65; and Guo Yuqing (2007), p. 117.

13. Taira (1982). Taira's view is supported by Wray (1989), pp. 44–47.

14. Ishii (2002). An illuminating indication of the importance of local deposits is provided by D. K. Lieu (1929, p. 86):

> Deposits of Chinese and foreign customers, especially savings and long term deposits, are invested by [the foreign banks] in [China] or other countries . . . although we are able to obtain their condensed balance sheets for all branches, it is impossible with a few exceptions to secure data concerning their China branches alone. As to the way they invest the deposits of their customers, detailed particulars for our purpose are also unavailable.

15. Guo Yuqing (2007), pp. 189, 191.

16. On the "chop loan" and the 1910–1912 financial crisis in Shanghai, see Bergère (1964); McElderry (1976); and Nishimura (2005).

17. On the Ta Ching Bank, see Kong (1991).

18. On the impact of the *fabi* reform on foreign bank note issuance in China, see Horesh (2009c).

19. Takatsuna (1995) and Guo Yuqing (2007). Cf. Remer (1933).

20. Kikuchi (1966), p. 182.

21. See for example *Santō shuppei to hai nikka undō* (1927).

22. See *Tsūshō kōhō* issues for June 16, 1919 (Changchun) and July 17, 1919 (Zhifu).

23. See for example JCAHR intelligence report dated November 20, 1919, reel no. 1-0517, folio 0273; retrieved on September 12, 2012, from www.jacar .go.jp/english/index.html.

On the longer-term Japanese mercantile anxiety that the May 4th boycott unleashed, see also Banno (1989), pp. 314–317. However, Banno does not discuss the impact of boycotts specifically on banking.

24. Fung (1991), p. 44.

25. Rinbara Fumiko's case study (1983, p. 47) well illustrates the failure to address boycotts of quasi-foreign banknotes as one of the most significant characteristics of antiforeign agitation in 1919–1937. Rinbara cursorily describes how students in Tianjin had tried to force merchants to encash Japanese-issued notes in 1919, but like other scholars he does not analyze the consequences for Japanese banks in the city at all. Notably, the first boycott against quasi-foreign banknotes in Tianjin had actually targeted the French-run Banque Industrielle de Chine as early as 1916. See Sheehan (2003), p. 82.

26. See *Wusi yundong zai Shanghai shiliao xuanji* (1961), pp. 11, 215.

27. See Ren Jianshu (1996), pp. 11–16, and *Wusi yundong zai Shanghai shiliao xuanji* (1961), pp. 212–213, 689–692.

28. Baster (1935) and Davis (1982). Cf. Horesh (2009a).

29. Remer (1933). Cf. Horesh (2009a).

30. See *Shanhai jijō* (1924), p. 131; and Orchard (1930), pp. 252–254; cf. Pan Liangui (2004), p. 130.

31. The boycott of Japanese-issued notes reawakened in 1923 in response to Japan's refusal to waive its territorial claims in northeast China. See *North-China Herald*, April 14, 1923, p. 81.

32. See for example an article by Arthur Sowerby, member of the Shanghai branch of the Royal Asiatic Society, in *North-China Herald*, August 8, 1925, p. 1925; cf. Orchard (1930), p. 256.

33. See for example *Shenbao*, November 27 1919, p. 6, and *Shenbao*, November 18, 1919, p. 10. For articles in similar vein during the May 30th Movement, see for example *Dongfang zazhi*, vol. 22 no. 22, November 25, 1925, pp. 59–63; and *Dongfang zazhi*, vol. 22, no. 24, December 25, 1925, pp. 59–63.

34. *Yokohama shōkin ginkō zenshi* (1984), vol. 2, p. 360, 385. YSB may have tried to increase its Hankou circulation in the early 1920s to offset the fall in demand in Shanghai.

35 *Yokohama shōkin ginkō zenshi* (1984), vol. 1, p. 336.

36. On Yuan Shikai's interventionism, see for example Cheng Linsun (2003), pp. 37–57.

37. Wray (1989) and Gerth (2003), passim.

38. Chung Young-Iob (2006), pp. 15–16.

39. Palais (1991), chapter 8; Duus (1998) pp. 90–96; Chung Young-Iob (2006), pp. 28–29, 58, 61–65; and Schiltz (2012a), chapter 3.

40. *Chōsen ginkō shi* (1987), pp. 26–29. Duus (1984, pp. 152–157) suggests that the great bulk of deposits in the Seoul branch of *Dai'ichi ginkō* in 1909 were by ethnic Korean individuals, the Yi court. Cf. Horesh (2009a). Customs Receipts, and other non-Japanese foreigners.

41. Sukawa (2009). Chinese-style paper money had been issued in Korea during the fifteenth century (K. *chŏhwa* 楮貨), but these notes went out of circulation over the following century.

42. *The History of Korean Money* (1969), pp. 136–149; *Chōsen ginkō shi* (1987), pp. 26–29; Oh Doo-Hwan (1987); and Pratt, Rutt, and Hoare (1999), p. 81.

43. McNamara (1990), p. 42, and Chung Young-Iob (2006), pp. 131–132, 156–194. During the economic boom that East Asia as a whole experienced during World War I, smaller privately run banks were established in Korea, including Korean-owned ones, but few survived into the late 1930s. The Industrial Bank of Chosen (*Chōsen shōkusan ginkō* 朝鮮殖産銀行) was dedicated to funding mining ventures, industry, and large-scale land acquisition by Japanese firms operating in Korea. An equivalent industrial-oriented *Tokushu ginkō* was *not* set up in Taiwan, a colony that remained in the prewar era largely reliant on the export of agricultural commodities (sugar, rice, tea). These were controlled by Japanese trading firms but cultivated for the most part by Chinese households owning small plots of land. See Helleiner (2003), p. 175.

44. *Chōsen ginkō shi* (1987), Historical Appendix.

45. *Chōsen ginkō ryakushi* (1960), pp. 7–10, 748.

46. The BoCS bank set up a branch in Andong (today, Dandong) as early as 1909. Its gold-yen notes were legal tender also in the Guandong leased territory.

Concomitantly, YSB silver-denominated notes were issued in Dairen. See Mitter (2000), p. 61.

47. Ishikawa (2002).

48. Suleski (1979), pp. 643–660, and Suleski (1994), pp. 75–88.

49. See *Chōsen ginkō shi* (1987), p. 11, Table 1, p. 227, Table 2-32. Rawski (1989, p. 377) similarly found that about one-third of the BoCS total issue circulated in Manchuria. The *Tsūshō kōhō* issue for July 17, 1917 reported that in Zhifu (Yantai) YSB and BoCS notes made up about one-fourth of the local currency stock.

50. Yasutomi (1997), pp. 53–54, and Yasutomi (1998), pp. 1–5.

51. Mitter (2000), p. 121; on the flight of silver from China in 1935, see Burdekin's ground-breaking empiric study (2008b). On the Great Depression in East Asia, see Shiroyama (2008).

52. Yasutomi (1998), pp. 5–7. Cf. Jones (1949), p. 124.

53. Dai Jianbing (2001).

54. Howe (2001), p. 38; and Andrade (2006).

55. Perez (1999), p. 173, and Tamaki (195), pp. 24–27. Cf. Chang and Myers (1963).

56. Davidson (1903), p. 173. Kishimoto (1997, pp. 359–363) suggests most privately drafted contracts in Taiwan had already been denominated in silver dollars rather than in taels as of the mid-eighteenth century, whereas on the mainland the transition from taels to silver-dollar terms would occur only in the late nineteenth century. Qing-backed rebels opposing the accession of Taiwan to Japan were probably the first to issue substantial amounts of paper notes on the island, but these disappeared once the uprising was quelled. See *Zhongguo jindai zhibi shi* (2001), Taiwan segment. After Japanese rule stabilized, many ethnic Chinese merchants relocated from Taiwan to the mainland as Japanese subjects. They consequently enjoyed extraterritorial protection and therefore maintained an edge over the local Chinese. Taiwanese remittance houses prospered in Xiamen in the 1910s and were able to divert much business from the Bank of Taiwan branch there. See Lin Man-houng (2005), pp. 230–231.

57. Chen I-Ten (1970).

58. Unlike Taiwan and Korea, Singapore had seen a full-fledged government issue replacing private bank notes by 1907. See Nelson (1984).

59. Davidson (1903), p. 618, and Schiltz (2012a), Chapter 2.

60. The Japanese brought silver and gold yen currency, minted in Osaka, into the island; they did not mint locally. Unlike Osaka-minted Korean currency, the coinage brought to Taiwan did not bear local inscriptions or images. Silver coinage in all its forms had all but disappeared on the island by World War I, a time when the world price of silver shot up. See Yuan Yingsheng (2001).

61. For a historical overview of the BoTW, see *Taiwan ginkō shi* (1964).

62. Boomgaard and Brown (2002).

63. Jansen (2002), p. 534, and Katō (1988), pp. 341–342.

64. Howe (2001), pp. 47–48; see also Ho (1978, 1984); Myers and Yamada (1984); Mizoguchi (1972); and Mizoguchi and Yamamoto (1984).

65. BoTW disbursed local silver-dollar notes only on the mainland. The first issues appear to have been in Xiamen (Amoy) (1905) and Fuzhou (1906), followed by Shantou (Swatow) (1908), Jiujiang (1913), Shanghai (1912), and Hankou (1915). See Pick (1990), vol. 1, p. 284.

66. In late 1904, the BoTW silver-yen note circulation on the island stood at ¥2,673,000. By late 1905, it had dropped to ¥318,000. In 1906, the silver issue formally ceased. In 1909, it was nominally at only ¥20,000. See *Taiwan ginkō yonjūnenshi* (1939), pp. 44–46.

67. As a whole, the BoTW mainland issue was thought to have accounted for about 10 percent of the total BoTW issue. See *Ziben zhuyi guojia* (1992), p. 32; Ji Zhaojin (2002), p. 143–145; and *Taiwan ginkō yonjūnenshi* (1939), p. 227. On the earlier European experience with low-denomination notes, see for example Helleiner (2003), pp. 55–57, 71–75. On Bank of Japan, BoCS, and BoTW note values, see Field (1934), pp. 328–329.

68. A comparison of data in *Taiwan ginkō yonjūnenshi* (1939, pp. 45–46) with that aligned *Chōsen ginkō shi* (1987, p. 202, Table 2-23) would suggest that the BoTW kept a relatively bigger metallic and overall reserve against its issue than the BoCS. In 1920, for example, the BoCS's total note circulation volume stood at a whopping ¥114 million, while its overall reserve was posted as ¥49.9 million, or just 43 percent of the total issue. In 1921, the BoTW total circulation was, on the other hand, much smaller. It was valued at ¥35.8 million, but the corresponding metallic (bullion) reserve *alone* was valued at ¥22.2 million, or 62 percent of the issue. BoTW's overall reserve that year typically constituted 100 percent of its issue.

69. See allusions to that effect in *Taiwan ginkō yonjūnenshi* (1939), pp. 58, 228.

70. Cf. aggregates in *Meiji taisho zaisei shi* (1955), vol. 16, pp. 321–325, 419–424, and vol. 15, pp. 87–93; on Korean living standard trends under colonial Japanese rule, see Kimura (1993). On Taiwan, see Howe (2001). For a conjoint assessment, see Mizoguchi (1972).

CHAPTER SEVEN

1. Wu, Pan, and Wang (2010), p. 64.
2. See for example Hefeker and Nabor (2005).
3. Olsen (1983) and Ritchie and Park (1987).
4. For a classical theoretical discussion see for example Von Mises (trans. 1982) and Menger (1909).
5. Wu, Pan, and Wang (2010), p. 66.
6. Wu, Pan, and Wang (2010), p. 79.
7. Cribb (1996) and Lucassen (2007), p. 35.
8. Sewell (1904); Sidebotham (1986), pp. 27–30; and Turner (1989). Small quantities of north Indian coins minted in the ninth and tenth centuries were discovered in the USSR west of the Urals. See Wink (2002), p. 128.
9. Hall (1999) and Van Aelst (2007), pp. 108–109.
10. Ghosh (1989), p. 196, and Honda (2007).

11. Kobata (1971). Segal (2011, pp. 59, 101–106, 184–213) suggests that Song coinage supplanted cloth and silk as the main popular media of exchange in late Kamakura Japan to the extent that the Kamakura shogunate reluctantly came to approve of its use.

12. Robequain (1944).

13. Wicks (1992), pp. 19–75, 157–161, 225–250.

14. Codrington (1975), p. 166, and Van Aelst (2007), pp. 97–106. The earliest Chinese bronze coins found in Sri Lanka appear to date back to the ninth century CE, although some of the Chinese coins found in South India date back to the seventh century CE.

15. Raschke (1978), pp. 1070–1071; and Greste (1010). On pre-modern Indian coins in Africa see, for example, Chittick (1980), p. 123.

16. Miyamoto and Shikano (2003), pp. 170–171; Kim (2005), p. 94; Honda (2007); and Segal (2011), pp. 203–2011.

17. Van Aelst (2007), p. 107.

18. Van Aelst (1995) and Heng (2006).

19. Reid (1993), pp. 107–108, and Wolters (2006).

20. Van der Eng (1999), pp. 63–66, and Helleiner (2003), p. 165.

21. Horesh (2008).

22. Vogel (1983), and Horesh (2008), pp. 5–8.

23. *Meiji-zen Nihon kōgyō gijutsu hattatsushi* (1982).

24. Horesh (2004).

25. Weber (rep. 1964), pp. 283–291.

26. Von Glahn (1996a), p. 145, and Kuroda (2000).

27. On billon, see Munro (1974).

28. Kuroda (2009).

29. Kuroda (2000), p. 187–188.

30. Horesh (2009c).

31. Burdekin and Whited (2005).

32. Schottenhammer (2001).

33. Shi Lei (1998), p. 20.

34. Chen Mingyuan (2009), p. 168.

35. *Zhongguo yinhang hangshi* (1995).

36. Naughton (1996), pp. 26–56; Lardy (1998), p. 61; Burdekin (2008a), pp. 76–82; and Zhang Jie (2010), p. 182.

37. Burdekin and Whited (2005). On Japanese forgeries, see for example Kotani (2009), p. 45; on alleged KMT forgeries, see for example Hung Yin-hang (1970).

38. On the evolution of RMB units, see PBC official data retrieved on September 19, 2012, from www.pbc.gov.cn/publish/huobijinyinju/387/1590/15901/15901_.html.

39. Burdekin (2008a), p. 14, and Zhang Jie (2010), p. 184; Liew and Wu (2007), pp. 29–49.

40. Li Ping and Qingfang Yang (1999), pp. 85–88.

41. Dukes (2001), pp. 101–107.

42. Schenk (2009), pp. 6–7.

43. The wording of this 1983 declaration as published in the CCP organ, the *People's Daily* (*Renmin ribao*) can be viewed at the newspaper's website; retrieved on September 19, 2012, from www.people.com.cn/item/flfgk/gwyfg/1983/112203198306.html.

44. The 1993 official pronouncement to that effect can be viewed at the People's Bank of China website; retrieved on September 19, 2012, from www.pbc.gov.cn/publish/bangongting/91/1590/15900/15900_.html.

45. Chung and Tongzon (2004).

46. Tao Yi-feng (2011), p. 116; Burdekin and Siklos (2008); and Singleton (2011), pp. 218–219.

47. Tseng Wanda (1994), p. 7; Drumm (1994–1995); and Lin and Schramm (2003).

48. Liew, Leong H. (2002) and Burdekin (2008a), pp. 20–21. See also Li Ping and Qingfang Yang (1999), p. 106–107, and Long Yuan (2011), pp. 7–10.

49. Ogawa (2002).

50. Prasad and Wei (2005), and Burdekin (2008a), pp. 26–27.

51. Chen Xiaoli and Yin-wong Cheung (2011).

52. Tao Yi-Feng (2011), pp. 118–124.

53. Wei Linglin (2011).

54. Shi Jianhui (2008), pp. 107–101.

55. Li Jing (2007).

56. Chambers (2011).

57. Le Yan (2007).

58. For an integrative discussion of globalization and China's changing political economy, see Zweig (2002) and Liew, Leong H. (2006).

59. Chen Xiaoli and Yin-wong Cheung (2011), pp. 7, 13.

60. For official news coverage of this bond issue see the English-language CCTV website, retrieved on September 19, 2012, from http://english.cntv.cn/20110614/103933.shtml.

61. Chen, Wang, and Yang (2005). Cf. Cheng, Ma and McCauley (2011).

62. Chen, Wang, and Yang (2005). The windfall was broken down to US$678 trillion in seigniorage-derived revenue and US$274 trillion in financial and transaction benefits.

63. Chen, Wang, and Yang (2005).

64. Renminbi guojihua yanjiu ketizu (2006).

65. Dobson and Masson (2009).

66. The wording of the June announcement can be viewed at the People's Bank of China website; retrieved on September 19, 2012, from www.pbc.gov.cn/publish/huobizhengceersi/3131/index.html.

67. Chen Xiaoli and Yin-wong Cheung (2011, pp. 5–6, 9–10) suggest for example that, contrary to popular perceptions, nonresidents currently own PRC equities equivalent to 24 percent of the country's GDP, while nonresidents of Japan own domestic equities amounting to only 17 percent of Japan's GDP. This factor, among others, seems to lead them to predict that more RMB-denominated bond issues and greater overseas trade volumes would of themselves turn the RMB into a global currency in the not-too-distant future.

68. Chen Xiaoli and Yin-wong Cheung (2011), pp. 5–6, 9–10.
69. Triffin (1960).
70. Eichengreen and Flandreau (2008).
71. Eichengreen and Flandreau (2008).
72. Tavlas (1991)
73. Carbaugh and Hedrick (2009).
74. Lardy (1998).
75. Ito (2010). See also Lee Jong-Wha (2010), p. 277, and Takagi (2010), p. 280.
76. Zhou Xiaochuan (2009), pp. 8–13.
77. Li Daokui and Liu Linlin (2008), pp. 42–43.
78. Zhang Wuchang (2010), p. 98.
79. Lang Xianping (2009).
80. Chen Zhiwu (2008).
81. Lin Yifu (2009).

CONCLUSION

1. For a recent detailed discussion see, for example, Munro (2012).
2. This is not to deny Qing de jure strictness with regard to counterfeiting coinage. See for example Greatrex (2013).
3. See for example Araujo and Camargo (2006). On the importance of information in tempering early modern domestic *coin* debasement, see also Gandal and Sussman (1997).
4. See for example Flandreau and Maurel (2001).
5. See Helleiner (2005a,b); and Hira and Dean (2004).
6. Coggan (2011).
7. Cassis (2006), p. 81.

Bibliography

This bibliography consists of books, chapters, and articles cited. All archival records, as well as gazetted data and contemporaneous media reports, are clearly identified in the notes.

Adachi Keiji 足立啓二. 2012. *Min Shin Chūgoku no keizai kōzō* 明清中国の経済構造. Tokyo: Kyūko Shoin.

Agricola, Georgius. *De Re Metallica*. [1556, rep. 1950]. Trans. by Herbert C. Hoover and Lou Henry Hoover. New York: Dover.

Allen, G. C., and Audrey G. Donnithorne. 1954. *Western Enterprise in Far Eastern Economic Development*. London: George Allen and Unwin.

Allen, Martin. 2012. *Mints and Money in Medieval England*. New York: Cambridge University Press.

Allen, Robert C. 2011. *Global Economic History: A Very Short Introduction*. Oxford, UK: Oxford University Press.

Allen, Robert C., Jean-Pascal Bassino, Ma Debin, Christine Moll-Murata, and Jan Luiten Van Zanden. 2011. "Wages, Prices, and Living Standards in China, 1738–1925: In Comparison with Europe, Japan, and India." *Economic History Review* 64.s1: 8–38.

Allsen, Thomas. T. 2001. *Culture and Conquest in Mongol Eurasia*. Cambridge, UK: Cambridge University Press.

Andrade, Tonio. 2006. "The Rise and Fall of Dutch Taiwan, 1624–1662: Cooperative Colonization and the Statist Model of European Expansion." *Journal of World History* 17.4: 429–450.

Andréadès, Andreas Michaël. [1922, rep. 1966]. *History of the Bank of England: 1640 to 1903*. Trans. by Meredith Christabel. London: King.

Araujo, Luis, and Braz Camargo. 2006. "Information, Learning and the Stability of Fiat Money." *Journal of Monetary Economics* 53: 1571–1591.

Arnold, Julean. 1919. *Commercial Handbook of China*. 2 vols. Washington, DC: Government Printing Office.

Arnon, Arie. 2011. *Monetary Theory and Policy from Hume and Smith to Wicksell: Money, Credit and the Economy*. New York: Cambridge University Press.

Ashworth, William. 2006. *An Economic History of England, 1870–1939*. London: Routledge.

Atwell, William S. 1982. "International Bullion Flows and the Chinese Economy Circa 1530-1650." *Past & Present* 95: 68–90.

Baba Kuwatarō 馬場鍬太郎. 1922. *Shina keizai chirishi*支那經濟地理誌. Shanghai: Uiki gakkai.

Badian, Ernst. 1972. *Publicans and Sinners: Private Enterprise in the Service of the Roman Republic*. Ithaca, NY: Cornell University Press.

Bagchi, Amiya Kumar. 1989. *The Presidency Banks and the Indian Economy*. Calcutta: Oxford University Press.

Banaji, Jairus. 2007. "Islam, the Mediterranean and the Rise of Capitalism." *Historical Materialism* 15.1: 47–74.

Bandarage, Asoka. 1983. *Colonialism in Sri Lanka: The Political Economy of the Kandyan Highlands, 1833–1886*. New York: Mouton.

Banno Junji. 1989. "Japanese Industrialists and Merchants and the Anti-Japanese Boycotts in China, 1919–1928." In Peter Duus, Ramon H. Myers, and Mark R. Peattie, eds., *The Japanese Informal Empire in China, 1895–1937*, 314–330. Princeton, NJ: Princeton University Press.

Barnard, Noel. 1983. "Further Evidence to Support the Hypothesis of Indigenous Origins of Metallurgy in Ancient China." In David N. Keightley, ed., *The Origins of Chinese Civilization*, 237–278. Berkeley: University of California Press.

Baskin, Jonathan Barron, and Paul J. Miranti Jr. 1997. *A History of Corporate Finance*. New York: Cambridge University Press.

Baster, A. S. J. 1929. *The Imperial Banks*. London: P. S. King and Son.

———. 1934. "The Origins of the British Exchange Banks in China." *Economic History* (Supplement to *The Economic Journal*) 3.9: 140–151.

———. [1935, rep. 1977]. *The International Banks*. New York: Arno Press.

Becker, Thomas W. 1969. *The Coin Makers*. New York: Doubleday.

Beckwith, Christopher I. 2011. *Empires of the Silk Road: A History of Central Eurasia from the Bronze Age to the Present*. Princeton, NJ: Princeton University Press.

Bentley, Jerry H. 2006. "Beyond Modern Centrism: Toward Fresh Visions of the Global Past." In Victor H. Mair, ed., *Contact and Exchange in the Ancient World*, 17–29. Honolulu: University of Hawai'i Press.

Bergère, Marie-Claire. 1964. *Une crise financière à shanghai à la fin de l'ancien régime*. Paris: Mouton.

Bernholz, Peter. 1997. "Paper Money Inflation, Gresham's Law and Exchange Rates in Ming China." *Kredit und Kapital* 30.1: 35–51.

———. 2003. *Monetary Regimes and Inflation: History, Economic and Political Relationships*. Northampton, MA: Edward Elgar.

Bickers, Robert A. 1999. *Britain in China: Community Culture and Colonialism, 1900–1949*. Manchester, UK: Manchester University Press.

Bivar, A. D. H. 1971. "A Hoard of Ingot-Currency of the Median Period from Nush-i-Jan, Near Malayir." *Iran* 9:97–130.

————. 1985. "Achaemenid Coins, Weights and Measures." In Ilya Gershevits, ed. *Cambridge History of Iran*, vol. 2, 610–639. Cambridge, UK: Cambridge University Press.

Blackburn, Mark. 2005. "Money and Coinage." In Paul Fouracre, ed., *The New Cambridge Medieval History c. 500–c. 700*, 660–675. New York: Cambridge University Press.

Blake, Robert P. 1937. "The Circulation of Silver in the Moslem East Down to the Mongol Epoch." *Harvard Journal of Asiatic Studies* 2.3/4: 291–328.

Blanchard, Ian. 2005. *Mining, Metallurgy, and Minting in the Middle Ages: Continuing Afro-European Supremacy, 1250–1450*. Berlin: Franz Steiner Verlag.

Bloch, K. 1935. "On the Copper Currencies in China." *Nankai Social & Economic Quarterly* 8.3: 616–632.

Block, Fred L. 1977. *The Origins of International Economic Disorder: A Study of United States International Monetary Policy from World War II to the Present*. Berkeley: University of California Press.

Bol, Peter K. 2010. *Neo-Confucianism in History*. Cambridge, MA: Harvard University Press.

Bolin, Sture. 1958. *State and Currency in the Roman Empire to 300 A.D.* Stockholm: Almqvist & Wiksell.

Boomgaard, Peter, and Ian Brown. 2002. "The Economies of Southeast Asia in the 1930s Depression: An Introduction." In idem., eds., *Weathering the Storm: The Economies of Southeast Asia in the 1930s Depression*, 1–19. Leiden: KITLV Press.

Bopearachchi, Osmund, and Aman ur Rahman. 1995. *Pre-Kushana Coins in Pakistan*. Karachi: Iftikar Rasul.

Bordo, Michael D. 1986. "Explorations in Monetary History: A Survey of the Literature." *Explorations in Economic History* 23.4: 339–415.

Bowen, H. V., and P. L. Cottrell. 1997. "Banking and the Evolution of the British Economy." In Alice Teichova, Ginette Kurgan-Van Hentenryk, and Dieter Ziegler, eds., *Banking, Trade and Industry: Europe, America and Asia from the Thirteenth to the Twentieth Century*, 89–112. Cambridge, UK: Cambridge University Press.

Braudel, Fernand. 1992. *Civilization and Capitalism, 15th–18th Century: The Perspective of the World*, vol. 2, *The Wheels of Commerce*. Trans. by Sîan Reynolds. Berkeley: University of California Press.

Bresson, Alain. 2009. "Electrum Coins, Currency Exchange and Transaction Costs in Archaic and Classical Greece." *Revue Belge de Numismatique et de sigillographie* 140: 71–80.

Bretton, Henry L. 1980. *The Power of Money: A Political-Economic Analysis with Special Emphasis on the American Political System*. Albany: State University of New York Press.

Brewer, John. 1988. *The Sinews of Power: War, Money and the English State, 1688–1783*. London: Unwin Hyman.

Briones, Ignacio, and Hugh Rockoff. 2005. "Do Economists Reach a Conclusion on Free-Banking Episodes?" *Econ Journal Watch* 2.2: 279–324.

Brook, Timothy. 1999. *The Confusions of Pleasure: Commerce and Culture in Ming China*. Berkeley: University of California Press.

Brooke, George C. 1950. *English Coins: From the Seventh Century to the Present Day*. London: Methuen.

Brown, C. J. 1967. *The Coins of India*. Chicago: Argonaut.

Brown, Rajeswary. 1994. *Capital and Entrepreneurship in South-East Asia*. New York: St. Martin's Press.

Bulmer-Thomas,Victor. 1994. *The Economic History of Latin America since Independence*. Cambridge, UK: Cambridge University Press.

Burdekin, Richard C. K. 2005. "Exporting Hyperinflation: The Long Arm of Chiang Kai-shek." *China Economic Review* 16.1: 71–89.

———. 2008a. *China's Monetary Challenges: Past Experiences and Future Prospects*. New York: Cambridge University Press.

———. 2008b. "US Pressure on China: Silver Flows, Deflation and the 1934 Shanghai Credit Crunch." *China Economic Review* 19.2: 170–182.

Burdekin, R. C. K., and Siklos, P. L. 2008. "What Has Driven Chinese Monetary Policy since 1990? Investigating the People's Bank Policy Rule." *Journal of International Money and Finance* 27: 847–859.

Burger, Werner. 2008. "Coin Production during the Qianlong and Jiaqing Reigns (1736–1820): Issues in Cash and Silver Supply." In Thomas Hirzel and Nanny Kim, eds., *Metals, Monies, and Markets in Early Modern Societies: East Asian and Global Perspectives*, 171–189. London: Global.

Burnett, Andrew. 1991. *Coins: Interpreting the Past*. Berkley: University of California Press.

Cameron, Rondo. 1967a. "England, 1750–1844." In Rondo Cameron, Olga Crisp, Hugh T.Patrick, and Richard Tilly, eds., *Banking in the Early Stages of Industrialization: A Study in Comparative Economic History*, 15–59. New York: Oxford University Press.

———. 1967b. "France, 1800, 1870." In Rondo Cameron, Olga Crisp, Hugh T. Patrick, and Richard Tilly eds., *Banking in the Early Stages of Industrialization: A Study in Comparative Economic History*, 100–128. New York: Oxford University Press.

Capie, Forrest, and Alan Webber. 1983. "Total Coin and Coin in Circulation in the United Kingdom, 1868–1914." *Journal of Money, Credit and Banking* 15.1: 24–39.

Carbaugh, Robert J., and David W. Hedrick. 2009. "Will the Dollar Be Dethroned as the Main Reserve Currency?" *Global Economy Journal* 9.3: 1–14.

Carothers, Neil. [1930, rep. 1967]. *Fractional Money: A History of the Small Coins and Fractional Paper Currency of the United States*. New York: A. M. Kelley.

Carradice, Ian. 1987. "The 'Regal' Coinage of the Persian Empire." In idem., ed., *Coinage and Administration in the Athenian and Persian Empires: The Ninth Oxford Symposium on Coinage and Monetary History*, 73–95. Oxford, UK: BAR.

Carson, R. A. G. 1970. *Coins: Ancient, Medieval & Modern*. London: Hutchison.

Cassis, Youssef. 1994. *City Bankers, 1890–1914*. Trans. from the French by Margaret Roques. Cambridge, UK: Cambridge University Press.

———. 2006. *Capital of Capitals: A History of International Financial Centres, 1780–2005*. Cambridge, UK: Cambridge University Press.

Challis, C. E. 1978. *The Tudor Coinage*. Manchester, UK: Manchester University Press.

Chalmers, Robert. 1893. *History of Currency in the British Colonies*. London: Her Majesty's Stationary Office.

Chambers, Matt. 2011, July 13. "It's Yuan for the Money for Twiggy Forrest." *The Australian* [online edition]; retrieved on August 1, 2011, from www.theaustralian.com.au/business/mining-energy/its-yuan-for-the-money-for-twiggy-forrest/story-e6frg9df-1226093397794

Chamley, Christophe. 2011. "Interest Reductions in the Politico-Financial Nexus of Eighteenth-Century England." *The Journal of Economic History* 71.3: 555–589.

Chan-kuo Ts'e [Zhanguo ce]. 1979. Trans. by J.I. Crump. San Francisco: Chinese Materials Center.

Chan, Wellington K. K. 1977. *Merchants, Mandarins and Modern Enterprise in Late Ch'ing China*. Cambridge, MA: Harvard University Press.

Chang Han-Yu and Ramon H. Myers. 1963. "Japanese Colonial Development Policy in Taiwan, 1895–1906: A Case of Bureaucratic Entrepreneurship." *Journal of Asian Studies* 24.4: 433–449.

Chang, James L. Y. 1987. "History of Chinese Economic Thought: Overview and Recent Works." *History of Political Economy* 19.3: 481–502.

"Chartered Bank of India, Australia & China: Conditions in Eastern Markets." *Bankers' Magazine* 121.1 (1926): 784–786.

Chaudhuri, K. N. 1975. *The Trading World of Asia and the East India Company, 1660–1760*. Cambridge, UK: Cambridge University Press.

———. 1985. *Trade and Civilisation in the Indian Ocean*. Cambridge, UK: Cambridge University Press.

———. 1990. *Asia before Europe: Economy and Civilisation of the Indian Ocean from the Rise of Islam to 1750*. Cambridge, UK: Cambridge University Press.

Chaudoir, B. M. 1842. *Recueil des monnaies de la Chine, du Japon et de la Coree*. Published Manuscript. St. Petersburg.

Checkland, S. G. 1953. "An English Merchant House in China after 1842." *Bulletin of the Historical Society* 27.3: 158–189.

Chen Chau-nan. 1975. "Flexible Bimetallic Exchange Rates in China, 1650–1850: A Historical Example of Optimum Currency Areas." *Journal of Money, Credit and Banking* 7.3: 359–376.

Chen Chau-nan, Chang Pin-tsun, and Chen Shikuan. 1995. "The Sung and Ming Paper Monies: Currency Competition and Currency Bubbles." *Journal of Macroeconomics* 17.2:273–288.

Chen I-Ten, Edward. 1970. "Japanese Colonialism in Korea and Formosa: A Comparison of the Systems of Political Control." *Harvard Journal of Asian Studies* 30: 126–158.

Ch'ên, Jerome. 1958. "The Hsien-Fêng Inflation." *Bulletin of the School of Oriental and African Studies,* 578–586.

———. 1980. *State Economic Policies of the Ch'ing Government, 1840–1895.* New York: Garland.

Chen, Joseph T. 1971. *The May Fourth Movement in Shanghai: The Makings of a Social Movement in Modern China.* Leiden: Brill.

Chen Limao 陳禮茂. 2003. "Zhang Zhidong zai Zhongguo tongshang yinhang chunagban guochengzhong de yanlun shuping" 張之洞在中國通商銀行創辦過程中的言論述評. *Anhui shixue 5:* 29–35.

Chen Longwen 陳隆文. 2006. "Shi yuanqian" 釋圜錢. *Renwen zazhi 5:* 140–143.

Chen Mingyuan 陳明遠. 2009. *Lishi de jianzheng: Si shi nian piaozheng he Renminbi shi* 曆史的見證: 四十年票證和人民幣史. Nanjing: Fenghuang chubanshe.

Chen Qixin 陳啟新. 1996. "Ming zhi shi kao" 冥紙史考. *Zhongguo zaozhi* 75–79.

Chen Shao-teh. [1932, rep. 1982]. *Étude sur le marché monetaire de Changhai.* New York: Garland.

Chen Xiaoli and Yin-Wong Cheung. 2011. "Renminbi Going Global." *China & World Economy* 19.2: 1–18.

Chen Yulu, Fang Wang, and Ming Yang. 2005. "Internationalization of Currency as a Transnational Competition Strategy: Evidential Experience of the US Dollar on the Globalization of the Renminbi." *Economic Research* 2: 35–44.

Chen Zhiwu 陳志武. 2008. "Renminbi sheng zhi guo man jia ju liu dong xing guo sheng" 人民幣升值過慢加劇流動性過剩 *Caifu luntan* 3: 129–130.

Cheng Linsun. 2003. *Banking in Modern China: Entrepreneurs, Professional Managers and the Development of Chinese Banks, 1897–1937.* New York: Cambridge University Press.

Chernykh, E. N. 1992. *Ancient Metallurgy in the USSR: The Early Metal Age.* Trans. by Sarah Wright. Cambridge, UK: Cambridge University Press.

Cheung Yin-Wong, Ma Guonan, and Robert N. McCauley. 2011. "Why Does China Attempt to Internationalise the Renminbi?" In Jane Golley and Ligang Song, eds., *Rising China: Global Challenges and Opportunities,* 45–68. Canberra: ANU e-Press.

Chiang Hai Ding. 1963. *A History of Straits Settlements Foreign Trade, 1870–1915.* Published PhD dissertation. Australian National University.

Chilosi, David, and Oliver Volckart. 2011. "Money, States, and Empire: Financial Integration and Institutional Change in Central Europe, 1400–1520." *Journal of Economic History* 13.71: 762–791.

Chittick, Neville. 1980. "Indian Relations with East Africa before the Arrival of the Portuguese." *Journal of the Royal Asiatic Society* 112.2: 117–127.

Chōsen Ginkō ryakushi 朝鮮銀行略史. 1960. Tokyo: Haibunsha.

Chōsen Ginkō shi 朝鮮銀行史. 1987. Tokyo: Tōyō Keizai shinpōsha.

Chown, John F. 1994. *A Histroy of Money from AD 800.* London: Routledge.

Chung, Connie Wee-Wee, and Jose L. Tongzon. 2004. "A Paradigm Shift for China's Central Banking System." *Journal of Post Keynesian Economics* 27.1: 87–104.

Chung Young-Iob. 2006. *Korea under Siege: Capital Formation and Economic Transformation* . New York: Oxford University Press.

Cibot, Pierre-Martial. c. 1776. "Mémoire sur l'intérêt de l'argent en Chine." In C. Batteux and L. G. O. F. de Brequigny, eds., *Memoires concernant l'histoire, les sciences, les arts, les moeurs, les usages, &c. des Chinois*. Paris: Chez Nyon.

Cipolla, Carlo M. 1967. *Money, Prices, and Civilization in the Mediterranean World, Fifth to Seventeenth Century*. New York: Guardian Press.

Clapham, J. H. 1944. *The Bank of England: A History*. Cambridge, UK: Cambridge University Press.

Clark, Gregory. 2008. *A Farewell to Alms: A Brief Economic History of the World*. Princeton, NJ: Princeton University Press.

Cleveland, Harold van B., and Thomas F. Huertas. 1985. *Citibank, 1812–1970*. Cambridge, MA: Harvard University Press.

Clifford, Nicholas R. 1991. *Spoilt Children of Empire: Westerners in Shanghai and the Chinese Revolution of the 1920s*. Hanover, NH: University Press of New England.

Cobbett, William. 1820. *Paper against Gold: Or, The History and Mystery of the Bank of England, of the Debt, of the Stocks, of the Sinking Fund, and of All the Other Tricks and Contrivances, Carried on by the Means of Paper Money*. London: C. Clement.

Cochran, Sherman. 1980. *Big Business in China: Sino-Foreign Rivalry in the Cigarette Industry, 1890–1930*. Cambridge, MA: Harvard University Press.

Codrington, Humphrey W. 1975. *Ceylon Coins and Currency*. Colombo: Colombo Museum.

Coggan, Philip. 2011. *Paper Promises: Money, Debt and the New World Order*. London: Allen Lane.

Conant, Charles Arthur. 1927. *History of Modern Banks of Issue*. New York: G. P. Putnam.

Cook, Constance A. 1997. "Wealth and the Western Zhou." *Bulletin of the School of Oriental and African Studies* 60.2: 253–294.

Coole, Arthur B. 1981. *Earliest Round Coins of China*. Lawrence, MA: Quarterman Publications.

Cooper, Denis R. 1988. *The Art and Craft of Coinmaking: A History of Minting Technology*. London: Spink & Son.

Craig, John Herbert McCutcheon. 1953 [rep. 2011]. *The Mint: A History of the London Mint from A.D. 287 to 1948*. Cambridge, UK: Cambridge University Press.

Crawford, Michael H. 1985. *Coinage and Money under the Roman Republic*. Berkeley: University of California Press.

Cribb, Joe. 1987. *Money in the Bank: An Illustrated Introduction to the Money Collection of the Hongkong and Shanghai Banking Corporation*. London: Spink & Son.

————. 1992. *Catalogue of Sycee in the British Museum*. London: British Museum.

————. 1996. "Chinese Coin Finds from Arabia and the Arabian Gulf." *Arabian Archaeology and Epigraphy* 7: 108–118.

Crisp, Olga. 1967. "Russia, 1860–1914." In Rondo Cameron, Olga Crisp, Hugh T. Patrick, and Richard Tilly, eds., *Banking in the Early Stages of Industrialization: A Study in Comparative Economic History*, 183–238. New York: Oxford University Press.

Curtin, Philip D. 1975. *Economic Change in Precolonial Africa*. Madison: University of Wisconsin Press.

————. 1983. "Africa and the Wider Monetray World, 1250–1850." In J. F. Richards, ed., *Precious Metals in the Later Medieval and Early Modern Worlds*, 231–268. Durham, NC: Carolina Academic Press.

Czeglédy, K. 1983. "From East to West: The Age of Nomadic Migrations in Eurasia." *Archivum Eurasiae Medii Aevi* 3: 25–125.

"The Dai Fook Dollar of Foochow." 1927. *Chinese Economic Journal* 2: 127–141.

Dai Hongjia 戴宏嘉. 1988. "Dong Zhuo xiaoqian ji qi dui liangjia de ying xiang" 董卓小錢及其對糧價的影響. *Zhejiang xuekan* 3: 32–40.

Dai Jianbing 戴建兵. 2001. "Riben touxiang qianhou dui Zhongguo jingji de zuihou zhaqu he zhaiwu zhuanyi" 日本投降前後對中國經濟的最後榨取和債務轉移. *Kang ri zhanzheng yan jiu* 1: 36–42.

Dai Zhiqiang and Zhou Weirong. 1993. "A Comparative Study of Early Metal Currency (7th–3rd Centuries B.C.) in China and the West." *Bulletin of the Metal Museum* 20.11.

Dardess, John. 1994. "Shun-ti and the end of Yüan rule in China." In Herbert Franke and Denis Twitchett, eds., *The Cambridge History of China*, vol. 6, *Alien Regimes and Border States, 907–1368*, 561–586. Cambridge, UK: Cambridge University Press.

Davenport-Hines, R. P. T., and Geoffrey Jones. 1989. "British Business in Asia since 1860." In idem., eds., *British Business in Asia since 1860*, 1–30. Cambridge, UK: Cambridge University Press.

Davidson, James W. 1903. *The Island of Formosa, Past and Present*. London: Macmillan.

Davies, Glyn. [1994, rep. 2002]. *A History of Money: From Ancient Times to the Present Day*. Cardiff: University of Wales.

Davis, Clarence B. 1982. "Financing Imperialism: British and American Bankers as Vectors of Imperial Expansion in China, 1908–1920." *Business History Review* 56.2: 236–264.

Dayer, Roberta Albert. 1981. *Bankers and Diplomats in China, 1917–1925: The Anglo-American Relationships*. London: Frank Cass.

De Cecco, Marcello. 1975. *Money and Empire: The International Gold Standard, 1890–1914*. Totowa, NJ: Rowman and Littlefield.

De Roover, Raymond. 1999. *Money, Banking and Credit in Medieval Bruges: Italian Merchant-Bankers, Lombards and Money-Changers: A Study in the Origins of Banking*. London: Routledge.

De Ryck, I., A. Adriaens, and F. Adams. 2005. "An Overview of Mesopotamian Bronze Metallurgy during the 3rd Millennium BC." *Journal of Cultural Heritage* 6: 261–268.

De Vries, Jan. 2010. "The Limits of Globalization in the Early Modern World." *Economic History Review* 63.3: 710–733.

Decourdemanche, J. A. 1913. *Traité Des Monnaies, Mesures et Poids Anciens et Modernes de L'Inde et de La Chine*. Paris: Leroux.

Defoe, Daniel. [1738, rep. 1989]. *The Complete English Trademan*. Manila: Historical Conservation Society.

Del Mar, Alex. 2004. *A History of the Precious Metals from the Earliest Times to the Present*. London: Kessinger.

Deng Fucheng 鄧成福. 1995. "Riben Hengbin zhengjin yinhang dui woguo de jinrong qinlüe" 日本横濱正金銀行對我國的金融侵略. *Beijing liaowang* 6: 27–64.

Deng Gang. 1999. *The Premodern Chinese Economy: Structural Equilibrium and Capitalist Sterility*. London: Routledge.

Deng, Stephen. 2011. *Coinage and State Formation in Early-Modern English Literature*. New York: Palgrave Macmillan.

Dennys, N. B., W. F. Mayers, and Charles King. 1867. *The Treaty Ports of China and Japan: A Complete Guide to the Open Ports of Those Countries, Together with Peking, Yedo, Hongkong and Macao. Forming a Guide Book & Vade Mecum for Travellers, Merchants, and Residents in General*. London: Trübner & Co.

Denzel, Markus A. 2010. *Handbook of World Exchange Rates, 1590–1914*. Aldershot, UK: Ashgate.

Dewey, Donald. 2007. "In Palmstruch We Trust." *Scandinavian Review* 95.1: 60–64.

Deyell, John. 1994. "The China Connection: Problems of Silver Supply in Medieval Bengal." In Sanjay Subrahmanyam, ed., *Money and the Market in India 1100–1700*. Delhi: Oxford University Press.

Dhavalikar, M. K. 1975. "The Beginning of Coinage in India." *World Archaeology* 6.3: 330–338.

Di Cosmo, Nicola. 2002. *Ancient China and Its Enemies: The Rise of Nomadic Power in East Asian History*. New York: Cambridge University Press.

Ding Guoliang 丁國良 and Zhang Yuncai 張運才. 1993. *Xiang E Gan geming genjudi huobi shi* 湘鄂贛革命根據地貨幣史. Beijing: Zhongguo jinrong chubanshe.

Ding Richu 丁日初. 1994. *Shanghai jindai jingji shi* 上海近代經濟史. 2 vols. Shanghai: Shanghai renmin chubanshe.

Dobson, Wendy, and Paul R. Masson. 2009. "Will the Renminbi Become a World Currency?" *China Economic Review* 20.1: 124–135.

Doolittle, the Reverend Justus. [1868, rep. 1966]. *Social Life of the Chinese*. 2 vols. Taipei: Chengwen chubanshe.

Doty, Richard. 1990. "The World Coin: Matthew Boulton and His Industrialisation of Coinage." *Interdisciplinary Science Reviews* 15.2: 177–186.

Dowd, Kevin, ed. 1992. *The Experience of Free Banking*. London: Routledge.

Drumm, Larry L. 1994–1995. "Changing Money: Foreign Exchange Reform in the People's Republic of China." *Hastings International & Comparative Law Review*, 359–396.

Du Halde, J. B. c. 1741. *Description of the Empire of China and Chinese-Tartary*. Trans. from the French. London: Gardner and Cave.

Du Xuncheng 杜恂诚. 2002. *Shanghai jinrong de zhidu, gongneng yu bianqian, 1897–1997* 上海金融的制度、功能與變遷, 1897–1997. Shanghai: Shanghai renmin chubanshe.

———. 2003. *Zhongguo jinrong tongshi: Beiyang zhengfu shiqi* 中國金融通史—北洋政府時期. Beijing: Zhongguo jinrong chubanshe.

Dukes, Paul. 2001. *Superpowers: A Short History*. London: Routledge.

Dunstan, Helen. 1992. "Safely Supping with the Devil: The Qing State and Its Merchant Suppliers of Copper." *Late Imperial China* 13.2: 42–81.

———. 1996a. *Conflicting Counsels to Confuse the Age: A Documentary Study of Political Economy in Qing China, 1644-1840*. Ann Arbor: University of Michigan Press.

———. 1996b. "'Orders Go Forth in the Morning and Are Changed by Nightfall': A Monetary Policy Cycle in Qing China, November 1744–June 1745." *T'oung pao* 82: 66–136.

———. 2006. *State or Merchant? Political Economy and Political Process in 1740s China*. Cambridge, MA: Harvard University Press.

Duus, Peter. 1984. "Economic Dimensions of Meiji Imperialism: The Case of Korea, 1895–1910." In Ramon H. Myers and Mark R. Peattie, eds., *The Japanese Colonial Empire, 1895–1945*, 128–171. Princeton, NJ: Princeton University Press.

———. 1998. *The Abacus and the Sword: The Japanese Penetration of Korea, 1895–1910*. Berkeley: University of California Press.

Eagly, Robert V. 1971. "Introduction." In *The Swedish Bullionist Controversy: P. N. Christiernin's Lectures on the High Price of Foreign Exchange in Sweden (1761)*. Philadelphia: American Philosophical Society.

Eckert, Carter J. 1996. *Offspring of Empire: The Koch'ang Kims and the Colonial Origins of Korean Capitalism, 1876–1945*. Seattle: University of Washington Press.

Ederer, R. J. 1964. *The Evolution of Money*. Washington, DC: Public Affairs Press.

Edkins, J. D. D. 1905. *Banking and Prices in China*. Shanghai: Presbyterian Press.

Edmondson, J. C. 1987. *Two Industries in Roman Lusitania: Mining and Garum Production*. Oxford, UK: B. A. R.

Ehrenkreutz, Andrew S. 1970. "Monetary Aspects of Medieval Near Eastern Economic History." In M.A. Cook, ed., *Studies in the Economic History of the Middle East*, 37–50. Oxford, UK: Oxford University Press.

Eichengreen, Barry J. 2008. *Globalizing Capital: A History of the International Monetary System*. Princeton, NJ: Princeton University Press.

Eichengreen, Barry J., and Marc Flandreau. 1997. "Editor's Introduction." In idem., eds., *The Gold Standard in Theory and History*, pp. 1–21. London: Routledge.

———. 2008. "The Rise and Fall of the Dollar, or When Did the Dollar Replace Sterling as the Leading International Currency?" *NBER Working Paper 14154.*

Einaudi, Luigi. 1953. "The Theory of Imaginary Money from Charlemagne to the French Revolution." In Frederic C. Lane and Jelle C. Riemersma, eds., *Enterprise and Secular Change: Readings in Economic History*, 229–261. London: Allen and Unwin.

Einzig, Paul. 1966. *Primitive Money in Its Ethnological, Historical and Economic Aspects.* New York: Pergamon Press.

Eldem, Edhem. *1998. A 135-Year-Old Treasure: Glimpses from the Past in the Ottoman Bank Archives.* Istanbul: Osmanli Bankasi.

El-Hibri, Tayeb. 1993. "Coinage Reform Under the 'Abbasid Caliph al-Ma'mun." *Journal of the Economic and Social History of the Orient* 36: 58–83.

Elman, Benjamin A. 2000. *A Cultural History of Civil Examinations in Late Imperial China.* Berkeley, CA: University of California Press.

Elvin, Mark. 1973. *The Pattern of the Chinese Past.* London: Eyre Methuen.

———. 1999. "*How Did the Cracks Open? The Origins of the Subversion of China's Late-Traditional Culture by the West.*" Thesis Eleven 57: 1–16.

———. 2006. *The Retreat of the Elephants: An Environmental History of China.* New Haven, CT: Yale University Press.

———. 2013. "Cash and commerce in the poems of Qing China," in Nanny Kim and Keiko Nagase-Reimer, eds., *Mining, Monies, and Culture in Early Modern Societies; East Asian and Global Perspectives*, pp. 209–260, vol. 4 of the series *Monies, Markets, and Finance in East Asia, 1600–1900*, Hans Ulrich Vogel, ed. Leiden: Brill.

———. 2009. "Why Intensify? The Outline of a Theory of the Institutional Causes Driving Long-Term Changes in Chinese Farming and the Consequent Modifications to the Environment." In Sverker Sörlin and Paul Warde, eds., *Nature's End: History and the Environment*, 273–303. Basingstoke, UK: Palgrave Macmillan.

———. Forthcoming. "Preface." In Ulrich Theobald, ed., *Small Currencies Matter.* Edited Volume in Preparation.

Engdahl, Torbjörnand Anders Ögren. 2008. "Multiple Paper Monies in Sweden 1789–1903: Substitution or Complementarity?" *Financial History Review* 15.1: 73–91.

Enoki, K., G. A. Koshelenko, and Z. Haidary. 1994. "The Yüeh-chih and Their Migrations." In J. Harmatta, ed., *History of Civilizations of Central Asia*, vol. 2, *The Development of Sedentary and Nomadic Civilizations: 700 B.C. to A.D. 250*, 171–189. Paris: UNESCO.

Erya zhushu 爾雅注疏. [rep. 1965]. Annotated by Guo Pu (CE 276–324) 郭璞 and Xing Bing 邢昺 (CE 932–1010). Taipei: Taiwan Zhonghua shuju.

"The Failure of the Oriental Bank". 1844. *Bankers' Magazine* 44: 613–616.

Fang Guoyu 方國瑜. 2001. *Yunnan shi liao cong kan* 雲南史料叢刊. Kunming: Yunnan daxue chubvanshe.

Farris, William W. 2009. *Japan to 1600: A Social and Economic History*. Honolulu: University of Hawai'I Press.

Farrokh, Kaveh. 2007. *Shadows in the Desert: Ancient Persia at War*. New York: Osprey.

Faulkner, Chris. 2004. "Holey Dollars and Other Bitts and Pieces of Prince Edward Island." In Richard G. Doty and John M. Kleeberg, eds., *Money of the Caribbean*, 191–215. New York: American Numismatic Society.

Faure, David. 2006. *China and Capitalism: A History of Business Enterprise in Modern China*. Hong Kong: Hong Kong University Press.

Ferguson, Niall. 2001. *The Cash Nexus: Money and Power in the Modern World, 1700–2000*. New York: Basic Books.

———. 2008. *The Ascent of Money: A Financial History of the World*. New York: Penguin.

Feuerwerker, Albert. 1958. *China's Early Industrialization: Sheng Hsuan-huai (1844–1916) and the Mandarin Enterprise*. Cambridge, MA: Harvard University Press.

Fewsmith, Joseph. 1985. *Party, State, and Local Elites in Republican China: Merchant Organizations and Politics in Shanghai, 1890–1930*. Honolulu: University of Hawai'i Press.

Field, Frederick V. 1934. *Economic Handbook of the Pacific Area*. New York: Doubleday.

Figueira, Thomas. 1998. *The Power of Money: Coinage and Politics in the Athenian Empire*. Philadelphia: University of Pennsylvania Press.

Finley, M. I. 1973. *The Ancient Economy*. Berkeley: University of California Press.

Fisher, Irving. 1929. *The Purchasing Power of Money*. New York: Macmillan.

Flandreau, Marc, and Mathilde Maurel. 2001. "Monetary Union, Trade Integration, and Business Cycles in 19th Century Europe: Just Do It." *CEPR Discussion Paper* 3087. Paris: Centre Maison des Sciences Economiques.

Flandreau, Marc, and Frédéric Zumer. 2004. *The Making of Global Finance 1880–1913*. Paris: OECD, Development Centre Studies.

Flynn, Dennis Owen, and Arturo Giráldez. 1994. "China and the Manila Galleons." In A. J. H. Latham and H. Kawakatsu, eds., *Japanese Industrialization and the Asian Economy*, 71–90. London: Routledge.

———. 1995a. "Born with a Silver Spoon: The Origin of World Trade in 1571." *Journal of World History* 6.2: 201–221.

———. 1995b. "Arbitrage, China, and World Trade in the Early Modern Period." *Journal of the Economic and Social History of the Orient* 38. 4: 429–448.

———. 2002. "Cycles of Silver: Global Economic Unity through the Mid-Eighteenth Century." *Journal of World History* 13.2: 391–427.

———. 2004. "Path Dependence, Time Lags and the Birth of Globalisation: A Critique of O'Rourke and Williamson." *European Review of Economic History* 8: 81–108.

———. 2010. *China and the Birth of Globalization in the 16th Century.* Farnham, UK: Ashgate.

Forbes, R. J. 1950. *Metallurgy in Antiquity.* Leiden: Brill.

The Foreign Trade of China 1925: Reports and Abstracts of Statistics. 1926. Comp. by the Chinese Maritime Customs. Shanghai: Inspector General of Customs.

Fortune, Robert. 1847. *Three Years' Wanderings in the Northern Provinces of China.* London: J. Murray.

Frank, Andre Gunder. 1998. *ReOrient: Global Economy in the Asian Age.* Berkeley: University of Californai Press.

Franke, Herbert. 1949. *Geld und Wirtschaft unter der Mongolen-Herrschaft.* Leipzig: Harrassowitz.

———. 1992. "The Chin Dynasty." In idem. and Denis Twitchett. eds., *The Cambridge History of China*, vol. 6, *Alien Regimes and Border States*, 907–1368, 215–320. Cambridge UK: Cambridge University Press.

Freeman-Grenville, G. S. P. 1960. "East African Coin Finds and Their Historical Significance." *The Journal of African History* 1.1: 31–43.

French, Doug. 2006. "The Dutch Monetary Environment during Tulipmania." *The Quarterly Journal of Australian Economics* 9.1: 3–14.

Friedman, M., and A. Schwartz. 1986. "Has Government Any Role in Money?" *Journal of Monetary Economics* 17: 37–62.

Friedman, Milton, and A. Schwartz. 1963. *A Monetary History of the United States, 1867–1960.* Princeton, NJ: Princeton University Press.

Friedman, Thomas L. 2003. *The World Is Flat: A Brief History of the 21st Century.* New York: Farrar, Straus and Giroux.

Frost, Peter. 1970. *The Bakumatsu Currency Crisis.* Cambridge, MA: Harvard University Press.

Fung, Edmund S. K. 1991. *The Diplomacy of Imperial Retreat: Britain's South China Policy, 1924–1931.* Hong Kong: Oxford University Press.

Galbraith, John Kenneth. 1975. *Money: Whence It Came, Where It Went.* Boston: Houghton Mifflin.

Galor, Oded, Omer Moav, and Dietrich Vollrath. 2009. "Inequality in Landownership, the Emergence of Human-Capital Promoting Institutions, and the Great Divergence." *Review of Economic Studies* 76.1: 143–179.

Gandal, Neil, and Nathan Sussman. 1997. "Asymmetric Information and Commodity Money: Tickling the Tolerance in Medieval France." *Journal of Money, Credit and Banking* 29.4: 440–457.

Gao Congming 高聰明. 1999. *Songdai huobi yu huobi liutong yanjiu* 宋代貨幣與貨幣流通研究. Baoding Shi: Hebei daxue chubanshe.

Gardner, Percy. [1918, rep. 1974]. *A History of Ancient Coinage, 700–300 BC.* Chicago: Ares.

Gavin, Francis J. 2003. *Gold, Dollars, and Power: The Politics of International Monetary Relations, 1958–1971.* Chapel Hill: University of North Carolina Press.

Geguo huobi huijia tongji shouce 各國貨幣匯價統計手冊. 1979. Comp. by the Bank of China. Beijing: Zhongguo caijing jingji chubanshe.

Gerth, Karl. 2003. *China Made: Consumer Culture and the Creation of the Nation*. Cambridge, MA: Harvard University Press.

Ghosh, A. 1989. *Encyclopaedia of Indian Archaeology*. New Delhi: Brill.

Gilbert, Emily, and Eric Helleiner. 1999. "Introduction." In idem., eds., *Nation-States and Money: The Past, Present and Future of National Currencies*, 1–21. London: Routledge.

Giráldez, Arturo. 2008. "China and Counterfeiting in 1650 Potosi." In Thomas Hirzel and Nanny Kim, eds., *Metals, Monies, and Markets in Early Modern Societies: East Asian and Global Perspectives*, 15–43. London: Global.

Glasner, David. 1989. *Free Banking and Monetary Reform*. New York: Cambridge University Press.

———. 1998. "An Evolution Theory of the State Monopoly over Money." In Kevin Dowd and Richard H. Timberlake, eds., *Money and the Nation-State*. Oakland, CA.: Independent Institute.

Glassman, Debra, and Angela Redish. 1988. "Currency Depreciation in Early Modern England and France." *Explorations in Economic History* 75–97.

Golas, Peter A. 1999. *Mining*. In Joseph Needham, ed., *Science and Civilisation in China* vol. 5, *Chemistry and Chemical Technology*, Part 13. Cambridge, UK: Cambridge University Press.

Goldsmith, R. W. 1983. *The Financial Development of India, 1860–1977*. New Haven: Yale University Press.

Goldstone, Jack A. 1993. *Revolution and Rebellion in the Early Modern World*. Berkeley: University of California Press.

Gongbuju dongshihui huiyilu 公部局董事會會議錄 ['The Minutes of the Shanghai Municipal Council']. 2001. Comp. by the Shanghai Municipal Archive. Shanghai: Shanghai guji chubanshe.

Gonjō Yasuo. *1993. Banque coloniale ou banque d'affaires: la Banque de l'Indochine sous la IIIe République*. Paris: Comité pour l'histoire économique et financière de la France.

Good, Irene. 1995. "On the Question of Silk in Pre-Han Eurasia." *Antiquity* 69: 959–968.

Goodman, Bryna. 1995. *Native Place, City, and Nation: Regional Networks and Identities in Shanghai, 1853–1937*. Berkeley: University of California Press.

Gorski, Philip S. 2003. *The Disciplinary Revolution: Calvinism and the Rise of the State in Early Modern Europe*. Chicago: University of Chicago Press.

Goudsmit, Simon. 2004. *The Limits of Money: Three Perceptions of Our Most Comprehensive Value System*. Delft: Eburon.

Gould, J. D. 1970. *The Great Debasement: Currency and the Economy in Mid-Tudor England*. Oxford, UK: Clarendon Press.

Grayson, J. H. 1985. *Early Buddhism and Christianity in Korea: A Study in the Emplantation of Religion*. Leiden: Brill.

Greatrex, Roger. 2013. "Administrative Regulations Concerning Counterfeiting and Their Implementation in Eighteenth-Century China." In Nanny Kim and Keiko Nagase-Reimer, eds., *Mining, Monies, and Culture in Early Modern Societies; East Asian and Global Perspectives*, pp. 185–208, vol. 4 of the series *Monies, Markets, and Finance in East Asia, 1600–1900,* Hans Ulrich Vogel, ed. Leiden: Brill.

Green, E. H. H. 1988. "Rentiers Versus Producers? The Political Economy of the Bimetallic Controversy c. 1880–1898." *The English Historical Review* 103.408: 588–612.

Green, Edwin, and Sara Kinsey. 1999. *The Paradise Bank: The Mercantile Bank of India, 1893–1984.* Aldershot, UK: Ashgate.

Greenberg, Michael. 1951. *British Trade and the Opening of China, 1800–42.* Cambridge, UK: Cambridge University Press.

Greif, Avner. 2006. *Institutions and the Path to the Modern Economy: Lessons from Medieval Trade.* New York: Cambridge University Press.

Greste, Peter. 2010. "Could a Rusty Coin Re-Write Chinese-African History?" October 18, 2010. BBC News Africa [online]; retrieved on September 15, 2012, from www.bbc.co.uk/news/world-africa-11531398.

Grierson, Philip. 1960. "The Monetary Reforms of 'Abd al-Malik: Their Metrological Basis and Their Financial Repercussions." *Journal of the Economic and Social History of the Orient* 3.3: 241–264.

———. 1999. *Byzantine Coinage.* Washington DC: Dumbarton Oaks Research Library and Colelction.

Griffiths, Percival. 1974. *A Licence to Trade: The History of English Chartered Companies.* London: Ernest Benn.

Grossman, Richard S. 2001. "Charters, Corporations and Codes: Entry Restrictions in Modern Banking Law." *Financial History Review* 8.2: 107–121.

Guanzi 管子. [rep. 1989]. Shanghai: Shanghai guji chubanshe.

Guo Yuqing 郭予慶. 2007. *Jindai Riben yinhang zai Hua jinrong huodong: Hengbin zhengjin yinhang 1894–1919* 近代日本銀行在華金融活動: 橫濱正金銀行 1894–1919. Beijing: Renmin chubanshe.

Guoyu 國語. [rep. 2008]. Changchun: Shidai wenyi chubanshe.

Gupta, P. L., and T. R. Hardaker. 1985. *Indian Silver Punchmarked Coins: Magadha-Maurya Karshapana Series.* New Delhi: Indian Institute of Research in Numismatic Studies.

Hall, Kenneth R. 1999. "Coinage, Trade and Economy in Early South India and its Southeast Asian Neighbours." *Indian Economic Social History Review* 36: 431–459.

Hall, Ray Ovid. 1921. *Chinese National Banks: From Their Founding to the Moratorium.* Berlin: s.n.

Hamashita Takeshi 濱下武志. 1980. *Chūgoku tsūshō ginkō no setsuritsu to Honkon Shanhai ginkō* 中国通商銀行の設立と香港上海銀行. *Hitotsubashi ronsō*: 84.4: 448–464.

———. 1989. *Chūgoku kindai keizaishi kenkyū* 中国近代経済史研究. Tokyo: Tokyo University.

Hamilton, Earl J. 1943. "Money and Economic Recovery in Spain under the First Bourbon, 1701–1746." *Journal of Modern History* 15.3: 192–206.

Hanashiro, Roy S. 1999. *Thomas William Kinder and the Japanese Imperial Mint, 1868–1875.* Leiden: Brill.

Hanna, Hugh H., Charles A. Conant, and Jeremiah W. Jenks. 1904. *Report on the Introduction of the Gold-Exchange Standardinto China, the Philippine Islands, Panama, and Other Silver-Using Countries.* Washington, DC: Government Printing Office.

Hanshu 漢書. [rep. 1956]. 40 vols. Taipei: Er shi wu shi bian kanguan.

Hao Yen-p'ing. 1986. *The Commercial Revolution in Nineteenth-Century China.* Berkeley: University of California Press.

———. 1970. *The Comprador in Nineteenth Century China: A Bridge between East and West.* Cambridge, MA: Harvard University Press.

Hargreaves, Eric Lyde. 1930. *The National Debt.* London: E. Arnold.

Harl, K. W. 1996. *Coinage in the Roman Economy, 300 BC to AD 700.* Baltimore: Johns Hopkins University Press.

Harmatta, J. 1994. "Languages and Literature in the Kushan Empire." In idem., ed., *History of Civilizations of Central Asia*, vol. 2, *The Development of Sedentary and Nomadic Civilizations: 700 B.C. to A.D. 250*, 417–440. Paris: UNESCO.

Hartwell, Robert. 1967. "A Cycle of Economic Change in Imperial China: Coal and Iron in Northeast China, 750–1350." *Journal of the Economic and Social History of the Orient* 10.1: 102–159.

Hasan, Aziza. 1969. "The Silver Currency Output of the Mughal Empire and Prices in India during the 16th and 17th Centuries." *Indian Economic and Social History Review* 6.85: 85–116.

He Wenkai. 2010. Book Review of Horesh (2009a). *Economic History Review* 63.2: 558–559.

He Ziquan 何兹全. 1949. "Dong Jin nanchao de qianbi shiyong yu qianbi wen ti" "東晉南朝的錢幣使用與錢幣問題." *Zhongyang yanjiuyuan lishi yuyan yanjiusuo jikan* 14: 21–56.

Headrick, Daniel R. 2010. *Power over Peoples: Technology, Environments and Western Imperialism, 1400 to the Present.* Princeton, NJ: Princeton University Press.

Heal, Ambrose. [1935, rep. 1972]. *The London Goldsmiths, 1200–1800: A Record of the Names and Addresses of the Craftsmen, Their Shop Signs and Trade-Cards.* London: Cambridge University Press.

Healy, John F. 1978. *Mining and Metallurgy in the Greek and Roman World.* London: Thames and Hudson.

Heckscher, Eli F. 1954. *An Economic History of Sweden.* Trans. from the Swedish by G. Ohlin. Cambridge, MA: Harvard University Press.

Hefeker, Carsten, and Andreas Nabor. 2005. "China's Role in East-Asian Monetary Integration." *International Journal of Finance and Economics* 10: 157–166.

Heilperin, Michael A. 1960. *Studies in Economic Nationalism.* Geneva: Droz.

Heimann, James. 1980. "Small Change and Ballast: Cowry Trade and Usage as an Example of Indian Ocean Economic History." *South Asia* 3.1: 48–67.

Helleiner, Eric. 1999. "Denationalising Money? Economic Liberalism and the 'National Question' in Currency Affairs." In Emily Gilbert and Eric Helleiner, eds., *Nation-States and Money: The Past, Present and Future of National Currencies*, 139–158. London: Routledge.

———. 2003. *The Making of National Money: Territorial Currencies in Historical Perspective*. Ithaca, NY: Cornell University Press.

———. 2005a. "Why Would Nationalists Not Want a National Currency: The Case of Quebec." In Eric Helleiner and Andreas Pickel, eds., *Economic Nationalism in a Globalizing World*, 164–182. Ithaca, NY: Cornell University Press.

———. 2005b. "Conclusion: The Meaning and Contemporary Significance of Economic Nationalism." In Eric Helleiner and Andreas Pickel, eds., *Economic Nationalism in a Globalizaing World*, 220–234. Ithaca, NY: Cornell University Press.

Hendy, Michael F. 2008. *Studies in the Byzantine Monetary Economy C. 300–1450*. Cambridge, UK: Cambridge University Press.

Heng, Derek. 2006. "Export Commodity and Regional Currency: The Role of Chinese Copper Coins in the Malacca Straits Region, Tenth to Fourteenth Centuries." *Journal of Southeast Asian Studies* 37.2: 179–203.

Herbert, Penelope A. 1976. "A Debate in T'ang China on the State Monopoly on Casting Coin." *T'oung Pao* 62.4/5: 253–292.

Hickson, C. R., and J. D. Turner. 2004. "Free Banking and the Stability of Early Joint-Stock Banking." *Cambridge Journal of Economics* 28: 903–919.

Higuchi, Takayasu. 1992. "Silk Road: A Culture of Imported Goods." *Senri Ethnological Studies* 32: 33–36.

Hill, George F. 1922. "Ancient Methods of Coining." *Numismatic Chronicle* 2: 1–42.

Hill, J. E. 2009. *Through the Jade Gate to Rome: A Study of the Silk Routes during the Later Han Dynasty 1st to 2nd Centuries CE*. Charleston, SC: Book Surge.

Hira, Anil, and James W. Dean. 2004. "Distributional Effects of Dollarisation: The Latin American Case." *Third World Quarterly* 25.3: 461–482.

Hirokichi Taya. 1980. "The Modernization of the Japanese Currency System." *Acta Asiatica* 39: 78–94.

The History of Korean Money. 1969. Compiled by the central Bank of Korea.

Ho Hon-wai 何漢威. 1993. "Cong yinqian huang dao tongyuan fanlan—Qingmo xin huobi de faxing ji qi yinxiang" 從銀錢荒到銅元汎濫——清末新貨幣的發行及其影響. *Zhongyang yanjiuyuan lishi yuyan yanjiusuo jikan 62.3: 389–494*.

Ho, Samuel P. S. 1978. *Economic Development of Taiwan 1860–1970*. New Haven, CT: Yale University Press.

———. 1984. "Colonialism and Development: Korea, Taiwan, and Kwantung." In Ramon H. Myers and Mark R. Peattie, eds., *The Japanese Colonial Empire, 1895–1945*, 347–397. Princeton, NJ: Princeton University Press.

Hobson, John M. 2004. *The Eastern Origins of Western Civilization*. New York: Cambridge University Press.

Hogendorn, Jan, and Marion Johnson. 1986. *The Shell Money of the Slave Trade*. New York: Cambridge University Press.

Homer, Sidney, and Richard Sylla. 2005. *A History of Interest Rates.* Hoboken, NJ: Wiley.

Honda, Hiroyuki. 2007. "Copper Coinage, Ruling Power and Local Society in Medieval Japan." *International Journal of Asian Studies* 4.2: 225–240.

Hong Jiaguan 洪葭管. 1989. *Jindai Shanghai jinrong shichang* 近代上海金融市場. Shanghai: Shanghai renmin chubanshe.

Horesh, Niv. 2004. "The Transition from Coinage to Paper Money in China: Hallmarks of Statehood in Global Perspective, 8th Century BC to 1935 AD." *Journal of the Institute of Asian Studies* 21.2: 1–26.

———. 2008. "Silk, Tea, and Treasure: Maritime Trade in Eighteenth-Century Literature." *Sungkyun Journal of East Asian Studies.* 8.2: 131–142.

———. 2009a. *Shanghai's Bund and Beyond: British Banks, Banknote Issuance and Monetary Policy in China, 1842–1937.* New Haven, CT: Yale University Press.

———. 2009b. "What Time Is the 'Great Divergence'? And Why Economic Historians Think It Matters." *China Review International* 16.1: 18–32.

———. 2009c. "Whitehall vs Old China Hands: The 1935–36 Leith-Ross Mission Revisited." *Asian Studies Review* 33.2: 211–227.

Hou Ching-Lang. 1975. *Monnaies D'offrande et la notion de tresorerie dans la religion Chinoise.* Paris: Institut de Hautes Etudes Chinoises.

Hou Hanshu 後漢書. [rep. 1999]. Beijing: Zhonghua shuju.

Hou Houji 侯厚吉and Wu Qijing 吳其敬. 1982. *Zhongguo jindai jingji sixiang shigao* 中國近代經濟思想史稿. Harbin: Heilongjiang renmin chubanshe.

Howe, A. C. 1990. "Bimetallism, c. 1880–1898: A Controversy Reopened?" *The English Historical Review* 105.415: 377–391.

Howe, Christopher. 2001. "Taiwan in the 20th Century: Model or Victim? Development Problems in a Small Asian Economy." *China Quarterly* 165: 37–60.

Howgego, Christopher J. 1995. *Ancient History from Coins.* London: Routledge.

Hozumi Fumio 穗積文雄. 1944. *Shina kahei ko* 支那貨幣考. Kyoto: Kyōto Inshokan.

Hsiao Ch'i-Ch'ing. 1994. "Mid-Yüan Politics." In Herbert Franke and Denis Twitchett, eds., *The Cambridge History of China,* vol. 6, *Alien Regimes and Border States, 907–1368,* 490–560. Cambridge, UK: Cambridge University Press.

Hsiao Liang-lin. 1974. *China's Foreign Trade Statistics, 1864–1949.* Cambridge, MA: Harvard University Press.

Hsu Yih-tzong 許義宗. 1997. *Qing dai zhibi tushuo* 清代紙幣圖説. Taipei: Hsu Yih-tzong.

———. 1998. *Zhongguo Huashang zhibi tushuo* 中國華商之筆圖説. Taipei: Hsu Yih-tzong.

Hu Jichuang 胡寄窗. 1988. *A Concise History of Chinese Economic Thought.* Beijing: Foreign Languages Press.

———. 1998. *Zhongguo jingji sixiang shi* 中國經濟思想史. Shanghai: Shanghai caijing daxue chubanshe.

Hua Jueming 華覺明. 1999. *Zhongguo gudai jinshu jishu: tong he tie zaojiu de wenming* 中國古代金屬技術：銅和鐵造就的文明. Zhengzhou: Daxiang chubanshe.

———. 2000. "On the Origins of Metallurgy in China." In Katheryn M. Linduff, Han Rubin, and Sun Shuyun, eds., *The Beginnings of Metallurgy in China*, 51–62. Lewiston, NY: Lampeter.

———. 2008. "Metallurgy in China." In Helaine Selin, ed., *Encyclopaedia of the History of Science, Technology, and Medicine in Non-Western Cultures, 1624–1626.* Berlin: Springer.

Huang Hengjun 黃亨俊. 2001. *Qingdai guanyin qianhao faxing shi* 清代官銀錢號發行史. Taipei: Guoli lishi bowuguan.

Huang Jianhui 黃鑒暉. 1992. *Shanxi piaohao shi* 山西票號史. Taiyuan: Shanxi jingji chubanshe.

———. 1994. *Zhongguo yinhang yeshi* 中國銀行業史. Taiyuan: Shanxi jingji chubanshe.

Huang, Ray. 1974. *Taxation and Government Finance in 16th Century Ming China*. New York: Cambridge University Press.

———. 1990. *China: A Macro History*. New York: M. E. Sharpe.

Huang Yihai and Wang Yunting. 2004. *Chinese Specimens Printed by the American Bank Note Company*, 3 vols. Hong Kong: Zhongguo tong chubanshe.

Huangchao jingshi wen tongbian 皇朝經世文統編. [rep. 1980]. 10 vols. Taipei: Wenhai chubanshe.

Huey, Herbert. 1985. "European Conceptions of the Chinese Economy, 1650–1750: French Jesuits' Views on China." *Papers on Far Eastern History* 31: 95–116.

"Huhehaoteshi fujin chutu de waiguo jinyin bi" 呼和浩特市附近出土的外國金銀幣. 1975. *Kaogu* 3: 182–186.

Hundred-Year Statistics of the Japanese Economy. 1966. Tokyo: Nihon Ginko tokeikyoku.

Hung Yin-hang. 1970. "A Great Victory for Mao Tse-Tung'S Thought on the Financial and Monetary Front—China's People's Currency Has Become an Exceptionally Stable Currency of the World." *Chinese Economy* 3.3: 179–190.

Husain, M. K. 1967. "The Silver Larin." *Journal of the Numismatic Society of India* 29.2: 54–72.

Ibn Battuta. [rep. 2009]. *The Travels of Ibn Battuta*. Trans. by Samuel Lee. New York: Cosimo.

Inalcik, Halil. 1970. "The Ottoman Economic Mind and Aspects of the Ottoman Economy." In M. A. Cook, ed., *Studies in the Economic History of the Middle East*, 207–218. Oxford, UK: Oxford University Press.

Ingram, James Carlton. 1971. *Economic Change in Thailand since 1850*. Stanford, CA: Stanford University Press.

Irigoin, Alejandra. 2009. "The End of a Silver Era: The Consequences of the Breakdown of the Spanish Peso Standard in China and the United States, 1780s–1850s." *Journal of World History* 20.2: 226–229.

Ishii Kanji 石井寛治. 2002. "British-Japanese Rivalry in Trading and Banking." In Janet E. Hunter and Sugiyama Shinya, eds., *The History of Anglo-Japanese Relations, 1600–2000*, vol. 4, 110–132. Basingstoke, UK: Macmillan.

———. 2007. *Keizai hatten to ryōgaeshō kin'yū* 経済発展と両替商金融. Tokyo: Yuhikaku.

Ishikawa Ryota 石川亮太. 2002. "1910 Nen Manshū ni okeru Chōsen ginkō no ryūtsū to chiiki keizai" 1910 年代満州における朝鮮銀行券の流通と地域経済. *Shakai keizai shigagu* 68.2: 127–144.

Ito Takatoshi. 2010. "China as Number One: How about the Renminbi?" *Asian Economic Policy Review* 5.2: 249–76.

Jackson, A. V. W. 1922. "The Persian Dominions in Northwestern India Down to the Time of Alexander's Invasion." In E. Rapson, ed., *Cambridge History of India*, 319–344. Cambridge, UK: Cambridge University Press.

Jacoud, Gilles. 2001. "Mollien's Contribution to the Analysis of the Bank of Issue1." *Financial History Review* 8.2: 123–141.

Jahn, K. 2009. "Čāo." In P. Bearman, Th. Bianquis, C. E. Bosworth, E. van Donzel, and W. P. Heinrichs Brill, eds., *Encyclopaedia of Islam*, second edition. Retrieved on September 15, 2012, from Brill Online at www.brillonline.nl.virtual.anu.edu.au/subscriber/entry?entry=islam_SIM-1591.

Jain, Lakshmi Chandra. 1929. *Indigenous Banking in India*. London: Macmillan.

Jansen, Marius B. 2002. *The Making of Modern Japan*. Cambridge, MA: Harvard University Press.

Jao Y. C. and Frank H. H. King. 1990. *Money in Hong Kong: Historical Perspective and Contemporary Analysis*. Hong Kong: The University of Hong Kong, Centre of Asian Studies.

Jernigan, T. R. 1904. *China's Business Methods and Policy*. Shanghai: Kelly & Walsh.

Ji Zhaojin. 2002. *A History of Modern Shanghai Banking*. Armonk, NY: M. E. Sharpe.

Jia Daquan 賈大泉. 1994a. "Xue Tian shi woguo he shijieshang zuizao de jiechu de zhibi zhuanjia" 薛田是我國和世界上最早的杰出的紙幣專家. *Xinan jinrong* 7: 51–53.

———. 1994b. "Zhang Yong, Xue Tian yu jiaozi—guanyu jiaozi de chansheng shijian, zhengdun he guan jiaoziwu de jianli" 張詠、薛田与交子—關于交子的產生時間、整頓和官交子務的建立. *Sichuan wenwu* 5: 58–61.

*Jia Yi Xinshu*賈誼新書. [rep. 2008]. Changchun: Shidai wenyi chubanshe.

Jiang Hongye姜宏業. 1991. *Zhongguo difang yinhang shi* 中國地方銀行. Changsha: Hunan chubanshe.

Johnson, Marion. 1970. "The Cowrie Currencies of West Africa." *Journal of African History* 11.3: 331–353.

Jones, F. C. 1949. *Manchuria since 1931*. New York: Oxford University Press.

Jones, Geoffrey. 1990. "Competitive Advantages in British Multinational Banking Since 1890." In idem., ed., *Banks as Multinationals*, 30–61. London: Routledge.

———. 1993. *British Multinational Banking, 1830–1990*. Oxford, UK: Clarendon Press.

Joslin, David Maelgwyn. 1963. *A Century of Banking in Latin America*. London: Oxford University Press.

Kahan, Arcadius. 1989. *Russian Economic History: The Nineteenth Century*. Chicago: University of Chicago Press.

Kakinuma Yōhei 柿沼陽平. 2011. *Chūgoku kodai kahei keizai shi kenkyū* 中国古代貨幣経済史研究. Tokyo: Kyūko shoin.

Kann, Eduard, 1927. *The Currencies of China*. Shanghai: Kelly & Walsh.

Kaplanis, Costas. 2003. "The Debasement of the 'Dollar of the Middle Ages.'" *The Journal of Economic History* 63.3: 768–801.

Katō Shigeru 加藤繁. 1963. *Zhongguo jingji shi kaozheng* 中國經濟史考證. 2 vols. Trans. from Japanese into Chinese by Wu Jie 吳傑. Beijing: Xinhua shudian.

———. 1944 [rep. 1970]. *Tang Song shidai jinyin zhi yanjiu*. 唐宋時代金銀之研究. 2 vols. Hong Kong: Longman shudian.

Katō Toshihiko 加藤俊彦. 1988. "Kin'yū kyōkō to Yokohama shōkin ginkō" 金融恐慌と横浜正金銀行. In Yamaguchi Kazuo 山口和雄 and Katō Toshiniko 加藤俊彦, eds., *Ryō taisenkan no Yokohama shōkin ginkō* 両大戦間の横浜正金銀行, 326–354. Tokyo: Nippon kei'ei.

Katsari, Constantina. 2011. *The Roman Monetary System: The Eastern Provinces from the First to the Third Century AD*. Cambridge, UK: Cambridge University Press.

Kawamura Tomotaka 川村朋貴. 2005. "Higashi Indo kaisha kaisan izen no isutan banku mondai, 1847–1857 nen" 東インド会社解散以前のイースタンバンク問題、１８４７-１８５７年. *Shakai keizai shigaku* 71.2: 25–47.

Kazui Tashihiro. 1991. "Exports of Gold and Silver during the Early Tokugawa Era, 1600–1750." In Eddy H. G. Van Cauwenberghe, ed., *Money, Coins and Commerce: Essays in the Monetary History of Asia and Europe*, 75–93. Leuven: Leuven University Press.

Kehoe, Dennis P. 2007. "The Early Roman Empire: Production." In Walter Scheidel, Ian Morris, and Richard Saller, eds. *Cambridge Economic History of the Greco-Roman World*, 543–569. Cambridge, UK: Cambridge University Press.

Kennedy, J. 1898. "The Early Commerce of Babylon with India 700–300 BC." *Journal of the Royal Asiatic Society of Great Britain* (New Series) 30.2: 241–288.

Keynes, John Maynard. 1926. *The End of Laissez-Faire*. London: Hogarth Press.

Khan, Muhammad Akram. 2003. *Islamic Economics and Finance: A Glossary*. London: Routledge.

Kikuchi Takaharu 菊池貴晴. 1966. *Chūgoku minzoku undō no kihon kōzō* 中国民族運動の基本構造. Tokyo: Daian.

Kim Chun-kil. 2005. *The History of Korea*. Westport, CT: Greenwood.

Kim Hyun Jin. 2009. *Ethnicity and Foreigners in Ancient Greece and China*. London: Duckworth.

Kimura Mitsuhiku. 1993. "Standards of Living in Colonial Korea: Did the Masses Become Worse Off or Better Off under Japanese Rule?" *Journal of Economic History* 53.3: 629–652.

Kindleberger, Charles P. 1984. *A Financial History of Western Europe.* London: Allen & Unwin.

———. 1986. *The World in Depression, 1929–1939.* Berkeley: University of California Press.

———. 1989. *Spenders and Hoarders: The World Distribution of Spanish American Silver, 1550–1750.* Singapore: ASEAN.

———. 2000. *Comparative Political Economy: A Retrospective.* Cambridge, MA: MIT Press.

King, Frank H. H. 1965. *Money and Monetary Policy in China, 1845–1895.* Cambridge, MA: Harvard University Press.

———. 1987. *The History of the Hongkong and Shanghai Banking Corporation.* 4 vols. New York: Cambridge University Press.

King, W. T. C. 1936. *History of the London Discount Market.* London: Routledge.

Kirshner, Jonathan. 1995. *Currency and Coercion: The Political Economy of International Monetary Power.* Princeton, NJ: Princeton University Press.

Kishimoto Mio 岸本美緒. 1997. *Shindai chūgoku no bukka to keizai hendō* 清代中国の物価と経済変. Tokyo: Kenbun.

Klaproth, J. 1823. *Origin of Paper Money.* London: Treuttel and Wurtz.

Kobata Atsushi 小葉田淳. [1930, rep. 1969]. *Nihon kahei ryutsushi* 日本貨幣流通史. Tokyo: Toko shoin.

———. 1965. "The Production and Uses of Gold and Silver in Sixteenth and Seventeenth-century Japan." *Economic History Review* 18.2: 245–266.

———. 1971. "Coinage from the Kamakura Period through the Edo Period." *Acta Asiatica* 21: 98–108.

Kolsky, Maurice, and Maurice Muszynski. 1996. *Les Billets de la Banque de L'Indochine.* Monaco: V. Gadoury.

Kong Xiangxian 孔祥賢. 1991. *Daqing yinhang hangshi* 大清銀行行史. Nanjing: Nanjing daxue chubanshe.

Kosambi, D. D. 1981. *Indian Numismatics.* New Delhi: Orient Longman.

Kotani, Ken. 2009. *Japanese Intelligence in World War II.* New York: Osprey.

Kotenev, Anatol M. 1927. *Shanghai: Its Municipality and the Chinese.* Shanghai: North-China Daily News and Herald.

Kraay, Colin M. 1976. *Archaic and Classical Greek Coins.* London: Methuen.

Krishnamurthy, R. 2000. *Non-Roman Ancient Foreign Coins from Karur India.* Chennai: Garnet.

Kroll, John H. 2001. "Observations on Monetary Instruments in Pre-Coinage Greece." In Miriam S. Balmuth, ed., *Hacksilber to Coinage: New Insights into the Monetary History of the Near East and Greece,* 77–92. New York: American Numismatic Society.

Ku Hung-ting. 1983. "Urban Mass Movement in Action: The Shakee Incident and the Canton-Hongkong Strike." In Academia Sinica, comp., *Proceedings* of the Conference on the Early History of the Republic of China, 1912–1927, 849–872. Taipei: Academia Sinica.

Kuppuram, K. and K. Kumudamani. 1990. *History of Science and Technology in India.* vol. 8, *Coins, Metallurgy.* Delhi: Sundeep Prakashan.

Kuroda, Akinobu 黒田明伸. 1987. "Kenryō no senki" 乾隆の銭貴. *Tōyōshi kenkyū* 45.4: 692–723.

———. 2000. "Another Monetary Economy: The Case of Traditional China." In A. J. H. Latham and Heita Kawakatsu, eds., *Asia Pacific Dynamism 1550–2000*, 187–198. London: Routledge.

———. 2003. *Kahei shisutemu no sekaishi: "hitaishosei" o yomu* 貨幣システムの世界史：〈非対称性〉をよむ. Tokyo: Iwanami shoten.

———. 2006. "Too Commercialised to Synchronise Currencies: Monetary Peasant Economy in Late Imperial China in Comparison with Contemporary Japan." Proceedings of the XIV International Economic History Congress in Helsinki. Retrieved on October 6, 2008, from www.helsinki.fi/iehc2006/papers3/Kuroda.pdf.

———. 2007. "The Maria Theresa Dollar in the Early Twentieth-Century Red Sea Region: A Complementary Interface between Multiple Markets." *Financial History Review* 14: 89–110.

———. 2008. "Concurrent but Non-Integrable Currency Circuits: Complementary Relationships among Monies in Modern China and Other Regions." *Financial History Review* 15.1: 17–36.

———. 2009. "The Eurasian Silver Century, 1276–1359: Commensurability and Multiplicity." *Journal of Global History* 4: 245–269.

Kuz'mina, Elena Efimivna. 2008. Trans. by Victor H. Mair. *The Prehistory of the Silk Road.* Philadelphia: University of Pennsylvania Press.

Labib, Subhi Y. 1969. "Capitalism in Medieval Islam." *The Journal of Economic History* 29.1: 79–96.

Lacouperie, Terrien de. 1894. *Western Origin of the Early Chinese Civilisation from 2,300 B.C. to 200 A.D.* London: Asher & Co.

Lane, F. C. and Reinhold C. Mueller. 1985. *Money and Banking in Medieval and Renaissance Venice.* Baltimore, MD: Johns Hopkins University Press.

Lane, Roger DeWart. 2008. *Encyclopaedia of Small Silver Coins.* Self-published.

Lang Xianping 郎咸平. 2009. "Renminbi shengzhi rang ni geng fuyu?" 人民幣升值讓你更富裕? *Shiye* 8: 40.

Lardy, Nicholas R. 1998. *China's Unfinished Economic Revolution.* Washington, DC: Brookings Institution Press.

Laufer, Berthold. [1919, rep. 1967]. *Sino-Iranica: Chinese Contributions to the History and Civilization in Ancient Iran.* Taipei: Ch'eng-Wen.

Le Yan. 2007. "China's Foreign Exchange Markets." In Salih N. Neftci and Michelle Yuan Ménager-Xu, eds., *China's Financial Markets: An Insider's Guide to How the Markets Work*, 112–134. Burlington, MA: Elsevier.

Lee, Frederic Edward. [1926, rep. 1982]. *Currency, Banking, and Finance in China.* New York: Garland.

Lee Jong-Wha. 2010. "Comment on 'China as Number One': How about the Renminbi?" *Asian Economic Policy Review* 5.2: 277–278.

Levine, Ari D. 2008. *Divided by a Common Language: Factional Conflict in Late Northern Song China.* Honolulu: University of Hawai'i Press.

Levintal, Oren, and Joseph Zeira. 2009. "The Evolution of Paper Money." *CEPR Working Paper.* Jeruslaem: Hebrew University Economics Department. Retrieved on September 17, 2012, from http://papers.ssrn.com/sol3/papers.cfm?abstract_id=1429724&http://papers.ssrn.com/sol3/papers.cfm?abstract_id=1429724

Lewis, Mark Edward. 2007. *The Early Chinese Empires: Qin and Han.* Cambridge, MA: Harvard University Press.

Li Daokui 李稻葵 and Liu Linlin 劉霖林. 2008. "Shuangguizhi tuijin Renminbi guojihua" 雙軌制推進人民幣國際化. *Zhongguo jinrong* 10: 42–43.

Li Dongrong 李東榮. 2006. *Renminbi hui jia hui bian: 1949–2005 nian* 人民幣匯價匯編: 1949–2005 年. People's Bank of China.

Li Gan 李幹. 1985. *Yuandai shehui jingji shigao* 元代社會經濟史稿. Hubei renmin chubanshe.

Li Jing. 2007. "The Rise of the Renminbi in Asia: Cost-Benefit Analysis and Road Map." *The Chinese Economy* 40.4: 29–43.

Li Jinlian 李金蓮. 2005. "Yunnan gudai dianchi diqu qingtong wenhua zhong de zhubeiqi zongshu" "雲南古代滇池地區青銅文化中的貯貝器綜述." *Chuxiong shifan xueyuan xuebao* 楚雄師範學院學報 2: 56–62.

Li Lonsheng 李隆生. 2010. *Qingdai de guoji maoyi* 清代的國際貿易. Taipei: Xiuwei.

Li Ming-Hsun. 1963. *The Great Recoinage of 1696 to 1699.* London: Weidenfeld and Nicolson.

Li Ping 李平 and Yang Qingfang 楊清仿. 1999. *Renminbi huilü, lilun, lishi, xianzhuang ji qi fazhan qushi* 人民幣匯率: 理論、曆史、現狀及其發展趨勢. Beijing: Jingji kexue chubanshe.

Li Taichu 李泰初. 1936. *Xianggang zhibi yu Guangzhou wujia guanxi zhi chubu yanjiu* 香港紙幣與廣州物價關係之初步研究. Guangzhou: Guangdong shengli rangqin daxue shangxue yuan.

Li Xizhu 李細珠. 2003. *Zhang Zhidong yu Qingmo xinzheng yanjiu* 張之洞與清末新政研究. Shanghai: Shanghai shudian.

Li Yu'an 李育安. 1996. "Qingdai de bizhi he zhibi liutong" 清代的幣制和紙幣流通. *Zhengzhou daxue xuebao* 6:84–89.

Li Yung-ti. 2006. "On the Function of Cowries in Shang and Western Zhou China." *Journal of East Asian Archaeology* 5.1–4: 1–26.

Liang Fangzhong 梁方仲. 1989. *Liang Fangzhong jingji shi lunwenji* 梁方仲經濟史論文集. Beijing: Zhonghua shu ju.

Lieu, D. K. 1929. *Foreign Investments in China.* Nanjing: Chinese Government Bureau of Statistics.

Liew, Leong H. 2002. "Policy Elites in the Political Economy of China's Exchange Rate Policymaking." *Journal of Contemporary China* 13.38: 21–51.

———. 2006. "Changing China's Political Economy: Uniting and Dividing Impacts of Globalisation." In Iyanatul Islam and Mozaaem Hossain, eds., *Glo-*

balisation and the Asia-Pacific: Contested Perspectives and Diverse Experiences, 131–149. Cheltenham, UK: Edward Elgar.

Liew, Leong H, and Harry X. Wu. 2007. *The Making of China's Exchange Rate Policy: From Plan to WTO Entry.* Cheltenham, UK: Edward Elgar.

Lin Guijun and Ronald M. Schramm. 2003. "China's Foreign Exchange Policies since 1979: A Review of Developments and an Assessment." *China Economic Review* 14.3: 246–280.

Lin Man-houng. 2005. "Taiwanese Merchants in the Economic Relations between Taiwan and China, 1895–1937." In Sugiyama Kaoru, ed., *Japan, China, and the Growth of the Asian International Economy, 1850–1949*, 217–244. New York: Oxford University Press.

———. 2006. *China Upside Down: Currency, Society and Ideologies, 1808–1856.* Cambridge, MA: Harvard University Press.

Lin Yifu 林毅夫. 2009. "Renminbi shangzhi keneng hui esha quanqiu fusu" 人民幣升值可能會扼殺全球复蘇. *Renmin luntan zhenglun shuangzhoukan* 22: 158.

Ling Yeqin 淩業勤. 1987. *Zhongguo gudai chuantong zhuzao jishu* 中國古代傳統鑄造技術. Beijing: Xinhua.

Liu Hengwu 劉恒武 and Yang Xinmin 楊心珉. 2010. "Mingdai de qianfa zuzhi wenti yu Huang Zongxi de qianfa sixiang" "明代的錢法阻滯問題與黄宗義的錢法思想." *Zhejiang shehui kexue* 9: 64–71.

Liu Qiugen 劉秋根. 2000. *Ming Qing gaolidai ziben* 明清高利貸資本. Beijing: Shehui kexue wenxian chubanshe.

Liu Sen 劉森. 2007. "Yuanchao 'chaoben' chutan" 元鈔'鈔本'初探. *Henan daxue xuebao* 47.2: 135–143.

Lo Cascio, Elio. 2007. "The Early-Roman Empire: The State and the Economy." In Walter Scheidel, Ian Morris, and Richard Saller, eds. *Cambridge Economic History of the Greco-Roman World*, 619–650. Cambridge, UK: Cambridge University Press.

Loehr, Max. 1949. "Weapons and Tools from Anyang, and Siberian Analogie." *American Journal of Archaeology* 53.2: 126–144.

Long Yuan. 2011. *Further Development of Renminbi's Exchange Rate Regime after Joining the WTO.* Norderstedt: Grin Verlag.

Lopez, Robert Sabatino. 1951. "The Dollar of the Middle Ages." *The Journal of Economic History* 11.3: 209–234.

———. 1953. "An Aristocracy of Money in the Middle Ages." *Speculum: A Journal of Medieval Studies* 28.1: 1–43.

Love, John R. 1991. *Antiquity and Capitalism: Max Weber and the Sociological Foundations of Roman Civilization.* London: Routledge.

Lowick, N. M. 1970. "Axumite Coins." *British Museum Quarterly* 34.3–4: 148–151.

Lu Hanchao. 2004. "The Art of History: A Conversation with Jonathan Spence." *Chinese Historical Review* 11.2: 133–154.

Lucassen, Jan. 2005. "Coin Production, Coin Circulation, and the Payment of Wages in Europe and China." In Christine Moll-Murata, Song Jianze, and

Hans Ulrich Vogel, eds., *Chinese Handicraft Regulations of the Qing Dynasty: Theory and Application*, 423–446. Pheonix: Arizona University Press.

———. 2007 "Introduction." In idem., ed., *Wages and Currency: Global Comparisons from Antiquity to the Twentieth Century*, 9–58. Berlin: Peter Lang.

Lüshi chunqiu 吕氏春秋. [rep. 1991]. Beijing: Zhonghua shuju.

Ma Chuande 馬傳德, Xu Yuan 徐淵, and Hu Youwen 胡幼文. 2000. *Shanghaitan huobi* 上海灘貨幣. Shanghai: Shanghai jiaoyu chubanshe.

Ma Debin. 2013. "Chinese Money and Monetary System, 1800–2000, Overview." In Gerard Caprio, ed., *Handbook of Key Global Financial Markets, Institutions, and Infrastructure*, vol. 1, 57–64. Oxford, UK: Elsevier.

Ma Tao 馬濤 and Song Dan 宋丹. 2009. "On the Features of Ancient Money Categories in China." *Journal of Finance and Economics* 11: 26–36.

Macdonald, George. 1916. *The Evolution of Coinage*. Cambridge, UK: Cambridge University Press.

Mackenzie, A. D. 1953. *The Bank of England Note Issue: A History of Its Printing*. Cambridge, UK: Cambridge University Press.

Mackenzie, Compton. 1954. *Realms of Silver: One Hundred Years of Banking in the East*. London: Routledge and Kegan Paul.

Maddison, Angus. 2007. *Chinese Economic Performance in the Long Run*. Paris: Development Centre of the Organisation for Economic Co-Operation and Development.

Magnusson, Lars. 2000. *An Economic History of Sweden*. London: Routledge.

Maity, S. K. 1970. *Early Indian Coins and Currency System*. Delhi: Munshiram Manoharlal.

Malmendier, Ulrike. 2005. "Roman Shares." In N. Goetzmann and K. Geer, eds., *The Origins of Value: The Financial Innovations That Created Modern Capital Markets*. Oxford, UK: Oxford University Press.

Manela, Erez. 2007. *The Wilsonian Moment: Self-Determination and the International Origins of Anticolonial Nationalism*. New York: Oxford University Press.

Mao King On. 1977. *History of Chinese Paper Currency*, 2 vols. Hong Kong: K. O. Mao.

Marcus, Harold G. 2002. *A History of Ethiopia*. Berkeley: University of California Press.

Markley, Robert. 2003. "Riches, Power, Trade and Religion: The Far East and the English Imagination, 1600–1720." *Renaissaince Studies* 17.3: 494–516.

Martin, David A. 1977. "The Changing Role of Foreign Money in the United States, 1782–1857." *Journal of Economic History*. 37.4: 1009–1027.

Maruyama Makoto. 1999. "Local Currencies in Pre-Industrial Japan." In Emily Gilbert and Eric Helleiner, eds., *Nation-States and Money: The Past, Present and Future of National Currencies*, 68–81. London: Routledge.

Marx, Karl. [1867, rep. 1967]. *Kapital: Kritik der politischen Ökonomie*. 3 vols. Frankfurt: Europaische Verlagsanstalt.

———. [rep. 1990]. *Capital: A Critique of Political Economy*. 3 Vols. Trans. from German by Ben Fowkes. London: Penguin Classics.

Marybon, Charles B. 1929. *Histoire de la concession française de changhai.* Paris: Plon.

Maspéro, Henri. 1955. *La Chine Antique.* Paris: Impr. Nationale.

Masters, Bruce. 1988. *The Origins of Western Economic Dominance in the Middle East: Mercantilism and the Islamic Economy in Aleppo, 1600–1750.* New York: New York University Press.

Mattingly, Harold. 1960. *Roman Coins: From the Earliest Times to the Fall of the Western Empire.* London: Methuen.

McElderry, Andrea Lee. 1976. *Shanghai Old-Style Banks (Ch'ien- Chuang), 1800–1925: A Traditional Institution in a Changing Society.* Ann Arbor: Center for Chinese Studies, University of Michigan.

McGuire, John. 2004. "The Rise and Fall of the Oriental Bank in the Nineteenth Century: A Product of the Transformation That Occurred in the World Economy or the Result of its Own Mismanagement." In *Proceedings of the Fifteenth Biennial Conference of the Asian Studies Association of Australia*, 1–20. Retrieved on September 19, 2012, from http://coombs.anu.edu.au/SpecialProj/ASAA/biennial-conference/2004/McGuire-J-ASAA2004.pdf.

McLean, David. 1976. "Finance and 'Informal Empire' before the First World War." *Economic History Review* 29.2: 291–305.

McNamara, Dennis L. 1990. *The Colonial Origins of Korean Enterprise, 1910–1945.* New York: Cambridge University Press.

Meiji taishō kokusei sōran 明治大正國勢總覽. 1975. Tokyo: Keizai Shinposha.

Meiji taishō zaisei shi 明治大正財政史. 1955. 20 vols. Tokyo: Keizai Ōraisha.

Meiji-zen Nihon kōgyō gijutsu hattatsushi 明治前日本鉱業技術発達史. 1982. Tokyo: Hatsubaijo Inoue shoten.

Menger, Carl. 1909. "Geld." In F. A. Hayek, ed., *Schriften über Geld und Währungspolitik*, 1–116. Tübingen: Mohr.

Metcalf, D. M. 1980–1981. "Continuity and Change in English Monetary History 973–1086." *British Numismatic Journal* 50, 51.

Metzler, Mark. 2006. *Lever of Empire: The International Gold Standard and the Crisis of Liberalism in Prewar Japan.* Berkeley: University of California Press.

Miao Mingyang 繆明楊. 1995. "Songdai zhibi faxing zhunbeijin shulüe" 宋代紙幣發行准備金述略. *Caijing kexue* 5: 75–76.

Michie, Ranald C. 2006. *The Global Securities Market: A History.* Oxford, UK: Oxford University Press.

Mihm, Stephen. 2007. *A Nation of Counterfeiters: Capitalists, Con Men and the Making of the United States.* Cambridge, MA: Harvard University Press.

Ming jingshi wenbian 明經世文編. [rep. 1964]. Comp. by Chen Zilong 陳子龍. 6 vols. Hong Kong: Zhuji shudian.

Ming shilu leizuan 明實錄類纂. [rep. 1993] Comp. by Li Guoxiang 李國祥 and Yang Chang 楊昶. Wuhan: Wuhan chubanshe.

Mira, W. J. D., and W. J. Noble. 1988. *The Holey Dollars of New South Wales.* Sydney: Australian Numismatic Society.

Miskimin, Harry A. 1983. "Money and Money Movements in France and England at the End of the Middle Ages." In J. F. Richard, ed., *Precious Metals in the Later Medieval and Early Modern Worlds*, 79–96. Durham, NC: Carolina Academic Press.

———. 1984. *Money and Power in Fifteenth-Century France*. New Haven, CT: Yale University Press.

Mitchiner, Michael. 1977. *Indo-Greek and Indo-Scythian Coinage*. London: Hawkins.

Mitter, Rana. 2000. *The Manchurian Myth: Nationalism, Resistance and Collaboration in Modern China*. Berkeley: University of California Press.

Miyamoto Matao and Shikano Yoshiaki. 2003. "The Emergence of the Tokugawa Monetary System in East Asian International Perspective." In Richard Von Glahn, Arturo Giráldez, and Dennis O. Flynn, eds., *Global Connections and Monetary History, 1470–1800*, 169–186. Aldershot, UK: Ashgate.

Miyazaki Ichisada 宮崎市定. 1977. *Chūgoku shi* 中國史. 2 vols. Tokyo: Iwanami shoten.

Mizoguchi Toshiyuki. 1972. "Consumer Prices and Real Wages in Taiwan and Korea under Japanese Rule." *Hitotsubashi Journal of Economics* 13.1: 40–56.

Mizoguchi Toshiyuki and Yamamoto Yuzo. 1984. "Capital Formation in Taiwan and Korea." In Ramon H. Myers and Mark R. Peattie, eds., *The Japanese Colonial Empire, 1895–1945*, 399–420. Princeton, NJ: Princeton University Press.

Mokyr, Joel. 2009. *The Enlightened Economy: An Economic History of Britain, 1700–1850*. New Haven, CT: Yale University Press.

Molenda, Danuta. 1976. "Investments in Ore Mining in Poland from the 13th to the 17th Centuries." *Journal of European Economic History* 15.1: 121–139.

Morelli, Roberta. 1976. "The Medici Silver Mines (1542–1592)." *Journal of European Economic History* 5.1: 121–139.

Morris-Suzuki, Tessa. 1989. *A History of Japanese Economic Thought*. London: Routledge.

Morrison, John Robert. 1848. *A Chinese Commercial Guide*. China s.n.

Morse, H. B. [1921, rep. 1967]. *The Trade and Administration of China*. New York: Russel and Russel.

Motomura, Akira. 1994. "The Best and Worst Currencies: Seigniorage and Currency Policy in Spain, 1597–1650." *Journal of Economic History* 54.1: 104–197.

Moulder, Frances V. 1977. *Japan, China and the Modern World Economy*. Cambridge, UK: Cambridge University Press.

Muirhead, Stuart. 1996. *Crisis Banking in the East: The History of the Chartered Mercantile Bank of India, London and China, 1853–93*. London: Scolar Press.

Mukhamedjanov, A. R. 1994. "Economy and Social System in Central Asia in the Kushan Age." In J. Harmatta, ed., *History of Civilizations of Central Asia*, vol. 2, *The Development of Sedentary and Nomadic Civilizations: 700 B.C. to A.D. 250*, 265–290. Paris: UNESCO.

Müller-Jabusch, Maximilian. 1940. *Fünfzig Jahre Deutsch-Asiatische Bank, 1890–1939.* Berlin: Die Bank.

Munro, John H. 1974. "Billon: From Byullion to Base Coinage." *Revue Belge de Philology et d'histoire.* 52.2: 293–305.

———. 1983. "Bullion Flows and Monetray Contraction in Late-Medieval England and the Low Countries." In J. F. Richards, ed., *Precious Metals in the Later Medieval and Early Modern Worlds*, 97–158. Durham, NC: Carolina Academic Press.

———. 2007. "South German Silver, European Textiles, and Venetian Trade with the Levant and Ottoman Empire, c. 1370 to c. 1720: A Non-Mercantilistic Approach." In Simonetta Cavaciocchi, ed., *Relazione Economichetra Europa e Mondo Islamico, Seccoli XIII-XVIII*, 905–1055. Tuscany: Fondazione Casa Risparmio di Prato.

———. 2012. "Introduction," in idem., ed., *Money in the Pre-Industrial World: Bullion, Debasements and Coin*, 1–14. London: Pickering & Chatto.

Murphey, Rhoads. 1953. *Shanghai: Key to Modern China.* Cambridge, MA: Harvard University Press.

Myers, Ramon H., and Yamada Saburo. 1984. "Agricultural Development in the Empire." In Ramon H. Myers and Mark R. Peattie, eds., *The Japanese Colonial Empire, 1895–1945*, 420–455. Princeton, NJ: Princeton University Press.

Narain, A. K. 1990. "Indo-Europeans in Inner Asia." In D. Sinor, ed., *The Cambridge History of Early Inner Asia*, 151–176. Cambridge, UK: Cambridge University Press.

"Native Banks in Foochow." 1932. *Chinese Economic Journal* 10.5: 440–447.

Naughton, Barry. 1996. *Growing Out of the Plan: Chinese Economic Reform, 1978–1993.* New York: Cambridge University Press.

Neal, Larry. 1993. *The Rise of Financial Capitalism: International Capital Markets in the Age of Reason.* New York: Cambridge University Press.

Needham, Joseph. 1974. *Spagyrical Discovery and Invention.* In Joseph Needham, ed., *Science and Civilisation in China*, vol. 5, *Chemistry and Chemical Technology*, Part 2. Cambridge, UK: Cambridge University Press.

Nef, John U. 1941. "Silver Production in Central Europe, 1450–1618." *The Journal of Political Economy* 49.4: 575–591.

Nelson, Evan W. 1984. *The Imperial Administration of Currency and British Banking in the Straits Settlements, 1867–1908.* Unpublished PhD dissertation, Duke University.

Nicholson, J. Shield. 1893. *Principles of Political Economy.* London: Black.

Nishimura, Shizuya. 2005. "The Foreign and Native Banks in China: Chop Loans in Shanghai and Hankow before 1914." *Modern Asian Studies* 39.1: 109–132.

Noda Masaho 野田正穂. 1980. *Nihon shōken shijō seiritsu* 日本証券市場成立史. Tokyo: Yu hikaku.

North, Douglass C., and Robert Thomas. 1973. *The Rise of the Western World: A New Economic History.* Cambridge, UK: Cambridge University Press.

O'Brien, Patrick K., and Philip A. Hunt. 1999. "England, 1485–1815." In Richard Bonney, ed., *The Rise of the Fiscal State in Europe, 1200–1815*, 53–100. Oxford, UK: Oxford University Press.

Ogawa Eiji. 2002. "Should East Asian Countries Return to a Dollar Peg Again?" In Peter Drysdale and Kenichi Ishigaki, eds., *East Asian Trade and Financial Integration: New Issues*, 159–184. Canberra: Asia Pacific Press.

Oh Doo-Hwan. 1987. "Currency Readjustment and Colonial Monetary System of 1905 in Korea." *Journal of Social Sciences and Humanities* 65: 53–86.

Olsen, John W. 1983. "An Analysis of East Asian Coins Excavated in Tuscon, Arizona." *Historical Archaeology* 17: 42–55.

Orbell, John, and Alison Turton. 2001. *British Banking: A Guide to Historical Records*. Aldershot, UK: Ashgate.

Orchard, Dorothy J. 1930. "China's Use of the Boycott as a Political Weapon." *The Annals of the American Academy of Political and Social Science—China* 152: 252–261.

Ormond, W. M. 1999. "England in the Middle Ages." In Richard Bonney, ed., *The Rise of the Fiscal State in Europe 1200–1815*, 19–52. Oxford, UK: Oxford University Press.

O'Rourke, Kevin H., and Jeffrey G. Williamson. 2004. "Once More: When Did Globalisation Begin?" *European Review of Economic History* 8: 109–117.

Osterhammel, Jürgen. 1989. "British Business in China, 1860s–1950s." In R. P. T. Davenport-Hines and Geoffrey Jones, eds., *British Business in Asia since 1860*, 189–216. Cambridge, UK: Cambridge University Press.

———. 1999. "Britain and China, 1842–1914." In Andrew Porter, ed., *The Oxford History of the British Empire* 3: 146–169. Oxford, UK: Oxford University Press.

Palais, James B. 1991. *Politics and Policy in Traditional Korea*. New York: Cambridge University Press.

Pamuk, Sevket. 1997. "In the Absence of Domestic Currency: Debased European Coinage in the Seventeenth-Century Ottoman Empire." *The Journal of Economic History* 57.2: 345–366.

———. 2000. *A Monetary History of the Ottoman Empire*. Cambridge, UK: Cambridge University Press.

———. 2004. "The Evolution of Financial Institutions in the Ottoman Empire, 1600–1914." *Financial History Review* 11: 7–32.

———. 2007. "The Black Death and the Origins of the 'Great Divergence' across Europe, 1300–1600." *European Review of Economic History* 11: 289–317.

Pan Liangui 潘連貴. 2004. *Shanghai huobi shi* 上海貨幣史. Shanghai: Shanghai renmin chubanshe.

Pan Ming-te. 1996. Rural Credit in Ming-Qing Jiangnan and the Concept of Peasant Petty Commodity Production. *The Journal of Asian Studies* 55.1: 94–117.

Parkes, H. 1852. "An Account of the Paper Currency and Banking System of Fuhchowfoo." *Royal Asiatic Society of Great Britain and Ireland* 13: 179–189.

Parsons, William Barclay. 1900. *An American Engineer in China*. New York McClure, Phillips & Co.

Pelcovits, Nathan A. 1948. *Old China Hands and the Foreign Office*. New York: King's Crown Press.

Peng Xinwei 彭信威. 1958 [rev. 1970, 1988, 2007]. *Zhongguo huobi shi* 中國貨幣史. Shanghai: Shanghai renmin chubanshe.

———. 1994. *A Monetary History of China*. Trans. by Edward H. Kaplan. Bellingham, WA: Western Washington.

Perez, Louis G. 1999. *Japan Comes of Age: Mutsu Munemitsu and the Revision of the Unequal Treaties*. Madison, NJ: Fairleigh Dickinson University Press.

Perlin, Frank. 1993. *The Invisible City: Monetary, Administrative, and Popular Infrastructures in Asia and Europe, 1500–1900*. Brookfield, VT: Ashgate.

Peters, Ken. 2002. *The Counterfeit Coin Story*. Kent, UK: Envoy Publicity.

Pezzolo, Luciano. 2005. "Bonds and Government Debt in Italian City-States, 1250-1650." In William N. Goetzmann and K. Geert Rouwenhorst, eds., *The Origins of Value: The Financial Innovations That Created Modern Capital Markets*, 145–164. Oxford, UK: Oxford University Press.

Philips, C. H. 1961. *The East India Company, 1784–1834*. London: Routledge.

Pick, Albert. 1990. *Standard Catalog of World Paper Money*. 2 vols. Iola, WI: Krause Publications.

Pigou, A. C. [rep. 1947, 1979]. *The Veil of Money*. Westport, CT: Greenwood Press.

Pines, Yuri. 2005. "Beasts or Humans: Pre-Imperial Origins of the 'Sino-Barbarian' Dichotomy." In Reuven Amitai and Michal Biran, eds., *Mongols, Turks, and Others: Eurasian Nomads and the Sedentary World*, 59–102. Leiden: Brill.

———. 2009. *Envisioning Eternal Empire: Chinese Political Thought of the Warring States Era*. Honolulu: University of Hawaii Press.

———. 2012. *The Everlasting Empire: The Political Culture of Ancient China and Its Imperial Legacy*. Princeton, NJ: Princeton University Press.

Pirenne, Henri, and Ivy E. Clegg. 2006. *An Economic and Social History of Medieval Europe*. London: Taylor & Francis.

Polanyi, Karl. 1944. *The Great Transformation*. New York: Rinehart.

Polo, Marco. [rep. 1903]. *The Book of Ser Marco Polo*. Trans. from the Venetian by Henry Yule. London: J. Murray.

———. [rep. 1987]. *The Travels of Marco Polo*. Trans. from the Venetian by R. E. Latham. Harmondsworth, UK: Penguin.

Pomeranz, Kenneth. 2001. *The Great Divergence*. Princeton, NJ: Princeton University Press.

Porter, David L. 2002. "Monstrous Beauty: Eighteenth-Century Fashion and Aesthetics of Chinese Taste." *Eighteenth-Century Studies* 35.3: 395–411.

Postan, Michael. 1987. "The Trade of Medieval Europe: The North." In M. M. Postan and Edward Miller, eds., *The Cambridge History of Europe: Trade and Industry in the Middle Ages*, vol. 2, Chapter 4. Cambridge, UK: Cambridge University Press.

Prakash, Om. 1987. "Foreign Merchants and Indian Mints in the Seventeenth and the Early Eighteenth Century." In J. F. Richards, ed., *The Imperial Monetary System of Mughal India*, 171–192. Bombay: Oxford University Press.

———. 1988. "On Coinage in Mughal India." *Indian Economic and Social History Review* 25: 475–491.

———. 1998. *European Commercial Enterprise in Pre-Colonial India*. New York: Cambridge University Press.

Prasad, Eswar S., and Wei Shang-jin. 2005. "The Chinese Approach to Capital Inflows: Patterns and Possible Explanations." *IMF Working Paper* No. 05/79.

Pratt, Keith L., Richard Rutt, and James Hoare. 1999. *Korea: A Historical and Cultural Dictionary*. London: Routledge.

Pugach, Noel H. 1997. *Same Bed, Different Dreams: A History of the Chinese American Bank of Commerce, 1919–1937*. Hong Kong: Centre of Asian Studies, Hong Kong University.

Pugachenkova, G. A., S. R. Dar, R. C. Sharma, M. A. Joyenda, and H. Siddiqi. 1994. "Kushan Art." In J. Harmatta, ed., *History of Civilizations of Central Asia*, vol. 2, *The Development of Sedentary and Nomadic Civilizations: 700 B.C. to A.D. 250*, 331–395. Paris: UNESCO.

Puk Wing-kin. 2010. "The Ming Salt Certificate: A Public Debt System in Sixteenth-Century China?" *Ming Studies* 61: 1–12.

Puri, B. N. 1994. "The Kushans." In J. Harmatta, ed., *History of Civilizations of Central Asia*, vol. 2, *The Development of Sedentary and Nomadic Civilizations: 700 B.C. to A.D. 250*, 247–263. Paris: UNESCO.

Qi Xia 漆俠. 1987. *Songdai jingji shi* 宋代經濟史. 2 vols. Shanghai: Shanghai renmin chubanshe.

Qian Jiaju 千家駒 and Guo Yangang 郭彥崗. 2005. *Zhongguo huobi yanbian shi* 中國貨幣演變史. Shanghai : Shanghai renmin chubanshe.

Qin Han jingji sixiang shi 秦漢經濟思想史. 1989. Comp. by the Shanghai Academy of Social Sciences. Beijing: Zhonghua shuju.

Qinding Hubu zeli 欽定戶部則例. [rep. 1968]. Taipei: Chengwen chubanshe.

Qingchao wenxian tongkao 清朝文獻通考.[rep. 1962]. Taipei: Xinxing shuju.

Quan Hansheng 全漢升. 1941. "Zhong gu ziran jingji" 中古自然經濟. *Zhongyang yanjiuyuan lishi yuyan yanjiusuo jikan* 10: 73–173.

———. 1972. *Zhongguo jingjishi luncong* 中國近代史論叢. 2 vols. Hong Kong: Chinese University of Hong Kong.

———. 1987. *Ming Qing jingji shi yanjiu* 明清經濟史研究. Taipei: Lian jing chuban shiye gongsi.

Quested, R. K. I. 1977. *The Russo-Chinese Bank: A Multinational Financial Base of Tsarism in China*. Birmingham, UK: Birmingham University Press.

Quinn, Stephen, and William Roberds. 2005. "The Big Problem of Large Bills: The Bank of Amsterdam and the Origins of Central Banking." *Federal Reserve Bank of Atlanta Working Paper*.

Rajan, Raghuram G., and Luigi Zingales. 2003. "The Great Reversals: The Politics of Financial Development in the Twentieth Century." *Journal of Financial Economics* 69.1: 5–50.

Rang Huey-shin [Zhang Huixin] 張惠信. 1988. *Zhongguo yinding* 中國銀錠. Taipei: Liu Qiuyan.

Raschke, M. G. 1978. "New Studies in Roman Commerce with the East." In Temporini, Hildegard ed., *Aufstieg und Niedergang der Römischen Welt* vol. 9, Part 2, 604-1361. Berlin: Gruyter.

Rawski, Thomas G. 1989. *Economic Growth in Prewar China*. Berkeley: University of California Press.

Rawson, Jessica. 1989. "Statesmen or Barbarians? The Western Zhou as Seen through Their Bronzes." *Proceedings of the British Academy* 75: 71–95.

Redish, Angela. 2000. *Bimetallism: An Economic and Historical Analysis*. New York: Cambridge University Press.

Reid, Anthony. 1993. *Southeast Asia in the Early Modern Era: Trade, Power, and Belief*. Ithaca, NY: Cornell University Press.

Remer, C. F. 1933. *A Study of Chinese Boycotts: With Special Reference to Their Economic Effectiveness*. Baltimore, MD: Johns Hopkins University Press.

Ren Jianshu 任建樹. 1996. Xiandai Shanghai da shiji 現代上海大事記. Shanghai: Shanghai cishu chubanshe.

Renminbi guojihua yanjiu ketizu [PBC Research Group for RMB Internationalization] 人民幣國際化研究課題組. 2006. "Renminbi guojihua de shiji, tujing ji celüe" 人民幣國際化的時機、途徑及策略. *Zhongguo jinrong* 5: 12–13.

Richards, J. F. 1987. "Introduction." In idem, ed., *The Imperial Monetary System of Mughal India*, 1–12. Bombay: Oxford University Press.

Rigby, Richard W. 1980. *The May 30 Movement: Events and Themes*. Canberra: Australian National University.

Rinbara Fumiko 林原文子. 1983. *Sō Sokkyū to Tenshin no kokka teishō undō* 宋則久と天津の国貨提唱運動. Kyoto: Dōhōsha.

Ritchie, Neville A., and Stuart Park. 1987. "Chinese Coins Down Under: Their Role on the New Zealand Goldfields." *Australian Historical Archeology* 5: 41–48.

Ritter, Joseph A. 1995. "The Transition from Barter to Fiat Money." *The American Economic Review* 85.1: 134–149.

Robbert, Louise. 1983. "Monetary Flows—Venice 1150–1400." In J. F. Richards, ed., *Precious Metals in the Later Medieval and Early Modern Worlds*, 53–78. Durham, NC: Carolina Academic Press.

Robequain, Charles. 1944. *The Economic Development of French Indo-China*. Trans. by Isabel A. Ward. Oxford, UK: Oxford University Press.

Robinson, K. G. 2004. *General Conclusions and Reflections*. In Joseph Needham, ed., *Science and Civilisation in China* vol. 7, *The Social Background*, Part 2. Cambridge, UK: Cambridge University Press.

Rolnick, Arthur J., Francois R. Velde, and Warren E. Weber. 1996. "The Debasement Puzzle: An Essay on Medieval Monetary History." *Journal of Economic History* 56: 789–808.

Rossabi, Morris. 1989. *Khubilai Khan: His Life and Times*. Berkeley: University of California Press.

————. 1994. "The Reign of Khubilai Khan." In Herbert Franke and Denis Twitchett, eds., *The Cambridge History of China*, vol. 6, *Alien Regimes and Border States, 907–1368*, 414–488. Cambridge, UK: Cambridge University Press.

Rowe, William T. 2005. "Provincial Monetary Practice in Eighteenth-Century China: Chen Hongmou in Jiangxi and Shaanxi." In Christine Moll-Murata, Jianze Song, and Hans Ulrich Vogel, eds., *Chinese Handicraft Regulations of the Qing Dynasty*. München: Iudicium.

————. 2010. "Money, Economy and Polity in the Daoguang-Era Paper Currency Debates." *Late Imperial China* 31.2: 69–96.

Rowlinson, Matthew. 1999. "'The Scotch Hate Gold': British Identity and Paper Money." In Emily Gilbert and Eric Helleiner, eds., *Nation-States and Money: The Past, Present and Future of National Currencies*, 47–67. London: Routledge.

Sagar, Krishna Chandra. 1992. *Foreign Influence on Ancient India*. New Delhi: Northern Book Centre.

Sahillioglu, Halil. 1983. "The Role of International Monetary and Metal Movements in Ottoman Monetary History, 1330–1750." In J. F. Richards, ed., *Precious Metals in the Later Medieval and Early Modern Worlds*, 269–304. Durham, NC: Carolina Academic Press.

Samuels, Richard J. 1994. *"Rich Nation, Strong Army": National Security and the Technological Transformation of Japan*. Ithaca, NY: Cornell University Press.

Santō shuppei to hai nikka undō 山東出兵と排日貨運動. 1927. Shanghai: Shanhai Nippon shōgyōkai gisha.

Sargent, Thomas J., and François R. Velde. 2002. *The Big Problem of Small Change*. Princeton, NJ: Princeton University Press.

Sawyer, P. H. 1982. *Kings and Vikings: Scandinavia and Europe AD 700–1100*. London: Routledge.

Schaps, David M. 2001. "The Conceptual Pre-History of Money and Its Impact on the Greek Economy." In Miriam S. Balmuth, ed., *Hacksilber to Coinage: New Insights into the Monetary History of the Near East and Greece*, 93–104. New York: American Numismatic Society.

————. 2004. *The Invention of Coinage and the Monetization of Ancient Greece*. Ann Arbor: University of Michigan Press.

————. 2006. "The Invention of Coinage in Lydia, in India, and in China." Proceedings of the XIV International Economic History Congress, Helsinki. Retrieved on September 20, 2012, from www.helsinki.fi/iehc2006/papers1/Schaps.pdf.

Scheidel, Walter. 2008. "The Divergent Evolution of Coinage in Eastern and Western Eurasia." In W. V. Harris, ed., *The Monetary Systems of the Greeks and Romans*, 267–288. New York: Oxford University Press.

————. 2009a. "Introduction." In idem., ed., *Rome and China: Comparative Perspectives on Ancient World Empires*, 3–10. New York: Oxford University Press.

————. 2009b. "The Monetary Systems of the Han and Roman Empires." In idem., ed., *Rome and China: Comparative Perspectives on Ancient World Empires*, 137–208. New York: Oxford University Press.

Schenk, Catherine R. 2000. "Another Asian Financial Crisis: Monetary Links between Hong Kong and China 1945–50." *Modern Asian Studies* 34.3: 739–764.

————. 2009. "Hong Kong's Monetary Challenges in Historical Perspective." In idem., ed., *Hong Kong SAR's Monetary and Exchange Rate Challenges: Historical Perspectives*, 3–14. Houndmills, UK: Palgrave Macmillan.

————. 2010. *The Decline of Sterling: Managing the Retreat of an International Currency, 1945–1992*. New York: Cambridge University Press.

Schifferli, Christoph. 1986. "Le système monétaire au sichuan vers la fin du Xe siècle." *T'oung Pao* 72: 269–290.

Schiltz, Michael. 2006. "An 'Ideal' Bank of Issue: the Banque Nationale de Belgique as a Model for the Bank of Japan." *Financial History Review* 13.2: 179–196.

————. 2012a. *The Money Doctors from Japan: Finance, Imperialism, and the Building of the Yen Bloc, 1895–1937*. Cambridge, MA: Harvard University Press.

————. 2012b. "Money on the Road to Empire: Japan's Adoption of Gold Monometallism, 1873–97." *Economic History Review* 63.5: 1147–1168.

Schlumberger, D. 1953. "L'Argent Grec dans l'Empire Achemenide." In R. Curiel and D. Schlumberger, eds., *Tresor Monétaire d'Afghanistan*, 3–62. Paris: Impr. Nationale.

Schottenhammer, Angela. 2001. "The Role of Metals and the Impact of the Introduction of Huizi Paper Notes in Quanzhou on the Development of Maritime Trade in the Song Period." In idem., ed., *The Emporium of the World, Maritime Quanzhou 1000–1400*, 95–176. Leiden: Brill.

Schuler, Kurt. 1992. "The World History of Free Banking: An Overview." In Kevin Dowd, ed., *The Experience of Free Banking*, 7–47. London: Routledge.

Schurmann, Franz Herbert. 1967. *Economic Structure of the Yüan Dynasty*. Cambridge, MA: Harvard University Press.

Schurtz, William L. 1959. *The Manila Galleon*. New York: E. P. Dutton.

Segal, Ethan Isaac. 2011. *Coins, Trade and the State: Economic Growth in Early Medieval Japan*. Cambridge, MA: Harvard University Press.

Selgin, George A. 1992. "Free Banking in Foochow." In Kevin Dowd, ed., *The Experience of Free Banking*, 103–122. London: Routledge.

————. 1996. "Salvaging Gresham's Law: The Good, the Bad, and the Illegal." *Journal of Money, Credit, and Banking* 28.4: 637–649.

————. 2008. *Good Money: Birmingham Button Makers, the Royal Mint, and the Beginnings of Modern Coinage, 1775–1821*. Ann Arbor: University of Michigan Press.

Sellwood, David. 1976. "Minting." In Donald Strong and David Brown, eds., *Roman Crafts*, 63–74. London: Duckworth.

Sewell, R. 1904. *Roman Coins Found in India*. London: Royal Asiatic Society of Great Britain.

Shanhai jijō 上海事情. 1924. Comp. by the Imperial Japanese Consulate to Shanghai. Tokyo: Gaimushō tsūshō kyoku.

Shanxi piaohao shiliao 山西票號史料. 1990. Taiyuan: Shanxi jingji chubanshe.

Shaughnessy, Edward L. 1988. "Historical Perspectives on the Introduction of the Chariot into China." Harvard Journal of Asiatic Studies 48.1: 189–237.

Sheehan, Brett. 2003. Trust in Troubled Times: Money, Banks and State–Society Relations in Republican Tianjin. Cambridge, MA: Harvard University Press.

Sherman, Sandra. 1996. Finance and Fictionality in the Early Eighteenth Century: Accounting for Defoe. New York: Cambridge University Press.

Shi Jianhui. 2008. "Are Currency Appreciations Contractionary in China?" In Ito Takatoshi and Andrew Rose, eds., International Financial Issues in the Pacific Rim: Global Imbalances, Financial Liberalization, and Exchange Rate Policy, 77–101. Chicago: University of Chicago Press.

Shiji 史記. [rep. 1959]. 10 vols. Beijing: Zhonghua shuju.

Shi Lei 石雷. 1998. Renminbi shihua 人民幣史話. Beijing: Zhongguo jinrong chubanshe.

Shi Yufu 石毓符. 1984. Zhongguo huobi jinrong shilüe 中國貨幣金融史略. Tianjin: Tianjin renmin chubanshe.

Shimada Ryuto. 2006. The Intra-Asian Trade in Japanese Copper by the Dutch East India Company during the Eighteenth Century. Leiden: Brill.

Shina kinyu kikan 支那金融機関. 1919. Tokyo: Hiagashi Ajia dobunkai.

Shiroyama, Tomoko. 2008. China during the Great Depression: Market, State, and the World Economy, 1929–1937. Cambridge, MA: Harvard University Press.

Sidebotham, Steven E. 1986. Roman Economic Policy in the Erythra Thalassa, 30 B.C.–A.D. 217. Leiden: Brill.

"Siglos Coins Found in Taxila." 1934. Indian Historical Quarterly 10.

Sihag, Balbir S. 2009. "Kautilya on Moral, Market, and Government Failures." International Journal of Hindu Studies 13.1: 83–102.

Singleton, John. 2011. Central Banking in the Twentieth Century. Cambridge, UK: Cambridge University Press.

Sinn, Elizabeth. 1994. Growing with Hong Kong: The Bank of East Asia, 1919–1994. Hong Kong: The Bank of East Asia.

Smith, Adam. [1805, rep. 1952]. An Inquiry into the Nature and Causes of the Wealth of Nations. Chicago: The University of Chicago Press.

Smith, Paul J. 1991. Taxing Heaven's Storehouse: Horses, Bureaucrats, and the Destruction of the Sichuan Tea Industry, 1074–1124. Cambridge, MA: Harvard University Press.

Snelling. Thomas. 1762. A View of the Silver Coin and Coinage of England: From the Norman Conquest to the Present Time, Consider'd with Regard to Type, Legend, Sorts, Rarity, Weight, Fitness and Value. London: printed for T. Snelling.

Snodgrass, Mary Ellen. 2003. Coins and Currency: An Historical Encyclopedia. Jefferson, NC: McFarland.

Song Yingxing 宋應星 [rep. 1987]. Annotated by Yang Weizeng 楊維增 *Tiangong kaiwu xinzhu yanjiu* 天工開物新注研究. Nanchang: Jiangxi kexue jishu chubanshe.

Songshi 宋史. [rep. 1984]. 9 vols. Taipei: Taiwan shangwu yinshuguan.

Spalding, William Frederick. 1924. *Eastern Exchange, Currency and Finance*. London: Pitman.

Spiegel, Henry William. 1991. *The Growth of Economic Thought*. Durham, NC: Duke University Press.

Spooner, Frank C. 1972. *The International Economy and Monetary Movements in France, 1493–1725*. Cambridge, MA: Harvard University Press.

Sprenger, Bernd. 1991. *Das Geld der Deutschen: Geldgeschichte Deutschlands von den Anfangen bis zur Gegenwart*. Paderborn: F. Schoningh.

Spufford, Peter. 1988a. *Money and Its Use in Medieval Europe*. Cambridge, UK: Cambridge University Press.

———. 1988b. "Mint Organisation in Late Medieval Europe." In N. J. Mayhew and idem, ed., *Later Medieval Mints: Organisation, Adminstration and Techniques*, 7-29. Oxford: BAR.

Stahl, Alan M. 2000. *Zecca: The Mint of Venice in the Middle Ages*. Baltimore, MD: Johns Hopkins University Press.

Staunton, George. 1799. *An Authentic Account of an Embassy from the King of Great Britain to the Emperor of China: Taken Chiefly from the Papers of His Excellency the Earl of Macartney*. Philadephia: Campbell.

Stronach, David, Michael Roaf, Ruth Stronach, and S. Bökönyi. 1978. "Excavations at Tepe Nush-i Jan." *Iran*, 16: 1–28.

Sukawa Hidenori. 2009. "Currency in Early Choseon Korea: Issuance, Principles and Controversies." *International Journal of Asian Studies* 6.1: 65–85.

Suleski, Ronald. 1979. "The Rise and Fall of the Fengtien Dollar, 1917–1928: Currency Reform in Warlord China." *Modern Asian Studies* 13.4: 643–660.

———. 1994. *The Modernization of Manchuria: An Annotated Bibliography*. Hong Kong: Chinese University Press.

Sundstrom, Lars. 1974. *The Exchange Economy of Pre-Colonial Tropical Africa*. London: Hurst.

Sussman, Nathan. 1998. "The Late Medieval Bullion Famine Reconsidered." *The Journal of Economic History* 58.1: 126–154.

Taira Tomoyuki 平智之. 1982. "Nihon teikoku shugi seiritsuki, chūgoku ni okeru Yokohama shōkin ginkō" 日本帝国主義成立期、中国における横浜正金銀行." *Tōkyō daigaku keizaigaku kenkyū* 25.11: 67–81.

Taiwan Ginko shi 臺灣銀行史. 1964. Tokyo: Taiwan ginko shi hensanshitsu.

Taiwan ginkō yonjūnenshi 臺灣銀行四十年誌. 1939. Tokyo: Dai Nihon Insatsu Kabushiki Kaisha.

Takagi Shinji. 2010. "Comment on 'China as Number One': How about the Renminbi?" *Asian Economic Policy Review* 5.2: 279–280.

Takahashi Hiro'omi. 高橋弘臣. 2000. *Genchō kahei seisaku seiritsu katei no kenkyū* 元朝貨幣政策成立過程の研究. Tokyo: Tōyō shoin.

Takahashi Kōsuke 高橋孝助 and Furumaya Tadao 古厩忠夫. 1995. *Shanhai shi: kyodai toshi no keisei to hitobito no itonami* 上海史: 巨大都市の形成と人々の営み. Tokyo: Tōhō shoten.

Takatsuna Hirofumi 高綱博文. 2009. *Kokusai toshi: Shanhai no nakara no Nihonjin* 国際都市: 上海のなかの日本人. Tokyo: Kenbun.

Tamagna, Frank. 1942. *Banking and Finance in China.* New York: Institute of Pacific Relations.

Tamaki, Norio. 1995. *Japanese Banking: A History, 1859–1959.* Cambridge, UK: Cambridge University Press.

Tanaka Issei 田仲一成, Kominami Ichiro 小南一郎, and Shiba Yoshinobu 斯波義信. 2009. *Chūgoku kinsei bungeiron: nōson saishi kara toshi geinō e* 中国近世文芸論: 農村祭祀から都市芸能へ. Tokyo: Tōyō bunko.

Tang Jing 唐景. 2009. "Lun Yuan chao de zhi bi guan ji zhi du" "論元朝的紙幣管理制度." *Guangzhou shehui zhuyi xueyuan xuebao* 3: 68–71.

T'ang Leang-Li. 1936. *China's New Currency System.* Shanghai: China United Press.

Tao Jing-Shen. 1983. "Barbarians or Northeners: Northern Sung Images of the Khitan." In Morris Rossabi, ed., *China among Equals: The Middle Kingdom and Its Neighbors, 10th–14th Centuries,* 66–86. Berkeley: University of California Press.

Tao Yi-Feng. 2011. "From a Socialist State to a Mercantilist State: Depoliticizing Central Banking and China's Economic Growth since 1993." In S. Philip Hsu, Yu-Shan Wu, and Suisheng Zhao, eds., *In Search of China's Development Model: Beyond the Beijing Consensus,* 111-127. London: Routledge.

Tavernier, Jean-Baptiste. 1677. *The Six Voyages of John Baptista Tavernier: Baron of Aubonne.* Trans. by John Phillips. London: Littlebury and Pitt.

Tavlas, George S. 1991. "On the International Use of Currencies: The Case of the Deutsche Mark." Washington, DC: International Monetary Fund.

Tawney, R. H. [1932, rep. 1972]. *Land and Labour in China.* New York: Octagon.

Taylor, James. 2006. *Creating Capitalism: Joint-Stock Enterprise in British Politics and Culture, 1800–1870.* Rochester, NY: Boydell Press.

Teare, Herbert. 1926. *The History, Theory and Practice of Australian Banking Currency and Exchange.* Sydney: Alexander Hamilton Institute of Australia Ltd.

Temin, Peter, and Hans-Joachim Voth. 2008. "Interest Rate Restrictions in a Natural Experiment: Loan Allocation and the Change in the Usury Laws in 1714." *Economic Journal* 118.528: 743–758.

Tennant, Charles. 1866. *The Bank of England: And the Organisation of Credit in England.* London: Longmans.

Thompson, C. M. 2003. "Sealed Silver in Iron Age Cisjordan and the 'Invention' of Coinage." *Oxford Journal of Archaeology* 22.1:67–107.

Tilly, Richard. 1967. "Germany, 1815–1870." In Rondo Cameron, Olga Crisp, Hugh T. Patrick, and Richard Tilly, eds., *Banking in the Early Stages of Industrialization: A Study in Comparative Economic History,* 151–182. New York: Oxford University Press.

Tom, C. F. Joseph. 1964. *The Entrepot Trade and the Monetary Standards of Hongkong, 1842–1941.* Hong Kong: K. Weiss.

Totman, Conrad D. 1993. *Early-Modern Japan.* Berkeley: University of California Press.

Triffin, Robert. 1960. *Gold and the Dollar Crisis: The Future of Convertibility.* New Haven, CT: Yale University Press.

———. 1985. "The Myths and Realities of the So-Called Gold Standard." In Barry Eichengreen, ed., *The Gold Standard in History and Theory,* 121–140. New York: Methuen.

Tsai Shih-Shan Henry. 1996. *The Eunuchs in the Ming Dynasty.* New York: State University of New York Press.

Tschoegl, Adrian. E. 2001. "Maria Theresa's Thaler: A Case of International Money." *Eastern Economic Journal* 27.4: 443–462.

Tseng Wanda. 1994. *Economic Reform in China: A New Phase.* Washington, DC: International Monetary Fund.

Tullock, Gordon. 1958. "Paper Money—A Cycle in Cathay." *Economic History Review* 9.3: 393–407.

Turner, Paula J. 1989. *Roman Coins from India.* London: Royal Numismatic Society.

Twitchett, Denis C. 1970. *Financial Administration under the T'ang Dynasty.* Cambridge, UK: Cambridge University Press.

Tylecote, R. F. 1976. *A History of Metallurgy.* London: Metals Society.

The Umayyads: The Rise of Islamic Art. 2000. London: AIRP.

Usher, Abbott Payson. 1914. "The Origin of the Bill of Exchange." *Journal of Political Economy* 22.6: 565–576.

Van Aelst, Arian. 1995. "Majapahit Picis: The Currency of a 'Moneyless' Society 1300–1700." *Bijdragen tot de Tall-. Land- en Volkenkunde* 151.3: 357–393.

———. 2007. "A South-Chinese Currency Zone between the Twelfth and Nineteenth Centuries." In Jan Lucassen, ed., *Wages and Currency: Global Comparisons from Antiquity to the Twentieth Century,* 97–112. Bern: Peter Lang.

Van der Eng, Pierre. 1999. "The Silver Standard and Asia's Integration into the World Economy, 1850–1914." *Journal of Asian and Pacific Studies* 18: 59–85.

Van der Wee, Herman. 1977. "Money Credit and Banking Systems." In John Harold Clapham, Michael Moïssey Postan, and Edwin Ernest Rich, eds., *The Cambridge Economic History of Europe,* 290–393. Cambridge, UK: Cambridge University Press.

Van Dormael, Armand. 1997. *The Power of Money.* London: Macmillan Press.

Van Dyke, Paul. 2005. *The Canton Trade: Life and Enterprise on the China Coast, 1700–1845.* Hong Kong: Hong Kong University Press.

Van Wickevoort Crommelin, B. 1998. "Die Parther und Die Parthische Geschichte Bei Pompeius Trogus-Iustin." In J Wiesehöfer,. ed., *Das Partherreich und Seine Zeugnisse,* 259–277. Stuttgart: Franz Steiner.

Vilar, Pierre. 1976. *A History of Gold and Money.* Trans. by Judith White. London: Humanities Press.

Vissering, G. 1914. *On Chinese Currency: Preliminary Remarks on the Monetary and Banking Reform in China* 2 vols. Amsterdam: De Bussy.

Vogel, Hans Ulrich. 1983. "Chinese Central Monetary Policy and Yunnan Copper Mining in the Early Qing." *Late Imperial China* 8.2: 1–52.

————. 1987. "Chinese Central Monetary Policy, 1644–1800." *Late Imperial China* 8.2: 1–51.

————. 1991. "Kupfererzeugung und handel in China und Europa, Mitte des 8. Bis Mitte des 19. Jahrhunderts: Einevergleeichende Studie." *Bochumer Jahrbuch zur Ostasienforschung* 15: 1–57.

————. 1993a. "Cowry Trade and Its Role in the Economy of Yunnan: From the Ninth to the Mid-Seventh Century. Part I." *Journal of the Economic and Social History of the Orient* 36. 3:211–252.

————. 1993b. "Cowry Trade and Its Role in the Economy of Yunnan: From the Ninth to the Mid-Seventh Century. Part II." *Journal of the Economic and Social History of the Orient* 36. 3:309–353.

————. 2006. "The Mining Industry in Traditional China: Intra- and Intercultural Comparisons." In Helga Nowotny, ed., *Cultures of Technology and the Quest for Innovation*, 167–188. New York: Berghahn Books.

————. 2013. *Marco Polo Was in China: New Evidence from Currencies, Salts and Revenues*. Leiden: Brill.

Vogel, Hans Ulrich, and Elisabeth Theisen-Vogel. 1989. "Der Kupferbergbau in der chinesischen Provinz Yunnan vom 18. Bis zur Mitte des 19. Jahrhunderts: Produktion, Administration, Finanzierung." *Der Anschnitt* 41.5: 146–158.

Von Falkenhausen, Lothar. 1999. "The Waning of the Bronze Age: Material Culture and Social Developments, 770–481 BC." In Michael Loewe and Edward L. Shaughnessy, eds., *The Cambridge History of Ancient China: From the Origins of Civilization to 221 BC*, 450–545. Cambridge, UK: Cambridge University Press.

Von Glahn, Richard. 1996a. *Fountain of Fortune: Money and Monetary Policy in China, 1000–1700*. Berkeley: University of California Press.

————. 1996b. "Comment on 'Arbitrage, China and World Trade in the Early Modern Period.'" *Journal of the Social and Economic History of the Orient* 39.3: 365–367.

————. 2005. "The Origins of Paper Money in China." In William N. Goetzmann and K. Geert Rouwenhorst, eds., *The Origins of Value: The Financial Innovations That Created Modern Capital Markets*, 65–89. New York: Oxford University Press.

————. 2007. "Foreign Silver Coins in the Market Culture of Nineteenth Century China." *International Journal of Asian Studies* 4.1: 51–78.

————. 2010. "Monies of Account and Monetary Transition in China, Twelfth to Fourteenth Centuries." *Journal of the Economic and Social History of the Orient* 53.3: 463–505.

Von Mises, Ludwig. [1912, Trans. 1982]. *The Theory of Money and Credit*. Trans. by H. E. Batson. Indianapolis: The Liberty Fund.

Vort-Ronald, Michael P. 1982. *Banks of Issue in Australia*. Whyalla Norrie: Vort-Ronald.

Wagel, Srinivas R. 1914 [rep. 1980]. *Finance in China*. New York: Garland.

———. 1915. *Chinese Currency and Banking*. Shanghai: North China Daily News and Herald.

Wagner, Donald. 2008. *Ferrous Metallurgy*. In Joseph Needham, ed., *Science and Civilisation in China* vol. 5, *Chemistry and Chemical Technology*, Part 11. Cambridge, UK: Cambridge University Press.

Wakeman, Frederic E. 1985. *The Great Enterprise: The Manchu Reconstruction of Imperial Order in Seventeenth-Century China*. 2 vols. Berkeley: University of California Press.

Waldron, Arthur. 1995. *From War to Nationalism: China's Turning Point, 1924–1925*. Cambridge, UK: Cambridge University Press.

Walker, Thomas. 1983. "The Italian Gold Revolution of 1255." In J. F. Richards, ed., *Precious Metals in the Later Medieval and Early Modern Worlds*, 5–29. Durham, NC: Carolina Academic Press.

Wang, Helen. 2004. *Money on the Silk Road: The Evidence from Eastern Central Asia to c. AD 800*. London: British Museum.

Wang Hongbin 王宏斌. 1987. "Qianlong shiqi yin gui qian jian wenti tanyuan" 乾隆時期銀貴錢賤問題探源. *Zhongguo shehui jingji shi yanjiu* 2: 86–92.

Wang Jingyu 汪敬虞.1983. "Cong Liru yinhang de lishi kan shijiu shiji waiguo yinhang qinlüe Zhongguo de tedian he jincheng" 從麗如銀行的歷史看十九世紀外國銀行侵略中國的特點和進程 *Zhongguo shehui kexueyuan: Jingji yanjiusuo jikan* 4: 218–277.

Wang Shengduo 汪聖鐸. 2003. *LiangSong huobi shi* 兩宋貨幣史. 2 vols. Beijing: Shehhui kexue wenxian chubanshe.

Wang Wencheng 王文成. 2000. *LiangSong yinhuobihua yanjiu* 兩宋銀貨幣化研究. Published PhD Dissertation. Yunan University.

Wang Xianguo 王顯國. 2006. "Qianlong wunian gaizhu 'qingqian' yuanyin chu tan" 乾隆五年改鑄 "青錢" 原因初探. *Zhongguo qianbi* 95: 9–15.

Wang Xipeng 汪錫鵬. 2009. "Bianwei de lupibi."变味的白鹿皮币. *Zhongguo chengshi jinrong* 9: 64–65.

Wang Yeh-chien [Wang Yejian] 王業鍵. 1973. *Land Taxation in Imperial China, 1750–1911*. Cambridge, MA: Harvard University Press.

———. 1981. *Zhongguo jindai huobi yu yinhang de yanjin (1644–1937)* 中國近代貨幣與銀行的演進 (1644–1937). Taipei: Academia Sinica.

Wang Yü-ch'üan [Wang Yuquan] 王毓銓. 1951. *Early Chinese Coinage*. New York: American Numismatic Society.

———. 1957. *Woguo gudai huobi de qiyuan he fazhan* 我國古代貨幣的起源和發展. Beijing: Kexue chubanshe.

Watson, A. M. 1967. "Back to Gold and Silver." *Economic History Review* 20.2: 1–18.

Weatherford, Jack. 1997. *The History of Money*. New York: Three Rivers Press.

Webber, Caroline, and Aaron Wildavsky. 1986. *History of Taxation in the Western World*. New York: Simon & Schuster.

Weber, Max. [rep. 1964]. *The Theory of Social Economic Organization*. New York: Free Press.

Wei Jianyou 魏建猷. 1986. *Zhongguo jindai huobisi* 中國近代貨幣史. Huang-shan shushe chuban.

Wei Linglin. 2011, January 12. "New Move to Make Yuan a Global Currency." *Wall Street Journal* [online edition]. Retrieved on July 1, 2011, from http://online.wsj.com/article/SB10001424052748703791904576076082178393532.html.

Wei Wen Pin. 1914. *The Currency Problem in China.* New York: Columbia University.

Wells, Kenneth. 1985. "The Rationale of Korean Economic Nationalism under Japanese Colonial Rule, 1922–1932: The Case of Cho Man-Sik's Products Promotion." *Modern Asian Studies* 19.4: 823–859.

Wennerlind, Carl. 2011. *Casualties of Credit: The English Financial Revolution, 1620–1720.* Cambridge, MA: Harvard University Press.

Whaley, Mark A. 2009. "A Middle Indo-Aryan Inscription from China." *Acta Orientalia* 69.4: 413–460.

White, Lawrence H. 1984. *Free Banking in Britain: Theory, Experience, and Debate, 1800–1845.* Cambridge, UK: Cambridge University Press.

Whitfield, Susan. 2004. *The Silk Road: Trade, Travel, War and Faith.* London: Serinda.

Wicks, Robert S. 1992. *Money, Markets and Trade in Early Southeast Asia: The Development of Indigenous Monetary Systems to AD 1400.* Ithaca: Cornell University Press.

Wilkins, Mira. 1986. "The Impacts of American Multinational Enterprise on American–Chinese Economic Relations, 1786–1949." In Ernest R. May and John K. Fairbank, eds., *America's China Trade in Historical Perspective: The Chinese and American Performance,* 259–292. Cambridge, MA: Harvard University Press.

Wilkinson, Endymion Porter. 2000. *Chinese History: A Manual.* Cambridge, MA: Harvard University Press.

Will, Pierre-Étienne. 1990. *Bureaucracy and Famine in Eighteenth-Century China.* Stanford, CA: Stanford University Press.

Will, Pierre-Étienne, and Roy Bin Wong. 1991. *Nourish the People: The State Civilian Granary System in China, 1650–1850.* Ann Arbor: University of Michigan Press.

Williams, S. W. 1851. "Paper Money among the Chinese." *Chinese Repository* 20.6: 289–296.

Williamson, Jeffrey G. 2008. "Globalization and the Great Divergence: Terms of Trade Booms, Volatility and the Poor Periphery, 1782–1913." *European Review of Economic History* 12.3: 355–391.

Wink, André. 2001. "India and the Turco-Mongol Frontier." In A. M. Khazanov and A.Wink, eds., *Nomads in the Sedentary World,* 211–233. New York: Routledge.

———. 2002. *Al-Hind: Early Medieval India and the Expansion of Islam, 7th–11th Centuries.* Leiden: Brill.

Wolters, Willem G. 2006. "Managing Multiple Currencies with Units of Account: Netherlands India 1600–1800." Proceedings of the XIV International

Economic History Congress, Helsinki. Retrieved on September 20, 2012, from www.helsinki.fi/iehc2006/papers2/Wolters.pdf.

Wood, Diana. 2002. *Medieval Economic Thought*. New York: Cambridge University Press.

Wray, William D. 1989. "Japan's Big-Three Service Enterprises in China, 1896–1936." In Peter Duus, Ramon H. Myers, and Mark R. Peattie, eds., *The Japanese Informal Empire in China, 1895–1937*, 31–64. Princeton, NJ: Princeton University Press.

Wright, Tim. 1984. *Coal Mining in China's Economy and Society, 1895–1937*. Cambridge, UK: Cambridge University Press.

Wu Baosan 巫寶三. 1990. *Zhongguo jingji sixiang shi ziliao zuanji* 中国经济思想史资料选辑. Beijing: Zhongguo shehui kexue chubanshe.

Wu Chouzhong 吳籌中. 1989. "Hengbin zhengjin yinhang ji qi zai wo guo faxing de chaopiao" 橫濱正金銀行及其在我國發行的鈔票. *Zhongguo qianbi* 3: 41–44.

Wu, Friedrich, Pan Rongfang, and Wang Di. 2010. "Renminbi's Potential to Become a Global Currency." *China & World Economy* 18.1: 63–81.

Wu Ping 吳平. 1994. *Huanan geming genjudi huobi shi* 華南革命根據地貨幣史. Beijing: Zhongguo jinrong chubanshe.

Wusa yundong shiliao 五卅運動史料. 1981. Comp. by the Shanghai Academy of Social Sciences. Shanghai: Shanghai renmin chubanshe.

Wusi yundong zai Shanghai shiliao xuanji 五四運動在上海史料選輯. 1961. Comp. by the Shanghai Academy of Social Sciences. Shanghai: Shanghai renmin chubanshe.

Xia Dongyuan 夏東元. 1981. *Zheng Guanying zhuan* 鄭觀應傳. Shanghai: Huadong shifan daxue chubanshe.

Xia Nai 夏鼐. 1966. *Hebei Ding xian taji sheli shihanzhong Bosi Sashan chao yinbi* 河北定縣塔基舍利石函中波斯薩珊朝銀幣. *Kaogu* 5: 269–270.

Xia Xiangrong 夏湘蓉 et al. 1980. *Zhongguo gudai kuangye kaifa shi* 中國古代礦業開發史. Beijing: Dizhi chubanshe.

Xiao Maosheng 肖茂盛 and Yang Ming 楊明. 2005. "Wang Mang bizhi gaige ji lishi te dian" 王莽幣制改革及歷史特點. *Hangzhou jinrong yanxiu xueyuan xuebao* 6: 63–64.

Xiao Qing 蕭清. 1984. *Zhongguo gudai huobi shi* 中國古代貨幣史. Beijing: Renmin chubanshe.

Xu Jinxiong 許進雄. 1988. *Zhongguo gudai shehui: wenzi yu renleixue de tou shi* 中國古代社會: 文字與人類學的透視. Taipei: Taiwan shangwu yinshu guan.

Xu Jiqing 徐寄廎. [1932, rep. 1970]. *Shanghai jinrong shi* 上海金融史. Taipei: Xuehai chubanshe.

Xu Ping'an 許平安. 2000. "Zhongguo zhibi zhi fu Zhang Yong jianyu Peng Xinwei xiansheng shangque" 中國紙幣之父張詠兼与彭信威先生商榷. *Xi'an jinrong* 8: 60–62.

Yamane Yukio. 1984. "Reforms in the Service Levy System in the Fifteenth and Sixteenth Centuries." Trans. from the Japanese by Helen Dunstan. In Linda Grove and Christian Daniels, eds., *State and Society in China: Japanese*

Perspectives on Ming-Qing Social and Economic History, 279–310. Tokyo: Tokyo University Press.

Yantielun 鹽鐵論. [rep. 1974]. Shanghai: Shanghai renmin chubanshe.

Yang Bin. 2004. "Horses, Silver, and Cowries: Yunnan in Global Perspective." *Journal of World History* 15.3: 281–322.

———. 2009. *Between Winds and Clouds: The Making of Yunnan (Second Century BCE to Twentieth Century CE)*. New York: Columbia University Press.

———. 2011. "The Rise and Fall of Cowrie Shells: The Asian Story." *Journal of World History* 22.1: 1–25.

Yang Duanliu 楊端六. 1962. *Qingdai huobi jinrong shigao* 清代貨幣金融史稿. Beijing: Shenghuo.

Yang Lien-sheng. 1952. *Money and Credit in China: A Short History*. Cambridge, MA: Harvard University Press.

Yang Yinpu 楊蔭溥. [1930, rep. 1972]. *Shanghai jinrong zuzhi gaiyao* 上海金融組織概要. Taipei: Xuehai chubanshe.

Yao Shuomin 姚朔民. 2003. "Jinchao zai Zhongguo gu zhibi fazhanzhong de diwei" 金鈔在中國古紙幣發展中的地位. *Neimenggu jinrong yanjiu* S1: 45–50.

Yasutomi Ayumu 安冨步. 1997. *Manshūkoku no kinyū* 満州国の金融. Tokyo: Sōbunsha.

———. 1998. *Finance in "Manchukuo."* London: London School of Economics.

Ye Shichang 葉世昌. 1996. "Shuo 'chengti'" 說 "稱提. *Huobi shi yanjiu* 1.56: 7–9.

———. 2002. *Zhongguo jinrong tongshi diyijuan: xian Qin zhi Qing yapian zhanzheng shiqi* 中國金融通史–先秦至清鴉片戰爭時期. Beijing: Zhongguo jinrong chubanshe.

———. 2003. *Gudai Zhongguo jingji sixiang shi* 古代中國經濟思想史. Shanghai: Fudan daxue chubanshe.

Ye Ziqi 葉子奇.[c. 1378, rep. 1959]. *Caomuzi* 草木子. Beijing: Zhonghua shuju.

Yokohama shōkin ginkō zenshi 横浜正金銀行全史. 1980–1984. Tokyo: The Bank of Tokyo.

Yokouchi Masao 横内正雄. 1996. "Dai'ichiji taisen mae ni okeru Tōyō kawase ginkō no soshiki teki kōdō" 第一次大戰前における東洋為替銀行の組織的行動. In Gonjō Yasuo 権上康男, Hirota Akira 廣田明, and Ōmori Hiroyoshi 大森弘喜, eds., *Nijū Seiki shi'hon shugi no seisei: jiyū to soshikika* 20 世紀資本主義の生成: 自由と組織化, 151–185. Tokyo: Tokyo University Press.

Young, Arthur N. 1971. *China's Nation-Building Effort, 1927–1937: The Financial and Economic Record*. Stanford, CA: Hoover Institution Press.

Yu Taishan. 2006. "A History of the Relationships between the Western and Eastern Han, Wei, Jin, Northern and Southern Dynasties and the Western Regions." *Sino-Platonic Papers* 173: 1–167. Retrieved on September 15, 2012, from www.sino-platonic.org/complete/spp173_chinese_dynasties_western0206 .pdf.

Yuan Shuiqing 袁水清. 2003. "Zhongguo gu jindai huobi shi 'zhi zui'" 中國古近代貨幣'之最'. *Xi'an jinrong* 9: 64.

Yuan Yingsheng 袁穎生. 2001. *Taiwan guangfu qian huobi shishu* 臺灣光復前貨幣史述. Nantou: Taiwan Sheng wenxian weiyuanhui.

Yuanshi 元史 [rep. 1976]. 15 vols. Beijing: Zhonghua shuju.

Zelin, Madeleine. 1984. *The Magistrate's Tael: Rationalizing Fiscal Reform in Eighteenth-Century Ch'ing China.* Berkeley: University of California Press.

Zeng Xianming 曾憲明. 2002. "Shanhai shōgyō chochiku ginkō ni miru chūgoku ginkōgyō no keisei katei" 上海商業儲蓄銀行にみる中国銀行業の形成過程 1920~1931年 ["The Establishment of Modern Banking in China: an Analysis of the Loan Business of the Shanghai Commercial and Savings Bank, 1920-1931"]. *Shakai keizai shigaku* 67.5: 71–88.

Zhang Jiaxiang 張家驤. 2001. *Zhongguo huobi sixiang shi* 中國貨幣思想史. Wuhan: Hubei renmin chubanshe.

Zhang Jie 張傑. 2010. *Yinhang zhidu gaige yu renminbi guojihua: lishi, lilun yu zhengce* 銀行制度改革與人民幣國際化: 歷史、理論與政策. Beijing: Zhongguo renmin daxue chubanshe.

Zhang Wuchang 張五常. 2010. "Renminbi yiding yao you ge mao" 人民幣一定要有個錨. *Shangjie pinglun* 9: 98.

Zhang Zhizhong 張志中. 1997. *Zhongguo jindai zhibi, piaoquan tujian* 中國近代紙幣、票券圖鑒. Beijing: Zhishi chubanshe.

Zhao Dexin 趙德馨. 1996. *Chuguo de huobi* 楚國的貨幣. Hankou: Hubei jiaoyu chubanshe.

Zhao Jing 趙靖. 1997. *Zhongguo jingji sixiang tongshi* 中國經濟思想通史. 4 vols. Beijing: Beijing daxue chubanshe.

Zheng Guanying 鄭觀應. [1921, rep.1969]. *Shengshi weiyan houbian* 盛世危言後編. Taipei: Taiwandatong shuju.

———. [rep. 1982]. *Zheng Guanying ji* 鄭觀應集. Shanghai: Shanghai ren min chubanshe.

Zheng Jin 鄭瑾. 2007. *Zhongguo gudai weibi yanjiu* 中國古代偽幣研究. Hangzhou: Zhejiang da xue chu ban she.

Zhongguo di yi jia yinhang 中國第一傢銀行. 1982. Comp. by the Institute of Modern History—Chinese Academy of Social Sciences. Beijing: Zhongguo shehui kexue chubanshe.

Zhongguo guchao tuji 中國古鈔圖輯. 1987. Comp. by the Numismatic Society of Inner Mongolia. Beijing: Zhongguo jinrong chubanshe.

Zhongguo jindai huobi shi ziliao 中國近代貨幣史資料. 1964. Comp. by the People's Bank of China. Beijing: Xinhua.

Zhongguo jindai zhibi shi 中國近代紙幣史. 2001. Comp. by Monetary Society of Jiangsu. Beijing: Zhongguo jinrong chubanshe.

Zhongguo jinrong baike quanshu 中國金融百科全書. 1990. Comp by Huang Da 黃達, Liu Hongru 劉鴻儒, and Zhang Xiao 張肖. Beijing: Jingji guanli chuban she.

Zhongguo lidai huobi 中國歷代貨幣. 1999. Comp. by the People's Bank of China. Beijing: Xinhua chubanshe.

Zhongguo yinhang hangshi 中國銀行行史. 1995. Comp. by the Bank of China. Beijing: Zhongguo jinrong chubanshe.

Zhongguo zhibi biaozhun tulu 中國紙幣標準圖錄. 1994. Comp. by Beijing shi qianbi xuehui 北京市錢幣學會. Beijing: Beijing chubanshe.

Zhonghua minguo huobishi ziliao 中華民國貨幣史資料. 1989. Comp. by the People's Bank of China. Shanghai: Shanghai renmin chubanshe.

Zhou Weirong 周衛榮. 2004. *Zhongguo gudai qianbi hejin chengfen yan jiu* 中國古代錢幣合金成分研究. Beijing: Zhonghua shuju.

———. 2009. "Fan sha gong yi—Zhongguo guadai zhuqianye de zhongda faming" 翻砂工藝: 中國古代鑄錢業的重大發明. *Zhongguo qianbi* 3.106: 14–17.

Zhou Xiaochuan 周小川. 2009. "Guanyu gaige guoji huobi tixi de sikao" 關於改革國際貨幣體系的思考. *Zhongguo jinrong* 7: 8–9.

Zhou Xingji 周行己. [rep. 1935]. *Fuzhi ji* 浮沚集. Shanghai: Shangwu yinshu guan.

Zhu Zhiqian 朱志騫. 1972. *Zhang Jian de shiye zhuzhang* 張謇的實業主張. Taipei: Guoli Taiwan daxue.

Ziben zhuyi guojia zai jiu Zhongguo faxing he liutong de huobi 資本主義國家在舊中國發行和流通的貨幣. 1992. Comp. by the People's Bank of China. Beijing: Wenwu.

Zimmermann, Hubert. 2002. *Money and Security: Troops, Monetary Policy and West Germany's Relations with the United States and Britain, 1950–1971*. Cambridge, UK: Cambridge University Press.

Zou Guishan 鄒桂山. 2011. *Shilun gudai jin yin qianbi* 試論古代金銀錢幣. *Shoucang jie* 2: 79–80.

Zou Jinwen 鄒進文 and Huang Ailan 黃愛蘭. 2010. "Zhongguo gudai de huobi zhengce sixiang: 'chengti' shulun" 中國古代的貨幣政策思想: "稱提" 述論. *Huazhong shifan daxue xuebao* 9: 56–61.

Zweig, David. 2002. *Internationalizing China: Domestic Interests and Global Linkages*. Ithaca, NY: Cornell University Press.

Glossary

bakufu 幕府
banliang 半兩
bao 薄
Bao Shichen 包世臣
baochao 寶鈔
bianmin 便民
bubi 布幣

Cai Zhiding 蔡之定
چاو *čāw*
chanxing 鏟形
chao 鈔
chaoben 鈔本
chaoguan 鈔貫
Chen Zilong 陳子龍
chengti 稱提
Chongzhen 崇禎
Chōsen ginkō 朝鮮銀行
Chu 楚
chupiao dian 出票店

Dai'ichi ginkō 第一銀行
daimyō 大名
dangshiqian 當十錢
Danshui 淡水
daobi 刀幣
Daoguang 道光
daqian 大錢
Daqing yinhang 大清銀行
daquan dangqian 大泉當錢
diao 弔

Dong Biwu 董必武
Dong Zhuo 董卓
Dongsansheng da yinhang 東三省大銀行
duanmo 短陌
duzhi bu 度支部

erizeni 撰錢
Erya 爾雅

fabi 法幣
Fan Ji 范濟
fanpiao 番票
feiqian 飛錢
Fengtian 奉天
fuguo qiangbing 富國強兵
Fuzhiji 浮沚集

gaige kaifang 改革開放
Gao Zecheng 高則誠
Ge Shouli 葛守禮
Gotō Shinpei 後藤新平
Gu Yanwu 顧炎武
guan 貫
guan yinqian hao 官銀錢號
Guannei 關內
guantie 官帖
Guanzi 管子
Guoyu 國語
guifang 櫃坊
guqian 古錢

han 藩
haijin 海禁
Hao Jing 郝敬
hansatsu 藩札
Hanshu 漢書
Hongzhi 弘治
Hu Zhiyu 胡祗遹
Huan Xuan 桓玄
Huang Zongxi 黃宗羲
Huang Zunxian 黃遵憲
Hubu 戶部
Hubu guanpiao 戶部官票
huilüsi 匯率司
huizi 會子
Huizong 徽宗

ji bu ke shi 飢不可食
Jiajing 嘉靖
Jiaqing 嘉慶
Jia Yi 賈誼
jianbian qian 剪邊錢
jianzubu 尖足布
Jiang Chen 蔣臣
Jianqian rifan zhengqian riwang
    奸錢日繁正錢日亡
jiaozi 交子
Jibin 罽賓
jie 界
Jin 金

kaiyuan tongbao 開元通寶
kaizhongfa 開中法
Kamakura 鎌倉
Kangxi 康熙
Kong Linzhi 孔琳之
Kou Jian 寇埅

lanfa 濫發
Li Zhizao 李之藻
lijia 里甲
liang 兩
Liang Qichao 梁啟超
Lin Zexu 林則徐
Liu Dingzhi 劉定之
Lu Bao 魯褒

lupibi 鹿皮幣
Lüshi chunqiu 呂氏春秋
Manshū chūō ginkō 滿洲中央銀行
Manzhou xingye yinhang 滿洲興業
    銀行
maoyi neibu 貿易內部
Matsutaka Masayoshi 松方正義
mingzhi 冥紙
mo 陌
Muromachi 室町

naqian qingjiao 納錢請交
Naigai Wata 內外棉
Nanzhao 南詔
Ni Yuanlu 倪元璐
nianhao 年號

piaohao 票號
piaotie 票帖
pingshoubu 平首布
pingzhunku 平準庫
(K.) *pobusang* 褓負商

Qi Junzao 祁寯藻
qian 錢
Qian Bingdeng 錢秉鐙
Qianbi chuyan 錢幣芻言
qianshu 錢樹
qianzhuang 錢莊
qianhuang 錢荒
Qianlong 乾隆
Qianshenlun 錢神論
qianyin 錢引
qianzhuang 錢莊
Qin 秦
qing 輕
qiyue 契約
Qiu Jun 邱濬

Renminbi 人民幣
Riben guozhi 日本國誌

Shan Qi 單旗
Shang Yang 商鞅
she 賒

Shen Kuo　沈括

Shen Qingzhi　沈慶之

Shen Yue　沈約

Sheng Xuanhuai　盛宣懷

Shenzong　神宗

shi　實

shisatsu　私札

Shu　蜀

shuaishu　衰叔

Shunzhi　順治

siqian　私錢

Song Yingxing　宋應星

Sun Quan　孫權

Suzuki shōten　鈴木商店

Taifu　臺伏

Tiangong kaiwu　天工開物

Tianqi　天啓

ting　鋌

Tokugawa　德川

tongjin　銅禁

tongqian　銅錢

tongyuan　銅元

Tongzhi　同治

Tsūshō kōhō　通商公報

Wanli　萬曆

Wang Anshi　王安石

Wang Fuzhi　王夫之

Wang Liu　王鎏

Wang Maoyin　王茂蔭

Wang Yide　王懿德

wangyan luanzheng　妄言亂政

Wei Yuan　魏源

wen　文

Wubaozhuan　烏寶傳

Wudi　武帝

Wusa　五卅

Wusi　五四

wuzhu　五銖

Xianfeng　咸豐

Xianzong　憲宗

xiaoqian　銷錢

Xixia　西夏

xu　虛

Xu Mei　許楣

xuquan　虛券

Xu Heng　許衡

Xuande　宣德

Xue Tian　薛田

xunqing　徇情

yanyin　鹽引

yanchao　鹽鈔

Yantielun　鹽鐵論

Yang Cheng　楊成

Ye Li　葉李

Ye Ziqi　葉子奇

yi　翼

Yi shi han xu　以實馭虛

yi tiao bianfa　一條變法

yibi qian　蟻鼻錢

yinding　銀錠

yinhao　銀號

yinyuan　銀圓

yinzi　銀子

Yizhou　益州

yingyuan　郢爰

Yokohama shōkin ginkō　橫濱正金銀行

Yongle　永樂

Yongzheng　雍正

Yuan Xie　袁燮

Yu Xiaqing [Yu Qiaqing]　虞洽卿

Yuan Shikai　袁世凱

yuanbao　元寶

yuanqian　圜錢

zaibatsu　財閥

zhan　斬

Zhang Jian　張謇

Zhang Jiuling　張九齡

Zhang Yong　張詠

Zhang Zhidong　張之洞

Zhang Zuolin　張作霖

Zheng Guanying　鄭觀應

Zheng He　鄭和

Zheng Jiefu　鄭介夫

Zhejiang xingye yinhang　浙江興業銀行

zhi 質

zhiji 質劑

zhiyuan 至元

zhizheng jiaochao 至正交鈔

zhong 重

zhongtong yuanbao chao 中統元
  寶鈔

Zhoushan 舟山

Zhou Xingji 周行己

zimu xiangquan 子母相權

Zongli yamen 總理衙門

zumo qian 足陌錢

Index

'Abd al-Malik ibn Marwan, 87, 88, 266n17
Acapulco, 63, 109, 122
Achaemenid Empire: astronomy in, 27; electrum/gold-coin standard in, 31–32; and India, 33, 34; round coinage in, 20, 30, 32, 38; silver ingots in, 32; silver standard in, 31–32
Addis, Charles, 157, 168, 175, 177
Africa: coinage in, 23, 213, 268n61; cowrie in, 109, 113–15; gold in, 6, 87, 88, 100, 101, 102, 103, 107, 108, 113, 114, 115, 139, 265n11; trade with Europe, 77, 87, 100, 102, 103
Agra Bank, 151
Agricola, Georgius, 105
Agricultural Bank of China, 224
Agricultural Development Bank of China, 224
Ahmad Fanakati, 59
Alexanders, 150
Alexander the Great, 20, 33–34, 38
Allen, Martin, 269n64
Allen, Robert, 75, 263n109
American Banknote Company, 80
American-Oriental Bank, 273n54
Amoy. See Xiamen
Anastasius I, 50
Anatolia, 21, 31–32
animal hide, 22, 23, 254n12
Annam, 213, 214
Ansei Treaties, 201
antiforeign boycotts: as anti-British, 14, 168–80, 181, 190, 191, 193–94, 281n99, 282nn106,113, 283n124, 285n143; as anti-Japanese, 14, 185,

190–96, 204–5, 206–7, 209, 245, 286nn23,24, 287n31
Argentina, 150
Aristophanes' *Frogs*, 25, 26
Aristotle: on money, 7
Artabanus, 35
Ashoka, 34
Asian Development Bank, 227
Asian Financial Crisis of 1997, 225
Asiatic Bank, 151
Asiatic Banking Corporation, 154
assaying, 121, 215
assignats, 4, 73, 128
Assyrian Empire, 31, 32
Australia: New South Wales, 75; private bank notes in, 281n
Austro-Hungary, 244
axe-shaped coinage, 23

Babylonian ring money, 31
Babylonian shekels, 32–33
Bactria, 12, 34, 35, 36, 37, 38. *See also* Greco-Bactrian coinage
Ban Chao, 35
Ban Gu's *Hanshu*, 36
bank deposits: in Chinese banks, 132, 140–41, 147, 169, 189, 282n102; in England, 80, 140; in India, 143; relationship to economic modernization, 141, 145, 147, 245; in United States, 145; YSB deposits in China, 188, 189, 190, 191, 192, 193, 196, 208, 286n14
Bank of Abyssinia, 275n5
Bank of Australasia, 149
Bank of Beihai, 220
Bank of China, 170, 184, 189, 190, 220, 224

Bank of Chosen (BoCS), 183, 202, 287n46; vs. BoTW, 204–5, 208–9; deposits in China, 200, 208; during May 4th Movement, 204–5; note issuance by, 185, 197–99, 200–201, 204, 207, 208, 287n46, 288n49, 289n68; reserve requirements, 198, 204, 207, 289n68; Seoul branch, 200; vs. YSB, 185, 187, 191, 192, 198, 207, 208, 209
Bank of Communications, 220
Bank of England, 4, 48, 81, 153, 177, 182, 259n29; bond issuance by, 98; bullion deposits, 73; bullion reserves held by, 73–74, 78, 253n33; and national debt, 48, 72–73, 79, 98–99; note issuance by, 72–74, 79–81, 98–99, 253n33
Bank of France, 253n33
Bank of Hindustan, 151
Bank of India, 151, 276n19
Bank of Japan (BoJ), 185, 186, 197–98, 204
Bank of Southern Hebei, 220
Bank of Taiwan (BoTW), 183, 185, 189, 192, 201–6, 288n56; vs. BoCS, 204–5, 208–9; deposits, 204, 205–6, 208; during May 4th Movement, 204–5, 209; note issuance by, 202–6, 207, 208, 289nn65–67; reserve requirements, 204, 205, 207, 289n68
Bank of the Northeast, 220
Bank of Tokyo, 285n7
Bank of Tokyo-Mitsubishi UFJ, 227
Bank of Western India, 151, 155, 276n17
Banno Junji, 286n23
Banque de L'Indochine, 150, 158, 166, 275n5, 276n32, 280n85
Banque Industrielle de Chine, 154, 286n25
Banque Nationale de Belgique, 186
Banque Russo-Asiatique, 154, 158
Bao Shichen, 126
Barclays, 149
Barlow, A. H., 173–74, 177–78, 179, 180, 283n120, 284n141
Barnard, Noel, 256n28
Baster, A. S. J., 276n27
Bayerische Hypotheken und Wechselbank, 144

Beijing, 59, 65, 76, 111, 135, 157, 158, 161, 186, 278n51; during May 4th Movement, 192; during May 30th Movement, 281n100; PBC headquarters in, 14, 224; YSB note circulation in, 187
Beijing ribao, 178
Beiyang period, 158–59
bent-bar coinage, 32, 33, 34
Bentley, Jerry, 15
Bernholz, Peter, 8, 253n26
bills of exchange. *See* exchange banking; exchange bills
Biringuccio, Vannoccio, 105
Black Death, 9
block-printing technology, 61–62
Bodin, Jean: on money creation, 4–5
Bopearachchi, Osmund, 257n52
Bordo, Michael D., 253n26
Boulton, Matthew, 84–85
Bradbury, Wilkinson & Co., 80
Bramante, Donato, 103
Brazil, 150
Bretton Woods monetary system, 6, 216, 218, 221, 228, 229, 236; collapse of, 2–4, 222, 246, 247
Brewer, John: on fiscal-military states, 72
British American Tobacco Company (BAT), 172
British colonialism, 72–73, 111, 112; British India, 6, 143, 151, 152, 154, 274n78, 276n28; vs. Japanese colonialism, 202, 208, 244–45
British East India Company. *See* East India Company (EIC)
British overseas banks, 137, 162, 276n28; banknotes issued by, 7, 8, 11, 14, 73–74, 122, 129, 130, 133, 135, 136, 140, 148–54, 155–56, 158, 159, 160, 163–68, 169, 172–82, 186, 193, 194, 196, 201, 204, 209, 245, 275n4, 276nn23,31,32, 278n59, 279nn70,71, 280nn76,80,85, 281nn94,99, 283nn120,124, 284nn134,141; vs. domestic banks, 149; and entrepôt trade, 152–53, 164–65; failures of, 151–52, 163–64, 182; vs. French overseas banks, 153; vs. Japanese banks, 183, 185, 186, 188, 205, 207, 209, 244–45; during May 30th Movement,

167–68, 169–80, 193, 194, 281n100, 282nn106,113, 283n122; reserve requirements, 135, 150, 163–68, 171, 174–77, 178, 179, 182, 207, 244–45, 276n31, 279nn70,71, 280n83; Treasury regulations on, 149–50, 152, 153, 154, 163–64, 166–67, 174–77, 178, 182, 204, 276n31, 280n76, 283n120
Bronze Age in China, 20–23, 27, 256n28
Brundisium, 41
Buddhism, 34, 35, 37, 38, 51, 65, 69
bullion flows, 4–5, 9, 10, 53, 61, 244; and Latin American silver deposits, 14, 19–20, 63, 64, 70–71, 78, 95, 101–2, 103, 106–7, 109, 112, 113, 116–17, 121, 138–39, 214, 215, 216, 235, 262n81; during Ming dynasty, 63, 65, 66–67; during Qing dynasty, 140, 152, 157; relevance to Great Divergence debate, 84, 86, 87, 91, 95, 96, 98, 100–102, 107–8, 109, 110, 111–12, 113, 115, 116–17; and West Africa, California and Nevada silver deposits, 6, 139
Burdekin, Richard C. K., 13, 225, 288n51
Burma, 152, 213
Butterfield, Swire and Co., 160
Byzantine Empire, 50, 86, 212, 216; copper coinage in, 87–88; gold nomisma (bezant), 88–89, 100; Pecheneg invasions, 88

Cai Yurong, 262n90
Cai Zhiding, 125
California School historians, 13–14, 83–84, 85
call loans, 44, 155, 276n27
Cambodia, 213
Cameron, Rondo, 264n116
Canada, 74–75; Quebec, 245
capital markets, 71, 210, 211, 237
Carolingian era, 84, 86
Carolus silver dollar, 74–75, 106–7, 116–17, 214, 215, 216, 241, 262n81
Cassis, Youssef, 70, 149
casting: of Chinese bronze coinage, 21–22, 24–25, 26, 27, 28, 29, 30–31, 38–39, 41, 42, 43, 58, 60, 61, 62, 63, 66, 67–68, 69, 85, 92, 93, 94, 109, 121, 137, 138, 213, 214, 216–17, 219,

236, 240, 241; of copper coinage, 12, 34, 37; of iron, 21–22, 37, 45, 46, 105–6; of lead coinage, 45; of silver coinage, 33–34. *See also* minting
Caterpillar, 227
CBIAC. *See* Chartered Bank of India Australia and China
Central America, 245
Central Bank of "Manchukuo," 199, 200–201
Central Bank of the Republic of China, 14
Central Bank of Western India, 151
central banks, 7, 130, 154, 182, 218, 224, 232, 245–46; and money supply, 148, 220, 221
Ceylon, 112, 152, 164, 213, 214–15, 290n14
Changchun, 191
Chartalism, 7, 252n23
Chartered Bank of India Australia and China (CBIAC): banknotes issued by, 152, 155, 158, 165, 166, 169, 172–73, 179, 180–81, 182, 193, 276n32, 279nn70,71, 280n85, 281n99, 284n141; during May 30th Movement, 169–70, 171–73, 282nn106,113, 283n121, 284n141; reserves, 165, 182, 279nn70,71, 280n83; Royal Charter of, 151, 155
Chartered Mercantile Bank of India, London and China (CMBILC), 151, 275n4
Chen Chau-nan, 137
Ch'ên, Jerome, 127
Chen Xiaoli, 226, 231, 291n67
Chen Yulu, 291n62
Chen Zhiwu, 13, 235
Chen Zilong, 68
Cheng Linsun, 13
Cheung, Steven Ng-Sheong, 234
Cheung Yin-Wong, 226, 231, 291n67
China Association, 172
China Construction Bank, 224
Chinese-American Bank of Commerce, 154
Chinese banks, 182, 187, 285n5; Bank of China, 170, 184, 189, 190, 220, 224; Central Bank of the Republic of China, 14; deposits in, 132, 140–41, 147, 169, 189, 282n102; failures of, 131, 135, 136, 139, 146, 186, 272n39;

Chinese banks (*continued*)
in Fuzhou, 130–34; Imperial Bank of
China, 161–62; and Japanese banks,
183, 184, 199–200; logos of, 14, 15,
23; during May 30th Movement,
169–70, 173, 178, 245, 281n98,
282n102; notes issued by, 128–29,
137, 187, 204, 218, 220; People's
Bank of China, 14, 220, 226, 228,
291nn44,66; provincial banks, 161,
162; relations with foreign banks,
122, 154–55, 183, 184, 199–200;
reserves, 159–60; Shanxi banks
(*piaohao*), 132–33, 135–36, 273n50.
See also money shops; People's Bank
of China
Chinese bronze coinage, 20–26, 42,
57, 136, 216–17, 254n7, 255n19,
256nn38,39, 260nn34,46; in Chinese
statecraft, 43, 50–52, 66, 90, 91, 109,
128, 217, 240, 241, 242, 266n25;
coin famines (*qianhuang*), 49, 50–51,
57, 79, 240, 241, 259n32; as copper "cash," 47, 49, 51, 54, 67, 85,
86, 90, 91, 93, 95, 96, 99, 101, 105,
108–9, 110, 111, 126, 128, 131, 132,
133–35, 137–39, 140, 146, 157, 211,
213, 216, 217, 236, 241, 259nn27,30,
261n79, 265n7, 266n25, 267n41,
272n41; heavy vs. light coinage, 25,
26, 49–50, 54, 66, 67–68, 93, 129,
241; during Jin dynasty, 55–56; during Ming dynasty, 61, 63, 64, 65–69,
81, 93–95, 213, 214, 215, 241, 242,
244; during Northern Song dynasty,
10, 11, 45–46, 48–49, 50, 51, 65–66,
93, 96–97, 104–5, 215, 219, 290n11;
origin of *banliang* design (round with
square holes), 22–23; vs. precious-
metal coinage, 11, 23, 25, 26, 38,
90, 95, 99, 102, 216, 217, 239–40;
during Qing dynasty, 63, 64, 66,
94, 96, 121, 127, 132, 133, 135, 136,
137, 138, 140, 146, 147, 156, 159,
199, 215, 241, 245, 259n32, 267n41;
round shape of, 15, 19, 20–21, 22–25,
26, 27–31, 32, 33, 34, 36, 38–40,
106, 254n13, 255n20, 256nn30,33,
257n52; short strings of cash (*duanmo*), 51; during Southern Song
dynasty, 50–51, 54, 58, 61, 62,
65–66, 212–13, 214, 241, 244;
square holes in, 15, 22–23, 28, 29,

85, 110, 138, 214; strings of 1,000
bronze coins (*guan/diao*), 47, 51,
58, 60, 67, 85, 105, 121, 132, 138,
217, 259n27, 261n63, 261n79; supply of coins, 10, 46, 48–49, 50–51,
57, 63, 79, 92, 93–94, 96–97, 98,
104–5, 125, 138–39, 159, 215, 240,
241, 259n32; during Tang dynasty,
37, 212, 254n13; as *tongyuan*, 85,
110, 121, 138; usage in India, 212,
213, 290n14; usage in Japan, 63, 96,
212–14; during Yuan dynasty, 58,
60–61, 217, 260n50. *See also daqian*
("big cash")
Chinese Communist Party, 6, 156,
219–20, 221, 223; Central Commission for Financial Affairs, 226;
Open Door Policy, 223; policies
regarding Hong Kong, 226; Regulatory Commission, 226. *See
also* People's Republic of China
(PRC)
Chinese Patriotic Tobacco Co., 176
Chinese statecraft: bronze coinage
in, 43, 50–52, 66, 90, 91, 109, 128,
217, 240, 241, 242, 266n25; *daqian*
in, 128, 242; dynastic decline in,
55; mining in, 66, 92, 240, 262n90;
paper money in, 26, 55, 66–67, 124,
128, 241, 242; peasants in, 25–26,
81, 242; state monopoly over coinage
in, 25–26, 90
Chongzhen Emperor, 94, 124–25
Chu, kingdom of, 22, 25, 29, 114,
254n10
Churchill, Winston, 175–76
Cibot, Pierre-Martial, 76, 264n128
Clapham, J. H., 73, 264n120
Clark, Gregory: on cost of capital, 75
clay coinage, 45
clipping, 31, 39, 42, 75, 85, 89, 101,
104, 106
CMBILC. *See* Chartered Mercantile
Bank of India, London and China
Cobbett, William, 67
Cochran, Sherman, 172
coffee, 70, 115
Coggan, Philip, 246
coin famines (*qianhuang*), 49, 50–51,
57, 79, 240, 241, 259n32
Columbus, Christopher, 101
Colvin & Co., 150
Commercial Bank of India, 151

commercial taxes, 70, 72
commodity money, 31, 43, 267n40, 290n11
Comptoir d'Escompte, 151
Confucianism, 22, 43–44, 51, 52, 57, 90, 217; neo-Confucianism, 48, 50, 67, 69, 95, 260n41
Constantine IX Monomachus, 88
Continental Bank Note Company, 80
convertibility, 64, 93, 272n32; convertible paper money, 4, 52–53, 54–55, 73, 81, 126, 130, 133, 144, 152, 154, 187, 199–200, 204, 207, 217, 218, 242, 263n97, 278n59; inconvertible paper money, 3, 55, 59, 60, 62, 65, 73, 78, 96, 125, 128, 143–44, 199–200, 221, 263n97, 271n17, 275n82; pound-gold convertibility, 4, 73; of RMB, 7, 211, 221, 222, 227, 231, 233–34, 246; U.S. dollar-gold convertibility, 2–4, 222, 246, 247; yen-gold convertibility, 6, 184, 186, 197, 201, 207, 208. *See also* exchange rates
Coole, Arthur B., 256n30
copper: Chinese regulations on, 10, 23, 48, 50, 92, 109, 240; exchange rate for silver, 110, 111, 114, 121, 126, 137; exported from Europe to Africa, 100, 102, 103, 115; mining of, 12, 21, 23, 41, 45, 48, 50, 86, 96, 97, 100, 101, 103, 109–10, 114, 125, 240, 259n32, 265n137, 267n41; price of, 93, 97
copper coinage: in Byzantine Empire, 87–88; casting of, 12, 34, 37; in China, 22, 25, 212; *duiten*, 214–15; as European token money, 25, 106, 107, 138; in France, 102, 107; in India, 34, 62, 79, 114–15, 219, 257n54, 269n74; in Ottoman Empire, 110, 270n85; *picis*, 214–15; in Rome, 217, 268n47; in Spain, 78–79, 101, 102, 106, 107, 239–40; in Sweden, 77–78, 81, 239–40. *See also* Chinese bronze coinage
Cornish, Sir Montagu, 171–72
counterfeiting. *See* forgery
counting houses (*guifang*), 44
cowrie: in Africa, 109, 113–15; in China, 21, 22, 23, 24, 28, 29, 51, 108, 109, 114, 213, 254nn8,10, 270n101; trade in, 108, 113–15, 116; in Yunnan, 24, 108, 109, 114, 213

credit economies, 44, 47, 53, 54, 72–73, 79, 80–81, 147
Cribb, Joe, 13
Crimean War, 144
Crisp, Olga, 275n82
Crusades, 100, 266n19
Cruttenden & Co., 150
cupro-nickel (*baitong*), 12
Curzon, George, 176
Cyprus, 41
Cyrus the Great, 34

Dai Zhiqiang, 28
"Dai Fook" [*taifu*] dollar, 272n40
Dai'ichi ginkō, 197, 287n40
Dairen, 186
Daoguang Emperor, 126, 129
Daoism, 51, 65
daqian ("big cash"), 50–51, 67–68, 125, 127–28, 140; in Chinese statecraft, 128, 242; forgery of, 66, 67, 68, 93; as inflationary, 49, 126
Darius, 34
David Sassoon & Co., 273n48
Da Vinci, Leonardo, 39
debasement: in Canada, 74–75; in China, 12, 25–26, 39, 42–43, 44, 49, 75, 81, 86, 90, 91, 93, 94, 95, 108, 110, 127, 133, 159, 160, 214, 217, 239, 240, 242, 244, 248; in Europe, 3, 4–5, 12, 15, 25, 26, 31, 39, 50, 53, 72, 78, 81, 86–87, 88–90, 91, 93, 98–99, 101, 104, 107, 108, 217, 239, 242, 244, 248; finance of war through, 3, 25, 26, 88; of gold dinars, 100; Great Debasement, 89–90, 98–99, 117; in Ottoman Empire, 107, 270n85; relevance to Great Divergence debate, 88, 89–90, 91, 92–93, 98–99, 117
deer-hide currency, 23, 66, 125, 140
Defoe, Daniel: *Complete English Tradesman*, 111; on global trade, 111; *New Voyage Round the World*, 111
Deng Xiaoping, 223
deniers, 87, 88, 99
Dennys, N. B., 131
design convergence, 24, 34, 39–40
design diffusion, 24–25, 32–38
Deutsch-Asiatrische Bank, 150, 154, 158
De Vries, Jan, 265n2

Di Cosmo, Nicola, 36–37
Diodorus of Sicily, 265n11
Discourse on the States (Guoyu), 25, 26
Dong Biwu, 220
Dong Zhuo, 42
Doolittle, Rev. Justus, 127, 133, 134–35
double liability, 163, 279n72
Du Xuncheng, 170
Dudley, Dud, 106
Du Halde, J. B.: on Chinese coinage, 94–95; *Description of the Empire of China*, 94–95
Dunstan, Helen, 91
Dutch East India Company (VOC), 80, 112, 114, 214–15
Duus, Peter, 287n40

Eastern Exchange Banks. *See* British overseas banks
Eastern Han dynasty, 85, 258n6; coinage during, 42–43, 93, 213, 242, 254n5
East India Company (EIC), 4, 150–51, 155, 182, 269n73
Ederer, R. J., 251n6
Edkins, Joseph, 141
Eichengreen, Barry, 5–6, 231
Einaudi, Luigi, 99
El Dorado, 101
electrum coinage, 31, 32
Elvin, Mark, 47, 258n18, 259nn25,28,33, 260n39, 265n2, 267n31, 268n42, 278n57
England: Alfred the Great, 89; Charles I, 80; vs. China, 47–48, 73–74, 82, 117, 140; vs. Continental Europe, 86, 102, 117, 243; debasement in, 89–90, 98–99, 102, 104, 117, 243, 244; East India Company (EIC), 4, 150–51, 155, 182, 269n73; Edward the Confessor, 89; Edward VI, 89; Elizabeth I, 105; foreign currency in, 91–92, 266n26; foreign trade, 70, 111, 151, 152, 171, 243–44; Glorious Revolution, 70; gold coinage in, 42, 85, 104–5; Great Debasement, 89–90, 98–99, 117; Henry VIII, 89; interest rates in, 48, 72, 80, 245, 264n128; London financial industry, 16, 182; London Mint, 49, 80, 89, 259n32; manufacturing in, 111; merchants in, 80, 92; mining in, 86, 105; minting in, 31, 49, 80, 84, 88, 89, 98,

99, 103, 104–5, 106, 110, 112, 116, 117, 259n32, 269n64; monetary policies in, 89–90, 98–99, 244; national debt, 5, 48, 70, 72–73, 74, 78, 79, 92, 98–99, 117, 218, 243, 264n134; paper money in, 67, 70, 71–74, 79–81, 83–84, 243, 264n116; Parliament, 76, 81; promissory notes in, 80; vs. Scotland, 79; silver pennies in, 42, 49, 87, 88, 89–90, 92, 98, 99, 104, 259n32; standardization of coinage in, 89, 104; vs. Sweden, 78; taxation in, 47, 48, 70, 81, 92, 93, 98, 243; trade with China, 111. *See also* Bank of England; British overseas banks
erizeni (shroffing in Japan), 214
Erya, 29
Ethiopia, 149; Bank of Abyssinia, 275n5; gold coinage in, 103; Menilek II, 104; round coinage (*aksum*) in, 23; silver coinage in, 103–4
euro, 2, 7, 210, 231, 232, 247
European banks, 77–78, 122, 148–50, 154, 156–58, 285n7. *See also* British overseas banks
European Monetary Union, 231
European Union (EU): economic conditions, 210
examination system, 51
exchange banking, 151–52, 155, 163–68, 188
Exchange Bank of China, 285n5
exchange bills, 51, 66, 71, 79, 150, 151–52, 155, 188, 277n38
exchange rates, 45, 95, 185, 211, 223–25; bronze-silver, 41, 267n38; copper-silver, 110, 121, 194; gold-cowrie, 115; gold-silver, 31–32, 88, 90, 91, 102, 104–5, 110–11, 115, 152, 200; Hong Kong dollar-U.S. dollar, 222, 223, 229; manipulation in the West, 26, 91, 92, 242; Mexican silver dollar-Chinese copper "cash," 131; Mexican silver dollar-rupee, 274n78; RMB-Hong Kong dollar, 223, 228; RMB-older Chinese currencies, 220, 221; RMB-U.S. dollar, 221, 222, 223, 224, 227; RMB-yen, 228; yen-U.S. dollar, 222, 228, 229
Export-Import Bank of China, 224

fabi reform, 181, 190, 194, 204, 218
famines, 91, 266n25

Fan Ji, 66, 67, 125, 140
Farmers' Bank of Northwest China, 220
Fatimids, 100, 266n19
feiqian (flying cash), 44–45, 260n46
Feng Sufu tombs, 37
Fengtian dollar, 199–200
fiat currency, 39, 55, 60, 73, 243, 261n72; and collapse of Bretton Woods monetary system, 2–4, 222, 246, 247; *fabi* reform, 181, 190, 194, 204, 218; universalization of, 3, 7, 16, 236, 244
financial speculators, 226, 230, 235
Financial Times, 283n121
First Emperor, 22, 29, 36, 38
Fisher, Irving, 3
fish-hook (*larin*) coinage, 24
Five Dynasties era, 44, 45, 53, 56, 78–79, 240–41, 255n20
Flandreau, Marc, 231
flat-plate coinage, 22, 25
Florentine banking, 76
Florentine gold florins, 100, 104
flying cash (*feiqian*), 44–45, 260n46
Flynn, Dennis Owen, 13, 109
foreign currency substitution, 5, 7, 89, 90, 91–92, 93, 121, 129, 158, 240–41, 242
Foreign Exchange Certificates (FECs), 225
foreign investment in China, 223, 224, 225, 226–27, 234
foreign trade, 104, 155, 219; China-England trade, 70, 111, 151, 152, 171; China-Japan trade, 63, 96, 98, 109, 110, 186, 191, 212–13, 214, 236, 281n94; in cowrie, 108, 113–15, 116; of England, 70, 111, 151, 152, 171, 243–44; Europe-Africa trade, 77, 87, 100, 102, 103; Japan-West trade, 6, 208; opium/Opium Wars, 70, 113, 121, 125, 126, 127, 140, 150, 151, 152, 160, 184; in porcelain, 116, 122, 212; relationship to joint-stock firms, 76; relationship to RMB, 223, 224, 225, 226–27, 228, 233, 235, 246, 291n67; role of gold dinars in, 88, 100; role of Spanish-American dollar in, 63, 106–7, 215, 216, 235; role of U.S. dollar in, 245–46; in silk, 14, 122, 151, 152, 215, 216; Adam Smith on, 71; in tea, 14, 70, 102, 122, 151,

152, 201, 202, 215, 216, 259n21. *See also* bullion flows
forgery: of Chinese coinage, 26, 43, 62, 65–66, 67, 68, 93–94, 95, 97, 214, 241; counterforgery measures, 39, 80, 85, 97, 110, 130, 131, 143–44, 240; of cowrie, 114; of European coinage, 107, 267n37, 268n47, 269n72; of paper money, 46, 80, 143–44, 159, 168, 194, 221, 242, 267n30, 281n94
Forrest, Andrew, 226–27
Fortescue Metals, 226–27
Fortune, Robert, 131, 272n33
France: *assignats* issued during Revolution, 4, 73, 128; banks in, 285n7; vs. Britain, 243; vs. China, 145; copper coinage in, 102, 107; debasement of coinage in, 89, 90, 102; gold coinage in, 104; Louis XV, 8; mints in, 99, 103, 106; monetary policies, 2, 8, 99, 102, 104, 107, 144–45; overseas banks, 153, 154; paper money in, 72, 144–45; Philip IV, 104; silver coinage in, 104; taxation in, 93
Frank, Herbert, 19–20
Franks, 86, 87, 88
free banking, 130–31, 145, 146, 155, 202, 246, 252n23
Friedman, Milton, 3
Fuggars, 98
Fujian province, 203–4
Fung, Edmund S. K., 191
Fuzhou, 127, 130–36, 146, 272nn33,39, 273n54, 289n65

G20, 227, 230, 237
Galbraith, John K.: on inflation, 8, 9
Galor, Oded, 265n2
Gao Zecheng's *Wubaozhuan*, 61
Gaykhatu, 61
Genghis Khan, 56, 62
Genoa, 100, 101
Germany: banks in, 285n7; vs. China, 144, 145; paper money in, 144, 145; silver coinage in, 6, 252n20
Ge Shouli, 94
Giráldez, Arturo, 13, 109
global financial crisis of 2008, 2, 9, 227, 232, 233
globalization, 15, 19–20, 23, 39, 79, 215, 227

global reserve currency: pound sterling as, 16, 210, 219, 231, 246, 247; requisites for, 211, 226, 230–31, 232; RMB as candidate for, 1, 2, 7, 14, 16, 210–11, 219, 230–31, 232, 245, 246–47, 291n67; U.S. dollar as, 7, 210, 229–30, 231–33, 234, 235, 236, 237, 247, 291n62

Goa, 112

gold: in Africa, 6, 87, 88, 100, 101, 102, 103, 107, 108, 113, 114, 115, 139, 265n11; and Buddhism, 69; flat golden plates (*yingyuan*), 22; as global commodity, 233, 234; gold ingots, 23; from Latin America, 101, 113, 116; mining of, 6, 41, 78, 87, 88, 96, 98, 265n11; monetary use in China, 11–12, 23, 42, 239, 258n6; during Shang dynasty, 21. *See also* bullion flows

gold coinage, 50, 53, 212, 213, 255n19, 266n17; Byzantine gold nomisma, 88–89, 100; daric, 32, 33, 34; dinar, 88, 100, 115, 266n19; in Europe, 25, 31, 36, 42, 64, 73, 78, 85, 86–87, 88–89, 90, 91, 95, 99–102, 100, 104–5, 107, 108, 117, 239, 242, 255n19; in India, 214, 236, 257n54, 269n74; in Japan, 96, 142, 216, 288n60; *larin* coins, 24; lira, 143; minted in England, 42, 85, 104–5; minted in Ethiopia, 103; solidi, 42, 86–87, 88; tremissis, 86–87, 88

gold convertibility: exchange rate for silver, 31–32, 88, 90, 91, 102, 104–5, 110–11, 115, 152, 200; gold standard, 2–3, 4, 5–7, 13, 31–32, 78, 89, 92, 99–102, 104–5, 107–8, 116, 117, 129, 139, 144, 160, 184, 186, 197, 201, 202, 203, 215, 217, 222, 236, 246, 252nn15,20, 275n82; of U.S. dollar, 2–4, 6, 7, 222

Goldsmith, R. W., 143

Good, Irene, 255n18

Goslar, 107

Gotō Shinpei, 184

Great Debasement, 89–90, 98–99, 117

Great Depression, 200

Great Divergence debate, 84, 86, 87, 91, 95, 96, 98, 100–102, 107–8, 109, 110, 111–12, 113, 115, 116–17

Greco-Bactrian coinage, 22, 30, 33, 34, 36, 37, 38, 257n52

Greece, 232, 239, 244; privately-issued bankotes in, 275n1; round coinage in, 20, 38, 256n39; silver drachma, 266n17; silver tetradrachm, 32, 37; Venetian coinage in, 101, 244

Greif, Avner, 9

Gresham's Law, 5, 25, 45, 252n16

groschen/groats/grossi, 93

Gu Yanwu, 68–69

Guangzhou, 121, 151, 156, 180, 276nn17,27, 277n38

Guanzi, 26, 255n27, 260n34

guifang (counting houses), 44

guilder, 215

Guo Yuqing, 188, 190–91

haiguan bank, 133

Hainan, 139

Halifax, Nova Scotia, 74

Hangzhou, 55, 161

Hankou, 161, 186, 194, 287n34, 289n65

Hao Jing, 68

Hao Yen-p'ing, 145, 272n41, 273n48

Harbin, 186

Hayek, Friedrich, 7, 130, 252n23

Headrick, Daniel R., 112

heavy vs. light coinage, 25, 26, 49–50, 54, 66, 67–68, 93, 129, 241

Hebei Province, 220

Helleiner, Eric: on foreign currencies, 5, 84

Hellenistic coinage, 33–34, 36, 37, 212, 251n6

Henan, 135; Jiaozuo, 169

High Imperialism, 19

Ho Hon-wai, 159

Hobson, John M., 19–20; *The Eastern Origins of Western Civilization*, 20

Hong Jianguan, 169, 282n102

Hong Kong, 151, 202, 276n17, 280n81; copper cash in, 157; Lunar New Year in, 166, 167, 280n80, 281n87; mint in, 110; PRC policies regarding, 226, 227, 230–31, 234, 237; private banknotes in, 79, 148, 163, 164, 165, 283n120; RMB-denominated deposits in, 231; RMB-denominated/"dim sum" bonds issued in, 227, 230; silver dollars in, 156–57, 167–68; U.S. dollar-denominated deposits in, 231

Hongkong and Shanghai Banking Corporation (HSBC), 170, 277n38; banknotes issued by, 8, 155, 157, 160, 163, 164, 165, 166–68, 172–79, 182, 186, 196, 276n32, 279nn70,71, 280n80, 283nn120,124, 284nn134,141; Hong Kong Ordinances, 163; and Imperial Bank of China, 161; during May 30th Movement, 168, 173–77, 178–80, 184n133, 282n113, 283nn121,122,124, 284nn134,141; reserves, 161, 182, 279nn70,71; Royal Charter of, 151, 155; Shanghai branch, 173–74, 176–78, 179, 180–81, 193; vs. Yokohama Specie Bank, 185, 186, 189, 190, 193, 196, 209

Hong Kong Blue Book, 165

Hong Kong dollar, 177, 222, 223, 284nn133,141

Hongzhi Emperor, 65–66, 94

hot money, 226, 230, 235

Hou Houji, 271nn4,15

Howgego, Christopher J., 251n1

HSBC. *See* Hongkong and Shanghai Banking Corporation

Hsiao Liang-lin, 143, 144, 274n78

Hu Jichuang, 251n7

Hua Jueming, 27, 29, 256n30

Huainan region, 55

Huan Xuan, 43

Huang, Ray, 259n30

Huang Zongxi, 68, 69, 125

Huang Zunxian, 129, 142

Huizong Emperor, 51

Hume, David: on bullion hoarding, 4

Hu Zhiyu, 60

Ibn Battuta, 3, 103

ICBC, 224

Imperial Bank of China, 161–62, 189, 190

Imperial Maritime Customs (IMC), 70, 135–36, 140; *Decennial Reports*, 131–32

India: and Achaemenid Empire, 33, 257n52; Alexander's invasion, 33–34, 38; and Bactria, 37, 38; bent-bar coinage, 32, 33, 34; Bombay, 188; British India, 6, 143, 151, 152, 154, 274n78, 276n28; Calcutta agency houses, 150; Chinese bronze coinage in, 212, 213, 290n14; copper coinage in, 34, 62, 79, 114–15, 219, 257n54, 269n74; cotton textiles, 116; cowrie in, 114; Delhi sultanate, 62;

Gandhara, 34, 35–36; gold coinage in, 214, 236, 257n54, 269n74; government rupee bonds, 164; Gupta Empire, 269n74; Kushan empire, 34, 35–36, 37, 38, 39; Magadha, 33, 34; Mauryan era, 34; mining in, 27; money supply under British rule, 143, 274n78; Mughals, 111–12, 117, 264n112, 269n74; opium grown in, 152, 160; paper money in, 153; pepper in, 101; private-order payment instruments (*hundi*) in, 71; punch-marked coinage, 31, 32, 33, 34; rectangular coinage in, 33, 34; Roman coins in, 212, 257n54; round coinage in, 20, 30, 33, 34, 38, 257n52; silver coinage in, 31, 32–33, 112, 117, 213, 214, 236, 257n54, 269n74; silver imports, 107, 116; taxation in, 264n112; Vedic literature, 32

Industrial Bank of Chosen (IBC), 197, 208, 287n43

Industrial Revolution, 14, 70, 83, 91, 113, 145, 243

inflation, 3, 5, 23, 62, 78, 110, 130, 218, 234, 247, 248, 252n23; *daqian* ("big cash") as inflationary, 49, 126; fear of, 8, 9; Galbraith on, 8, 9; and global reserve currency, 232; in Japan, 129; during Ming dynasty, 11, 63, 65, 67; paper money as inflationary, 11, 59–60, 61, 63, 65, 67, 78, 124, 126, 127, 129, 146, 147, 160; during Qing dynasty, 124, 126, 127, 159; in Republican China, 218; and RMB, 211, 221, 224, 230, 234; during Yuan dynasty, 59–60, 61, 65

inscriptions on coinage, 26, 37, 103, 197; in China, 26, 31, 85, 94–95, 216; in Europe, 94–95, 112, 216, 239

interest rates, 5, 9, 132, 136, 152–53, 234, 264n127; in China vs. Europe, 71, 75–76, 145, 264n128, 276n27; in England, 48, 72, 80, 245, 264n128

International Banking Corporation, 154

International Finance Corporation (IFC), 227

International Monetary Fund (IMF), 237, 252n17

Ionian-Greeks, 30

Iran: Mongol rule in, 56–57, 61–62; Naksh-i-Rustam, 34; Nush-i-Jan, 31, 32; paper money in, 61–62; Persepolis, 34; Sassanid Empire, 37, 87, 212, 257n49
Ireland, 232
iron: cast-iron weaponry, 21; iron coinage, 11, 25, 26, 45–46, 49, 51, 52, 55, 56, 58, 77, 93, 128, 133, 255n20
Islamic world, 61, 71, 87–88, 99, 102, 107, 214, 216; gold dinars in, 88, 100, 115, 266n19
Italian city-states, 100–101, 102, 104, 112–13, 263nn104,108, 269n65
Italian mints, 103
Ito Takotoshi, 233

jade discs and coinage, 28, 29, 256nn33,39
Japan, 28, 59, 274n72; banks in, 122, 153, 154, 197, 203, 205, 285n7; British colonialism vs. colonial policies of, 202, 208, 244–45; vs. China, 6, 52, 96, 129, 139, 142–43, 147, 183, 184, 212–13, 232; coinage in, 63–64, 96, 139, 142, 212–14, 216, 236, 262n82, 267n40, 288n60; copper mining in, 79, 96, 101, 109, 114; economic conditions, 190, 193, 196, 203, 205, 210, 232; foreign banks in, 153, 165–66; foreign currency in, 142; gold mining in, 96, 98, 216; government bonds in, 129; inflation in, 129; Kamakura era, 212–13, 290n11; Kobe, 166; Lost Decade of 1990s, 232; and Marco Polo Bridge Incident, 201; Meiji reforms, 52, 129, 142; minting in, 197, 288n60; monetary policies in, 6, 7, 15–16, 96, 129, 139, 142–43, 144, 183, 184, 185–87, 197, 201, 202, 203, 207–8, 209, 213–14, 244–45, 288n60; Muromachi era, 63–64, 98, 213, 214, 262n82; Osaka mint, 197, 288n60; paper money in, 7, 80, 96, 129, 142–43, 184, 185–86, 204, 281n94; recession of 1920s, 190, 193, 196, 203, 205; Samurai class, 142; silver mining in, 64, 96, 98, 109, 114, 214, 216, 262n82; Tokugawa era, 52, 61, 63, 64, 96, 142, 213–14, 262n82; trade with China, 63, 96, 98, 109, 110, 186, 191, 212–13, 214, 236, 281n94; trade with West, 6, 208;

Treasury, 186, 207; Yokohama, 166; zaibatsu, 197
Japanese Kanto Army, 187
Jardine, Matheson & Co., 277n38
Java, 212, 213, 214–15
Javasche Bank, 215
Jenks, Jeremiah, 253n36, 278n46
Jernigan, T. R., 136, 271n3, 273n50
Jesuits, 14, 76, 94, 263n109, 264n128
Ji Zhaojin, 259n27
Jia Yi, 25–26, 129, 255n27; Jia Yi Xinshu, 255n24
Jiajing Emperor, 94; "Single Whip" reform, 63, 109
Jiang Chen, 68, 263n97, 271n15
Jiaqing Emperor, 125
Jibin, kingdom of, 36
Jilin City, 198, 199
Jinan, 186
Jin dynasty, 47; bronze coinage during, 55–56; inflation during, 124; paper money during, 56, 57, 58, 124; taxation during, 56
Jiujiang, 289n65
joint-stock firms, 72, 76, 80–81, 113, 145, 182; joint-stock banks, 146, 148–50, 151–52, 185–86, 285n5
Jurchens, 47, 48, 55–56

Kahan, Arcadius, 144
Kaifeng, 47
kaiyuan tongbao coin, 37
Kangxi Emperor, 262n90
Kanishka, 34, 35
Kanto earthquake, 203
Katō Shigeru, 13, 256n33
Kehoe, Dennis, 10
Kemmerer, E. W., 253n36
Keynes, John Maynard, 1, 4
Khitans, 46
Kikuchi Takaharu, 191
Kilwa sultanate, 268n61
King, Frank, 280n80
Kirshner, Jonathan, 16
Kishmoto Mio, 288n56
Knapp, Georg, 252n23
knife-shaped coinage (daobi), 21, 22, 23, 25, 27, 29, 34, 36–37, 256n30
Kong Linzhi, 43
Korea, 64, 92, 236; commodity money in, 267n40; Japanese banks in, 7, 185, 187, 197, 200, 207–9, 244–45, 287n40; as Japanese colony, 197–98,

200, 203; as Japanese protectorate, 197; March 1st Movement, 185; mint in, 196; monetary policies of, 96, 143, 184, 196–97, 213–14, 287n41; paper money in, 96, 185, 197, 200, 207–8, 287n41; peasants in, 197; silver in, 197, 198; taxation in, 197; yen coinage in, 197; Yi/Choson dynasty, 196–97, 213–14

Kou Jian, 46

Kroll, John H., 251n6

Khublai Khan, 56, 57, 58–59

Kufic script, 88

Kujula Kadphises, 35

Kuroda, Akinobu, 13, 84, 91, 107, 108, 217, 265n2

Kushan empire, 34, 35–36, 37, 38, 39

Kutna Hura, 102, 107

Kuz'mina, Elena Efimivna, 27

Lacouperie, Terrien: on Chinese coinage, 28, 33; *Western Origin of the Early Chinese Civilization*, 20, 28

Lang, Hsien-Ping (Lang Xianping), 234–35

Lardy, Nicholas, 232

Later Shu dynasty, 45, 46, 79

Latin America: European banks in, 150; gold from, 101, 113, 116; Latin Union monetary policies, 6; silver from, 14, 19, 63, 64, 70–71, 78, 95, 101–2, 103, 106–7, 109, 112, 113, 116, 117, 121, 138–39, 214, 215, 216, 235, 262n81; U.S. banks in, 155

Law, John, 8

lead coinage, 45

legalism, 43–44, 57

Leith-Ross, Sir Frederick, 253n36

Levant, 27, 88, 100, 104, 107, 115, 251n6, 256n30, 263n108, 266n19

level-head coinage, 22

Lewis, Mark E., 43

Li Daokui, 233–34

Li Yu'an, 124

Li Zhizao, 68

Liang Fangzhong, 95

Liang Qichao, 129

liang standard, 28, 37

Liaodong peninsula, 186, 201

Lieu, D. K., 286n14

Liew, Liong H., 225

limited liability, 149–50, 151, 154, 161, 182, 276n17

Lin Man-houng, 96, 271n4

Lin Yifu, 235

Lin Zexu, 125, 126

Liu Dingzhi, 67

Liu Zhi, 255n27

Lloyd's, 149

Locke, John, 4

Lombards, 86

London-centric international gold standard, 5–6

London financial industry, 16, 182

London Mint, 49, 80, 89, 259n32

long-distance drafts (*piaotie*), 132–33, 162

Louis XV, 8

Low Countries, 112–13. *See also* Netherlands

Lowndes, William, 4

Lowson, A. B., 180

Lu Bao's *Qianshenlun*, 43

Lüshi chunqiu, 29

Lydia: bronze casting in, 30–31; electrum/gold-coin standard in, 31–32; iron smelting in, 31; round coinage in, 3, 20, 27, 28, 30, 31, 32, 38, 251n6, 256n30

Macdonald, George, 254n5

Macedonia, 42

Mackay Treaty, 162

Macleod, H. D.: on Gresham's Law, 252n16

Macquarie, Lachlan, 75

Maddison, Angus, 143

Majapahit Empire, 213

Malaya, 148, 275n4

Maldives, 113, 114, 115

Mali, 103

"Manchukuo," 183, 185, 198–99, 200–201, 207, 208

Manilha brassware ornaments, 115

Mao Zedong, 1, 223

Marco Polo Bridge Incident, 201

Maria Theresa thalers (MTT), 103–4

Marx, Karl, 8; *Das Kapital*, 128; on Wang Maoyin, 128

Maspéro, Henri, 27

Matsutaka Masayoshi, 186

Mattingly, Harold, 268n47

Mauritius, 152

May 4th Movement, 181, 185, 286nn23,25; YSB during, 190–94, 204, 206–7, 209, 245

May 30th Movement, 168–81, 185, 191, 283n123, 285n143; British manufactured goods during, 169, 171, 172; British overseas banks during, 167–68, 169–80, 193, 194, 281n100, 282nn106,113, 283n122; CBIAC during, 169–70, 171–73, 282nn106,113, 283n121, 284n141; Chinese banks during, 169–70, 173, 178, 245, 281n98, 282n102; HSBC during, 168, 173–77, 178–80, 184n133, 282n113, 283nn121,122,124, 284nn134,141
MBI. *See* Mercantile Bank of India
McDonald's, 227
Median Empire, 31
Medicis, 98
Mercantile Bank of Bombay, 151
Mercantile Bank of India (MBI), 165, 172, 283n121
mercantilism, 91, 94, 100–101, 186, 245
merchants, 122, 188, 259n21, 267n30, 277n38, 279n69; in Canada, 74; in China, 44, 46–47, 51, 53, 54–55, 57, 67, 69–70, 95, 125, 140, 155, 158, 169, 171, 215, 267n30, 272n33, 286n25, 288n56; in England, 80; in Japan, 212; in Korea, 196, 197; in Sweden, 4, 77, 79
Mesopotamia, 21, 27, 32, 254n7, 256nn28,30
Metzler, Mark, 184
Mexico, 19; silver dollars minted in, 75, 106, 121–22, 131, 137, 138–39, 142, 145, 154, 156, 163, 167, 177, 179, 201, 215, 274n78; trade with U.S., 122
Middle Ages and Great Divergence debate, 83, 84, 85–99, 105–7
Ming dynasty, 24, 59; bronze coinage during, 61, 63, 64, 65–69, 81, 93–95, 213, 214, 215, 241, 242, 244; inflation during, 11, 63, 65, 67; isolationism during, 105–6; metallurgy during, 105–6; mining during, 9–10, 65, 66, 109, 114, 215–16, 268n43; monetary policies during, 53, 61, 62–69, 94, 95, 108–9, 124–25, 241, 242, 244, 261n72, 262n84, 266n25, 271n15; paper money (*baochao*) during, 11, 12, 62, 63, 64–65, 66–68, 69, 81, 95, 108, 109, 124–25, 217–18, 243, 260n50, 261n72, 262n84; salt

certificates (*yanyin*) during, 69–70, 82; silver bullion during, 63, 64, 65–67, 68–69, 73, 81, 95, 109, 110, 112, 114, 215, 239; taxation during, 47, 63, 66–67, 70, 95, 109, 259n30, 262n80
mining: of copper, 12, 21, 23, 41, 45, 48, 50, 86, 96, 97, 100, 109–10, 114, 125, 240, 265n137, 267n41; in England, 86, 105; in Europe vs. China, 9, 10, 12, 27, 30, 97–98, 102–3, 105, 108, 109–10, 243, 268n44; of gold, 41, 78, 87, 88, 98, 265n11; at Kutna Hora, 102, 107; during Ming dynasty, 65, 66, 109, 114, 215–16, 268n43; during Northern Song dynasty, 10, 47, 48–49, 50, 53, 56, 96–97; as private, 9, 10, 68, 92, 97, 98, 109, 125, 262nn82,90, 268n43; during Qing dynasty, 109–10, 114, 125, 215–16, 267n41, 268n43; relevance to Great Divergence debate, 84, 97–98, 102–3, 107, 116; in Roman Empire, 10; in Roman Republic, 10, 30; in Sardinia, 102, 107; of silver, 14, 19, 41, 61, 62, 63, 64, 68, 70–71, 78, 95, 96, 98, 101, 102–3, 104, 106–7, 108, 109, 112, 113, 116, 117, 121, 129, 138–39, 214, 215, 216, 235, 259n32, 262n81, 262n82; as state monopoly, 27, 48, 49, 50, 56, 79, 88, 125; use of gunpowder in, 268n44
minting, 38, 39, 101, 216–17, 240, 266n17; coin hammering, 85, 103; consistency in, 116–17; in England, 31, 49, 80, 84, 88, 89, 98, 99, 103, 104–5, 106, 110, 112, 116, 117, 259n32, 269n64; mint hearts, 49; private coinage, 23, 31, 42, 43, 85, 86, 90, 104, 112, 138, 214, 215, 217, 269n64; relevance to Great Divergence debate, 84–85, 103, 104–5, 116–17; remintage of coins, 89, 90, 93, 98, 99, 101, 242; roller press, 103; screw press, 31, 85, 103; as state monopoly, 20, 23, 26–27, 29, 43, 88, 90, 92, 117, 137, 217, 254n5, 266n19; steam-powered mints, 10, 24, 31, 83, 84–85, 105, 116, 117, 138, 139, 141, 142, 211, 236. *See also* casting
Mitchell Report, 279n69
Mithradates II, 35
Mitsubishi Tokyo Bank, 285n7

Moav, Omer, 265n2
Mollien, Nicholas François, 126, 271n17
monetary policies, Chinese, 1–2, 11–12, 16, 254n13, 258n6, 260n34; First Emperor, 22, 29, 36, 38; vs. German policies, 6; vs. Japanese policies, 6, 7; mother and child trope, 26, 54, 60, 63, 69; during Northern Song dynasty, 11, 44–47, 48–49, 50, 51–55, 57, 58, 60, 96–97, 260n50; in PRC, 219–28; during Qing dynasty, 64, 85, 96, 122–29, 131, 138–40, 146–47, 159–62, 181–82, 184, 193, 241, 253n36, 259n32, 261n72, 267n38, 278n53; in Republican China, 180, 181–82, 184–85, 187, 190, 194, 195, 198–200, 204, 218, 219, 221, 253n36, 285n5; during Southern Song dynasty, 50–51, 54–55, 56, 57, 58, 61; vs. Western monetary policies, 4, 5, 6, 12, 13, 20, 21, 25–27, 31, 39–40, 41–44, 47–48, 49–50, 53–54, 64, 69–71, 72, 73–74, 76–77, 78–79, 81–82, 90–94, 99, 104–5, 108–9, 138–39, 140–45, 147, 247–48; during Yuan dynasty, 3, 11, 12, 53, 56–62, 63, 65, 107, 108, 109, 212, 217, 242, 243, 244, 260n50, 261n63
money shops: during Qing dynasty, 64, 96, 122–29, 131, 133–34, 136, 139, 146–47, 156, 159–62, 161, 181–82, 184, 188, 189, 244, 271n4, 272n32, 273n48; in Republican China, 155, 169, 182, 192, 220, 282n106. *See also* Chinese banks
money supply, 9, 14, 78, 147, 245; in British India, 143, 274n78; and central banks, 148, 220, 221; coin famines (*qianhuang*), 49, 50–51, 57, 79, 240, 241, 259n32; in France, 144–45; during Northern Song dynasty, 10, 46, 48–49, 50–51, 57, 104–5, 215; during Qing dynasty, 63, 138–39, 140–41, 143, 215, 259n32
Mongolia, 36–37; Huhehot, 37, 212
Mongols: bronze coins of, 55; in Central Asia (Chagatai), 56–57, 61; in Iran (Ilkhanate), 56–57, 61–62, 88; paper money of, 19, 56, 57–62; in Russia (Golden Horde), 56–57, 88; silver-based currency of, 56–60, 108. *See also* Yuan dynasty

Morganthau, Henry Jr., 252n17
Mughal currency, 111–12, 117, 269n73
Mun, Thomas: on East India Company's specie trade, 4

Nanjing, 161, 181
Nanyang Bros., 172
Nanzhao kingdom, 213
Napoleonic Wars, 4, 113
National Bank of Egypt, 275n5
National Commercial Bank, 170
national debt, 2, 7, 9, 12, 82, 95; of England, 5, 48, 70, 72–73, 74, 78, 79, 92, 98–99, 117, 218, 243, 264n134; of Netherlands, 264n134; relationship to debasement, 90, 92, 98–99, 117; relationship to economic modernization, 72–74, 98–99, 117, 218, 243, 245; relationship to paper money, 69, 72–73, 74, 78, 98, 99, 218, 245; of Sweden, 77, 78; of United States, 234, 246, 247
nation-state: monetary sovereignty, 39–40; money as abstraction of, 2, 3, 7, 9, 14, 218, 239, 251n3; monopoly over coinage, 20, 23, 26–27, 29, 43, 88, 90, 92, 117, 137, 217, 254n5, 266n19; territorial currency, 84, 112, 138. *See also* fiat currency
Needham, Joseph, 12
Nef, John U., 259n32
neoclassical economics, 11
neo-Confucianism, 48, 50, 67, 69, 95, 260n41
neoliberalism, 235, 237, 246
Netherlands, 240, 243; Bank of Amsterdam, 79–80; monetary policies, 6; national debt, 264n134; paper money in, 79–80, 264n134
New Institutional Economics (NIE), 9, 11, 253n29
Newton, Isaac, 105
New York financial industry, 16
Ni Yuanlu, 125, 271n15
Niuzhuang, 186
Nixon, Richard M.: policy regarding U.S. dollar and gold, 2–4, 222, 246, 247
noble, 42
nomisma (bezant), 88–89, 100
nongovernmental organizations (NGOs), 227
North America, 141

North-China Herald, 273n48, 281n100, 282n105, 283n121
North, Douglass C., 9, 253n29
Northern Song dynasty, 48–56, 63, 212, 255n20; bronze coinage during, 10, 11, 45–46, 48–49, 50–51, 65–66, 93, 96–97, 104–5, 215, 219, 260n50, 290n11; economic conditions during, 14, 44–47, 219, 243, 244; gold coinage during, 258n6; iron production during, 105; merchants during, 46–47, 69; mining during, 10, 47, 48–49, 50, 53, 56, 96–97, 265n137; monetary policies during, 48–49, 50, 51–52, 53, 96–97, 105, 265n137; money supply during, 10, 46, 48–49, 50–51, 57, 104–5, 215; neo-Confucianism during, 48, 50; paper money during, 11, 44–47, 52–55, 57, 58, 60, 66, 81, 92–93, 95, 102, 242, 243, 260nn46,50; Sichuan iron coinage during, 52–53, 55; silver during, 53, 105, 261n79; *Taiping tongbao*, 258n6; taxation during, 47, 53, 97, 243, 261n79
North Western Bank of India, 151
Nubia, 87, 88, 103, 265n11

Official Bank of the Three Eastern Provinces, 199–200
Ogawa, Eiji, 225
opium, 113, 125, 140, 150, 151, 152, 160
Opium Wars, 70, 121, 126, 127, 184. *See also* treaty ports
Oresme, Nicholas: on currency debasement, 4–5
Oriental Bank Corporation (OBC), 140, 151, 152, 155, 193, 276n23; failure of, 163–64, 182, 280n73
O'Rourke, Kevin H., 265n2
Ostrogoths, 86
Ottoman Empire, 88, 107, 149; copper coinage in, 110, 270n85; Imperial Ottoman Bank, 144; silver akçe, 110; treasury notes (*kaime*) in, 143–44
Overend Gurney crisis, 151–52
overseas Chinese, 214, 223, 225, 282n115

Palmer, John Horsley, 74
Palmers, 150
Palmstruch, Johan, 4, 77, 79

Pamuk, Şevket, 107, 143
Pan Rongfang, 211
paper money, 2, 6–7, 50, 271n3; attitudes of Chinese regarding, 1, 11, 12, 49, 55, 66–67, 124–25, 128, 129, 147, 164, 167, 202–3, 207, 218, 241, 242, 243, 245, 262n84; bronze-coin denominated notes (*qianyin*), 47, 54–55, 56; *chaoguan*, 124; in Chinese statecraft, 26, 55, 66–67, 124, 128, 241, 242; as convertible, 4, 52–53, 54–55, 73, 81, 126, 130, 133, 144, 152, 154, 187, 199–200, 204, 207, 217, 218, 242, 263n97, 278n59; in England, 67, 70, 71–74, 79–81, 83–84, 243, 264n116; in Europe, 4, 8, 11, 12, 30, 42, 53–54, 64, 67, 69, 71–74, 75–78, 79–81, 83–84, 130, 137, 142, 217–18, 236, 242–43, 244, 264nn116,133, 267n30; *guantie*, 198, 199; horizontal style, 128; *huizi*, 54–55, 57, 66, 67; as inconvertible, 3, 55, 59, 60, 62, 65, 73, 78, 96, 125, 128, 143–44, 199–200, 221, 263n97, 271n17, 275n82; as inflationary, 11, 59–60, 61, 63, 65, 67, 78, 124, 126, 127, 129, 146, 147, 160; in Japan, 7, 80, 96, 129, 142–43, 184, 185–86, 204, 281n94; *jiaozi*, 46–47, 53, 54, 66, 260n46; during Jin dynasty, 56, 57, 58, 124; light (*qing*) vs. heavy (*zhong*), 54; during Ming dynasty *baochao*, 11, 12, 62, 63, 64–65, 66–68, 69, 81, 95, 108, 109, 124–25, 217–18, 243, 260n50, 261n72, 262n84; during Northern Song dynasty, 11, 44–47, 52–55, 57, 58, 60, 66, 81, 92–93, 95, 102, 242, 243, 260nn46,50; note denominations, 11, 26, 45, 46, 47, 52, 53, 54–55, 56, 58, 66, 67, 122, 123, 125, 126–27, 133–34, 136, 137, 138, 140, 143–44, 148, 153–54, 156, 157, 163, 166, 167, 179, 186, 187, 192, 194, 197, 198–99, 200, 201, 202, 203, 204, 207, 215, 217–18, 267n30, 271n4, 272n41, 274n57, 284n141, 289n65; overprinting of, 12, 47, 54, 57, 60, 61, 65, 67, 72, 128, 218, 242, 243; as privately issued, 7, 8, 11, 14, 15, 46, 49, 51, 52, 54, 76–77, 78, 79–80, 82, 122, 129, 130–36, 139, 140, 148–54, 155–56, 159, 160, 163–68, 169, 172–82,

184–86, 220, 244–45, 271n4, 273nn48,50, 275nn1,4,5, 277n40, 278n59, 279n72, 280nn76,80,85, 281nn92,94, 283n120, 284nn134,141, 286n25, 287nn31,46, 288nn49,56, 289nn65–67; during Qing dynasty, 15, 64, 121–47, 155–56, 158, 159, 160, 161–62, 198, 199, 244, 261n72, 272nn33,40, 273n47,48,50,54; relationship to economic modernization, 141, 146–47, 245; relationship to national debt, 69, 72–73, 74, 78, 98, 99, 218, 245; in Sichuan, 45, 46–47, 76–77, 81; silver-backed notes (*zhongtong*), 58–60; during Southern Song dynasty, 54–55, 56, 57, 58, 61, 66, 67, 107, 241; in Sweden, 4, 76–78, 79, 81, 264n133; trust in, 12, 57, 60–61, 64, 65, 72, 122, 127, 131, 133, 134, 135, 146, 181–82, 202–3, 207, 219, 273n47; vertical style, 123–24, 259n19; during Yuan dynasty, 3, 11, 12, 53, 56–62, 63, 65, 66, 72, 81, 95, 102, 107, 108, 212, 213, 217, 242, 243, 244, 260n50, 261n63. *See also* reserves
Parkes, Harry, 134, 272n39
Parsons, William, 141–42
Parthia, 35
path dependency, 11, 40, 216–17, 242; relevance to Great Divergence debate, 83, 90, 92
Paul, Ron, 246
PBC. *See* People's Bank of China
peasants, 46, 53, 81, 223, 242, 267n38, 272n41
Peking Syndicate mines, 169
Penang, 279n71
Peng Xinwei, 13, 255n20, 265n2; on Chinese round coinage, 28, 29, 256n38; on stock of currency in late Qing, 137, 138–39, 140–41, 143; on Yuan dynasty, 124
People's Bank of China (PBC), 220–21, 228, 233; central bank functions, 221, 223, 224; commercial banking functions, 221, 223; Exchange Rates Department, 230; logo of, 14, 23; provincial branches, 224; tourists in, 225; and trade surplus with West, 227; U.S. dollars in reserves, 225–26; views on RMB tradability, 228–31, 237

People's Liberation Army (PLA), 219
People's Republic of China (PRC): commercial banking functions in, 221, 223, 230; economic growth in, 232–33; economists in, 233–35, 237; in era of central planning, 219–23; financial markets in, 210, 225, 226, 227, 230, 234, 236; monetary policies, 219–28; policies regarding Hong Kong, 226, 227, 230–31, 234, 237; scholarship on numismatics in, 21, 27–28; trade with U.S., 216, 225–26. *See also* renminbi (RMB)
pepper, 101
Perkins, Jacob, 80
Perlin, Frank, 265n2
Persian Gulf, 24
Peru, 19
Pharaonic Egypt, 23
Philippines, 213, 214
Phraates II, 35
physiocracy, 66, 94, 97
picis, 214–15
pieces of eight. *See* Spanish-American silver dollar
Pigou, A. C., 251n3
Pines, Yuri, 260n41
Pittman, Key, 252n15
Pliny the Elder, 10, 30
pointed-feet coinage, 22
Polish coinage, 42
Polo, Marco, 3, 56, 57, 59, 71, 108, 251n4
Pomeranz, Kenneth, 134
porcelain, 116, 122, 212
Portugal, 101, 113, 114, 115, 116, 240, 243
postmodernity, 19–20
pound sterling, 4–5, 6, 143, 152, 202; convertibility of, 4, 73; as global reserve currency, 16, 210, 219, 231, 246, 247; Great Debasement, 89–90, 98–99; vs. RMB, 246; as unit of account, 89, 192; vs. U.S. dollar, 219, 231, 247
Prakash, Om, 101
Presidency Banks, 153, 276n28
Prince Edward Island, 74–75
promissory notes, 45, 80, 142, 263n108
property bubble in China, 226, 230
property rights, 9, 98
Prussian Bank, 144
public debt. *See* national debt

punch-marked coinage, 31, 32, 33, 34
Pyrrhic War, first, 41

Qi Junzao, 140
Qian Bingdeng, 68, 263n97
Qianlong Emperor, 66, 93, 94, 96, 271n4
Qin dynasty, 22–23, 29, 36, 38, 39, 43, 254n13
Qingdao, 186, 191
Qing dynasty: bronze coinage during, 64, 66, 94, 96, 121, 127, 132, 133, 135, 136, 137, 138, 140, 146, 147, 156, 159, 199, 215, 241, 245, 259n32, 267n41; coinage from earlier dynasties (*guqian*) during, 94, 129, 142; fall of, 133, 167, 186; foreign silver dollars during, 121, 125, 137, 138–39; government bonds, 164, 166; government-issued paper money during, 122–23, 137, 138, 140, 146, 156, 161–62, 198, 199; inflation during, 124, 126, 127, 159; metallurgic technology during, 106; mining during, 9–10, 109–10, 114, 125, 215–16, 267n41, 268n43; monetary policies during, 64, 85, 96, 122–29, 131, 138–40, 146–47, 159–62, 181–82, 184, 193, 241, 253n36, 259n32, 261n72, 267n38, 278n53; money shops during, 126–27, 128, 131, 133–34, 136, 139, 146, 156, 159, 161, 188, 189, 244, 271n4, 272n32, 273n48; money supply during, 63, 138–39, 140–41, 143, 215, 259n32; paper money during, 64, 121–47, 155–56, 158, 159, 160, 161–62, 198, 199, 244, 261n72, 272nn33,40, 273n47,48,50,54; privately-issued paper money during, 15, 122–23, 126–27, 130–34, 136, 137, 138, 139–40, 142, 146, 155–56, 158, 159, 160, 161, 272n40, 273nn48,50,54; Shunzhi Emperor, 64, 123–26, 128, 146; silver ingots (*sycee*) during, 121, 137, 138, 140, 156, 239, 267n38; Taiping rebellion, 64, 126, 127–28; taxation during, 47, 121, 126, 127, 133, 198, 215, 259n27, 267n38, 268n43; Treasury (*Hubu*) during, 127, 129, 136, 267n41. *See also* Opium Wars; treaty ports
Qin State, 28, 29, 35, 36

Qiu Jun, 67
Quan Hansheng, 261n79

Rahman, Aman ur, 257n52
Rawski, Thomas G., 141, 288n49
Rawson, Jessica, 27
rebasement, 89, 91, 94, 241
rectangular coinage, 33–34
Redish, Angela, 39, 267n30
Remer, C. F., 181
remittances from overseas Chinese, 223, 225
Renaissance, 39
renminbi (RMB): convertibility of, 7, 211, 221, 222, 227, 231, 233–34, 246; devaluation of, 223, 224, 235, 246–47; and domestic capital markets, 210, 211, 237; during era of central planning, 219–23; vs. euro, 210; exchange rate for U.S. dollar, 221, 222, 223, 224, 227; global prominence of, 1, 2, 7, 14, 16, 210–11, 219, 230–31, 232, 245, 246–47, 291n67; and inflation, 211, 221, 224, 230, 234; issuance of bonds denominated in, 291n67; vs. pound sterling, 210, 246; and prices of domestic goods, 234–35; during reform era, 223–28; relationship to China's economic growth, 232–33, 234, 236–37, 246–47; relationship to China's financial markets, 210, 225, 226, 227, 230, 234, 236; relationship to foreign trade, 223, 224, 225, 226–27, 233, 235, 237, 246, 291n67; revaluation of, 222, 223, 227, 228, 234–35, 237; tradability of, 226, 228–31, 237; and trade with Asia, 233, 237; undervaluation of, 216; vs. U.S. dollar, 3, 16, 210, 216, 219, 221, 222, 223, 224, 227, 232, 235, 236, 237, 246; views of Chinese economists regarding, 233–35, 237; views of PBC regarding, 228–31, 237
Republican China, 154–55, 158–59; *fabi* reform, 181, 190, 194, 204, 218; gold yuan notes, 221; KMT government, 180, 181, 190, 195, 218, 219, 220, 253n36; Maritime Customs, 180; monetary policies during, 180, 181–82, 184–85, 187, 190, 194, 195, 198–200, 204, 218, 219, 221, 253n36, 285n5; silver dollar in,

199–200; taxation in, 184–85; Yuan Shikai, 184, 187, 195, 199. *See also* May 4th Movement; May 30th Movement

reserves, 72, 81, 129, 132, 142, 144, 242–43; of Bank of England, 73–74, 78, 253n33; of BoCS, 198, 204, 207, 289n68; of BoTW, 204, 205, 207, 289n68; of British overseas banks, 73–74, 122, 135, 150, 163–68, 171, 174–77, 178, 179, 182, 207, 244–45, 276n31, 279nn70,71, 280n83; bullion reserves, 49, 54, 73–74, 82, 153, 164, 171, 177, 207, 279n71, 289n68; of CBIAC, 165, 182, 279nn70,71, 280n83; as *chengti*, 54, 61; of HSBC, 161, 182, 279nn70,71; during Ming dynasty, 62–63, 65, 139, 217–18, 260n50; one-third cover, 73–74, 129, 153, 163, 207, 253n33, 279n70; during Qing dynasty, 127, 147, 159, 161–62; two-thirds cover, 1, 11, 49–50, 55, 74, 175, 253n33; of YSB, 192, 207; during Yuan dynasty, 57, 58, 59–61, 108; Zhou Xingji on, 1, 11, 49, 55, 74

Rexue ribao, 178
rice, 201, 287n43
Richards, J. F., 112
Rigby, Richard, 172
Rinbara Fumiko, 286n25
Rio Tinto, 227
Rome: *aes* coinage, 25; bronze/copper coinage in, 25, 41, 42, 217, 268n47; vs. China, 41–44; civilian bureaucracy in, 43–44; coinage in, 25, 37, 41–42, 86–87, 88, 106, 217, 239, 268n47; counterfeiting in, 268n47; as empire, 10, 42, 43–44, 86–87, 268n47; gold solidi, 42, 86–87, 88; gold tremissis, 86–87, 88; mining, 10, 30, 41, 243; as republic, 1, 10, 30, 42, 212, 217; silver denarii, 42, 266n17
Rossabi, Morris, 57
round coinage, 15, 19, 22–25, 26, 36, 106, 254n13, 255n20, 256n33; in Achaemenid Empire, 20, 30, 32, 38; exogeneity vs. endogeneity of Chinese premodern round coinage, 20–21, 27–31, 33, 38–40; in Greece, 20, 38, 256n39; in India, 20, 30, 33, 34, 38, 257n52; in Lydia, 3, 20, 27, 28, 30, 31, 32, 38, 251n6, 256n30

Rovenson, John, 106
Royal Charters, 76, 77, 81, 133, 149–50, 151, 155, 182
ruble, 222, 275n82
Russia: Bolshevik Revolution, 198; coinage in, 99; monetary policies in, 275n82; paper money in, 144, 198, 199, 244; Siberia, 149
Russo-Japanese War, 186–87, 198

Sai (Saka), 35, 36
Sakatani, Baron Yoshio, 184
salt monopoly, 47, 50, 53, 69–70, 82
salt slabs, 260n37
Sang Hongyang, 255n27, 258n6
Sangha, 59
Sardinia: mining in, 102, 107
Sassanids, 212; Sassanid coins, 37, 87, 257n49
Scandinavia: coinage in, 42, 99, 258n4; monetary policies, 6. *See also* Sweden
Schaps, David M., 32, 251n6
Scheidel, Walter, 30, 43–44, 256n39
Schwartz, Anna, 3
Scotland: private banknotes in, 79, 275n1
Scythian-Tocharian peoples, 35, 36, 38, 39
Segal, Ethan Isaac, 274n72, 290n11
seigniorage revenue: in China, 49, 68, 92, 93–94, 95, 99, 159, 217, 229, 236, 240, 242; in Europe, 89–90, 92, 95, 99, 117, 217, 236, 240, 244; in Korea, 196–97
Seleucus I, 33
Selgin, George, 130–31, 133, 134
Sellassie, Haile, 275n5
Senkaku/Diaoyu islets, 245
Seven Years' War, 70, 78
Shaanxi province: Wei River Valley, 37–38
Shan Qi, 25, 54, 241
Shandong, 135, 191
Shang Yang, 51
Shang dynasty, 21, 27
Shanghai, 153, 154, 158, 161, 190, 202, 273n48; British banks in, 81, 130, 155, 157, 159, 162, 166, 167–68, 169–80, 173–74, 176–78, 179, 180–81, 193, 208, 276n17, 277n38, 279n70, 281nn99,100, 282n106; British-owned department stores in, 282n115; chop loans in, 188, 273n48;

Shanghai *(continued)*
  extraterritorial privileges in, 184–85;
  Japanese banks in, 192–94, 203,
  287n34, 289n65; during May 4th
  Movement, 192–94; during May
  30th Movement, 168–80, 193–94,
  282n106; money shops in, 188,
  272n32, 273n48; Municipal Police,
  193; Naigai Wata, 190; *North-China
  Herald*, 170; *Shenbao*, 170, 282n106;
  silver coinage in, 157; *Yinhang zhou-
  bao*, 171; YSB branch in, 186, 187,
  188, 189
Shanghai Commercial & Savings Bank,
  171
Shanghai's Bund and Beyond, 8
Shantou, 289n65
Shanxi province, 136
Shaughnessy, Edward L., 27
she, 45
Sheehan, Brett, 13
Shen Kuo, 50, 53
Shen Qingzhi, 43
Shen Yue, 43
Sheng Xuanhuai, 161
Shenzong Emperor, 48
Sherman, Sandra, 72
Shijiazhuang, 220
shroffs, in China, 131
Shunzhi Emperor, 64, 123–26, 128, 146
Siam, 213; foreign banks in, 153,
  165–66, 276n32, 280n85; monetary
  policies, 276n32
Sichuan: iron coinage in, 51, 52, 55,
  58, 77, 78, 78–79, 81, 255n20; paper money in, 45, 46–47, 76–77, 81;
  Shanxi banks (*piaohao*) in, 135–36;
  vs. Sweden, 76–77, 78–79, 81
silk, 22, 63, 212, 214, 255n18; foreign
  trade in, 14, 122, 151, 152, 215, 216
Silk Road: numismatic evidence from,
  21, 35–38, 212, 255n18, 289n8
silver: California deposits, 6, 139; flat
  bars (*ting*), 53; Latin American deposits, 14, 19, 63, 64, 70–71, 78, 95,
  101–2, 103, 106–7, 109, 112, 113,
  116–17, 121, 138–39, 214, 215, 216,
  235, 262n81; during Ming dynasty,
  63, 64, 65–67, 68–69, 73, 81, 95,
  109, 110, 112, 114, 215, 239; mining
  of, 6, 14, 19, 41, 61, 62, 63, 64, 68,
  70–71, 78, 95, 98, 101, 102–3, 104,
  106–7, 108, 109, 112, 113, 116, 117,

121, 129, 138–39, 214, 215, 216, 235,
  259n32, 262n81, 262n82; Nevada
  deposits, 6, 139; prices of, 6, 199; silver bar (*hacksilber*), 251n6; silver bar
  (*yinding*), 58; silver ingots (*sycee*),
  15, 85, 91, 93, 109, 121, 129, 137,
  140, 156, 198, 201, 215, 217, 239,
  241, 281n87; silver ingots (*yinzi*),
  95; silver ingots during Western Han
  dynasty, 23; silver ingots in Achaemenid Empire, 32; silver reserve, 58, 60,
  61, 62, 108, 127; silver sigloi, 32, 33;
  silver tael, 58, 67, 121, 126, 128, 138,
  154, 156, 157, 163, 167, 186, 187,
  192, 200, 262n79, 271n4, 277n42,
  288n56; West African deposits, 6,
  139; during Yuan dynasty, 58, 59, 60,
  61. *See also* bullion flows
silver coinage, 57, 61, 101–2, 125, 140,
  196, 255n19; akçe, 110; didrachm,
  41; dirham, 88, 99, 258n4, 266n17;
  drachma, 266n17; Dutch *guilder*,
  215; during Eastern Han dynasty,
  258n6; English silver pennies, 42,
  49, 87, 88, 89–90, 92, 98, 99, 107,
  259n32; in Europe, 25, 36, 42, 49,
  74–75, 78, 86–87, 88–90, 91, 92, 95,
  98, 99, 100, 106–7, 116–17, 214, 215,
  216, 239, 241, 242, 259n32, 262n81;
  European groschen, 93; in Germany,
  6, 252n20; Hong Kong silver dollars, 156–57, 167–68; in India, 31,
  32–33, 112, 117, 213, 214, 236,
  257n54, 269n74; in Japan, 96, 142,
  216, 288n60; Maria Theresa thalers
  (MTT), 103–4; during Qing dynasty,
  11–12, 138, 141, 199; Sassanid silver
  coinage, 87; Spanish-American silver
  dollar, 63, 74–75, 106–7, 116–17,
  121–22, 131, 137, 138–39, 142, 145,
  154, 156, 163, 167, 177, 179, 201,
  214, 215, 216, 235, 241, 262n81,
  274n78; tetradrachm, 32, 37; in
  United States, 6, 252n20; during
  Western Han dynasty, 23, 239
silver convertibility: exchange rate for
  copper, 110, 111, 114, 121, 126, 137;
  exchange rate for gold, 31–32, 88, 90,
  91, 102, 104–5, 110, 115, 152, 200;
  silver standard, 6, 31, 190, 197, 200,
  204, 208, 218, 264n133, 278n53
silver-gold bimetallists, 6
Sima Guang, 50

Sima Qian's *Records of the Grand Historian*, 51
Singapore, 202, 208, 279n71
Sino-foreign joint venture banks, 285n5
Sino-Japanese War, first, 186, 201
Sino-Kharosthi, 37–38
Six Dynasties era, 43
slavery, 10, 30, 44, 97, 113, 114–15, 265n11
Smith, Adam: on bullion hoarding, 4; on Chinese economy, 71; on foreign trade, 71; on paper money, 126, 271n17; on tax revenue in Mughal-ruled Bengal, 264n112
Sofala (Mozambique), 103
Song dynasty. *See* Northern Song dynasty; Southern Song dynasty
Song Yingxing, 68, 267n30; *Tiangong kaiwu*, 93
South China Morning Post, 283n122
Southern Song dynasty, 11, 47–48, 60; bronze coinage during, 50–51, 54, 58, 61, 62, 65–66, 212–13, 214, 241, 244, 260n50; paper money during, 54–55, 56, 57, 58, 61, 66, 67, 107
Soviet Union (USSR), 222
spade-shaped coinage (*bubi*), 14–15, 21, 22, 23, 25, 27, 28, 29, 34, 256nn30,33
Spain: vs. Britain, 243; Carolus silver dollar, 74–75, 106–7, 116–17, 214, 215, 216, 241, 262n81; colonialism of, 111; copper coinage in, 78–79, 101, 102, 107, 239–40; economic conditions, 232; gold coinage in, 87, 100; mints in, 116; monetary policies in, 102, 107; silver coinage in, 74–75, 100, 106–7, 214, 215, 216, 241, 262n81
Spanish-American silver dollar: Carolus dollar, 74–75, 106–7, 116–17, 214, 215, 216, 241, 262n81; as global currency, 63, 106, 215, 216, 235; Mexican dollar, 75, 106, 121–22, 131, 137, 138–39, 142, 145, 154, 156, 163, 167, 177, 179, 201, 215, 274n78
Special Drawing Rights (SDRs), 233
special economic zones, 223
Spence, Jonathan, 8–9
Sprenger, Bernd, 144
Spring and Autumn era, 21, 23, 29, 114
Spufford, Peter: on European mining, 102; on minting in Middle Ages, 269n65

square holes in coinage, 15, 22–23, 28, 29, 85, 110, 138, 214
Sri Lanka. *See* Ceylon
standardization of currency, 19, 20, 22–23, 31, 39, 84, 88, 117, 254n13
State Development Bank of China, 224
Staunton, George, 263n109
steelmaking in China vs. Europe, 105
Stitt, G. H., 173–74, 177–78, 179, 283n124, 284n134
Stockholms Banco, 4, 77
Stolberg emergency issue, 144
stone spinning whorls and coinage, 28, 29
Straits Settlements, 148, 163, 164, 165, 166, 280nn80,81,83
strings of cash: short strings of cash (*duanmo*), 51; strings of 1,000 bronze coins (*guan/diao*), 47, 51, 58, 60, 67, 85, 105, 121, 132, 138, 217, 259n27, 261n63, 261n79
Sturtevant, Simon, 106
subprime mortgage crisis of 2007, 232
Sudan, 113
sugar, 70, 115, 201, 203, 287n43
Sumatra, 213, 214–15
Sun Quan, 42–43
Supreme Command of the Allied Powers (SCAP), 285n7
Surat, 112
Suzhou, 161
Suzuki shōten, 203
Sweden: copper coinage in, 77–78, 81, 239–40; copper mines in, 79, 265n137; vs. England, 78, 79; Gustavus Adolphus, 78; monetary policies in, 264n133; national debt, 77, 78; paper money in, 4, 76–78, 79, 81, 264n133; Riksbank, 77–78; vs. Sichuan, 76–77, 78–79, 81; Stockholms Banco, 4, 77, 79
Switzerland, 275n1

Ta Ching Imperial Bank, 161–62, 189, 190
taipans, 160, 180
Taiping rebellion, 64, 126, 127–28
Taiping tongbao, 258n6
Taira Tomoyuki, 188
Taiwan, 139, 183, 201–6, 207–9, 221, 244–45, 287n43, 288nn56,60
Takatsuna Hirofumi, 190

Tang dynasty, 20, 49, 51, 69, 84, 92, 255n27, 259n26; bronze coinage during, 37, 212, 254n13; flying cash (*feiqian*) during, 44–45, 260n46; *kaiyuan tongbao* coin, 37; paper money during, 66, 71, 81

Tanguts, 46, 55

Tarim basin, 35, 212

Tavernier, Jean-Baptiste, 112

taxation, 51, 53, 54, 57, 62, 99, 108, 204, 214, 266n25; commercial taxes, 70, 72, 92, 259n27; in England, 47, 48, 70, 81, 92, 93, 98, 243; during Jin dynasty, 56; land taxes, 17, 47–48, 63, 70, 86, 92, 109, 198, 243, 259nn26,27,30, 264n112, 274n72; during Ming dynasty, 47, 63, 66–67, 70, 95, 109, 259n30, 262n80; during Northern Song dynasty, 47, 53, 97, 243, 261n79; during Qing dynasty, 47, 121, 126, 127, 133, 198, 215, 259n27, 267n38, 268n43; in Republican China, 184–85; during Yuan dynasty, 58, 59

tea, 47, 272n33; foreign trade in, 14, 70, 102, 122, 151, 152, 201, 202, 215, 216, 259n21

Temür, 59–60, 65

Tennant, Charles, 74

Terauchi Masatake, 187

territorial currency, 84, 112, 138

tetradrachm, 32, 37

Thomas, Robert, 253n29

Tianjin, 158, 167, 176, 180, 186, 188; during May 4th Movement, 192, 286n25; YSB note circulation in, 187

Tianqi Emperor, 68, 94, 262n89

Tibet, 11

tobacco, 70, 141, 172, 176

Toghto, 59, 65

Tongzhi Emperor, 126

Treaty of Versailles, 185, 191

Treaty of Westphalia, 84

treaty ports, 163, 164–65, 182, 208, 279n69; extraterritoriality in, 154, 156, 158, 169, 172, 173, 184–85, 278n51; foreign banknotes in, 122, 130–36, 139–40, 153–54, 156–58, 159, 162, 278n59, 279n71. *See also* British overseas banks; Fuzhou; May 30th Movement; Shanghai; Tianjin

Triffin, Robert, 231

Tughlaq, Sultan Muhammad ibn, 62

Umayyads, 87, 100

Union Bank of Australia, 149

United Kingdom: Bank of England Act of 1844, 253n33; Colonial Office, 153, 164, 177, 186; Colonial Ordinances, 182; economic conditions, 210; Foreign Office, 163, 172, 177, 279n69; Opium Wars, 70, 121, 126, 127, 184; Treasury, 149–50, 152, 153, 154, 159, 163–64, 165, 166–67, 173, 176, 178, 182, 204, 280n76, 283n120

United States: balance of payment deficits, 2–3; banks in, 122, 145, 154, 155, 183; vs. China, 145; Congress, 75; economic conditions, 210; financial markets in, 232, 233; monetary policies, 2–4, 6, 222, 246, 247; money supply, 145; New York financial industry, 16; overseas banking, 277n37; paper money in, 145; regulation of banks in, 130; silver coinage in, 6, 252n20; subprime mortgage crisis, 130. *See also* U.S. dollar

unlimited liability, 163, 279n72

Uruguay: Banco de la República, 150; River Plate Bank, 150

U.S. dollar, 225, 226, 233; and Asian trade, 233; and Bretton Woods accords, 221; devaluations of, 231; vs. euro, 231, 232, 247; exchange rate for RMB, 221, 222, 223, 224, 227; and the *fabi*, 218; as global reserve currency, 7, 210, 229–30, 231–33, 234, 235, 236, 237, 247, 291n62; gold convertibility, 2–4, 6, 7, 222; vs. pound sterling, 219, 231, 247; vs. RMB, 3, 16, 210, 216, 219, 221, 222, 223, 224, 227, 232, 235, 236, 237, 246; vs. Spanish/Mexican silver dollar, 75; and trade with China, 216, 235; Treasury bonds, 216, 245–46; and U.S. economy, 231, 232, 247

Usher, Abbot Payson, 263n108

Van Dormael, Armand, 252n17

Venice: foreign coins in, 101; Venetian coinage in Greek colonies, 101, 244; Venetian ducat, 88, 100; Venetian mining, 104, 268n44

Vietnam, 213; Vietnam War, 2

Vikings, 258n4

Vilar, Pierre, 101

Visigoths, 86, 100

Vissering, G., 253n36
Vogel, Hans Ulrich, 13, 96, 97, 105, 108
Vollrath, Dietrich, 265n2
Von Glahn, Richard, 13, 109, 265n2

Wales: paper money in, 72
wampum, 114
Wang Anshi, 48–49, 50, 51–52, 53, 97, 260n41, 265n137
Wang Di, 211
Wang Fang, 291n62
Wang Fuzhi, 68
Wang Ji, 266n25
Wang Liu, 140, 271n15; "Random Thoughts on Currency," 125, 126, 128
Wang Mang, 23, 254n13
Wang Maoyin, 128, 160
Wang Wencheng, 260n46
Wang Xiaobo, 259n21
Wang Yeh-chien, 139–40, 274n57
Wang Yide, 139–40
Wang Yuquan, 28
Wanli Emperor, 65, 94, 262n79
Warring States era, 22, 28, 29–30, 36
Washington Consensus, 233
Weatherford, Jack: on Chinese monetary rules, 1, 2
Weber, Max, 8, 217
Wei Yuan, 125, 126
Wei State, 28, 29–30, 256n38
Western Han dynasty, 10, 43, 44, 239, 254n13; coinage during, 20, 22, 23, 51; deer-hide currency during, 23, 66, 125, 140; Wudi Emperor, 23, 66, 125, 140
Whaley, Mark, 37–38
Williamson, Jeffrey G., 265n2
Williams, S. W., 135, 273n47
wine monopoly, 47
Wing On and Sincere, 282n115
World Bank, 227, 235, 237
World Economic Conference of 1933, 252n15
World Trade Organization (WTO), 227, 230
World War I, 154, 193, 195, 203, 283n120, 287n43; Treaty of Versailles, 185, 191
World War II, 16, 231, 247
Wu, Friedrich, 211
Wu Qijing, 271nn4,15
Wu, kingdom of, 42–43

Wudi Emperor, 23, 66, 125, 140
Wuling of Zhao, King, 36
Wusa Movement. *See* May 30th Movement
Wusi Movement. *See* May 4th Movement
Wusun, 36
wuzhu coinage, 42–43, 213

Xiamen, 136, 190, 202, 288n56, 289n65
Xianfeng Emperor, 64, 126–29, 140, 146
Xianzong Emperor, 44
Xiao Qing, 13, 27, 261n72
Xinjiang, 11, 35, 212; oasis of Khotan, 37
Xiongnu, 35, 37
Xu Heng, 60–61
Xu Jinxiong, 254n7
Xu Mei, 126
Xuande Emperor, 65
Xue Tian, 46, 54

Yamane Yukio, 261n79
Yang Cheng, 68
Yang Duanliu, 127
Yang Ming, 291n62
Yantielun, 26
YBS. *See* Yokohama Specie Bank
Ye Li, 60
Ye Shichang, 13
Ye Ziqi, 66, 67, 260n50
Yellow River basin, 21, 28
yen, 6, 15–16, 222, 228, 229, 232
Yokohama Specie Bank (YSB), 158, 184, 203, 285n11; before 1919, 185–90, 206; vs. Bank of Chosen, 185, 187, 191, 192, 198, 207, 208, 209; vs. Bank of Taiwan, 185, 189, 190, 192, 204, 205, 207, 208, 209; vs. CBIAC, 193; deposits in China, 188, 189, 190, 191, 192, 193, 196, 208, 286n14; vs. HSBC, 185, 186, 189, 190, 193, 196, 209; during May 4th Movement, 190–94, 204, 206–7, 209, 245; note issuance in China by, 136, 185, 186–88, 188, 190, 191–93, 194–96, 198, 199, 200, 204, 206, 207, 208, 245, 287n34, 288n46; reserve requirements, 192, 207; Shanghai branch, 186, 187, 188, 189; after WWII, 285n7
Yongle Emperor, 65, 66, 109, 213

Yongzheng Emperor, 268n43
Young, Arthur, 253n36
Yu Xiaqing, 178, 285n130
Yuan Shikai, 184, 187, 195, 199
Yuan Xie, 55
Yuan dynasty: bronze coinage during, 58, 60–61, 217, 260n50; inflation during, 59–60, 61, 65; monetary policies during, 3, 11, 12, 53, 56–62, 63, 65, 107, 108, 109, 212, 217, 242, 243, 244, 260n50, 261n63; paper money during, 3, 11, 12, 53, 56–62, 63, 65, 66, 72, 81, 95, 102, 107, 108, 212, 213, 217, 242, 243, 244, 260n50, 261n63; silver bullion during, 58, 59, 60, 61; taxation during, 58, 59
Yuezhi, 35–36, 257n57
Yunnan: copper mining in, 96, 97–98, 109–10, 267n41; cowrie in, 24, 108, 109, 114, 213

Zanzibar, 213
Zelin, Madeleine, 259n27, 267n38
Zhang Jian, 159, 278n49

Zhang Jiuling, 92
Zhang Wuchang, 234
Zhang Yong, 46
Zhang Zhidong, 85, 159, 161
Zhang Zuolin, 199–200
Zhao State, 36
Zheng Guanying, 159–60, 278n53
Zheng He, 65, 213
Zheng Jiefu, 60
Zhifu, 191, 288n49
Zhongzhou Farmers Bank, 220
Zhou dynasty, 21, 25, 27
Zhou Weirong, 13, 28
Zhou Xiaochuan, 233, 234, 237, 246
Zhou Xingji, 54; on metallic reserve ratio, 1, 11, 49, 55, 74; on paper money vs. coin, 1, 11, 49
Zhoushan, 124
Zhu Rongji, 226
Zhu Yuanzhang, 59, 62, 66; attitude regarding mining, 268n43; *lijia* reform, 63, 261n79
zinc, 12
Zoellick, Robert, 246

Printed and bound by CPI Group (UK) Ltd, Croydon, CR0 4YY

23/04/2025

14660939-0003